50% OFF
Online SAT Prep Course!

By Mometrix

Dear Customer,

We consider it an honor and a privilege that you chose our SAT Study Guide. As a way of showing our appreciation and to help us better serve you, we are offering **50% off our online SAT Prep Course.** Many SAT courses are needlessly expensive and don't deliver enough value. With our course, you get access to the best SAT prep material, and **you only pay half price.**

We have structured our online course to perfectly complement your printed study guide. The SAT Prep Course contains **in-depth lessons** that cover all the most important topics, **240+ video reviews** that explain difficult concepts, over **1,250+ practice questions** to ensure you feel prepared, and more than **500 digital flashcards**, so you can study while you're on the go.

Online SAT Prep Course

Topics Covered:

- Reading
  - Literary Analysis
  - Inferences in a Text or Texts
  - Author's Use of Language
- Writing
  - Foundations of Grammar
  - Essay Revision and Sentence Logic
  - Agreement and Sentence Structure
- Mathematics
  - Algebra and Functions
  - Geometry and Measurement
  - Data Analysis, Statistics, and Probability

Course Features:

- SAT Study Guide
  - Get content that complements our best-selling study guide.
- Full-Length Practice Tests
  - With over 1,250+ practice questions, you can test yourself again and again.
- Mobile Friendly
  - If you need to study on the go, the course is easily accessible from your mobile device.
- SAT Flashcards
  - Our course includes a flashcards mode with over 500 content cards for you to study.

To receive this discount, visit our website at mometrix.com/university/sat or simply scan this QR code with your smartphone. At the checkout page, enter the discount code: **sat50off**

If you have any questions or concerns, please contact us at support@mometrix.com.

Sincerely,

TEST PREPARATION

FREE Study Skills Videos/DVD Offer

Dear Customer,

Thank you for your purchase from Mometrix! We consider it an honor and a privilege that you have purchased our product and we want to ensure your satisfaction.

As part of our ongoing effort to meet the needs of test takers, we have developed a set of Study Skills Videos that we would like to give you for FREE. These videos cover our *best practices* for getting ready for your exam, from how to use our study materials to how to best prepare for the day of the test.

All that we ask is that you email us with feedback that would describe your experience so far with our product. Good, bad, or indifferent, we want to know what you think!

To get your FREE Study Skills Videos, you can use the **QR code** below, or send us an **email** at studyvideos@mometrix.com with *FREE VIDEOS* in the subject line and the following information in the body of the email:

- The name of the product you purchased.
- Your product rating on a scale of 1-5, with 5 being the highest rating.
- Your feedback. It can be long, short, or anything in between. We just want to know your impressions and experience so far with our product. (Good feedback might include how our study material met your needs and ways we might be able to make it even better. You could highlight features that you found helpful or features that you think we should add.)

If you have any questions or concerns, please don't hesitate to contact me directly.

Thanks again!

Sincerely,

Jay Willis
Vice President
jay.willis@mometrix.com
1-800-673-8175

Mometrix

TEST PREPARATION

Digital SAT®

Study Guide
2024-2025

3 Full-Length Exams

SAT® Prep Book Secrets with Practice Tests for the Math, Reading, and Writing Sections

9th Edition

Written and edited by the Mometrix College Admissions Test Team

Printed in the United States of America

This paper meets the requirements of ANSI/NISO Z39.48-1992 (Permanence of Paper).

Mometrix offers volume discount pricing to institutions. For more information or a price quote, please contact our sales department at sales@mometrix.com or 888-248-1219.

Mometrix Media LLC is not affiliated with or endorsed by any official testing organization. All organizational and test names are trademarks of their respective owners.

Paperback
ISBN 13: 978-1-5167-2561-8

DEAR FUTURE EXAM SUCCESS STORY

First of all, **THANK YOU** for purchasing Mometrix study materials!

Second, congratulations! You are one of the few determined test-takers who are committed to doing whatever it takes to excel on your exam. **You have come to the right place.** We developed these study materials with one goal in mind: to deliver you the information you need in a format that's concise and easy to use.

In addition to optimizing your guide for the content of the test, we've outlined our recommended steps for breaking down the preparation process into small, attainable goals so you can make sure you stay on track.

We've also analyzed the entire test-taking process, identifying the most common pitfalls and showing how you can overcome them and be ready for any curveball the test throws you.

Standardized testing is one of the biggest obstacles on your road to success, which only increases the importance of doing well in the high-pressure, high-stakes environment of test day. Your results on this test could have a significant impact on your future, and this guide provides the information and practical advice to help you achieve your full potential on test day.

Your success is our success

We would love to hear from you! If you would like to share the story of your exam success or if you have any questions or comments in regard to our products, please contact us at **800-673-8175** or **support@mometrix.com**.

Thanks again for your business and we wish you continued success!

Sincerely,
The Mometrix Test Preparation Team

Need more help? Check out our flashcards at:
http://MometrixFlashcards.com/SAT

TABLE OF CONTENTS

Introduction

Thank you for purchasing this resource! You have made the choice to prepare yourself for a test that could have a huge impact on your future, and this guide is designed to help you be fully ready for test day. Obviously, it's important to have a solid understanding of the test material, but you also need to be prepared for the unique environment and stressors of the test, so that you can perform to the best of your abilities.

For this purpose, the first section that appears in this guide is the **Secret Keys**. We've devoted countless hours to meticulously researching what works and what doesn't, and we've boiled down our findings to the five most impactful steps you can take to improve your performance on the test. We start at the beginning with study planning and move through the preparation process, all the way to the testing strategies that will help you get the most out of what you know when you're finally sitting in front of the test.

We recommend that you start preparing for your test as far in advance as possible. However, if you've bought this guide as a last-minute study resource and only have a few days before your test, we recommend that you skip over the first two Secret Keys since they address a long-term study plan.

If you struggle with **test anxiety**, we strongly encourage you to check out our recommendations for how you can overcome it. Test anxiety is a formidable foe, but it can be beaten, and we want to make sure you have the tools you need to defeat it.

Secret Key #1 – Plan Big, Study Small

There's a lot riding on your performance. If you want to ace this test, you're going to need to keep your skills sharp and the material fresh in your mind. You need a plan that lets you review everything you need to know while still fitting in your schedule. We'll break this strategy down into three categories.

Information Organization

Start with the information you already have: the official test outline. From this, you can make a complete list of all the concepts you need to cover before the test. Organize these concepts into groups that can be studied together, and create a list of any related vocabulary you need to learn so you can brush up on any difficult terms. You'll want to keep this vocabulary list handy once you actually start studying since you may need to add to it along the way.

Time Management

Once you have your set of study concepts, decide how to spread them out over the time you have left before the test. Break your study plan into small, clear goals so you have a manageable task for each day and know exactly what you're doing. Then just focus on one small step at a time. When you manage your time this way, you don't need to spend hours at a time studying. Studying a small block of content for a short period each day helps you retain information better and avoid stressing over how much you have left to do. You can relax knowing that you have a plan to cover everything in time. In order for this strategy to be effective though, you have to start studying early and stick to your schedule. Avoid the exhaustion and futility that comes from last-minute cramming!

Study Environment

The environment you study in has a big impact on your learning. Studying in a coffee shop, while probably more enjoyable, is not likely to be as fruitful as studying in a quiet room. It's important to keep distractions to a minimum. You're only planning to study for a short block of time, so make the most of it. Don't pause to check your phone or get up to find a snack. It's also important to **avoid multitasking**. Research has consistently shown that multitasking will make your studying dramatically less effective. Your study area should also be comfortable and well-lit so you don't have the distraction of straining your eyes or sitting on an uncomfortable chair.

 The time of day you study is also important. You want to be rested and alert. Don't wait until just before bedtime. Study when you'll be most likely to comprehend and remember. Even better, if you know what time of day your test will be, set that time aside for study. That way your brain will be used to working on that subject at that specific time and you'll have a better chance of recalling information.

Finally, it can be helpful to team up with others who are studying for the same test. Your actual studying should be done in as isolated an environment as possible, but the work of organizing the information and setting up the study plan can be divided up. In between study sessions, you can discuss with your teammates the concepts that you're all studying and quiz each other on the details. Just be sure that your teammates are as serious about the test as you are. If you find that your study time is being replaced with social time, you might need to find a new team.

2

Secret Key #2 – Make Your Studying Count

You're devoting a lot of time and effort to preparing for this test, so you want to be absolutely certain it will pay off. This means doing more than just reading the content and hoping you can remember it on test day. It's important to make every minute of study count. There are two main areas you can focus on to make your studying count.

Retention

It doesn't matter how much time you study if you can't remember the material. You need to make sure you are retaining the concepts. To check your retention of the information you're learning, try recalling it at later times with minimal prompting. Try carrying around flashcards and glance at one or two from time to time or ask a friend who's also studying for the test to quiz you.

To enhance your retention, look for ways to put the information into practice so that you can apply it rather than simply recalling it. If you're using the information in practical ways, it will be much easier to remember. Similarly, it helps to solidify a concept in your mind if you're not only reading it to yourself but also explaining it to someone else. Ask a friend to let you teach them about a concept you're a little shaky on (or speak aloud to an imaginary audience if necessary). As you try to summarize, define, give examples, and answer your friend's questions, you'll understand the concepts better and they will stay with you longer. Finally, step back for a big picture view and ask yourself how each piece of information fits with the whole subject. When you link the different concepts together and see them working together as a whole, it's easier to remember the individual components.

Finally, practice showing your work on any multi-step problems, even if you're just studying. Writing out each step you take to solve a problem will help solidify the process in your mind, and you'll be more likely to remember it during the test.

Modality

Modality simply refers to the means or method by which you study. Choosing a study modality that fits your own individual learning style is crucial. No two people learn best in exactly the same way, so it's important to know your strengths and use them to your advantage.

For example, if you learn best by visualization, focus on visualizing a concept in your mind and draw an image or a diagram. Try color-coding your notes, illustrating them, or creating symbols that will trigger your mind to recall a learned concept. If you learn best by hearing or discussing information, find a study partner who learns the same way or read aloud to yourself. Think about how to put the information in your own words. Imagine that you are giving a lecture on the topic and record yourself so you can listen to it later.

For any learning style, flashcards can be helpful. Organize the information so you can take advantage of spare moments to review. Underline key words or phrases. Use different colors for different categories. Mnemonic devices (such as creating a short list in which every item starts with the same letter) can also help with retention. Find what works best for you and use it to store the information in your mind most effectively and easily.

Secret Key #3 – Practice the Right Way

Your success on test day depends not only on how many hours you put into preparing, but also on whether you prepared the right way. It's good to check along the way to see if your studying is paying off. One of the most effective ways to do this is by taking practice tests to evaluate your progress. Practice tests are useful because they show exactly where you need to improve. Every time you take a practice test, pay special attention to these three groups of questions:

- The questions you got wrong
- The questions you had to guess on, even if you guessed right
- The questions you found difficult or slow to work through

This will show you exactly what your weak areas are, and where you need to devote more study time. Ask yourself why each of these questions gave you trouble. Was it because you didn't understand the material? Was it because you didn't remember the vocabulary? Do you need more repetitions on this type of question to build speed and confidence? Dig into those questions and figure out how you can strengthen your weak areas as you go back to review the material.

 Additionally, many practice tests have a section explaining the answer choices. It can be tempting to read the explanation and think that you now have a good understanding of the concept. However, an explanation likely only covers part of the question's broader context. Even if the explanation makes perfect sense, **go back and investigate** every concept related to the question until you're positive you have a thorough understanding.

As you go along, keep in mind that the practice test is just that: practice. Memorizing these questions and answers will not be very helpful on the actual test because it is unlikely to have any of the same exact questions. If you only know the right answers to the sample questions, you won't be prepared for the real thing. **Study the concepts** until you understand them fully, and then you'll be able to answer any question that shows up on the test.

It's important to wait on the practice tests until you're ready. If you take a test on your first day of study, you may be overwhelmed by the amount of material covered and how much you need to learn. Work up to it gradually.

On test day, you'll need to be prepared for answering questions, managing your time, and using the test-taking strategies you've learned. It's a lot to balance, like a mental marathon that will have a big impact on your future. Like training for a marathon, you'll need to start slowly and work your way up. When test day arrives, you'll be ready.

Start with the strategies you've read in the first two Secret Keys—plan your course and study in the way that works best for you. If you have time, consider using multiple study resources to get different approaches to the same concepts. It can be helpful to see difficult concepts from more than one angle. Then find a good source for practice tests. Many times, the test website will suggest potential study resources or provide sample tests.

4

Practice Test Strategy

If you're able to find at least three practice tests, we recommend this strategy:

UNTIMED AND OPEN-BOOK PRACTICE

Take the first test with no time constraints and with your notes and study guide handy. Take your time and focus on applying the strategies you've learned.

TIMED AND OPEN-BOOK PRACTICE

Take the second practice test open-book as well, but set a timer and practice pacing yourself to finish in time.

TIMED AND CLOSED-BOOK PRACTICE

Take any other practice tests as if it were test day. Set a timer and put away your study materials. Sit at a table or desk in a quiet room, imagine yourself at the testing center, and answer questions as quickly and accurately as possible.

Keep repeating timed and closed-book tests on a regular basis until you run out of practice tests or it's time for the actual test. Your mind will be ready for the schedule and stress of test day, and you'll be able to focus on recalling the material you've learned.

Secret Key #4 – Pace Yourself

Once you're fully prepared for the material on the test, your biggest challenge on test day will be managing your time. Just knowing that the clock is ticking can make you panic even if you have plenty of time left. Work on pacing yourself so you can build confidence against the time constraints of the exam. Pacing is a difficult skill to master, especially in a high-pressure environment, so **practice is vital**.

Set time expectations for your pace based on how much time is available. For example, if a section has 60 questions and the time limit is 30 minutes, you know you have to average 30 seconds or less per question in order to answer them all. Although 30 seconds is the hard limit, set 25 seconds per question as your goal, so you reserve extra time to spend on harder questions. When you budget extra time for the harder questions, you no longer have any reason to stress when those questions take longer to answer.

Don't let this time expectation distract you from working through the test at a calm, steady pace, but keep it in mind so you don't spend too much time on any one question. Recognize that taking extra time on one question you don't understand may keep you from answering two that you do understand later in the test. If your time limit for a question is up and you're still not sure of the answer, mark it and move on, and come back to it later if the time and the test format allow. If the testing format doesn't allow you to return to earlier questions, just make an educated guess; then put it out of your mind and move on.

On the easier questions, be careful not to rush. It may seem wise to hurry through them so you have more time for the challenging ones, but it's not worth missing one if you know the concept and just didn't take the time to read the question fully. Work efficiently but make sure you understand the question and have looked at all of the answer choices, since more than one may seem right at first.

Even if you're paying attention to the time, you may find yourself a little behind at some point. You should speed up to get back on track, but do so wisely. Don't panic; just take a few seconds less on each question until you're caught up. Don't guess without thinking, but do look through the answer choices and eliminate any you know are wrong. If you can get down to two choices, it is often worthwhile to guess from those. Once you've chosen an answer, move on and don't dwell on any that you skipped or had to hurry through. If a question was taking too long, chances are it was one of the harder ones, so you weren't as likely to get it right anyway.

On the other hand, if you find yourself getting ahead of schedule, it may be beneficial to slow down a little. The more quickly you work, the more likely you are to make a careless mistake that will affect your score. You've budgeted time for each question, so don't be afraid to spend that time. Practice an efficient but careful pace to get the most out of the time you have.

Secret Key #5 – Have a Plan for Guessing

When you're taking the test, you may find yourself stuck on a question. Some of the answer choices seem better than others, but you don't see the one answer choice that is obviously correct. What do you do?

The scenario described above is very common, yet most test takers have not effectively prepared for it. Developing and practicing a plan for guessing may be one of the single most effective uses of your time as you get ready for the exam.

In developing your plan for guessing, there are three questions to address:

1. When should you start the guessing process?
2. How should you narrow down the choices?
3. Which answer should you choose?

When to Start the Guessing Process

Unless your plan for guessing is to select C every time (which, despite its merits, is not what we recommend), you need to leave yourself enough time to apply your answer elimination strategies. Since you have a limited amount of time for each question, that means that if you're going to give yourself the best shot at guessing correctly, you have to decide quickly whether or not you will guess.

Of course, the best-case scenario is that you don't have to guess at all, so first, see if you can answer the question based on your knowledge of the subject and basic reasoning skills. Focus on the key words in the question and try to jog your memory of related topics. Give yourself a chance to bring the knowledge to mind, but once you realize that you don't have (or you can't access) the knowledge you need to answer the question, it's time to start the guessing process.

It's almost always better to start the guessing process too early than too late. It only takes a few seconds to remember something and answer the question from knowledge. Carefully eliminating wrong answer choices takes longer. Plus, going through the process of eliminating answer choices can actually help jog your memory.

Summary: Start the guessing process as soon as you decide that you can't answer the question based on your knowledge.

How to Narrow Down the Choices

The next chapter in this book (**Test-Taking Strategies**) includes a wide range of strategies for how to approach questions and how to look for answer choices to eliminate. You will definitely want to read those carefully, practice them, and figure out which ones work best for you. Here though, we're going to address a mindset rather than a particular strategy.

Your odds of guessing an answer correctly depend on how many options you are choosing from.

Number of options left	5	4	3	2	1
Odds of guessing correctly	20%	25%	33%	50%	100%

You can see from this chart just how valuable it is to be able to eliminate incorrect answers and make an educated guess, but there are two things that many test takers do that cause them to miss out on the benefits of guessing:

1. Accidentally eliminating the correct answer
2. Selecting an answer based on an impression

We'll look at the first one here, and the second one in the next section.

To avoid accidentally eliminating the correct answer, we recommend a thought exercise called **the $5 challenge**. In this challenge, you only eliminate an answer choice from contention if you are willing to bet $5 on it being wrong. Why $5? Five dollars is a small but not insignificant amount of money. It's an amount you could afford to lose but wouldn't want to throw away. And while losing

$5 once might not hurt too much, doing it twenty times will set you back $100. In the same way, each small decision you make—eliminating a choice here, guessing on a question there—won't by itself impact your score very much, but when you put them all together, they can make a big difference. By holding each answer choice elimination decision to a higher standard, you can reduce the risk of accidentally eliminating the correct answer.

The $5 challenge can also be applied in a positive sense: If you are willing to bet $5 that an answer choice *is* correct, go ahead and mark it as correct.

Summary: Only eliminate an answer choice if you are willing to bet $5 that it is wrong.

8

Which Answer to Choose

You're taking the test. You've run into a hard question and decided you'll have to guess. You've eliminated all the answer choices you're willing to bet $5 on. Now you have to pick an answer. Why do we even need to talk about this? Why can't you just pick whichever one you feel like when the time comes?

The answer to these questions is that if you don't come into the test with a plan, you'll rely on your impression to select an answer choice, and if you do that, you risk falling into a trap. The test writers know that everyone who takes their test will be guessing on some of the questions, so they intentionally write wrong answer choices to seem plausible. You still have to pick an answer though, and if the wrong answer choices are designed to look right, how can you ever be sure that you're not falling for their trap? The best solution we've found to this dilemma is to take the decision out of your hands entirely. Here is the process we recommend:

Once you've eliminated any choices that you are confident (willing to bet $5) are wrong, select the first remaining choice as your answer.

Whether you choose to select the first remaining choice, the second, or the last, the important thing is that you use some preselected standard. Using this approach guarantees that you will not be enticed into selecting an answer choice that looks right, because you are not basing your decision on how the answer choices look.

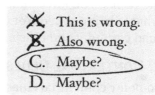

This is not meant to make you question your knowledge. Instead, it is to help you recognize the difference between your knowledge and your impressions. There's a huge difference between thinking an answer is right because of what you know, and thinking an answer is right because it looks or sounds like it should be right.

Summary: To ensure that your selection is appropriately random, make a predetermined selection from among all answer choices you have not eliminated.

Test-Taking Strategies

This section contains a list of test-taking strategies that you may find helpful as you work through the test. By taking what you know and applying logical thought, you can maximize your chances of answering any question correctly!

It is very important to realize that every question is different and every person is different: no single strategy will work on every question, and no single strategy will work for every person. That's why we've included all of them here, so you can try them out and determine which ones work best for different types of questions and which ones work best for you.

Question Strategies

☑ READ CAREFULLY

Read the question and the answer choices carefully. Don't miss the question because you misread the terms. You have plenty of time to read each question thoroughly and make sure you understand what is being asked. Yet a happy medium must be attained, so don't waste too much time. You must read carefully and efficiently.

☑ CONTEXTUAL CLUES

Look for contextual clues. If the question includes a word you are not familiar with, look at the immediate context for some indication of what the word might mean. Contextual clues can often give you all the information you need to decipher the meaning of an unfamiliar word. Even if you can't determine the meaning, you may be able to narrow down the possibilities enough to make a solid guess at the answer to the question.

☑ PREFIXES

If you're having trouble with a word in the question or answer choices, try dissecting it. Take advantage of every clue that the word might include. Prefixes can be a huge help. Usually, they allow you to determine a basic meaning. *Pre-* means before, *post-* means after, *pro-* is positive, *de-* is negative. From prefixes, you can get an idea of the general meaning of the word and try to put it into context.

☑ HEDGE WORDS

Watch out for critical hedge words, such as *likely, may, can, sometimes, often, almost, mostly, usually, generally, rarely,* and *sometimes.* Question writers insert these hedge phrases to cover every possibility. Often an answer choice will be wrong simply because it leaves no room for exception. Be on guard for answer choices that have definitive words such as *exactly* and *always.*

☑ SWITCHBACK WORDS

Stay alert for *switchbacks.* These are the words and phrases frequently used to alert you to shifts in thought. The most common switchback words are *but, although,* and *however.* Others include *nevertheless, on the other hand, even though, while, in spite of, despite,* and *regardless of.* Switchback words are important to catch because they can change the direction of the question or an answer choice.

10

☑ FACE VALUE

When in doubt, use common sense. Accept the situation in the problem at face value. Don't read too much into it. These problems will not require you to make wild assumptions. If you have to go beyond creativity and warp time or space in order to have an answer choice fit the question, then you should move on and consider the other answer choices. These are normal problems rooted in reality. The applicable relationship or explanation may not be readily apparent, but it is there for you to figure out. Use your common sense to interpret anything that isn't clear.

Answer Choice Strategies

☑ ANSWER SELECTION

The most thorough way to pick an answer choice is to identify and eliminate wrong answers until only one is left, then confirm it is the correct answer. Sometimes an answer choice may immediately seem right, but be careful. The test writers will usually put more than one reasonable answer choice on each question, so take a second to read all of them and make sure that the other choices are not equally obvious. As long as you have time left, it is better to read every answer choice than to pick the first one that looks right without checking the others.

☑ ANSWER CHOICE FAMILIES

An answer choice family consists of two (in rare cases, three) answer choices that are very similar in construction and cannot all be true at the same time. If you see two answer choices that are direct opposites or parallels, one of them is usually the correct answer. For instance, if one answer choice says that quantity x increases and another either says that quantity x decreases (opposite) or says that quantity y increases (parallel), then those answer choices would fall into the same family. An answer choice that doesn't match the construction of the answer choice family is more likely to be incorrect. Most questions will not have answer choice families, but when they do appear, you should be prepared to recognize them.

☑ ELIMINATE ANSWERS

Eliminate answer choices as soon as you realize they are wrong, but make sure you consider all possibilities. If you are eliminating answer choices and realize that the last one you are left with is also wrong, don't panic. Start over and consider each choice again. There may be something you missed the first time that you will realize on the second pass.

☑ AVOID FACT TRAPS

Don't be distracted by an answer choice that is factually true but doesn't answer the question. You are looking for the choice that answers the question. Stay focused on what the question is asking for so you don't accidentally pick an answer that is true but incorrect. Always go back to the question and make sure the answer choice you've selected actually answers the question and is not merely a true statement.

☑ EXTREME STATEMENTS

In general, you should avoid answers that put forth extreme actions as standard practice or proclaim controversial ideas as established fact. An answer choice that states the "process should be used in certain situations, if…" is much more likely to be correct than one that states the "process should be discontinued completely." The first is a calm rational statement and doesn't even make a definitive, uncompromising stance, using a hedge word *if* to provide wiggle room, whereas the second choice is far more extreme.

⊘ BENCHMARK

As you read through the answer choices and you come across one that seems to answer the question well, mentally select that answer choice. This is not your final answer, but it's the one that will help you evaluate the other answer choices. The one that you selected is your benchmark or standard for judging each of the other answer choices. Every other answer choice must be compared to your benchmark. That choice is correct until proven otherwise by another answer choice beating it. If you find a better answer, then that one becomes your new benchmark. Once you've decided that no other choice answers the question as well as your benchmark, you have your final answer.

⊘ PREDICT THE ANSWER

Before you even start looking at the answer choices, it is often best to try to predict the answer. When you come up with the answer on your own, it is easier to avoid distractions and traps because you will know exactly what to look for. The right answer choice is unlikely to be word-for-word what you came up with, but it should be a close match. Even if you are confident that you have the right answer, you should still take the time to read each option before moving on.

General Strategies

⊘ TOUGH QUESTIONS

If you are stumped on a problem or it appears too hard or too difficult, don't waste time. Move on! Remember though, if you can quickly check for obviously incorrect answer choices, your chances of guessing correctly are greatly improved. Before you completely give up, at least try to knock out a couple of possible answers. Eliminate what you can and then guess at the remaining answer choices before moving on.

⊘ CHECK YOUR WORK

Since you will probably not know every term listed and the answer to every question, it is important that you get credit for the ones that you do know. Don't miss any questions through careless mistakes. If at all possible, try to take a second to look back over your answer selection and make sure you've selected the correct answer choice and haven't made a costly careless mistake (such as marking an answer choice that you didn't mean to mark). This quick double check should more than pay for itself in caught mistakes for the time it costs.

⊘ PACE YOURSELF

It's easy to be overwhelmed when you're looking at a page full of questions; your mind is confused and full of random thoughts, and the clock is ticking down faster than you would like. Calm down and maintain the pace that you have set for yourself. Especially as you get down to the last few minutes of the test, don't let the small numbers on the clock make you panic. As long as you are on track by monitoring your pace, you are guaranteed to have time for each question.

⊘ DON'T RUSH

It is very easy to make errors when you are in a hurry. Maintaining a fast pace in answering questions is pointless if it makes you miss questions that you would have gotten right otherwise. Test writers like to include distracting information and wrong answers that seem right. Taking a little extra time to avoid careless mistakes can make all the difference in your test score. Find a pace that allows you to be confident in the answers that you select.

⊘ KEEP MOVING

Panicking will not help you pass the test, so do your best to stay calm and keep moving. Taking deep breaths and going through the answer elimination steps you practiced can help to break through a stress barrier and keep your pace.

Final Notes

The combination of a solid foundation of content knowledge and the confidence that comes from practicing your plan for applying that knowledge is the key to maximizing your performance on test day. As your foundation of content knowledge is built up and strengthened, you'll find that the strategies included in this chapter become more and more effective in helping you quickly sift through the distractions and traps of the test to isolate the correct answer.

Now that you're preparing to move forward into the test content chapters of this book, be sure to keep your goal in mind. As you read, think about how you will be able to apply this information on the test. If you've already seen sample questions for the test and you have an idea of the question format and style, try to come up with questions of your own that you can answer based on what you're reading. This will give you valuable practice applying your knowledge in the same ways you can expect to on test day.

Good luck and good studying!

Three-Week SAT Study Plan

On the next few pages, we've provided an optional study plan to help you use this study guide to its fullest potential over the course of three weeks. If you have six weeks available and want to spread it out more, spend two weeks on each section of the plan.

Below is a quick summary of the subjects covered in each week of the plan.

- Week 1: Reading and Writing Test: Part 1
- Week 2: Reading and Writing Test: Part 2
- Week 3: Mathematics Test

Please note that not all subjects will take the same amount of time to work through.

Two full-length practice tests are included in this study guide. We recommend saving any additional practice tests until after you've completed the study plan. Take this practice test timed and without any reference materials a day or two before the real thing as one last practice run to get you in the mode of answering questions at a good pace.

Week 1: Reading and Writing Test

INSTRUCTIONAL CONTENT

First, read carefully through the first two sections of the Reading and Writing chapter in this book, checking off your progress as you go. These two sections deal mostly with reading comprehension.

- ❏ Craft and Structure
- ❏ Information and Ideas

As you read, do the following:

- Highlight any sections, terms, or concepts you think are important
- Draw an asterisk (*) next to any areas you are struggling with
- Watch the review videos to gain more understanding of a particular topic
- Take notes in your notebook or in the margins of this book

After you've read through everything, go back and review any sections that you highlighted or that you drew an asterisk next to, referencing your notes along the way.

PRACTICE TEST #1, MODULE 1

Now that you've read over the instructional content, it's time to take a practice test. Complete Module 1 of the Reading and Writing Test section of Practice Test #1. Take this test with **no time constraints**, and feel free to reference the applicable sections of this guide as you go. Once you've finished, check your answers against the provided answer key. For any questions you answered incorrectly, review the answer rationale, and then **go back and review** the applicable sections of the book. The goal in this stage is to understand why you answered the question incorrectly, and make sure that the next time you see a similar question, you will get it right.

PRACTICE TEST #1, MODULE 2

Next, complete Module 2 of the Reading and Writing Test section of Practice Test #1. This time, give yourself **32 minutes** (the amount of time you will have per module on the real SAT) to complete all of the questions. You should again feel free to reference the guide and your notes, but be mindful of the clock. If you run out of time before you finish all of the questions, mark where you were when time expired, but go ahead and finish taking the practice test. Once you've finished, check your answers against the provided answer key and as before, review the answer rationale for any that you answered incorrectly and go back and review the associated instructional content. Your goal is still to increase understanding of the content but also to get used to the time constraints you will face on the test.

Week 2: Writing and Language Test

INSTRUCTIONAL CONTENT

First, read carefully through the last two sections of the Reading and Writing chapter in this book, checking off your progress as you go. These two sections deal mostly with English language conventions and writing skills.

❏ Standard English Conventions
❏ Expression of Ideas

As you read, do the following:

- Highlight any sections, terms, or concepts you think are important
- Draw an asterisk (*) next to any areas you are struggling with
- Watch the review videos to gain more understanding of a particular topic
- Take notes in your notebook or in the margins of this book

After you've read through everything, go back and review any sections that you highlighted or that you drew an asterisk next to, referencing your notes along the way.

PRACTICE TEST #2, MODULE 1

Now that you've read over the instructional content, it's time to take a practice test. Complete Module 1 of the Reading and Writing section of Practice Test #2. Take this test with **a stopwatch,** recording the time it takes you to complete each question. If you find yourself taking each question too slowly, then try to speed up until you are consistently answering each question as quickly as you need to. After completing a question feel free to reference the applicable sections of this guide as you go. Once you've finished, check your answers against the provided answer key. For any questions you answered incorrectly, review the answer rationale, and then **go back and review** the applicable sections of the book. The goal in this stage is to understand why you answered the question incorrectly, and make sure that the next time you see a similar question, you will get it right.

PRACTICE TEST #2, MODULE 2

Next, take the Writing and Language Test section of Practice Test #2. This time, give yourself **32 minutes** (the amount of time you will have on the real SAT) to complete all of the questions. Your goal is to simulate taking the real test. If you run out of time before you finish all of the questions, mark where you were when time expired, but go ahead and finish taking the practice test. Once you've finished, check your answers against the provided answer key, and as before, review the answer rationale for any that you answered incorrectly and then go back and review the associated instructional content. Your goal is still to increase understanding of the content but also to get used to the time constraints you will face on the test.

Week 3: Mathematics Test

INSTRUCTIONAL CONTENT

First, read carefully through the Mathematics Test chapter in this book, checking off your progress as you go:

- ❏ Introductory Information
- ❏ Algebra
- ❏ Advanced Math
- ❏ Problem-Solving and Data Analysis
- ❏ Geometry and Trigonometry

As you read, do the following:

- Highlight any sections, terms, or concepts you think are important
- Draw an asterisk (*) next to any areas you are struggling with
- Watch the review videos to gain more understanding of a particular topic
- Take notes in your notebook or in the margins of this book

After you've read through everything, go back and review any sections that you highlighted or that you drew an asterisk next to, referencing your notes along the way.

PRACTICE TEST #1

Now that you've read over the instructional content, it's time to take a practice test. Complete the Mathematics Test section of Practice Test #1. Take this test with **no time constraints**, and feel free to reference the applicable sections of this guide as you go. Once you've finished, check your answers against the provided answer key. For any questions you answered incorrectly, review the answer rationale, and then **go back and review** the applicable sections of the book. The goal in this stage is to understand why you answered the question incorrectly, and make sure that the next time you see a similar question, you will get it right.

PRACTICE TEST #2

Next, take the Mathematics section of Practice Test #2. This time, give yourself **35 minutes** to complete each module (the amount of time you will have on the real SAT). If you found yourself struggling to complete the first module on time, try speeding up when you take the second module. You should again feel free to reference the guide and your notes, but be mindful of the clock. If you run out of time before you finish all of the questions, mark where you were when time expired, but go ahead and finish taking the practice test. Once you've finished, check your answers against the provided answer key, and as before, review the answer rationale for any that you answered incorrectly and then go back and review the associated instructional content. Your goal is still to increase understanding of the content but also to get used to the time constraints you will face on the test.

Reading and Writing

Reading and Writing Overview

READING AND WRITING SECTION OVERVIEW

The reading and writing section of the Digital SAT consists of two modules with 27 questions each for a combined total of 54 questions. The test-taker has 32 minutes to complete each of the reading and writing modules. In previous versions of the SAT, the test-taker would read four longer passages with several associated questions. Instead, this version of the SAT requires the test taker to read a short passage for each question.

The first module always contains a balance of easy, moderate, and hard questions to help gauge the test-taker's skills. Based on how the test-taker does in the first module, the second module will be adjusted in difficulty. This helps to accurately gauge the test-taker's abilities, while keeping the test from being extremely long.

QUESTION TYPES

Unlike on older versions of the SAT, this version of the test combines the reading and writing sections into one section. Each module is a mixture of questions pertaining to reading ability and writing skills. The first two domains, Craft and Structure and Information and Ideas, both pertain mostly to reading skills, whereas the last two domains, Standard English Conventions and Expression of Ideas, pertain mostly to English language knowledge and writing skills.

Question Types	Percentage	Question Count (for both modules)
Craft and Structure	28%	12-14 Questions
Information and Ideas	26%	13-15 Questions
Standard English Conventions	26%	8-12 Questions
Expression of Ideas	20%	11-15 Questions

CRAFT AND STRUCTURE

This domain is made up of three question types and makes up about 28% of the questions:

- **Words in Context** – These questions require the test-taker to read a short passage and identify the most accurate meaning for a word or phrase as it relates to the context.
- **Text Structure and Purpose** – These questions require the test-taker to read a short passage and identify either the organizing structure or the author's purpose in writing the passage.
- **Cross-Text Connections** – These questions pertain to a pair of related passages. The test-taker must read both and draw a connection relating the two passages to each other. Passage pairs may either agree or disagree with each other.

INFORMATION AND IDEAS

This domain is made up of three question types and makes up about 26% of the questions:

- **Central Ideas and Details** – These questions require the test-taker to read a short passage and determine a main idea or identify specific details to demonstrate comprehension of the events of the passage and the ability to find information.

- **Command of Evidence** – These questions require the test-taker to read a short passage and use details from the passage or quantitative information found in a graphic to support a specific idea.
- **Inferences** – These questions require the test-taker to read a short passage and draw conclusions about ideas that are not explicitly stated in the passage. Test-takers will need to draw upon explicit or implied information to draw a conclusion.

STANDARD ENGLISH CONVENTIONS

This domain is made up of two question types and makes up about 26% of the questions:

- **Boundaries** – These questions require the test taker to choose an answer that completes a selection from the passage. These questions require the test-taker to use both context from the passage and English language conventions to select the correct choice.
- **Form, Structure, and Sense** – These questions require the test-taker to edit a selection from the passage to meet English language standards. Standards that are commonly tested include agreement, tense, and use of punctuation.

EXPRESSION OF IDEAS

This domain is made up of two question types and makes up about 20% of the questions:

- **Rhetorical Synthesis** - These questions require the test-taker to revise a selection from the passage to meet a particular rhetorical goal. The revisions in question can include removals from, additions to, or moves of sentences within the selection.
- **Transitions** – These questions require the test-taker to select from a variety of transition words to choose the one that best fits the context and logically coordinate ideas.

PASSAGE TYPES

The Reading and Writing section of the Digital SAT requires reading passages from a variety of academic disciplines. Unlike previous SAT formats, this format requires the test-taker to read one short passage per question. Passages generally range in length from 25-150 words per passage. Passage types include selections from literature, history or social studies, the humanities, and science. Literary passages can include prose fiction, poetry, drama, or literary nonfiction, meaning that test-takers will need to be prepared to read a variety of literary forms. Some question types require the test-taker to relate information from more than one passage, meaning that they will need to read two short passages at a time for particular questions. Some questions will require the test-taker to review quantitative information found in charts, tables, or graphs and relate the information to the written passage.

RECOMMENDED PACE

The Digital SAT requires the test-taker to answer 27 questions in 32 minutes, allowing just over 1 minute per question. This includes the time that it takes to read each passage and answer the question. Our recommendation for practice is to try practicing at pace, aiming for an average pace of 1-minute per question. At this pace, the test-taker will finish the test with with 5 minutes left to review any questions that were particularly troublesome. The test-taker is allowed to go back and review questions that they skipped earlier in the test.

Craft and Structure

WORD ROOTS AND PREFIXES AND SUFFIXES

AFFIXES

Affixes in the English language are morphemes that are added to words to create related but different words. Derivational affixes form new words based on and related to the original words. For example, the affix *–ness* added to the end of the adjective *happy* forms the noun *happiness.* Inflectional affixes form different grammatical versions of words. For example, the plural affix *–s* changes the singular noun *book* to the plural noun *books,* and the past tense affix *–ed* changes the present tense verb *look* to the past tense *looked.* Prefixes are affixes placed in front of words. For example, *heat* means to make hot; *preheat* means to heat in advance. Suffixes are affixes placed at the ends of words. The *happiness* example above contains the suffix *–ness.* Circumfixes add parts both before and after words, such as how *light* becomes *enlighten* with the prefix *en-* and the suffix *–en.* Interfixes create compound words via central affixes: *speed* and *meter* become *speedometer* via the interfix *–o–.*

> **Review Video: Affixes**
> Visit mometrix.com/academy and enter code: 782422

WORD ROOTS, PREFIXES, AND SUFFIXES TO HELP DETERMINE MEANINGS OF WORDS

Many English words were formed from combining multiple sources. For example, the Latin *habēre* means "to have," and the prefixes *in-* and *im-* mean a lack or prevention of something, as in *insufficient* and *imperfect.* Latin combined *in-* with *habēre* to form *inhibēre,* whose past participle was *inhibitus.* This is the origin of the English word *inhibit,* meaning to prevent from having. Hence by knowing the meanings of both the prefix and the root, one can decipher the word meaning. In Greek, the root *enkephalo-* refers to the brain. Many medical terms are based on this root, such as encephalitis and hydrocephalus. Understanding the prefix and suffix meanings (*-itis* means inflammation; *hydro-* means water) allows a person to deduce that encephalitis refers to brain inflammation and hydrocephalus refers to water (or other fluid) in the brain.

> **Review Video: Determining Word Meanings**
> Visit mometrix.com/academy and enter code: 894894

PREFIXES

Knowing common prefixes is helpful for all readers as they try to determining meanings or definitions of unfamiliar words. For example, a common word used when cooking is *preheat.* Knowing that *pre-* means in advance can also inform them that *presume* means to assume in advance, that *prejudice* means advance judgment, and that this understanding can be applied to many other words beginning with *pre-*. Knowing that the prefix *dis-* indicates opposition informs the meanings of words like *disbar, disagree, disestablish,* and many more. Knowing *dys-* means bad, impaired, abnormal, or difficult informs *dyslogistic, dysfunctional, dysphagia,* and *dysplasia.*

SUFFIXES

In English, certain suffixes generally indicate both that a word is a noun, and that the noun represents a state of being or quality. For example, *-ness* is commonly used to change an adjective into its noun form, as with *happy* and *happiness, nice* and *niceness,* and so on. The suffix *–tion* is commonly used to transform a verb into its noun form, as with *converse* and *conversation or move* and *motion*. Thus, if readers are unfamiliar with the second form of a word, knowing the meaning of the transforming suffix can help them determine meaning.

PREFIXES FOR NUMBERS

Prefix	Definition	Examples
bi-	two	bisect, biennial
mono-	one, single	monogamy, monologue
poly-	many	polymorphous, polygamous
semi-	half, partly	semicircle, semicolon
uni-	one	uniform, unity

PREFIXES FOR TIME, DIRECTION, AND SPACE

Prefix	Definition	Examples
a-	in, on, of, up, to	abed, afoot
ab-	from, away, off	abdicate, abjure
ad-	to, toward	advance, adventure
ante-	before, previous	antecedent, antedate
anti-	against, opposing	antipathy, antidote
cata-	down, away, thoroughly	catastrophe, cataclysm
circum-	around	circumspect, circumference
com-	with, together, very	commotion, complicate
contra-	against, opposing	contradict, contravene
de-	from	depart
dia-	through, across, apart	diameter, diagnose
dis-	away, off, down, not	dissent, disappear
epi-	upon	epilogue
ex-	out	extract, excerpt
hypo-	under, beneath	hypodermic, hypothesis
inter-	among, between	intercede, interrupt
intra-	within	intramural, intrastate
ob-	against, opposing	objection
per-	through	perceive, permit
peri-	around	periscope, perimeter
post-	after, following	postpone, postscript
pre-	before, previous	prevent, preclude
pro-	forward, in place of	propel, pronoun
retro-	back, backward	retrospect, retrograde
sub-	under, beneath	subjugate, substitute
super-	above, extra	supersede, supernumerary
trans-	across, beyond, over	transact, transport
ultra-	beyond, excessively	ultramodern, ultrasonic

NEGATIVE PREFIXES

Prefix	Definition	Examples
a-	without, lacking	atheist, agnostic
in-	not, opposing	incapable, ineligible
non-	not	nonentity, nonsense
un-	not, reverse of	unhappy, unlock

22

EXTRA PREFIXES

Prefix	Definition	Examples
for-	away, off, from	forget, forswear
fore-	previous	foretell, forefathers
homo-	same, equal	homogenized, homonym
hyper-	excessive, over	hypercritical, hypertension
in-	in, into	intrude, invade
mal-	bad, poorly, not	malfunction, malpractice
mis-	bad, poorly, not	misspell, misfire
neo-	new	Neolithic, neoconservative
omni-	all, everywhere	omniscient, omnivore
ortho-	right, straight	orthogonal, orthodox
over-	above	overbearing, oversight
pan-	all, entire	panorama, pandemonium
para-	beside, beyond	parallel, paradox
re-	backward, again	revoke, recur
sym-	with, together	sympathy, symphony

Below is a list of common suffixes and their meanings:

ADJECTIVE SUFFIXES

Suffix	Definition	Examples
-able (-ible)	capable of being	toler*able*, ed*ible*
-esque	in the style of, like	picturesque, grotesque
-ful	filled with, marked by	thankful, zestful
-ific	make, cause	terrific, beatific
-ish	suggesting, like	churlish, childish
-less	lacking, without	hopeless, countless
-ous	marked by, given to	religious, riotous

NOUN SUFFIXES

Suffix	Definition	Examples
-acy	state, condition	accuracy, privacy
-ance	act, condition, fact	acceptance, vigilance
-ard	one that does excessively	drunkard, sluggard
-ation	action, state, result	occupation, starvation
-dom	state, rank, condition	serfdom, wisdom
-er (-or)	office, action	teacher, elevator, honor
-ess	feminine	waitress, duchess
-hood	state, condition	manhood, statehood
-ion	action, result, state	union, fusion
-ism	act, manner, doctrine	barbarism, socialism
-ist	worker, follower	monopolist, socialist
-ity (-ty)	state, quality, condition	acidity, civility, twenty
-ment	result, action	Refreshment
-ness	quality, state	greatness, tallness
-ship	position	internship, statesmanship
-sion (-tion)	state, result	revision, expedition
-th	act, state, quality	warmth, width
-tude	quality, state, result	magnitude, fortitude

VERB SUFFIXES

Suffix	Definition	Examples
-ate	having, showing	separate, desolate
-en	cause to be, become	deepen, strengthen
-fy	make, cause to have	glorify, fortify
-ize	cause to be, treat with	sterilize, mechanize

NUANCE AND WORD MEANINGS

SYNONYMS AND ANTONYMS

When you understand how words relate to each other, you will discover more in a passage. This is explained by understanding **synonyms** (e.g., words that mean the same thing) and **antonyms** (e.g., words that mean the opposite of one another). As an example, *dry* and *arid* are synonyms, and *dry* and *wet* are antonyms.

There are many pairs of words in English that can be considered synonyms, despite having slightly different definitions. For instance, the words *friendly* and *collegial* can both be used to describe a warm interpersonal relationship, and one would be correct to call them synonyms. However, *collegial* (kin to *colleague*) is often used in reference to professional or academic relationships, and *friendly* has no such connotation.

If the difference between the two words is too great, then they should not be called synonyms. *Hot* and *warm* are not synonyms because their meanings are too distinct. A good way to determine whether two words are synonyms is to substitute one word for the other word and verify that the meaning of the sentence has not changed. Substituting *warm* for *hot* in a sentence would convey a different meaning. Although warm and hot may seem close in meaning, warm generally means that the temperature is moderate, and hot generally means that the temperature is excessively high.

24

Antonyms are words with opposite meanings. *Light* and *dark*, *up* and *down*, *right* and *left*, *good* and *bad*: these are all sets of antonyms. Be careful to distinguish between antonyms and pairs of words that are simply different. *Black* and *gray*, for instance, are not antonyms because gray is not the opposite of black. *Black* and *white*, on the other hand, are antonyms.

Not every word has an antonym. For instance, many nouns do not. What would be the antonym of *chair*? During your exam, the questions related to antonyms are more likely to concern adjectives. You will recall that adjectives are words that describe a noun. Some common adjectives include *purple*, *fast*, *skinny*, and *sweet*. From those four adjectives, *purple* is the item that lacks a group of obvious antonyms.

> **Review Video: What Are Synonyms and Antonyms?**
> Visit mometrix.com/academy and enter code: 105612

DENOTATIVE VS. CONNOTATIVE MEANING

The **denotative** meaning of a word is the literal meaning. The **connotative** meaning goes beyond the denotative meaning to include the emotional reaction that a word may invoke. The connotative meaning often takes the denotative meaning a step further due to associations the reader makes with the denotative meaning. Readers can differentiate between the denotative and connotative meanings by first recognizing how authors use each meaning. Most non-fiction, for example, is fact-based and authors do not use flowery, figurative language. The reader can assume that the writer is using the denotative meaning of words. In fiction, the author may use the connotative meaning. Readers can determine whether the author is using the denotative or connotative meaning of a word by implementing context clues.

> **Review Video: Connotation and Denotation**
> Visit mometrix.com/academy and enter code: 310092

NUANCES OF WORD MEANING RELATIVE TO CONNOTATION, DENOTATION, DICTION, AND USAGE

A word's denotation is simply its objective dictionary definition. However, its connotation refers to the subjective associations, often emotional, that specific words evoke in listeners and readers. Two or more words can have the same dictionary meaning, but very different connotations. Writers use diction (word choice) to convey various nuances of thought and emotion by selecting synonyms for other words that best communicate the associations they want to trigger for readers. For example, a car engine is naturally greasy; in this sense, "greasy" is a neutral term. But when a person's smile, appearance, or clothing is described as "greasy," it has a negative connotation. Some words have even gained additional or different meanings over time. For example, *awful* used to be used to describe things that evoked a sense of awe. When *awful* is separated into its root word, awe, and suffix, -ful, it can be understood to mean "full of awe." However, the word is now commonly used to describe things that evoke repulsion, terror, or another intense, negative reaction.

> **Review Video: Word Usage in Sentences**
> Visit mometrix.com/academy and enter code: 197863

USING CONTEXT TO DETERMINE MEANING
CONTEXT CLUES

Readers of all levels will encounter words that they have either never seen or have encountered only on a limited basis. The best way to define a word in **context** is to look for nearby words that can assist in revealing the meaning of the word. For instance, unfamiliar nouns are often accompanied by examples that provide a definition. Consider the following sentence: *Dave arrived* *at the party in hilarious garb: a leopard-print shirt, buckskin trousers, and bright green sneakers.* If a reader was unfamiliar with the meaning of garb, he or she could read the examples (i.e., a leopard-print shirt, buckskin trousers, and high heels) and quickly determine that the word means *clothing*. Examples will not always be this obvious. Consider this sentence: *Parsley, lemon, and flowers were just a few of the items he used as garnishes.* Here, the word *garnishes* is exemplified by parsley, lemon, and flowers. Readers who have eaten in a variety of restaurants will probably be able to identify a garnish as something used to decorate a plate.

USING CONTRAST IN CONTEXT CLUES

In addition to looking at the context of a passage, readers can use contrast to define an unfamiliar word in context. In many sentences, the author will not describe the unfamiliar word directly; instead, he or she will describe the opposite of the unfamiliar word. Thus, you are provided with some information that will bring you closer to defining the word. Consider the following example: *Despite his intelligence, Hector's low brow and bad posture made him look obtuse.* The author writes that Hector's appearance does not convey intelligence. Therefore, *obtuse* must mean unintelligent. Here is another example: *Despite the horrible weather, we were beatific about our trip to Alaska.* The word *despite* indicates that the speaker's feelings were at odds with the weather. Since the weather is described as *horrible*, then *beatific* must mean something positive.

SUBSTITUTION TO FIND MEANING

In some cases, there will be very few contextual clues to help a reader define the meaning of an unfamiliar word. When this happens, one strategy that readers may employ is **substitution**. A good reader will brainstorm some possible synonyms for the given word, and he or she will substitute these words into the sentence. If the sentence and the surrounding passage continue to make sense, then the substitution has revealed at least some information about the unfamiliar word. Consider the sentence: *Frank's admonition rang in her ears as she climbed the mountain.* A reader unfamiliar with *admonition* might come up with some substitutions like *vow, promise, advice, complaint*, or *compliment*. All of these words make general sense of the sentence, though their meanings are diverse. However, this process has suggested that an admonition is some sort of message. The substitution strategy is rarely able to pinpoint a precise definition, but this process can be effective as a last resort.

Occasionally, you will be able to define an unfamiliar word by looking at the descriptive words in the context. Consider the following sentence: *Fred dragged the recalcitrant boy kicking and screaming up the stairs.* The words *dragged, kicking*, and *screaming* all suggest that the boy does not want to go up the stairs. The reader may assume that *recalcitrant* means something like unwilling or protesting. In this example, an unfamiliar adjective was identified.

Additionally, using description to define an unfamiliar noun is a common practice compared to unfamiliar adjectives, as in this sentence: *Don's wrinkled frown and constantly shaking fist identified him as a curmudgeon of the first order.* Don is described as having a *wrinkled frown and constantly shaking fist*, suggesting that a *curmudgeon* must be a grumpy person. Contrasts do not always provide detailed information about the unfamiliar word, but they at least give the reader some clues.

WORDS WITH MULTIPLE MEANINGS

When a word has more than one meaning, readers can have difficulty determining how the word is being used in a given sentence. For instance, the verb *cleave*, can mean either *join* or *separate*. When

26

readers come upon this word, they will have to select the definition that makes the most sense. Consider the following sentence: *Hermione's knife cleaved the bread cleanly.* Since a knife cannot join bread together, the word must indicate separation. A slightly more difficult example would be the sentence: *The birds cleaved to one another as they flew from the oak tree.* Immediately, the presence of the words *to one another* should suggest that in this sentence *cleave* is being used to mean *join.* Discovering the intent of a word with multiple meanings requires the same tricks as defining an unknown word: look for contextual clues and evaluate the substituted words.

CONTEXT CLUES TO HELP DETERMINE MEANINGS OF WORDS

If readers simply bypass unknown words, they can reach unclear conclusions about what they read. However, looking for the definition of every unfamiliar word in the dictionary can slow their reading progress. Moreover, the dictionary may list multiple definitions for a word, so readers must search the word's context for meaning. Hence context is important to new vocabulary regardless of reader methods. Four types of context clues are examples, definitions, descriptive words, and opposites. Authors may use a certain word, and then follow it with several different examples of what it describes. Sometimes authors actually supply a definition of a word they use, which is especially true in informational and technical texts. Authors may use descriptive words that elaborate upon a vocabulary word they just used. Authors may also use opposites with negation that help define meaning.

EXAMPLES AND DEFINITIONS

An author may use a word and then give examples that illustrate its meaning. Consider this text: "Teachers who do not know how to use sign language can help students who are deaf or hard of hearing understand certain instructions by using gestures instead, like pointing their fingers to indicate which direction to look or go; holding up a hand, palm outward, to indicate stopping; holding the hands flat, palms up, curling a finger toward oneself in a beckoning motion to indicate 'come here'; or curling all fingers toward oneself repeatedly to indicate 'come on', 'more', or 'continue.'" The author of this text has used the word "gestures" and then followed it with examples, so a reader unfamiliar with the word could deduce from the examples that "gestures" means "hand motions." Readers can find examples by looking for signal words "for example," "for instance," "like," "such as," and "e.g."

While readers sometimes have to look for definitions of unfamiliar words in a dictionary or do some work to determine a word's meaning from its surrounding context, at other times an author may make it easier for readers by defining certain words. For example, an author may write, "The company did not have sufficient capital, that is, available money, to continue operations." The author defined "capital" as "available money," and heralded the definition with the phrase "that is." Another way that authors supply word definitions is with appositives. Rather than being introduced by a signal phrase like "that is," "namely," or "meaning," an appositive comes after the vocabulary word it defines and is enclosed within two commas. For example, an author may write, "The Indians introduced the Pilgrims to pemmican, cakes they made of lean meat dried and mixed with fat, which proved greatly beneficial to keep settlers from starving while trapping." In this example, the appositive phrase following "pemmican" and preceding "which" defines the word "pemmican."

DESCRIPTIONS

When readers encounter a word they do not recognize in a text, the author may expand on that word to illustrate it better. While the author may do this to make the prose more picturesque and vivid, the reader can also take advantage of this description to provide context clues to the meaning of the unfamiliar word. For example, an author may write, "The man sitting next to me on the airplane was obese. His shirt stretched across his vast expanse of flesh, strained almost to bursting."

The descriptive second sentence elaborates on and helps to define the previous sentence's word "obese" to mean extremely fat. A reader unfamiliar with the word "repugnant" can decipher its meaning through an author's accompanying description: "The way the child grimaced and shuddered as he swallowed the medicine showed that its taste was particularly repugnant."

OPPOSITES

Text authors sometimes introduce a contrasting or opposing idea before or after a concept they present. They may do this to emphasize or heighten the idea they present by contrasting it with something that is the reverse. However, readers can also use these context clues to understand familiar words. For example, an author may write, "Our conversation was not cheery. We sat and talked very solemnly about his experience and a number of similar events." The reader who is not familiar with the word "solemnly" can deduce by the author's preceding use of "not cheery" that "solemn" means the opposite of cheery or happy, so it must mean serious or sad. Or if someone writes, "Don't condemn his entire project because you couldn't find anything good to say about it," readers unfamiliar with "condemn" can understand from the sentence structure that it means the opposite of saying anything good, so it must mean reject, dismiss, or disapprove. "Entire" adds another context clue, meaning total or complete rejection.

SYNTAX TO DETERMINE PART OF SPEECH AND MEANINGS OF WORDS

Syntax refers to sentence structure and word order. Suppose that a reader encounters an unfamiliar word when reading a text. To illustrate, consider an invented word like "splunch." If this word is used in a sentence like "Please splunch that ball to me," the reader can assume from syntactic context that "splunch" is a verb. We would not use a noun, adjective, adverb, or preposition with the object "that ball," and the prepositional phrase "to me" further indicates "splunch" represents an action. However, in the sentence, "Please hand that splunch to me," the reader can assume that "splunch" is a noun. Demonstrative adjectives like "that" modify nouns. Also, we hand someone some*thing*—a thing being a noun; we do not hand someone a verb, adjective, or adverb. Some sentences contain further clues. For example, from the sentence, "The princess wore the glittering splunch on her head," the reader can deduce that it is a crown, tiara, or something similar from the syntactic context, without knowing the word.

SYNTAX TO INDICATE DIFFERENT MEANINGS OF SIMILAR SENTENCES

The syntax, or structure, of a sentence affords grammatical cues that aid readers in comprehending the meanings of words, phrases, and sentences in the texts that they read. Seemingly minor differences in how the words or phrases in a sentence are ordered can make major differences in meaning. For example, two sentences can use exactly the same words but have different meanings based on the word order:

- "The man with a broken arm sat in a chair."
- "The man sat in a chair with a broken arm."

While both sentences indicate that a man sat in a chair, differing syntax indicates whether the man's or chair's arm was broken.

DETERMINING MEANING OF PHRASES AND PARAGRAPHS

Like unknown words, the meanings of phrases, paragraphs, and entire works can also be difficult to discern. Each of these can be better understood with added context. However, for larger groups of words, more context is needed. Unclear phrases are similar to unclear words, and the same methods can be used to understand their meaning. However, it is also important to consider how the individual words in the phrase work together. Paragraphs are a bit more complicated. Just as words must be compared to other words in a sentence, paragraphs must be compared to other paragraphs in a composition or a section.

DETERMINING MEANING IN VARIOUS TYPES OF COMPOSITIONS

To understand the meaning of an entire composition, the type of composition must be considered. **Expository writing** is generally organized so that each paragraph focuses on explaining one idea, or part of an idea, and its relevance. **Persuasive writing** uses paragraphs for different purposes to organize the parts of the argument. **Unclear paragraphs** must be read in the context of the paragraphs around them for their meaning to be fully understood. The meaning of full texts can also be unclear at times. The purpose of composition is also important for understanding the meaning of a text. To quickly understand the broad meaning of a text, look to the introductory and concluding paragraphs. Fictional texts are different. Some fictional works have implicit meanings, but some do not. The target audience must be considered for understanding texts that do have an implicit meaning, as most children's fiction will clearly state any lessons or morals. For other fiction, the application of literary theories and criticism may be helpful for understanding the text.

PLOT AND STORY STRUCTURE
PLOT AND STORY STRUCTURE

The **plot** includes the events that happen in a story and the order in which they are told to the reader. There are several types of plot structures, as stories can be told in many ways. The most common plot structure is the chronological plot, which presents the events to the reader in the same order they occur for the characters in the story. Chronological plots usually have five main parts, the **exposition**, **rising action**, the **climax**, **falling action**, and the **resolution**. This type of plot structure guides the reader through the story's events as the characters experience them and is the easiest structure to understand and identify. While this is the most common plot structure, many stories are nonlinear, which means the plot does not sequence events in the same order the characters experience them. Such stories might include elements like flashbacks that cause the story to be nonlinear.

> **Review Video: How to Make a Story Map**
> Visit mometrix.com/academy and enter code: 261719

EXPOSITION

The **exposition** is at the beginning of the story and generally takes place before the rising action begins. The purpose of the exposition is to give the reader context for the story, which the author may do by introducing one or more characters, describing the setting or world, or explaining the events leading up to the point where the story begins. The exposition may still include events that contribute to the plot, but the **rising action** and main conflict of the story are not part of the exposition. Some narratives skip the exposition and begin the story with the beginning of the rising action, which causes the reader to learn the context as the story intensifies.

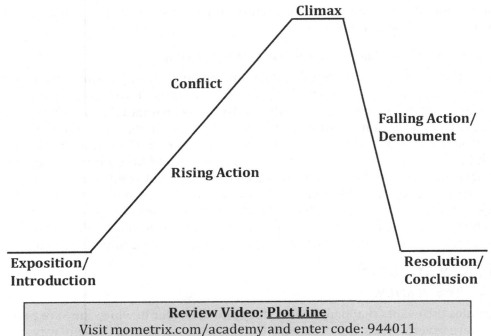

<u>CONFLICT</u>

A **conflict** is a problem to be solved. Literary plots typically include one conflict or more. Characters' attempts to resolve conflicts drive the narrative's forward movement. **Conflict resolution** is often the protagonist's primary occupation. Physical conflicts like exploring, wars, and escapes tend to make plots most suspenseful and exciting. Emotional, mental, or moral conflicts tend to make stories more personally gratifying or rewarding for many audiences. Conflicts can be external or internal. A major type of internal conflict is some inner personal battle, or **man versus self**. Major types of external conflicts include **man versus nature**, **man versus man**, and **man versus society**. Readers can identify conflicts in literary plots by identifying the protagonist and antagonist and asking why they conflict, what events develop the conflict, where the climax occurs, and how they identify with the characters.

Read the following paragraph and discuss the type of conflict present:

> Timothy was shocked out of sleep by the appearance of a bear just outside his tent. After panicking for a moment, he remembered some advice he had read in preparation for this trip: he should make noise so the bear would not be startled. As Timothy started to hum and sing, the bear wandered away.

There are three main types of conflict in literature: **man versus man**, **man versus nature**, and **man versus self**. This paragraph is an example of man versus nature. Timothy is in conflict with the bear. Even though no physical conflict like an attack exists, Timothy is pitted against the bear.

Timothy uses his knowledge to "defeat" the bear and keep himself safe. The solution to the conflict is that Timothy makes noise, the bear wanders away, and Timothy is safe.

> **Review Video: <u>Conflict</u>**
> Visit mometrix.com/academy and enter code: 559550
>
> **Review Video: <u>Determining Relationships in a Story</u>**
> Visit mometrix.com/academy and enter code: 929925

RISING ACTION

The **rising action** is the part of the story where conflict **intensifies**. The rising action begins with an event that prompts the main conflict of the story. This may also be called the **inciting incident**. The main conflict generally occurs between the protagonist and an antagonist, but this is not the only type of conflict that may occur in a narrative. After this event, the protagonist works to resolve the main conflict by preparing for an altercation, pursuing a goal, fleeing an antagonist, or doing some other action that will end the conflict. The rising action is composed of several additional events that increase the story's tension. Most often, other developments will occur alongside the growth of the main conflict, such as character development or the development of minor conflicts. The rising action ends with the **climax**, which is the point of highest tension in the story.

CLIMAX

The **climax** is the event in the narrative that marks the height of the story's conflict or tension. The event that takes place at the story's climax will end the rising action and bring about the results of the main conflict. If the conflict was between a good protagonist and an evil antagonist, the climax may be a final battle between the two characters. If the conflict is an adventurer looking for heavily guarded treasure, the climax may be the adventurer's encounter with the final obstacle that protects the treasure. The climax may be made of multiple scenes, but can usually be summarized as one event. Once the conflict and climax are complete, the **falling action** begins.

FALLING ACTION

The **falling action** shows what happens in the story between the climax and the resolution. The falling action often composes a much smaller portion of the story than the rising action does. While the climax includes the end of the main conflict, the falling action may show the results of any minor conflicts in the story. For example, if the protagonist encountered a troll on the way to find some treasure, and the troll demanded the protagonist share the treasure after retrieving it, the falling action would include the protagonist returning to share the treasure with the troll. Similarly, any unexplained major events are usually made clear during the falling action. Once all significant elements of the story are resolved or addressed, the story's resolution will occur. The **resolution** is the end of the story, which shows the final result of the plot's events and shows what life is like for the main characters once they are no longer experiencing the story's conflicts.

RESOLUTION

The way the conflict is **resolved** depends on the type of conflict. The plot of any book starts with the lead up to the conflict, then the conflict itself, and finally the solution, or **resolution**, to the conflict. In **man versus man** conflicts, the conflict is often resolved by two parties coming to some sort of agreement or by one party triumphing over the other party. In **man versus nature** conflicts, the conflict is often resolved by man coming to some realization about some aspect of nature. In

man versus self conflicts, the conflict is often resolved by the character growing or coming to an understanding about part of himself.

THEME

A **theme** is a central idea demonstrated by a passage. Often, a theme is a lesson or moral contained in the text, but it does not have to be. It also is a unifying idea that is used throughout the text; it can take the form of a common setting, idea, symbol, design, or recurring event. A passage can have two or more themes that convey its overall idea. The theme or themes of a passage are often based on **universal themes**. They can frequently be expressed using well-known sayings about life, society, or human nature, such as "Hard work pays off" or "Good triumphs over evil." Themes are not usually stated **explicitly**. The reader must figure them out by carefully reading the passage. Themes are created through descriptive language or events in the plot. The events of a story help shape the themes of a passage.

EXAMPLE

Explain why "if you care about something, you need to take care of it" accurately describes the theme of the following excerpt.

> Luca collected baseball cards, but he wasn't very careful with them. He left them around the house. His dog liked to chew. One day, Luca and his friend Bart were looking at his collection. Then they went outside. When Luca got home, he saw his dog chewing on his cards. They were ruined.

This excerpt tells the story of a boy who is careless with his baseball cards and leaves them lying around. His dog ends up chewing them and ruining them. The lesson is that if you care about something, you need to take care of it. This is the theme, or point, of the story. Some stories have more than one theme, but this is not really true of this excerpt. The reader needs to figure out the theme based on what happens in the story. Sometimes, as in the case of fables, the theme is stated directly in the text. However, this is not usually the case.

> **Review Video: Themes in Literature**
> Visit mometrix.com/academy and enter code: 732074

NARRATOR'S POINT OF VIEW
POINT OF VIEW

Another element that impacts a text is the author's point of view. The **point of view** of a text is the perspective from which a passage is told. An author will always have a point of view about a story before he or she draws up a plot line. The author will know what events they want to take place, how they want the characters to interact, and how they want the story to resolve. An author will also have an opinion on the topic or series of events which is presented in the story that is based on their prior experience and beliefs.

The two main points of view that authors use, especially in a work of fiction, are first person and third person. If the narrator of the story is also the main character, or *protagonist*, the text is written in first-person point of view. In first person, the author writes from the perspective of *I*. Third-person point of view is probably the most common that authors use in their passages. Using third person, authors refer to each character by using *he* or *she*. In third-person omniscient, the narrator is not a character in the story and tells the story of all of the characters at the same time.

> **Review Video: Point of View**
> Visit mometrix.com/academy and enter code: 383336

FIRST-PERSON NARRATION

First-person narratives let narrators express inner feelings and thoughts, especially when the narrator is the protagonist as Lemuel Gulliver is in Jonathan Swift's *Gulliver's Travels.* The narrator may be a close friend of the protagonist, like Dr. Watson in Sir Arthur Conan Doyle's *Sherlock Holmes.* Or, the narrator can be less involved with the main characters and plot, like Nick Carraway in F. Scott Fitzgerald's *The Great Gatsby.* When a narrator reports others' narratives, she or he is a "**frame narrator**," like the nameless narrator of Joseph Conrad's *Heart of Darkness* or Mr. Lockwood in Emily Brontë's *Wuthering Heights.* **First-person plural** is unusual but can be effective. Isaac Asimov's *I, Robot*, William Faulkner's *A Rose for Emily*, Maxim Gorky's *Twenty-Six Men and a Girl*, and Jeffrey Eugenides' *The Virgin Suicides* all use first-person plural narration. Author Kurt Vonnegut is the first-person narrator in his semi-autobiographical novel *Timequake.* Also unusual, but effective, is a **first-person omniscient** (rather than the more common third-person omniscient) narrator, like Death in Markus Zusak's *The Book Thief* and the ghost in Alice Sebold's *The Lovely Bones.*

SECOND-PERSON NARRATION

While **second-person** address is very commonplace in popular song lyrics, it is the least used form of narrative voice in literary works. Popular serial books of the 1980s like *Fighting Fantasy* or *Choose Your Own Adventure* employed second-person narratives. In some cases, a narrative combines both second-person and first-person voices, using the pronouns *you* and *I*. This can draw readers into the story, and it can also enable the authors to compare directly "your" and "my" feelings, thoughts, and actions. When the narrator is also a character in the story, as in Edgar Allan Poe's short story "The Tell-Tale Heart" or Jay McInerney's novel *Bright Lights, Big City,* the narrative is better defined as first-person despite it also addressing "you."

THIRD-PERSON NARRATION

Narration in the third person is the most prevalent type, as it allows authors the most flexibility. It is so common that readers simply assume without needing to be informed that the narrator is not a character in the story, or involved in its events. **Third-person singular** is used more frequently than **third-person plural**, though some authors have also effectively used plural. However, both singular and plural are most often included in stories according to which characters are being described. The third-person narrator may be either objective or subjective, and either omniscient or limited. **Objective third-person** narration does not include what the characters described are thinking or feeling, while **subjective third-person** narration does. The **third-person omniscient** narrator knows everything about all characters, including their thoughts and emotions, and all related places, times, and events. However, the **third-person limited** narrator may know everything about a particular character, but is limited to that character. In other words, the narrator cannot speak about anything that character does not know.

ALTERNATING-PERSON NARRATION

Although authors more commonly write stories from one point of view, there are also instances wherein they alternate the narrative voice within the same book. For example, they may sometimes use an omniscient third-person narrator and a more intimate first-person narrator at other times. In J. K. Rowling's series of *Harry Potter* novels, she often writes in a third-person limited narrative, but sometimes changes to narration by characters other than the protagonist. George R. R. Martin's series *A Song of Ice and Fire* changes the point of view to coincide with divisions between chapters. The same technique is used by Erin Hunter (a pseudonym for several authors of the *Warriors, Seekers,* and *Survivors* book series). Authors using first-person narrative sometimes switch to third-person to describe significant action scenes, especially those where the narrator was absent or uninvolved, as Barbara Kingsolver does in her novel *The Poisonwood Bible.*

SETTING, MOOD, AND TONE
SETTING AND TIME FRAME

A literary text has both a setting and time frame. A **setting** is the place in which the story as a whole is set. The **time frame** is the period in which the story is set. This may refer to the historical period the story takes place in or if the story takes place over a single day. Both setting and time frame are relevant to a text's meaning because they help the reader place the story in time and space. An author uses setting and time frame to anchor a text, create a mood, and enhance its meaning. This helps a reader understand why a character acts the way he does, or why certain events in the story are important. The setting impacts the **plot** and character **motivations**, while the time frame helps place the story in **chronological context**.

EXAMPLE

Read the following excerpt from The Adventures of Huckleberry Finn by Mark Twain and analyze the relevance of setting to the text's meaning:

> We said there warn't no home like a raft, after all. Other places do seem so cramped up and smothery, but a raft don't. You feel mighty free and easy and comfortable on a raft.

This excerpt from *The Adventures of Huckleberry Finn* by Mark Twain reveals information about the **setting** of the book. By understanding that the main character, Huckleberry Finn, lives on a raft, the reader can place the story on a river, in this case, the Mississippi River in the South before the Civil War. The information about the setting also gives the reader clues about the **character** of Huck Finn: he clearly values independence and freedom, and he likes the outdoors. The information about the setting in the quote helps the reader to better understand the rest of the text.

SYNTAX AND WORD CHOICE

Authors use words and **syntax**, or sentence structure, to make their texts unique, convey their own writing style, and sometimes to make a point or emphasis. They know that word choice and syntax contribute to the reader's understanding of the text as well as to the tone and mood of a text.

> **Review Video: What is Syntax?**
> Visit mometrix.com/academy and enter code: 242280

MOOD AND TONE

Mood is a story's atmosphere, or the feelings the reader gets from reading it. The way authors set the mood in writing is comparable to the way filmmakers use music to set the mood in movies. Instead of music, though, writers judiciously select descriptive words to evoke certain **moods**. The mood of a work may convey joy, anger, bitterness, hope, gloom, fear, apprehension, or any other emotion the author wants the reader to feel. In addition to vocabulary choices, authors also use figurative expressions, particular sentence structures, and choices of diction that project and reinforce the moods they want to create. Whereas mood is the reader's emotions evoked by reading what is written, **tone** is the emotions and attitudes of the writer that she or he expresses in the writing. Authors use the same literary techniques to establish tone as they do to establish mood. An author may use a humorous tone, an angry or sad tone, a sentimental or unsentimental tone, or something else entirely.

MOOD AND TONE IN THE GREAT GATSBY

To understand the difference between mood and tone, look at this excerpt from F. Scott Fitzgerald's *The Great Gatsby*. In this passage, Nick Caraway, the novel's narrator, is describing his affordable house, which sits in a neighborhood full of expensive mansions.

> "I lived at West Egg, the—well the less fashionable of the two, though this is a most superficial tag to express the bizarre and not a little sinister contrast between them. My house was at the very tip of the egg, only fifty yard from the Sound, and squeezed between two huge places that rented for twelve or fifteen thousand a season ... My own house was an eyesore, but it was a small eyesore, and it had been overlooked, so I had a view of the water, a partial view of my neighbor's lawn, and the consoling proximity of millionaires—all for eighty dollars a month."

In this description, the mood created for the reader does not match the tone created through the narrator. The mood in this passage is one of dissatisfaction and inferiority. Nick compares his home to his neighbors', saying he lives in the "less fashionable" neighborhood and that his house is "overlooked," an "eyesore," and "squeezed between two huge" mansions. He also adds that his placement allows him the "consoling proximity of millionaires." A literal reading of these details leads the reader to have negative feelings toward Nick's house and his economic inferiority to his neighbors, creating the mood.

However, Fitzgerald also conveys an opposing attitude, or tone, through Nick's description. Nick calls the distinction between the neighborhoods "superficial," showing a suspicion of the value suggested by the neighborhoods' titles, properties, and residents. Nick also undermines his critique of his own home by calling it "a small eyesore" and claiming it has "been overlooked." However, he follows these statements with a description of his surroundings, claiming that he has "a view of the water" and can see some of his wealthy neighbor's property from his home, and a comparison between the properties' rent. While the mental image created for the reader depicts a small house shoved between looming mansions, the tone suggests that Nick enjoys these qualities about his home, or at least finds it charming. He acknowledges its shortcomings, but includes the benefits of his home's unassuming appearance.

> **Review Video: Style, Tone, and Mood**
> Visit mometrix.com/academy and enter code: 416961

HISTORICAL AND SOCIAL CONTEXT

Fiction that is heavily influenced by a historical or social context cannot be comprehended as the author intended if the reader does not keep this context in mind. Many important elements of the text will be influenced by any context, including symbols, allusions, settings, and plot events. These contexts, as well as the identity of the work's author, can help to inform the reader about the author's concerns and intended meanings. For example, George Orwell published his novel *1984* in the year 1949, soon after the end of World War II. At that time, following the defeat of the Nazis, the Cold War began between the Western Allied nations and the Eastern Soviet Communists. People were therefore concerned about the conflict between the freedoms afforded by Western democracies versus the oppression represented by Communism. Orwell had also previously fought in the Spanish Civil War against a Spanish regime that he and his fellows viewed as oppressive. From this information, readers can infer that Orwell was concerned about oppression by

totalitarian governments. This informs *1984*'s story of Winston Smith's rebellion against the oppressive "Big Brother" government, of the fictional dictatorial state of Oceania, and his capture, torture, and ultimate conversion by that government. Some literary theories also seek to use historical and social contexts to reveal deeper meanings and implications in a text.

Information and Ideas

MAIN IDEAS AND SUPPORTING DETAILS
IDENTIFYING TOPICS AND MAIN IDEAS

One of the most important skills in reading comprehension is the identification of **topics** and **main ideas**. There is a subtle difference between these two features. The topic is the subject of a text (i.e., what the text is all about). The main idea, on the other hand, is the most important point being made by the author. The topic is usually expressed in a few words at the most while the main idea often needs a full sentence to be completely defined. As an example, a short passage might be written on the topic of penguins, and the main idea could be written as *Penguins are different from other birds in many ways.* In most nonfiction writing, the topic and the main idea will be **stated directly** and often appear in a sentence at the very beginning or end of the text. When being tested on an understanding of the author's topic, you may be able to skim the passage for the general idea by reading only the first sentence of each paragraph. A body paragraph's first sentence is often— but not always—the main **topic sentence** which gives you a summary of the content in the paragraph.

However, there are cases in which the reader must figure out an **unstated** topic or main idea. In these instances, you must read every sentence of the text and try to come up with an overarching idea that is supported by each of those sentences.

Note: The main idea should not be confused with the thesis statement. While the main idea gives a brief, general summary of a text, the thesis statement provides a **specific perspective** on an issue that the author supports with evidence.

> **Review Video: <u>Topics and Main Ideas</u>**
> Visit mometrix.com/academy and enter code: 407801

SUPPORTING DETAILS

Supporting details are smaller pieces of evidence that provide backing for the main point. In order to show that a main idea is correct or valid, an author must add details that prove their point. All texts contain details, but they are only classified as supporting details when they serve to reinforce some larger point. Supporting details are most commonly found in informative and persuasive texts. In some cases, they will be clearly indicated with terms like *for example* or *for instance*, or they will be enumerated with terms like *first*, *second*, and *last*. However, you need to be prepared for texts that do not contain those indicators. As a reader, you should consider whether the author's supporting details really back up his or her main point. Details can be factual and correct, yet they may not be **relevant** to the author's point. Conversely, details can be relevant, but be ineffective because they are based on opinion or assertions that cannot be proven.

> **Review Video: <u>Supporting Details</u>**
> Visit mometrix.com/academy and enter code: 396297

AUTHOR'S PURPOSE
AUTHOR'S PURPOSE

Usually, identifying the author's **purpose** is easier than identifying his or her **position**. In most cases, the author has no interest in hiding his or her purpose. A text that is meant to entertain, for instance, should be written to please the reader. Most narratives, or stories, are written to entertain, though they may also inform or persuade. Informative texts are easy to identify, while the most difficult purpose of a text to identify is persuasion because the author has an interest in making this purpose hard to detect. When a reader discovers that the author is trying to persuade, he or she should be skeptical of the argument. For this reason, persuasive texts often try to establish an entertaining tone and hope to amuse the reader into agreement. On the other hand, an informative tone may be implemented to create an appearance of authority and objectivity.

An author's purpose is evident often in the **organization** of the text (e.g., section headings in bold font points to an informative text). However, you may not have such organization available to you in your exam. Instead, if the author makes his or her main idea clear from the beginning, then the likely purpose of the text is to **inform**. If the author begins by making a claim and provides various arguments to support that claim, then the purpose is probably to **persuade**. If the author tells a story or wants to gain the reader's attention more than to push a particular point or deliver information, then his or her purpose is most likely to **entertain**. As a reader, you must judge authors on how well they accomplish their purpose. In other words, you need to consider the type of passage (e.g., technical, persuasive, etc.) that the author has written and if the author has followed the requirements of the passage type.

> **Review Video: Understanding the Author's Intent**
> Visit mometrix.com/academy and enter code: 511819

INFORMATIONAL TEXTS

An **informational text** is written to educate and enlighten readers. Informational texts are almost always nonfiction and are rarely structured as a story. The intention of an informational text is to deliver information in the most comprehensible way. So, look for the structure of the text to be very clear. In an informational text, the thesis statement is one or two sentences that normally appears at the end of the first paragraph. The author may use some colorful language, but he or she is likely to put more emphasis on clarity and precision. Informational essays do not typically appeal to the emotions. They often contain facts and figures and rarely include the opinion of the author; however, readers should remain aware of the possibility for bias as those facts are presented. Sometimes a persuasive essay can resemble an informative essay, especially if the author maintains an even tone and presents his or her views as if they were established fact.

> **Review Video: Informational Text**
> Visit mometrix.com/academy and enter code: 924964

PERSUASIVE WRITING

In a persuasive essay, the author is attempting to change the reader's mind or **convince** him or her of something that he or she did not believe previously. There are several identifying characteristics of **persuasive writing**. One is **opinion presented as fact**. When authors attempt to persuade readers, they often present their opinions as if they were fact. Readers must be on guard for statements that sound factual but which cannot be subjected to research, observation, or experiment. Another characteristic of persuasive writing is **emotional language**. An author will often try to play on the emotions of readers by appealing to their sympathy or sense of morality. When an author uses colorful or evocative language with the intent of arousing the reader's

passions, then the author may be attempting to persuade. Finally, in many cases, a persuasive text will give an **unfair explanation of opposing positions**, if these positions are mentioned at all.

ENTERTAINING TEXTS

The success or failure of an author's intent to **entertain** is determined by those who read the author's work. Entertaining texts may be either fiction or nonfiction, and they may describe real or imagined people, places, and events. Entertaining texts are often narratives or poems. A text that is written to entertain is likely to contain **colorful language** that engages the imagination and the emotions. Such writing often features a great deal of figurative language, which typically enlivens the subject matter with images and analogies.

Though an entertaining text is not usually written to persuade or inform, authors may accomplish both of these tasks in their work. An entertaining text may *appeal to the reader's emotions* and cause him or her to think differently about a particular subject. In any case, entertaining texts tend to showcase the personality of the author more than other types of writing.

DESCRIPTIVE TEXT

In a sense, almost all writing is descriptive, insofar as an author seeks to describe events, ideas, or people to the reader. Some texts, however, are primarily concerned with **description**. A descriptive text focuses on a particular subject and attempts to depict the subject in a way that will be clear to readers. Descriptive texts contain many adjectives and adverbs (i.e., words that give shades of meaning and create a more detailed mental picture for the reader). A descriptive text fails when it is unclear to the reader. A descriptive text will certainly be informative and may be persuasive and entertaining as well.

> **Review Video: Descriptive Texts**
> Visit mometrix.com/academy and enter code: 174903

EXPRESSION OF FEELINGS

When an author intends to **express feelings**, he or she may use **expressive and bold language**. An author may write with emotion for any number of reasons. Sometimes, authors will express feelings because they are describing a personal situation of great pain or happiness. In other situations, authors will attempt to persuade the reader and will use emotion to stir up the passions. This kind of expression is easy to identify when the writer uses phrases like *I felt* and *I sense*. However, readers may find that the author will simply describe feelings without introducing them. As a reader, you must know the importance of recognizing when an author is expressing emotion and not to become overwhelmed by sympathy or passion. Readers should maintain some **detachment** so that they can still evaluate the strength of the author's argument or the quality of the writing.

> **Review Video: Emotional Language in Literature**
> Visit mometrix.com/academy and enter code: 759390

EXPOSITORY PASSAGE

An **expository** passage aims to **inform** and enlighten readers. Expository passages are nonfiction and usually center around a simple, easily defined topic. Since the goal of exposition is to teach, such a passage should be as clear as possible. Often, an expository passage contains helpful organizing words, like *first, next, for example,* and *therefore*. These words keep the reader **oriented** in the text. Although expository passages do not need to feature colorful language and artful writing, they are often more effective with these features. For a reader, the challenge of expository

38

passages is to maintain steady attention. Expository passages are not always about subjects that will naturally interest a reader, so the writer is often more concerned with **clarity** and **comprehensibility** than with engaging the reader. By reading actively, you can ensure a good habit of focus when reading an expository passage.

> **Review Video: Expository Passages**
> Visit mometrix.com/academy and enter code: 256515

NARRATIVE PASSAGE

A **narrative** passage is a story that can be fiction or nonfiction. However, there are a few elements that a text must have in order to be classified as a narrative. First, the text must have a **plot** (i.e., a series of events). Narratives often proceed in a clear sequence, but this is not a requirement. If the narrative is good, then these events will be interesting to readers. Second, a narrative has **characters**. These characters could be people, animals, or even inanimate objects—so long as they participate in the plot. Third, a narrative passage often contains **figurative language** which is meant to stimulate the imagination of readers by making comparisons and observations. For instance, a *metaphor*, a common piece of figurative language, is a description of one thing in terms of another. *The moon was a frosty snowball* is an example of a metaphor. In the literal sense this is obviously untrue, but the comparison suggests a certain mood for the reader.

TECHNICAL PASSAGE

A **technical** passage is written to *describe* a complex object or process. Technical writing is common in medical and technological fields, in which complex ideas of mathematics, science, and engineering need to be explained *simply* and *clearly*. To ease comprehension, a technical passage usually proceeds in a very logical order. Technical passages often have clear headings and subheadings, which are used to keep the reader oriented in the text. Additionally, you will find that these passages divide sections up with numbers or letters. Many technical passages look more like an outline than a piece of prose. The amount of **jargon** or difficult vocabulary will vary in a technical passage depending on the intended audience. As much as possible, technical passages try to avoid language that the reader will have to research in order to understand the message, yet readers will find that jargon cannot always be avoided.

> **Review Video: Technical Passages**
> Visit mometrix.com/academy and enter code: 478923

COMMON ORGANIZATIONS OF TEXTS
ORGANIZATION OF THE TEXT

The way a text is organized can help readers understand the author's intent and his or her conclusions. There are various ways to organize a text, and each one has a purpose and use. Usually, authors will organize information logically in a passage so the reader can follow and locate the information within the text. However, since not all passages are written with the same logical structure, you need to be familiar with several different types of passage structure.

> **Review Video: Organizational Methods to Structure Text**
> Visit mometrix.com/academy and enter code: 606263
>
> **Review Video: Sequence of Events in a Story**
> Visit mometrix.com/academy and enter code: 807512

CHRONOLOGICAL

When using **chronological** order, the author presents information in the order that it happened. For example, biographies are typically written in chronological order. The subject's birth and childhood are presented first, followed by their adult life, and lastly the events leading up to the person's death.

CAUSE AND EFFECT

One of the most common text structures is **cause and effect**. A **cause** is an act or event that makes something happen, and an **effect** is the thing that happens as a result of the cause. A cause-and-effect relationship is not always explicit, but there are some terms in English that signal causes, such as *since*, *because*, and *due to*. Furthermore, terms that signal effects include *consequently, therefore, this leads to*. As an example, consider the sentence *Because the sky was clear, Ron did not bring an umbrella*. The cause is the clear sky, and the effect is that Ron did not bring an umbrella. However, readers may find that sometimes the cause-and-effect relationship will not be clearly noted. For instance, the sentence *He was late and missed the meeting* does not contain any signaling words, but the sentence still contains a cause (he was late) and an effect (he missed the meeting).

> **Review Video: Cause and Effect**
> Visit mometrix.com/academy and enter code: 868099
>
> **Review Video: Rhetorical Strategy of Cause and Effect Analysis**
> Visit mometrix.com/academy and enter code: 725944

MULTIPLE EFFECTS

Be aware of the possibility for a single cause to have **multiple effects.** (e.g., *Single cause*: Because you left your homework on the table, your dog engulfed the assignment. *Multiple effects*: As a result, you receive a failing grade, your parents do not allow you to go out with your friends, you miss out on the new movie, and one of your classmates spoils it for you before you have another chance to watch it).

MULTIPLE CAUSES

Also, there is the possibility for a single effect to have **multiple causes.** (e.g., *Single effect*: Alan has a fever. *Multiple causes*: An unexpected cold front came through the area, and Alan forgot to take his multi-vitamin to avoid getting sick.) Additionally, an effect can in turn be the cause of another effect, in what is known as a cause-and-effect chain. (e.g., As a result of her disdain for procrastination, Lynn prepared for her exam. This led to her passing her test with high marks. Hence, her resume was accepted and her application was approved.)

CAUSE AND EFFECT IN PERSUASIVE ESSAYS

Persuasive essays, in which an author tries to make a convincing argument and change the minds of readers, usually include cause-and-effect relationships. However, these relationships should not always be taken at face value. Frequently, an author will assume a cause or take an effect for granted. To read a persuasive essay effectively, readers need to judge the cause-and-effect relationships that the author is presenting. For instance, imagine an author wrote the following: *The parking deck has been unprofitable because people would prefer to ride their bikes.* The relationship is clear: the cause is that people prefer to ride their bikes, and the effect is that the parking deck has been unprofitable. However, readers should consider whether this argument is conclusive. Perhaps there are other reasons for the failure of the parking deck: a down economy, excessive fees, etc. Too often, authors present causal relationships as if they are fact rather than opinion. Readers should be on the alert for these dubious claims.

40

PROBLEM-SOLUTION

Some nonfiction texts are organized to **present a problem** followed by a solution. For this type of text, the problem is often explained before the solution is offered. In some cases, as when the problem is well known, the solution may be introduced briefly at the beginning. Other passages may focus on the solution, and the problem will be referenced only occasionally. Some texts will outline multiple solutions to a problem, leaving readers to choose among them. If the author has an interest or an allegiance to one solution, he or she may fail to mention or describe accurately some of the other solutions. Readers should be careful of the author's agenda when reading a problem-solution text. Only by understanding the author's perspective and interests can one develop a proper judgment of the proposed solution.

COMPARE AND CONTRAST

Many texts follow the **compare-and-contrast** model in which the similarities and differences between two ideas or things are explored. Analysis of the similarities between ideas is called **comparison**. In an ideal comparison, the author places ideas or things in an equivalent structure, i.e., the author presents the ideas in the same way. If an author wants to show the similarities between cricket and baseball, then he or she may do so by summarizing the equipment and rules for each game. Be mindful of the similarities as they appear in the passage and take note of any differences that are mentioned. Often, these small differences will only reinforce the more general similarity.

Review Video: **Compare and Contrast**
Visit mometrix.com/academy and enter code: 798319

Thinking critically about ideas and conclusions can seem like a daunting task. One way to ease this task is to understand the basic elements of ideas and writing techniques. Looking at the ways different ideas relate to each other can be a good way for readers to begin their analysis. For instance, sometimes authors will write about two ideas that are in opposition to each other. Or, one author will provide his or her ideas on a topic, and another author may respond in opposition. The analysis of these opposing ideas is known as **contrast**. Contrast is often marred by the author's obvious partiality to one of the ideas. A discerning reader will be put off by an author who does not engage in a fair fight. In an analysis of opposing ideas, both ideas should be presented in clear and reasonable terms. If the author does prefer a side, you need to read carefully to determine the areas where the author shows or avoids this preference. In an analysis of opposing ideas, you should proceed through the passage by marking the major differences point by point with an eye that is looking for an explanation of each side's view. For instance, in an analysis of capitalism and communism, there is an importance in outlining each side's view on labor, markets, prices, personal responsibility, etc. Additionally, as you read through the passages, you should note whether the opposing views present each side in a similar manner.

SEQUENCE

Readers must be able to identify a text's **sequence**, or the order in which things happen. Often, when the sequence is very important to the author, the text is indicated with signal words like *first*, *then*, *next*, and *last*. However, a sequence can be merely implied and must be noted by the reader. Consider the sentence *He walked through the garden and gave water and fertilizer to the plants*. Clearly, the man did not walk through the garden before he collected water and fertilizer for the plants. So, the implied sequence is that he first collected water, then he collected fertilizer, next he walked through the garden, and last he gave water or fertilizer as necessary to the plants. Texts do not always proceed in an orderly sequence from first to last. Sometimes they begin at the end and

41

start over at the beginning. As a reader, you can enhance your understanding of the passage by taking brief notes to clarify the sequence.

> **Review Video: <u>Sequence</u>**
> Visit mometrix.com/academy and enter code: 489027

MAKING AND EVALUATING PREDICTIONS
MAKING PREDICTIONS

When we read literature, **making predictions** about what will happen in the writing reinforces our purpose for reading and prepares us mentally. A **prediction** is a guess about what will happen next. Readers constantly make predictions based on what they have read and what they already know. We can make predictions before we begin reading and during our reading. Consider the following sentence: *Staring at the computer screen in shock, Kim blindly reached over for the brimming glass of water on the shelf to her side.* The sentence suggests that Kim is distracted, and that she is not looking at the glass that she is going to pick up. So, a reader might predict that Kim is going to knock over the glass. Of course, not every prediction will be accurate: perhaps Kim will pick the glass up cleanly. Nevertheless, the author has certainly created the expectation that the water might be spilled.

As we read on, we can test the accuracy of our predictions, revise them in light of additional reading, and confirm or refute our predictions. Predictions are always subject to revision as the reader acquires more information. A reader can make predictions by observing the title and illustrations; noting the structure, characters, and subject; drawing on existing knowledge relative to the subject; and asking "why" and "who" questions. Connecting reading to what we already know enables us to learn new information and construct meaning. For example, before third-graders read a book about Johnny Appleseed, they may start a KWL chart—a list of what they *Know*, what they *Want* to know or learn, and what they have *Learned* after reading. Activating existing background knowledge and thinking about the text before reading improves comprehension.

> **Review Video: <u>Predictive Reading</u>**
> Visit mometrix.com/academy and enter code: 437248

Test-taking tip: To respond to questions requiring future predictions, your answers should be based on evidence of past or present behavior and events.

EVALUATING PREDICTIONS

When making predictions, readers should be able to explain how they developed their prediction. One way readers can defend their thought process is by citing textual evidence. Textual evidence to evaluate reader predictions about literature includes specific synopses of the work, paraphrases of the work or parts of it, and direct quotations from the work. These references to the text must support the prediction by indicating, clearly or unclearly, what will happen later in the story. A text may provide these indications through literary devices such as foreshadowing. Foreshadowing is anything in a text that gives the reader a hint about what is to come by emphasizing the likelihood of an event or development. Foreshadowing can occur through descriptions, exposition, and dialogue. Foreshadowing in dialogue usually occurs when a character gives a warning or expresses a strong feeling that a certain event will occur. Foreshadowing can also occur through irony. However, unlike other forms of foreshadowing, the events that seem the most likely are the opposite of what actually happens. Instances of foreshadowing and irony can be summarized, paraphrased, or quoted to defend a reader's prediction.

MAKING INFERENCES AND DRAWING CONCLUSIONS

Inferences are logical conclusions that readers make based on their observations and previous knowledge. An inference is based on both what is found in a passage or a story and what is known from personal experience. For instance, a story may say that a character is frightened and can hear howling in the distance. Based on both what is in the text and personal knowledge, it is a logical conclusion that the character is frightened because he hears the sound of wolves. A good inference is supported by the information in a passage.

IMPLICIT AND EXPLICIT INFORMATION

By inferring, readers construct meanings from text that are personally relevant. By combining their own schemas or concepts and their background information pertinent to the text with what they read, readers interpret it according to both what the author has conveyed and their own unique perspectives. Inferences are different from **explicit information**, which is clearly stated in a passage. Authors do not always explicitly spell out every meaning in what they write; many meanings are implicit. Through inference, readers can comprehend implied meanings in the text, and also derive personal significance from it, making the text meaningful and memorable to them. Inference is a natural process in everyday life. When readers infer, they can draw conclusions about what the author is saying, predict what may reasonably follow, amend these predictions as they continue to read, interpret the import of themes, and analyze the characters' feelings and motivations through their actions.

EXAMPLE OF DRAWING CONCLUSIONS FROM INFERENCES

Read the excerpt and decide why Jana finally relaxed.

> Jana loved her job, but the work was very demanding. She had trouble relaxing. She called a friend, but she still thought about work. She ordered a pizza, but eating it did not help. Then, her kitten jumped on her lap and began to purr. Jana leaned back and began to hum a little tune. She felt better.

You can draw the conclusion that Jana relaxed because her kitten jumped on her lap. The kitten purred, and Jana leaned back and hummed a tune. Then she felt better. The excerpt does not explicitly say that this is the reason why she was able to relax. The text leaves the matter unclear, but the reader can infer or make a "best guess" that this is the reason she is relaxing. This is a logical conclusion based on the information in the passage. It is the best conclusion a reader can make based on the information he or she has read. Inferences are based on the information in a passage, but they are not directly stated in the passage.

Test-taking tip: While being tested on your ability to make correct inferences, you must look for **contextual clues**. An answer can be true, but not the best or most correct answer. The contextual clues will help you find the answer that is the **best answer** out of the given choices. Be careful in your reading to understand the context in which a phrase is stated. When asked for the implied meaning of a statement made in the passage, you should immediately locate the statement and read the **context** in which the statement was made. Also, look for an answer choice that has a similar phrase to the statement in question.

> **Review Video: Inference**
> Visit mometrix.com/academy and enter code: 379203
>
> **Review Video: How to Support a Conclusion**
> Visit mometrix.com/academy and enter code: 281653

READING COMPREHENSION AND CONNECTING WITH TEXTS

COMPARING TWO STORIES

When presented with two different stories, there will be **similarities** and **differences** between the two. A reader needs to make a list, or other graphic organizer, of the points presented in each story. Once the reader has written down the main point and supporting points for each story, the two sets of ideas can be compared. The reader can then present each idea and show how it is the same or different in the other story. This is called **comparing and contrasting ideas**.

The reader can compare ideas by stating, for example: "In Story 1, the author believes that humankind will one day land on Mars, whereas in Story 2, the author believes that Mars is too far away for humans to ever step foot on." Note that the two viewpoints are different in each story that the reader is comparing. A reader may state that: "Both stories discussed the likelihood of humankind landing on Mars." This statement shows how the viewpoint presented in both stories is based on the same topic, rather than how each viewpoint is different. The reader will complete a comparison of two stories with a conclusion.

> **Review Video: How to Compare and Contrast**
> Visit mometrix.com/academy and enter code: 833765

OUTLINING A PASSAGE

As an aid to drawing conclusions, **outlining** the information contained in the passage should be a familiar skill to readers. An effective outline will reveal the structure of the passage and will lead to solid conclusions. An effective outline will have a title that refers to the basic subject of the text, though the title does not need to restate the main idea. In most outlines, the main idea will be the first major section. Each major idea in the passage will be established as the head of a category. For instance, the most common outline format calls for the main ideas of the passage to be indicated with Roman numerals. In an effective outline of this kind, each of the main ideas will be represented by a Roman numeral and none of the Roman numerals will designate minor details or secondary ideas. Moreover, all supporting ideas and details should be placed in the appropriate place on the outline. An outline does not need to include every detail listed in the text, but it should feature all of those that are central to the argument or message. Each of these details should be listed under the corresponding main idea.

> **Review Video: Outlining as an Aid to Drawing Conclusions**
> Visit mometrix.com/academy and enter code: 584445

USING GRAPHIC ORGANIZERS

Ideas from a text can also be organized using **graphic organizers**. A graphic organizer is a way to simplify information and take key points from the text. A graphic organizer such as a timeline may have an event listed for a corresponding date on the timeline, while an outline may have an event listed under a key point that occurs in the text. Each reader needs to create the type of graphic organizer that works the best for him or her in terms of being able to recall information from a story. Examples include a spider-map, which takes a main idea from the story and places it in a bubble with supporting points branching off the main idea. An outline is useful for diagramming the main and supporting points of the entire story, and a Venn diagram compares and contrasts characteristics of two or more ideas.

> **Review Video: Graphic Organizers**
> Visit mometrix.com/academy and enter code: 665513

MAKING LOGICAL CONCLUSIONS ABOUT A PASSAGE

A reader should always be drawing conclusions from the text. Sometimes conclusions are **implied** from written information, and other times the information is **stated directly** within the passage. One should always aim to draw conclusions from information stated within a passage, rather than to draw them from mere implications. At times an author may provide some information and then describe a counterargument. Readers should be alert for direct statements that are subsequently rejected or weakened by the author. Furthermore, you should always read through the entire passage before drawing conclusions. Many readers are trained to expect the author's conclusions at either the beginning or the end of the passage, but many texts do not adhere to this format.

Drawing conclusions from information implied within a passage requires confidence on the part of the reader. **Implications** are things that the author does not state directly, but readers can assume based on what the author does say. Consider the following passage: *I stepped outside and opened my umbrella. By the time I got to work, the cuffs of my pants were soaked*. The author never states that it is raining, but this fact is clearly implied. Conclusions based on implication must be well supported by the text. In order to draw a solid conclusion, readers should have **multiple pieces of evidence**. If readers have only one piece, they must be assured that there is no other possible explanation than their conclusion. A good reader will be able to draw many conclusions from information implied by the text, which will be a great help on the exam.

DRAWING CONCLUSIONS

A common type of inference that a reader has to make is **drawing a conclusion**. The reader makes this conclusion based on the information provided within a text. Certain facts are included to help a reader come to a specific conclusion. For example, a story may open with a man trudging through the snow on a cold winter day, dragging a sled behind him. The reader can logically **infer** from the setting of the story that the man is wearing heavy winter clothes in order to stay warm. Information is implied based on the setting of a story, which is why **setting** is an important element of the text. If the same man in the example was trudging down a beach on a hot summer day, dragging a surf board behind him, the reader would assume that the man is not wearing heavy clothes. The reader makes inferences based on their own experiences and the information presented to them in the story.

Test-taking tip: When asked to identify a conclusion that may be drawn, look for critical "hedge" phrases, such as *likely*, *may*, *can*, and *will often*, among many others. When you are being tested on this knowledge, remember the question that writers insert into these hedge phrases to cover every possibility. Often an answer will be wrong simply because there is no room for exception. Extreme positive or negative answers (such as *always* or *never*) are usually not correct. When answering these questions, the reader **should not** use any outside knowledge that is not gathered directly or reasonably inferred from the passage. Correct answers can be derived straight from the passage.

EXAMPLE

Read the following sentence from *Little Women* by Louisa May Alcott and draw a conclusion based upon the information presented:

> *You know the reason Mother proposed not having any presents this Christmas was because it is going to be a hard winter for everyone; and she thinks we ought not to spend money for pleasure, when our men are suffering so in the army.*

Based on the information in the sentence, the reader can conclude, or **infer**, that the men are away at war while the women are still at home. The pronoun *our* gives a clue to the reader that the character is speaking about men she knows. In addition, the reader can assume that the character is speaking to a brother or sister, since the term "Mother" is used by the character while speaking to another person. The reader can also come to the conclusion that the characters celebrate Christmas, since it is mentioned in the **context** of the sentence. In the sentence, the mother is presented as an unselfish character who is opinionated and thinks about the wellbeing of other people.

SUMMARIZING

A helpful tool is the ability to **summarize** the information that you have read in a paragraph or passage format. This process is similar to creating an effective outline. First, a summary should accurately define the main idea of the passage, though the summary does not need to explain this main idea in exhaustive detail. The summary should continue by laying out the most important supporting details or arguments from the passage. All of the significant supporting details should be included, and none of the details included should be irrelevant or insignificant. Also, the summary should accurately report all of these details. Too often, the desire for brevity in a summary leads to the sacrifice of clarity or accuracy. Summaries are often difficult to read because they omit all of the graceful language, digressions, and asides that distinguish great writing. However, an effective summary should communicate the same overall message as the original text.

> **Review Video: Summarizing Text**
> Visit mometrix.com/academy and enter code: 172903

PARAPHRASING

Paraphrasing is another method that the reader can use to aid in comprehension. When paraphrasing, one puts what they have read into their own words by rephrasing what the author has written, or one "translates" all of what the author shared into their own words by including as many details as they can.

EVALUATING A PASSAGE

It is important to understand the logical conclusion of the ideas presented in an informational text. **Identifying a logical conclusion** can help you determine whether you agree with the writer or not. Coming to this conclusion is much like making an inference: the approach requires you to combine the information given by the text with what you already know and make a logical conclusion. If the author intended for the reader to draw a certain conclusion, then you can expect the author's argumentation and detail to be leading in that direction.

One way to approach the task of drawing conclusions is to make brief **notes** of all the points made by the author. When the notes are arranged on paper, they may clarify the logical conclusion. Another way to approach conclusions is to consider whether the reasoning of the author raises any pertinent questions. Sometimes you will be able to draw several conclusions from a passage. On occasion these will be conclusions that were never imagined by the author. Therefore, be aware that these conclusions must be **supported directly by the text**.

EVALUATION OF SUMMARIES

A summary of a literary passage is a condensation in the reader's own words of the passage's main points. Several guidelines can be used in evaluating a summary. The summary should be complete yet concise. It should be accurate, balanced, fair, neutral, and objective, excluding the reader's own opinions or reactions. It should reflect in similar proportion how much each point summarized was covered in the original passage. Summary writers should include tags of attribution, like "Macaulay argues that" to reference the original author whose ideas are represented in the summary. Summary writers should not overuse quotations; they should only quote central concepts or phrases they cannot precisely convey in words other than those of the original author. Another aspect of evaluating a summary is considering whether it can stand alone as a coherent, unified composition. In addition, evaluation of a summary should include whether its writer has cited the original source of the passage they have summarized so that readers can find it.

MAKING CONNECTIONS TO ENHANCE COMPREHENSION

Reading involves thinking. For good comprehension, readers make **text-to-self**, **text-to-text**, and **text-to-world connections**. Making connections helps readers understand text better and predict what might occur next based on what they already know, such as how characters in the story feel or what happened in another text. Text-to-self connections with the reader's life and experiences make literature more personally relevant and meaningful to readers. Readers can make connections before, during, and after reading—including whenever the text reminds them of something similar they have encountered in life or other texts. The genre, setting, characters, plot elements, literary structure and devices, and themes an author uses allow a reader to make connections to other works of literature or to people and events in their own lives. Venn diagrams and other graphic organizers help visualize connections. Readers can also make double-entry notes: key content, ideas, events, words, and quotations on one side, and the connections with these on the other.

COMPARING TWO TEXTS
SYNTHESIS OF MULTIPLE TEXTS

Synthesizing, i.e., understanding and integrating, information from multiple texts can at times be among the most challenging skills for some students to succeed with on tests and in school, and yet it is also among the most important. Students who read at the highest cognitive levels can select related material from different text sources and construct coherent arguments that account for these varied information sources. Synthesizing ideas and information from multiple texts actually combines other reading skills that students should have mastered previously in reading one text at a time, and applies them in the context of reading more than one text. For example, students are required to read texts closely, including identifying explicit and implicit meanings; use critical thinking and reading; draw inferences; assess author reasoning; analyze supporting evidence; and formulate opinions they can justify, based on more passages than one. When two paired texts represent opposing sides of the same argument, students can find analyzing them easier; but this is not always the case.

SIMILARITIES IN TEXTS

When students are called upon to compare things two texts share in common, the most obvious commonality might be the same subject matter or specific topic. However, two texts need not be about the same thing to compare them. Some other features texts can share include structural characteristics. For example, they may both be written using a sequential format, such as narrating

47

events or giving instructions in chronological order; listing and/or discussing subtopics by order of importance; or describing a place spatially in sequence from each point to the next. They may both use a comparison-contrast structure, identifying similarities and differences between, among, or within topics. They might both organize information by identifying cause-and-effect relationships. Texts can be similar in type, e.g., description, narration, persuasion, or exposition. They can be similar in using technical vocabulary or using formal or informal language. They may share similar tones and/or styles, e.g., humorous, satirical, serious, etc. They can share similar purposes, e.g., to alarm audiences, incite them to action, reassure them, inspire them, provoke strong emotional responses, etc.

CONTRASTS IN TEXTS

When analyzing paired or multiple texts, students might observe differences in tone; for example, one text might take a serious approach while another uses a humorous one. Even within approaches or treatments, style can differ: one text may be humorous in a witty, sophisticated, clever way while another may exercise broad, "lowbrow" humor; another may employ mordant sarcasm; another may use satire, couching outrageous suggestions in a "deadpan" logical voice to lampoon social attitudes and behaviors as Jonathan Swift did in *A Modest Proposal.* Serious writing can range from darkly pessimistic to alarmist to objective and unemotional. Texts might have similar information, yet organize it using different structures. One text may support points or ideas using logical arguments, while another may seek to persuade its audience by appealing to their emotions. A very obvious difference in text is genre: for example, the same mythological or traditional stories have been told as oral folk tales, written dramas, written novels, etc.; and/or set in different times and places (e.g., Shakespeare's *Romeo and Juliet* vs. Laurents, Bernstein, and Sondheim's *West Side Story*).

READING INFORMATIONAL TEXTS

LANGUAGE USE

LITERAL AND FIGURATIVE LANGUAGE

As in fictional literature, informational text also uses both **literal language**, which means just what it says, and **figurative language**, which imparts more than literal meaning. For example, an informational text author might use a simile or direct comparison, such as writing that a racehorse "ran like the wind." Informational text authors also use metaphors or implied comparisons, such as "the cloud of the Great Depression." Imagery may also appear in informational texts to increase the reader's understanding of ideas and concepts discussed in the text.

EXPLICIT AND IMPLICIT INFORMATION

When informational text states something explicitly, the reader is told by the author exactly what is meant, which can include the author's interpretation or perspective of events. For example, a professor writes, "I have seen students go into an absolute panic just because they weren't able to complete the exam in the time they were allotted." This explicitly tells the reader that the students were afraid, and by using the words "just because," the writer indicates their fear was exaggerated out of proportion relative to what happened. However, another professor writes, "I have had students come to me, their faces drained of all color, saying 'We weren't able to finish the exam.'" This is an example of implicit meaning: the second writer did not state explicitly that the students were panicked. Instead, he wrote a description of their faces being "drained of all color." From this description, the reader can infer that the students were so frightened that their faces paled.

> **Review Video: Explicit and Implicit Information**
> Visit mometrix.com/academy and enter code: 735771

48

MAKING INFERENCES ABOUT INFORMATIONAL TEXT

With informational text, reader comprehension depends not only on recalling important statements and details, but also on reader inferences based on examples and details. Readers add information from the text to what they already know to draw inferences about the text. These inferences help the readers to fill in the information that the text does not explicitly state, enabling them to understand the text better. When reading a nonfictional autobiography or biography, for example, the most appropriate inferences might concern the events in the book, the actions of the subject of the autobiography or biography, and the message the author means to convey. When reading a nonfictional expository (informational) text, the reader would best draw inferences about problems and their solutions, and causes and their effects. When reading a nonfictional persuasive text, the reader will want to infer ideas supporting the author's message and intent.

STRUCTURES OR ORGANIZATIONAL PATTERNS IN INFORMATIONAL TEXTS

Informational text can be **descriptive**, appealing to the five senses and answering the questions what, who, when, where, and why. Another method of structuring informational text is sequence and order. **Chronological** texts relate events in the sequence that they occurred, from start to finish, while how-to texts organize information into a series of instructions in the sequence in which the steps should be followed. **Comparison-contrast** structures of informational text describe various ideas to their readers by pointing out how things or ideas are similar and how they are different. **Cause and effect** structures of informational text describe events that occurred and identify the causes or reasons that those events occurred. **Problem and solution** structures of informational texts introduce and describe problems and offer one or more solutions for each problem described.

DETERMINING AN INFORMATIONAL AUTHOR'S PURPOSE

Informational authors' purposes are why they write texts. Readers must determine authors' motivations and goals. Readers gain greater insight into a text by considering the author's motivation. This develops critical reading skills. Readers perceive writing as a person's voice, not simply printed words. Uncovering author motivations and purposes empowers readers to know what to expect from the text, read for relevant details, evaluate authors and their work critically, and respond effectively to the motivations and persuasions of the text. The main idea of a text is what the reader is supposed to understand from reading it; the purpose of the text is why the author has written it and what the author wants readers to do with its information. Authors state some purposes clearly, while other purposes may be unstated but equally significant. When stated purposes contradict other parts of a text, the author may have a hidden agenda. Readers can better evaluate a text's effectiveness, whether they agree or disagree with it, and why they agree or disagree through identifying unstated author purposes.

IDENTIFYING AUTHOR'S POINT OF VIEW OR PURPOSE

In some informational texts, readers find it easy to identify the author's point of view and purpose, such as when the author explicitly states his or her position and reason for writing. But other texts are more difficult, either because of the content or because the authors give neutral or balanced viewpoints. This is particularly true in scientific texts, in which authors may state the purpose of their research in the report, but never state their point of view except by interpreting evidence or data.

To analyze text and identify point of view or purpose, readers should ask themselves the following four questions:

1. With what main point or idea does this author want to persuade readers to agree?
2. How does this author's word choice affect the way that readers consider this subject?
3. How do this author's choices of examples and facts affect the way that readers consider this subject?
4. What is it that this author wants to accomplish by writing this text?

> **Review Video: Understanding the Author's Intent**
> Visit mometrix.com/academy and enter code: 511819
>
> **Review Video: Author's Position**
> Visit mometrix.com/academy and enter code: 827954

EVALUATING ARGUMENTS MADE BY INFORMATIONAL TEXT WRITERS

When evaluating an informational text, the first step is to identify the argument's conclusion. Then identify the author's premises that support the conclusion. Try to paraphrase premises for clarification and make the conclusion and premises fit. List all premises first, sequentially numbered, then finish with the conclusion. Identify any premises or assumptions not stated by the author but required for the stated premises to support the conclusion. Read word assumptions sympathetically, as the author might. Evaluate whether premises reasonably support the conclusion. For inductive reasoning, the reader should ask if the premises are true, if they support the conclusion, and if so, how strongly. For deductive reasoning, the reader should ask if the argument is valid or invalid. If all premises are true, then the argument is valid unless the conclusion can be false. If it can, then the argument is invalid. An invalid argument can be made valid through alterations such as the addition of needed premises.

USE OF RHETORIC IN INFORMATIONAL TEXTS

There are many ways authors can support their claims, arguments, beliefs, ideas, and reasons for writing in informational texts. For example, authors can appeal to readers' sense of **logic** by communicating their reasoning through a carefully sequenced series of logical steps to help "prove" the points made. Authors can appeal to readers' **emotions** by using descriptions and words that evoke feelings of sympathy, sadness, anger, righteous indignation, hope, happiness, or any other emotion to reinforce what they express and share with their audience. Authors may appeal to the **moral** or **ethical values** of readers by using words and descriptions that can convince readers that something is right or wrong. By relating personal anecdotes, authors can supply readers with more accessible, realistic examples of points they make, as well as appealing to their emotions. They can provide supporting evidence by reporting case studies. They can also illustrate their points by making analogies to which readers can better relate.

TECHNICAL LANGUAGE

TECHNICAL LANGUAGE

Technical language is more impersonal than literary and vernacular language. Passive voice makes the tone impersonal. For example, instead of writing, "We found this a central component of protein metabolism," scientists write, "This was found a central component of protein metabolism." While science professors have traditionally instructed students to avoid active voice because it leads to first-person ("I" and "we") usage, science editors today find passive voice dull and weak. Many journal articles combine both. Tone in technical science writing should be detached, concise, and professional. While one may normally write, "This chemical has to be available for proteins to be digested," professionals write technically, "The presence of this chemical is required for the enzyme to break the covalent bonds of proteins." The use of technical language appeals to both technical and non-technical audiences by displaying the author or speaker's understanding of the subject and suggesting their credibility regarding the message they are communicating.

TECHNICAL MATERIAL FOR NON-TECHNICAL READERS

Writing about **technical subjects** for **non-technical readers** differs from writing for colleagues because authors place more importance on delivering a critical message than on imparting the maximum technical content possible. Technical authors also must assume that non-technical audiences do not have the expertise to comprehend extremely scientific or technical messages, concepts, and terminology. They must resist the temptation to impress audiences with their scientific knowledge and expertise and remember that their primary purpose is to communicate a message that non-technical readers will understand, feel, and respond to. Non-technical and technical styles include similarities. Both should formally cite any references or other authors' work utilized in the text. Both must follow intellectual property and copyright regulations. This includes the author's protecting his or her own rights, or a public domain statement, as he or she chooses.

> **Review Video: Technical Passages**
> Visit mometrix.com/academy and enter code: 478923

NON-TECHNICAL AUDIENCES

Writers of technical or scientific material may need to write for many non-technical audiences. Some readers have no technical or scientific background, and those who do may not be in the same field as the authors. Government and corporate policymakers and budget managers need technical information they can understand for decision-making. Citizens affected by technology or science are a different audience. Non-governmental organizations can encompass many of the preceding groups. Elementary and secondary school programs also need non-technical language for presenting technical subject matter. Additionally, technical authors will need to use non-technical language when collecting consumer responses to surveys, presenting scientific or para-scientific material to the public, writing about the history of science, and writing about science and technology in developing countries.

USE OF EVERYDAY LANGUAGE

Authors of technical information sometimes must write using non-technical language that readers outside their disciplinary fields can comprehend. They should use not only non-technical terms, but also normal, everyday language to accommodate readers whose native language is different than the language the text is written in. For example, instead of writing that "eustatic changes like thermal expansion are causing hazardous conditions in the littoral zone," an author would do better to write that "a rising sea level is threatening the coast." When technical terms cannot be avoided, authors should also define or explain them using non-technical language. Although authors must cite references and acknowledge their use of others' work, they should avoid the kinds of references or citations that they would use in scientific journals—unless they reinforce author messages. They should not use endnotes, footnotes, or any other complicated referential techniques because non-technical journal publishers usually do not accept them. Including high-resolution illustrations, photos, maps, or satellite images and incorporating multimedia into digital publications will enhance non-technical writing about technical subjects. Technical authors may publish using non-technical language in e-journals, trade journals, specialty newsletters, and daily newspapers.

VISUAL INFORMATION IN INFORMATIONAL TEXTS
CHARTS, GRAPHS, AND VISUALS
PIE CHART

A pie chart, also known as a circle graph, is useful for depicting how a single unit or category is divided. The standard pie chart is a circle with designated wedges. Each wedge is **proportional** in size to a part of the whole. For instance, consider Shawna, a student at City College, who uses a pie chart to represent her budget. If she spends half of her money on rent, then the pie chart will represent that amount with a line through the center of the pie. If she spends a quarter of her money on food, there will be a line extending from the edge of the circle to the center at a right angle to the line depicting rent. This illustration would make it clear that the student spends twice the amount of money on rent as she does on food.

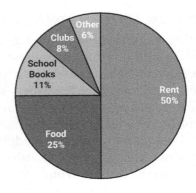

A pie chart is effective at showing how a single entity is divided into parts. They are not effective at demonstrating the relationships between parts of different wholes. For example, an unhelpful use of a pie chart would be to compare the respective amounts of state and federal spending devoted to infrastructure since these values are only meaningful in the context of the entire budget.

BAR GRAPH

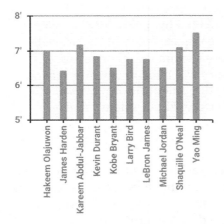

The bar graph is one of the most common visual representations of information. **Bar graphs** are used to illustrate sets of numerical **data**. The graph has a vertical axis (along which numbers are listed) and a horizontal axis (along which categories, words, or some other indicators are placed). One example of a bar graph is a depiction of the respective heights of famous basketball players: the vertical axis would contain numbers ranging from five to eight feet, and the horizontal axis would contain the names of the players. The length of the bar above the player's name would illustrate his height, and the top of the bar would stop perpendicular to the height listed along the left side. In this representation, one would see that Yao Ming is taller than Michael Jordan because Yao's bar would be higher.

52

LINE GRAPH

A line graph is a type of graph that is typically used for measuring trends over time. The graph is set up along a vertical and a horizontal **axis**. The variables being measured are listed along the left side and the bottom side of the axes. Points are then plotted along the graph as they correspond with their values for each variable. For instance, consider a line graph measuring a person's income for each month of the year. If the person earned $1500 in January, there should be a point directly above January (perpendicular to the horizontal axis) and directly to the right of $1500 (perpendicular to the vertical axis). Once all of the lines are plotted, they are connected with a line from left to right. This line provides a nice visual illustration of the general **trends** of the data, if they exist. For instance, using the earlier example, if the line sloped up, then one would see that the person's income had increased over the course of the year.

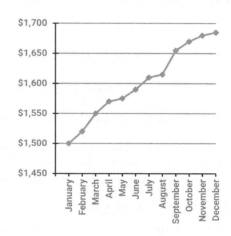

PICTOGRAPHS

A **pictograph** is a graph, generally in the horizontal orientation, that uses pictures or symbols to represent the data. Each pictograph must have a key that defines the picture or symbol and gives the quantity each picture or symbol represents. Pictures or symbols on a pictograph are not always shown as whole elements. In this case, the fraction of the picture or symbol shown represents the same fraction of the quantity a whole picture or symbol stands for.

> **Review Video: Pictographs**
> Visit mometrix.com/academy and enter code: 147860

Standard English Conventions

PARTS OF SPEECH

NOUNS

A noun is a person, place, thing, or idea. The two main types of nouns are **common** and **proper** nouns. Nouns can also be categorized as abstract (i.e., general) or concrete (i.e., specific).

COMMON NOUNS

Common nouns are generic names for people, places, and things. Common nouns are not usually capitalized.

Examples of common nouns:

People: boy, girl, worker, manager

Places: school, bank, library, home

Things: dog, cat, truck, car

> **Review Video: What is a Noun?**
> Visit mometrix.com/academy and enter code: 344028

PROPER NOUNS

Proper nouns name specific people, places, or things. All proper nouns are capitalized.

Examples of proper nouns:

People: Abraham Lincoln, George Washington, Martin Luther King, Jr.

Places: Los Angeles, California; New York; Asia

Things: Statue of Liberty, Earth, Lincoln Memorial

Note: Some nouns can be either common or proper depending on their use. For example, when referring to the planet that we live on, *Earth* is a proper noun and is capitalized. When referring to the dirt, rocks, or land on our planet, *earth* is a common noun and is not capitalized.

GENERAL AND SPECIFIC NOUNS

General nouns are the names of conditions or ideas. **Specific nouns** name people, places, and things that are understood by using your senses.

General nouns:

Condition: beauty, strength

Idea: truth, peace

Specific nouns:

People: baby, friend, father

Places: town, park, city hall

Things: rainbow, cough, apple, silk, gasoline

COLLECTIVE NOUNS

Collective nouns are the names for a group of people, places, or things that may act as a whole. The following are examples of collective nouns: *class, company, dozen, group, herd, team,* and *public*. Collective nouns usually require an article, which denotes the noun as being a single unit. For instance, a choir is a group of singers. Even though there are many singers in a choir, the word choir is grammatically treated as a single unit. If we refer to the members of the group, and not the group itself, it is no longer a collective noun.

Incorrect: The *choir are* going to compete nationally this year.

Correct: The *choir is* going to compete nationally this year.

Incorrect: The *members* of the choir *is* competing nationally this year.

Correct: The *members* of the choir *are* competing nationally this year.

PRONOUNS

Pronouns are words that are used to stand in for nouns. A pronoun may be classified as personal, intensive, relative, interrogative, demonstrative, indefinite, and reciprocal.

Personal: *Nominative* is the case for nouns and pronouns that are the subject of a sentence. *Objective* is the case for nouns and pronouns that are an object in a sentence. *Possessive* is the case for nouns and pronouns that show possession or ownership.

Singular

	Nominative	Objective	Possessive
First Person	I	me	my, mine
Second Person	you	you	your, yours
Third Person	he, she, it	him, her, it	his, her, hers, its

Plural

	Nominative	Objective	Possessive
First Person	we	us	our, ours
Second Person	you	you	your, yours
Third Person	they	them	their, theirs

Intensive: I myself, you yourself, he himself, she herself, the (thing) itself, we ourselves, you yourselves, they themselves

Relative: which, who, whom, whose

Interrogative: what, which, who, whom, whose

Demonstrative: this, that, these, those

Indefinite: all, any, each, everyone, either/neither, one, some, several

Reciprocal: each other, one another

> **Review Video: Nouns and Pronouns**
> Visit mometrix.com/academy and enter code: 312073

VERBS

A verb is a word or group of words that indicates action or being. In other words, the verb shows something's action or state of being or the action that has been done to something. If you want to write a sentence, then you need a verb. Without a verb, you have no sentence.

TRANSITIVE AND INTRANSITIVE VERBS

A **transitive verb** is a verb whose action indicates a receiver. **Intransitive verbs** do not indicate a receiver of an action. In other words, the action of the verb does not point to an object.

Transitive: He drives a car. | She feeds the dog.

Intransitive: He runs every day. | She voted in the last election.

A dictionary will tell you whether a verb is transitive or intransitive. Some verbs can be transitive or intransitive.

ACTION VERBS AND LINKING VERBS

Action verbs show what the subject is doing. In other words, an action verb shows action. Unlike most types of words, a single action verb, in the right context, can be an entire sentence. **Linking**

55

verbs link the subject of a sentence to a noun or pronoun, or they link a subject with an adjective. You always need a verb if you want a complete sentence. However, linking verbs on their own cannot be a complete sentence.

Common linking verbs include *appear, be, become, feel, grow, look, seem, smell, sound,* and *taste.* However, any verb that shows a condition and connects to a noun, pronoun, or adjective that describes the subject of a sentence is a linking verb.

Action: He sings. | Run! | Go! | I talk with him every day. | She reads.

Linking:

Incorrect: I am.

Correct: I am John. | The roses smell lovely. | I feel tired.

Note: Some verbs are followed by words that look like prepositions, but they are a part of the verb and a part of the verb's meaning. These are known as phrasal verbs, and examples include *call off, look up,* and *drop off.*

> **Review Video: Action Verbs and Linking Verbs**
> Visit mometrix.com/academy and enter code: 743142

VOICE

Transitive verbs may be in active voice or passive voice. The difference between active voice and passive voice is whether the subject is acting or being acted upon. When the subject of the sentence is doing the action, the verb is in **active voice**. When the subject is being acted upon, the verb is in **passive voice**.

Active: Jon drew the picture. (The subject *Jon* is doing the action of *drawing a picture.*)

Passive: The picture is drawn by Jon. (The subject *picture* is receiving the action from Jon.)

VERB TENSES

Verb **tense** is a property of a verb that indicates when the action being described takes place (past, present, or future) and whether or not the action is completed (simple or perfect). Describing an action taking place in the present (*I talk*) requires a different verb tense than describing an action that took place in the past (*I talked*). Some verb tenses require an auxiliary (helping) verb. These helping verbs include *am, are, is | have, has, had | was, were, will* (or *shall*).

Present: I talk	Present perfect: I have talked
Past: I talked	Past perfect: I had talked
Future: I will talk	Future perfect: I will have talked

Present: The action is happening at the current time.

Example: He *walks* to the store every morning.

To show that something is happening right now, use the progressive present tense: I *am walking*.

Past: The action happened in the past.

Example: She *walked* to the store an hour ago.

56

Future: The action will happen later.

Example: I *will walk* to the store tomorrow.

Present perfect: The action started in the past and continues into the present or took place previously at an unspecified time.

Example: I *have walked* to the store three times today.

Past perfect: The action was completed at some point in the past. This tense is usually used to describe an action that was completed before some other reference time or event.

Example: I *had eaten* already before they arrived.

Future perfect: The action will be completed before some point in the future. This tense may be used to describe an action that has already begun or has yet to begin.

Example: The project *will have been completed* by the deadline.

> **Review Video: <u>Present Perfect, Past Perfect, and Future Perfect Verb Tenses</u>**
> Visit mometrix.com/academy and enter code: 269472

CONJUGATING VERBS

When you need to change the form of a verb, you are **conjugating** a verb. The key forms of a verb are present tense (sing/sings), past tense (sang), present participle (singing), and past participle (sung). By combining these forms with helping verbs, you can make almost any verb tense. The following table demonstrate some of the different ways to conjugate a verb:

Tense	First Person	Second Person	Third Person Singular	Third Person Plural
Simple Present	I sing	You sing	He, she, it sings	They sing
Simple Past	I sang	You sang	He, she, it sang	They sang
Simple Future	I will sing	You will sing	He, she, it will sing	They will sing
Present Progressive	I am singing	You are singing	He, she, it is singing	They are singing
Past Progressive	I was singing	You were singing	He, she, it was singing	They were singing
Present Perfect	I have sung	You have sung	He, she, it has sung	They have sung
Past Perfect	I had sung	You had sung	He, she, it had sung	They had sung

MOOD

There are three **moods** in English: the indicative, the imperative, and the subjunctive.

The **indicative mood** is used for facts, opinions, and questions.

Fact: You can do this.

Opinion: I think that you can do this.

Question: Do you know that you can do this?

57

The **imperative** is used for orders or requests.

> Order: You are going to do this!

> Request: Will you do this for me?

The **subjunctive mood** is for wishes and statements that go against fact.

> Wish: I wish that I were famous.

> Statement against fact: If I were you, I would do this. (This goes against fact because I am not you. You have the chance to do this, and I do not have the chance.)

ADJECTIVES

An **adjective** is a word that is used to modify a noun or pronoun. An adjective answers a question: *Which one? What kind?* or *How many?* Usually, adjectives come before the words that they modify, but they may also come after a linking verb.

> Which one? The *third* suit is my favorite.

> What kind? This suit is *navy blue*.

> How many? I am going to buy *four* pairs of socks to match the suit.

> **Review Video: Descriptive Text**
> Visit mometrix.com/academy and enter code: 174903

ARTICLES

Articles are adjectives that are used to distinguish nouns as definite or indefinite. *A*, *an*, and *the* are the only articles. **Definite** nouns are preceded by *the* and indicate a specific person, place, thing, or idea. **Indefinite** nouns are preceded by *a* or *an* and do not indicate a specific person, place, thing, or idea.

Note: *An* comes before words that start with a vowel sound. For example, "Are you going to get an **u**mbrella?"

> **Definite**: I lost *the* bottle that belongs to me.

> **Indefinite**: Does anyone have *a* bottle to share?

> **Review Video: Function of Articles in a Sentence**
> Visit mometrix.com/academy and enter code: 449383

COMPARISON WITH ADJECTIVES

Some adjectives are relative and other adjectives are absolute. Adjectives that are **relative** can show the comparison between things. **Absolute** adjectives can also show comparison, but they do so in a different way. Let's say that you are reading two books. You think that one book is perfect, and the other book is not exactly perfect. It is not possible for one book to be more perfect than the other. Either you think that the book is perfect, or you think that the book is imperfect. In this case, perfect and imperfect are absolute adjectives.

Relative adjectives will show the different **degrees** of something or someone to something else or someone else. The three degrees of adjectives include positive, comparative, and superlative.

The **positive** degree is the normal form of an adjective.

Example: This work is *difficult*. | She is *smart*.

The **comparative** degree compares one person or thing to another person or thing.

Example: This work is *more difficult* than your work. | She is *smarter* than me.

The **superlative** degree compares more than two people or things.

Example: This is the *most difficult* work of my life. | She is the *smartest* lady in school.

> **Review Video: What is an Adjective?**
> Visit mometrix.com/academy and enter code: 470154

ADVERBS

An **adverb** is a word that is used to **modify** a verb, an adjective, or another adverb. Usually, adverbs answer one of these questions: *When? Where? How?* and *Why?* The negatives *not* and *never* are considered adverbs. Adverbs that modify adjectives or other adverbs **strengthen** or **weaken** the words that they modify.

Examples:

He walks *quickly* through the crowd.

The water flows *smoothly* on the rocks.

Note: Adverbs are usually indicated by the morpheme *-ly*, which has been added to the root word. For instance, *quick* can be made into an adverb by adding *-ly* to construct *quickly*. Some words that end in *-ly* do not follow this rule and can behave as other parts of speech. Examples of adjectives ending in *-ly* include: *early, friendly, holy, lonely, silly*, and *ugly*. To know if a word that ends in *-ly* is an adjective or adverb, check your dictionary. Also, while many adverbs end in *-ly*, you need to remember that not all adverbs end in *-ly*.

Examples:

He is *never* angry.

You are *too* irresponsible to travel alone.

> **Review Video: What is an Adverb?**
> Visit mometrix.com/academy and enter code: 713951
>
> **Review Video: Adverbs that Modify Adjectives**
> Visit mometrix.com/academy and enter code: 122570

COMPARISON WITH ADVERBS

The rules for comparing adverbs are the same as the rules for adjectives.

The **positive** degree is the standard form of an adverb.

Example: He arrives *soon*. | She speaks *softly* to her friends.

The **comparative** degree compares one person or thing to another person or thing.

Example: He arrives *sooner* than Sarah. | She speaks *more softly* than him.

The **superlative** degree compares more than two people or things.

Example: He arrives *soonest* of the group. | She speaks the *most softly* of any of her friends.

PREPOSITIONS

A **preposition** is a word placed before a noun or pronoun that shows the relationship between that noun or pronoun and another word in the sentence.

Common prepositions:

about	before	during	on	under
after	beneath	for	over	until
against	between	from	past	up
among	beyond	in	through	with
around	by	of	to	within
at	down	off	toward	without

Examples:

The napkin is *in* the drawer.

The Earth rotates *around* the Sun.

The needle is *beneath* the haystack.

Can you find "me" *among* the words?

> **Review Video: Prepositions**
> Visit mometrix.com/academy and enter code: 946763

CONJUNCTIONS

Conjunctions join words, phrases, or clauses and they show the connection between the joined pieces. **Coordinating conjunctions** connect equal parts of sentences. **Correlative conjunctions** show the connection between pairs. **Subordinating conjunctions** join subordinate (i.e., dependent) clauses with independent clauses.

COORDINATING CONJUNCTIONS

The **coordinating conjunctions** include: *and, but, yet, or, nor, for,* and *so*

Examples:

The rock was small, *but* it was heavy.

She drove in the night, *and* he drove in the day.

CORRELATIVE CONJUNCTIONS

The **correlative conjunctions** are: *either...or* | *neither...nor* | *not only...but also*

Examples:

> *Either* you are coming *or* you are staying.

> He *not only* ran three miles *but also* swam 200 yards.

> **Review Video: <u>Coordinating and Correlative Conjunctions</u>**
> Visit mometrix.com/academy and enter code: 390329
>
> **Review Video: <u>Adverb Equal Comparisons</u>**
> Visit mometrix.com/academy and enter code: 231291

SUBORDINATING CONJUNCTIONS

Common **subordinating conjunctions** include:

after	since	whenever
although	so that	where
because	unless	wherever
before	until	whether
in order that	when	while

Examples:

> I am hungry *because* I did not eat breakfast.

> He went home *when* everyone left.

> **Review Video: <u>Subordinating Conjunctions</u>**
> Visit mometrix.com/academy and enter code: 958913

INTERJECTIONS

Interjections are words of exclamation (i.e., audible expression of great feeling) that are used alone or as a part of a sentence. Often, they are used at the beginning of a sentence for an introduction. Sometimes, they can be used in the middle of a sentence to show a change in thought or attitude.

> Common Interjections: Hey! | Oh, | Ouch! | Please! | Wow!

AGREEMENT AND SENTENCE STRUCTURE

SUBJECTS AND PREDICATES

SUBJECTS

The **subject** of a sentence names who or what the sentence is about. The subject may be directly stated in a sentence, or the subject may be the implied *you*. The **complete subject** includes the simple subject and all of its modifiers. To find the complete subject, ask *Who* or *What* and insert the verb to complete the question. The answer, including any modifiers (adjectives, prepositional phrases, etc.), is the complete subject. To find the **simple subject**, remove all of the modifiers in the complete subject. Being able to locate the subject of a sentence helps with many problems, such as those involving sentence fragments and subject-verb agreement.

Examples:

The small, red <u>car</u> is the one that he wants for Christmas.

simple subject = car
complete subject = The small, red car

The young <u>artist</u> is coming over for dinner.

simple subject = artist
complete subject = The young artist

In **imperative** sentences, the verb's subject is understood (e.g., [You] Run to the store), but is not actually present in the sentence. Normally, the subject comes before the verb. However, the subject comes after the verb in sentences that begin with *There are* or *There was*.

Direct:

John knows the way to the park.	Who knows the way to the park?	John
The cookies need ten more minutes.	What needs ten minutes?	The cookies
By five o'clock, Bill will need to leave.	Who needs to leave?	Bill
There are five letters on the table for him.	What is on the table?	Five letters
There were coffee and doughnuts in the house.	What was in the house?	Coffee and doughnuts

Implied:

Go to the post office for me.	Who is going to the post office?	You
Come and sit with me, please?	Who needs to come and sit?	You

PREDICATES

In a sentence, you always have a predicate and a subject. The subject tells who or what the sentence is about, and the **predicate** explains or describes the subject. The predicate includes the verb or verb phrase and any direct or indirect objects of the verb, as well as any words or phrases modifying these.

Think about the sentence *He sings.* In this sentence, we have a subject (He) and a predicate (sings). This is all that is needed for a sentence to be complete. Most sentences contain more information, but if this is all the information that you are given, then you have a complete sentence.

Now, let's look at another sentence: *John and Jane sing on Tuesday nights at the dance hall.*

subject   predicate

John and Jane   sing on Tuesday nights at the dance hall.

> **Review Video: What is a Complete Predicate?**
> Visit mometrix.com/academy and enter code: 293942

SUBJECT-VERB AGREEMENT

Verbs must **agree** with their subjects in number and in person. To agree in number, singular subjects need singular verbs and plural subjects need plural verbs. A **singular** noun refers to **one** person, place, or thing. A **plural** noun refers to **more than one** person, place, or thing. To agree in person, the correct verb form must be chosen to match the first, second, or third person subject. The present tense ending *-s* or *-es* is used on a verb if its subject is third person singular; otherwise, the verb's ending is not modified.

> **Review Video: Subject-Verb Agreement**
> Visit mometrix.com/academy and enter code: 479190

NUMBER AGREEMENT EXAMPLES:

singular   singular
subject   verb

Single Subject and Verb: Dan   calls   home.

Dan is one person. So, the singular verb *calls* is needed.

plural   plural
subject   verb

Plural Subject and Verb: Dan and Bob call home.

More than one person needs the plural verb *call*.

PERSON AGREEMENT EXAMPLES:

First Person: I *am* walking.

Second Person: You *are* walking.

Third Person: He *is* walking.

COMPLICATIONS WITH SUBJECT-VERB AGREEMENT
WORDS BETWEEN SUBJECT AND VERB

Words that come between the simple subject and the verb have no bearing on subject-verb agreement.

Examples:

singular   singular
subject   verb

The joy of my life returns home tonight.

63

The phrase *of my life* does not influence the verb *returns*.

singular
subject   singular
verb

The question that still remains unanswered is "Who are you?"

Don't let the phrase "*that still remains…*" trouble you. The subject *question* goes with *is*.

COMPOUND SUBJECTS

A compound subject is formed when two or more nouns joined by *and*, *or*, or *nor* jointly act as the subject of the sentence.

JOINED BY AND

When a compound subject is joined by *and*, it is treated as a plural subject and requires a plural verb.

Examples:

You and Jon are invited to come to my house.

The pencil and paper belong to me.

JOINED BY OR/NOR

For a compound subject joined by *or* or *nor*, the verb must agree in number with the part of the subject that is closest to the verb (italicized in the examples below).

Examples:

Today or tomorrow is the day.

Stan or Phil wants to read the book.

Neither the pen nor the book is on the desk.

Either the blanket or pillows arrive this afternoon.

INDEFINITE PRONOUNS AS SUBJECT

An indefinite pronoun is a pronoun that does not refer to a specific noun. Some indefinite pronouns function as only singular, some function as only plural, and some can function as either singular or plural depending on how they are used.

ALWAYS SINGULAR

Pronouns such as *each*, *either*, *everybody*, *anybody*, *somebody*, and *nobody* are always singular.

Examples:

singular
subject

singular
verb

Each of the runners has a different bib number.

singular singular
verb   subject

Is either of you ready for the game?

Note: The words *each* and *either* can also be used as adjectives (e.g., *each* person is unique). When one of these adjectives modifies the subject of a sentence, it is always a singular subject.

singular
subject   singular
            verb

Everybody grows a day older every day.

singular singular
subject verb

Anybody is welcome to bring a tent.

ALWAYS PLURAL

Pronouns such as *both*, *several*, and *many* are always plural.

Examples:

plural
subject

plural
verb

Both of the siblings were too tired to argue.

plural plural
subject verb

Many have tried, but none have succeeded.

DEPEND ON CONTEXT

Pronouns such as *some*, *any*, *all*, *none*, *more*, and *most* can be either singular or plural depending on what they are representing in the context of the sentence.

Examples:

singular
subject

singular
verb

All of my dog's food was still there in his bowl.

plural
subject

plural
verb

By the end of the night, all of my guests were already excited about coming to my next party.

65

Other Cases Involving Plural or Irregular Form

Some nouns are **singular in meaning but plural in form**: news, mathematics, physics, and economics.

> The *news is* coming on now.

> *Mathematics is* my favorite class.

Some nouns are plural in form and meaning, and have **no singular equivalent**: scissors and pants.

> Do these *pants come* with a shirt?

> The *scissors are* for my project.

Mathematical operations are **irregular** in their construction, but are normally considered to be **singular in meaning**.

> *One plus one is* two.

> *Three times three is* nine.

Note: Look to your **dictionary** for help when you aren't sure whether a noun with a plural form has a singular or plural meaning.

Complements

A complement is a noun, pronoun, or adjective that is used to give more information about the subject or object in the sentence.

Direct Objects

A direct object is a noun or pronoun that tells who or what **receives** the action of the verb. A sentence will only include a direct object if the verb is a transitive verb. If the verb is an intransitive verb or a linking verb, there will be no direct object. When you are looking for a direct object, find the verb and ask *who* or *what.*

Examples:

> I took *the blanket.*

> Jane read *books.*

Indirect Objects

An indirect object is a noun or pronoun that indicates what or whom the action had an **influence** on. If there is an indirect object in a sentence, then there will also be a direct object. When you are looking for the indirect object, find the verb and ask *to/for whom or what.*

Examples:

indirect   direct
object   object

We taught the old dog a new trick.

indirect   direct
object   object

I gave them a math lesson.

> **Review Video: Direct and Indirect Objects**
> Visit mometrix.com/academy and enter code: 817385

PREDICATE NOMINATIVES AND PREDICATE ADJECTIVES

As we looked at previously, verbs may be classified as either action verbs or linking verbs. A linking verb is so named because it links the subject to words in the predicate that describe or define the subject. These words are called predicate nominatives (if nouns or pronouns) or predicate adjectives (if adjectives).

Examples:

subject   predicate
nominative

My father is a lawyer.

subject   predicate
adjective

Your mother is patient.

PRONOUN USAGE

The **antecedent** is the noun that has been replaced by a pronoun. A pronoun and its antecedent **agree** when they have the same number (singular or plural) and gender (male, female, or neutral).

Examples:

     antecedent   pronoun

Singular agreement: John came into town, and he played for us.

     antecedent   pronoun

Plural agreement: John and Rick came into town, and they played for us.

To determine which is the correct pronoun to use in a compound subject or object, try each pronoun **alone** in place of the compound in the sentence. Your knowledge of pronouns will tell you which one is correct.

Example:

Bob and (I, me) will be going.

Test: (1) *I will be going* or (2) *Me will be going*. The second choice cannot be correct because *me* cannot be used as the subject of a sentence. Instead, *me* is used as an object.

Answer: Bob and I will be going.

67

When a pronoun is used with a noun immediately following (as in "we boys"), try the sentence **without the added noun**.

Example:

(We/Us) boys played football last year.

Test: (1) *We played football last ye*ar or (2) *Us played football last year*. Again, the second choice cannot be correct because *us* cannot be used as a subject of a sentence. Instead, *us* is used as an object.

Answer: We boys played football last year.

> **Review Video: Pronoun Usage**
> Visit mometrix.com/academy and enter code: 666500
>
> **Review Video: What is Pronoun-Antecedent Agreement?**
> Visit mometrix.com/academy and enter code: 919704

A pronoun should point clearly to the **antecedent**. Here is how a pronoun reference can be unhelpful if it is puzzling or not directly stated.

               antecedent   pronoun

Unhelpful: Ron and Jim went to the store, and he bought soda.

Who bought soda? Ron or Jim?

            antecedent   pronoun

Helpful: Jim went to the store, and he bought soda.

The sentence is clear. Jim bought the soda.

Some pronouns change their form by their placement in a sentence. A pronoun that is a **subject** in a sentence comes in the **subjective case**. Pronouns that serve as **objects** appear in the **objective case**. Finally, the pronouns that are used as **possessives** appear in the **possessive case**.

Examples:

Subjective case: *He* is coming to the show.

The pronoun *He* is the subject of the sentence.

Objective case: Josh drove *him* to the airport.

The pronoun *him* is the object of the sentence.

Possessive case: The flowers are *mine*.

The pronoun *mine* shows ownership of the flowers.

The word *who* is a subjective-case pronoun that can be used as a **subject**. The word *whom* is an objective-case pronoun that can be used as an **object**. The words *who* and *whom* are common in subordinate clauses or in questions.

Examples:

$$\text{He knows } \overbrace{\text{who}}^{\text{subject}} \overbrace{\text{wants}}^{\text{verb}} \text{ to come.}$$

$$\text{He knows the man } \overbrace{\text{whom}}^{\text{object}} \text{ we } \overbrace{\text{want}}^{\text{verb}} \text{ at the party.}$$

CLAUSES

A clause is a group of words that contains both a subject and a predicate (verb). There are two types of clauses: independent and dependent. An **independent clause** contains a complete thought, while a **dependent (or subordinate) clause** does not. A dependent clause includes a subject and a verb, and may also contain objects or complements, but it cannot stand as a complete thought without being joined to an independent clause. Dependent clauses function within sentences as adjectives, adverbs, or nouns.

Example:

I am running (independent clause) | because I want to stay in shape (dependent clause).

The clause *I am running* is an independent clause: it has a subject and a verb, and it gives a complete thought. The clause *because I want to stay in shape* is a dependent clause: it has a subject and a verb, but it does not express a complete thought. It adds detail to the independent clause to which it is attached.

> **Review Video: What is a Clause?**
> Visit mometrix.com/academy and enter code: 940170
>
> **Review Video: Independent and Dependent Clauses**
> Visit mometrix.com/academy and enter code: 556903

TYPES OF DEPENDENT CLAUSES

ADJECTIVE CLAUSES

An **adjective clause** is a dependent clause that modifies a noun or a pronoun. Adjective clauses begin with a relative pronoun (*who, whose, whom, which,* and *that*) or a relative adverb (*where, when,* and *why*).

Also, adjective clauses usually come immediately after the noun that the clause needs to explain or rename. This is done to ensure that it is clear which noun or pronoun the clause is modifying.

Examples:

I learned the reason (independent clause) | why I won the award (adjective clause).

This is the place (independent clause) | where I started my first job (adjective clause).

An adjective clause can be an essential or nonessential clause. An essential clause is very important to the sentence. **Essential clauses** explain or define a person or thing. **Nonessential clauses** give more information about a person or thing but are not necessary to define them. Nonessential clauses are set off with commas while essential clauses are not.

Examples:

A person <u>who works hard at first</u> can often rest later in life.
(essential clause)

Neil Armstrong, <u>who walked on the moon,</u> is my hero.
(nonessential clause)

Review Video: Adjective Clauses and Phrases
Visit mometrix.com/academy and enter code: 520888

ADVERB CLAUSES

An **adverb clause** is a dependent clause that modifies a verb, adjective, or adverb. In sentences with multiple dependent clauses, adverb clauses are usually placed immediately before or after the independent clause. An adverb clause is introduced with words such as *after, although, as, before, because, if, since, so, unless, when, where*, and *while*.

Examples:

<u>When you walked outside,</u> I called the manager.
(adverb clause)

I will go with you <u>unless you want to stay.</u>
(adverb clause)

NOUN CLAUSES

A **noun clause** is a dependent clause that can be used as a subject, object, or complement. Noun clauses begin with words such as *how, that, what, whether, which, who*, and *why*. These words can also come with an adjective clause. Unless the noun clause is being used as the subject of the sentence, it should come after the verb of the independent clause.

Examples:

The real mystery is <u>how you avoided serious injury.</u>
(noun clause)

<u>What you learn from each other</u> depends on your honesty with others.
(noun clause)

SUBORDINATION

When two related ideas are not of equal importance, the ideal way to combine them is to make the more important idea an independent clause and the less important idea a dependent or subordinate clause. This is called **subordination**.

70

Example:

>**Separate ideas**: The team had a perfect regular season. The team lost the championship.

>**Subordinated**: Despite having a perfect regular season, *the team lost the championship.*

PHRASES

A phrase is a group of words that functions as a single part of speech, usually a noun, adjective, or adverb. A **phrase** is not a complete thought and does not contain a subject and predicate, but it adds detail or explanation to a sentence, or renames something within the sentence.

PREPOSITIONAL PHRASES

One of the most common types of phrases is the prepositional phrase. A **prepositional phrase** begins with a preposition and ends with a noun or pronoun that is the object of the preposition. Normally, the prepositional phrase functions as an **adjective** or an **adverb** within the sentence.

Examples:

>prepositional
>phrase
>The picnic is on the blanket.

>prepositional
>phrase
>I am sick with a fever today.

>prepositional
>phrase
>Among the many flowers, John found a four-leaf clover.

VERBAL PHRASES

A **verbal** is a word or phrase that is formed from a verb but does not function as a verb. Depending on its particular form, it may be used as a noun, adjective, or adverb. A verbal does **not** replace a verb in a sentence.

Examples:

>verb
>Correct: Walk a mile daily.

>This is a complete sentence with the implied subject *you*.

>verbal
>Incorrect: To walk a mile.

>This is not a sentence since there is no functional verb.

There are three types of verbal: **participles**, **gerunds**, and **infinitives**. Each type of verbal has a corresponding **phrase** that consists of the verbal itself along with any complements or modifiers.

71

PARTICIPLES

A **participle** is a type of verbal that always functions as an adjective. The present participle always ends with -*ing*. Past participles end with -*d, -ed, -n,* or -*t*. Participles are combined with helping verbs to form certain verb tenses, but a participle by itself cannot function as a verb.

Examples:
verb | present participle | past participle
dance | dancing | danced

Participial phrases most often come right before or right after the noun or pronoun that they modify.

Examples:

participial phrase
Shipwrecked on an island, the boys started to fish for food.

participial phrase
Having been seated for five hours, we got out of the car to stretch our legs.

participial phrase
Praised for their work, the group accepted the first-place trophy.

GERUNDS

A **gerund** is a type of verbal that always functions as a **noun**. Like present participles, gerunds always end with -*ing*, but they can be easily distinguished from participles by the part of speech they represent (participles always function as adjectives). Since a gerund or gerund phrase always functions as a noun, it can be used as the subject of a sentence, the predicate nominative, or the object of a verb or preposition.

Examples:

gerund
We want to be known for teaching the poor.
object of preposition

gerund
Coaching this team is the best job of my life.
subject

gerund
We like practicing our songs in the basement.
object of verb

INFINITIVES

An **infinitive** is a type of verbal that can function as a noun, an adjective, or an adverb. An infinitive is made of the word *to* and the basic form of the verb. As with all other types of verbal phrases, an infinitive phrase includes the verbal itself and all of its complements or modifiers.

Examples:

infinitive
<u>To join</u> the team is my goal in life.
noun

infinitive
The animals have enough food <u>to eat</u> for the night.
adjective

infinitive
People lift weights <u>to exercise</u> their muscles.
adverb

> **Review Video: Verbals**
> Visit mometrix.com/academy and enter code: 915480

APPOSITIVE PHRASES

An **appositive** is a word or phrase that is used to explain or rename nouns or pronouns. Noun phrases, gerund phrases, and infinitive phrases can all be used as appositives.

Examples:

appositive
Terriers, <u>hunters at heart,</u> have been dressed up to look like lap dogs.

The noun phrase *hunters at heart* renames the noun *terriers*.

appositive
His plan, <u>to save and invest his money,</u> was proven as a safe approach.

The infinitive phrase explains what the plan is.

Appositive phrases can be **essential** or **nonessential**. An appositive phrase is essential if the person, place, or thing being described or renamed is too general for its meaning to be understood without the appositive.

Examples:

essential
Two of America's Founding Fathers, <u>George Washington and Thomas Jefferson,</u> served as presidents.

nonessential
George Washington and Thomas Jefferson, <u>two Founding Fathers,</u> served as presidents.

ABSOLUTE PHRASES

An absolute phrase is a phrase that consists of **a noun followed by a participle**. An absolute phrase provides **context** to what is being described in the sentence, but it does not modify or explain any particular word; it is essentially independent.

73

Examples:

noun   participle
The alarm ringing, he pushed the snooze button.
absolute
phrase

noun   participle
The music paused, she continued to dance through the crowd.
absolute
phrase

PARALLELISM

When multiple items or ideas are presented in a sentence in series, such as in a list, the items or ideas must be stated in grammatically equivalent ways. For example, if two ideas are listed in parallel and the first is stated in gerund form, the second cannot be stated in infinitive form. (e.g., *I enjoy reading and to study.* [incorrect]) An infinitive and a gerund are not grammatically equivalent. Instead, you should write *I enjoy reading and studying* OR *I like to read and to study.* In lists of more than two, all items must be parallel.

Example:

Incorrect: He stopped at the office, grocery store, and the pharmacy before heading home.

The first and third items in the list of places include the article *the*, so the second item needs it as well.

Correct: He stopped at the office, *the* grocery store, and the pharmacy before heading home.

Example:

Incorrect: While vacationing in Europe, she went biking, skiing, and climbed mountains.

The first and second items in the list are gerunds, so the third item must be as well.

Correct: While vacationing in Europe, she went biking, skiing, and *mountain climbing*.

> **Review Video: Parallel Sentence Construction**
> Visit mometrix.com/academy and enter code: 831988

SENTENCE PURPOSE

There are four types of sentences: declarative, imperative, interrogative, and exclamatory.

A **declarative** sentence states a fact and ends with a period.

The football game starts at seven o'clock.

An **imperative** sentence tells someone to do something and generally ends with a period. An urgent command might end with an exclamation point instead.

Don't forget to buy your ticket.

An **interrogative** sentence asks a question and ends with a question mark.

Are you going to the game on Friday?

An **exclamatory** sentence shows strong emotion and ends with an exclamation point.

I can't believe we won the game!

SENTENCE STRUCTURE

Sentences are classified by structure based on the type and number of clauses present. The four classifications of sentence structure are the following:

Simple: A simple sentence has one independent clause with no dependent clauses. A simple sentence may have **compound elements** (i.e., compound subject or verb).

Examples:

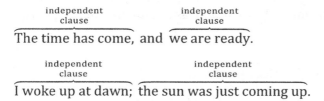

single subject   single verb
Judy watered the lawn.

compound subject   single verb
Judy and Alan watered the lawn.

single subject   compound verb   compound verb
Judy watered the lawn and pulled weeds.

compound subject   compound verb   compound verb
Judy and Alan watered the lawn and pulled weeds.

Compound: A compound sentence has two or more independent clauses with no dependent clauses. Usually, the independent clauses are joined with a comma and a coordinating conjunction or with a semicolon.

Examples:

independent clause   independent clause
The time has come, and we are ready.

independent clause   independent clause
I woke up at dawn; the sun was just coming up.

Complex: A complex sentence has one independent clause and at least one dependent clause.

Examples:

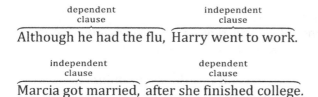

dependent clause   independent clause
Although he had the flu, Harry went to work.

independent clause   dependent clause
Marcia got married, after she finished college.

Compound-Complex: A compound-complex sentence has at least two independent clauses and at least one dependent clause.

Examples:

independent   dependent   independent
clause   clause   clause

John is my friend who went to India, and he brought back souvenirs.

independent   independent   dependent
clause   clause   clause

You may not realize this, but we heard the music that you played last night.

> **Review Video: Sentence Structure**
> Visit mometrix.com/academy and enter code: 700478

Sentence variety is important to consider when writing an essay or speech. A variety of sentence lengths and types creates rhythm, makes a passage more engaging, and gives writers an opportunity to demonstrate their writing style. Writing that uses the same length or type of sentence without variation can be boring or difficult to read. To evaluate a passage for effective sentence variety, it is helpful to note whether the passage contains diverse sentence structures and lengths. It is also important to pay attention to the way each sentence starts and avoid beginning with the same words or phrases.

SENTENCE FRAGMENTS

Recall that a group of words must contain at least one **independent clause** in order to be considered a sentence. If it doesn't contain even one independent clause, it is called a **sentence fragment**.

The appropriate process for **repairing** a sentence fragment depends on what type of fragment it is. If the fragment is a dependent clause, it can sometimes be as simple as removing a subordinating word (e.g., when, because, if) from the beginning of the fragment. Alternatively, a dependent clause can be incorporated into a closely related neighboring sentence. If the fragment is missing some required part, like a subject or a verb, the fix might be as simple as adding the missing part.

Examples:

Fragment: Because he wanted to sail the Mediterranean.

Removed subordinating word: He wanted to sail the Mediterranean.

Combined with another sentence: Because he wanted to sail the Mediterranean, he booked a Greek island cruise.

RUN-ON SENTENCES

Run-on sentences consist of multiple independent clauses that have not been joined together properly. Run-on sentences can be corrected in several different ways:

Join clauses properly: This can be done with a comma and coordinating conjunction, with a semicolon, or with a colon or dash if the second clause is explaining something in the first.

Example:

>**Incorrect**: I went on the trip, we visited lots of castles.

>**Corrected**: I went on the trip, and we visited lots of castles.

Split into separate sentences: This correction is most effective when the independent clauses are very long or when they are not closely related.

Example:

>**Incorrect**: The drive to New York takes ten hours, my uncle lives in Boston.

>**Corrected**: The drive to New York takes ten hours. My uncle lives in Boston.

Make one clause dependent: This is the easiest way to make the sentence correct and more interesting at the same time. It's often as simple as adding a subordinating word between the two clauses or before the first clause.

Example:

>**Incorrect**: I finally made it to the store and I bought some eggs.

>**Corrected**: When I finally made it to the store, I bought some eggs.

Reduce to one clause with a compound verb: If both clauses have the same subject, remove the subject from the second clause, and you now have just one clause with a compound verb.

Example:

>**Incorrect**: The drive to New York takes ten hours, it makes me very tired.

>**Corrected**: The drive to New York takes ten hours and makes me very tired.

Note: While these are the simplest ways to correct a run-on sentence, often the best way is to completely reorganize the thoughts in the sentence and rewrite it.

>**Review Video: Fragments and Run-on Sentences**
>Visit mometrix.com/academy and enter code: 541989

DANGLING AND MISPLACED MODIFIERS
DANGLING MODIFIERS

A dangling modifier is a dependent clause or verbal phrase that does not have a clear logical connection to a word in the sentence.

Example:

Incorrect: Reading each magazine article, the stories caught my attention.

dangling modifier

The word *stories* cannot be modified by *Reading each magazine article*. People can read, but stories cannot read. Therefore, the subject of the sentence must be a person.

Corrected: Reading each magazine article, I was entertained by the stories.

gerund phrase

Example:

Incorrect: Ever since childhood, my grandparents have visited me for Christmas.

dangling modifier

The speaker in this sentence can't have been visited by her grandparents when *they* were children, since she wouldn't have been born yet. Either the modifier should be clarified or the sentence should be rearranged to specify whose childhood is being referenced.

Clarified: Ever since I was a child, my grandparents have visited for Christmas.

dependent clause

Rearranged: Ever since childhood, I have enjoyed my grandparents visiting for Christmas.

adverb phrase

MISPLACED MODIFIERS

Because modifiers are grammatically versatile, they can be put in many different places within the structure of a sentence. The danger of this versatility is that a modifier can accidentally be placed where it is modifying the wrong word or where it is not clear which word it is modifying.

Example:

Incorrect: She read the book to a crowd that was filled with beautiful pictures.

modifier

The book was filled with beautiful pictures, not the crowd.

Corrected: She read the book that was filled with beautiful pictures to a crowd.

modifier

Example:

Ambiguous: Derek saw a bus nearly hit a man $\overbrace{\text{on his way to work}}^{\text{modifier}}$.

Was Derek on his way to work or was the other man?

Derek: $\overbrace{\text{On his way to work,}}^{\text{modifier}}$ Derek saw a bus nearly hit a man.

The other man: Derek saw a bus nearly hit a man $\overbrace{\text{who was on his way to work}}^{\text{modifier}}$.

SPLIT INFINITIVES

A split infinitive occurs when a modifying word comes between the word *to* and the verb that pairs with *to*.

Example: To *clearly* explain vs. *To explain* clearly | To *softly* sing vs. *To sing* softly

Though considered improper by some, split infinitives may provide better clarity and simplicity in some cases than the alternatives. As such, avoiding them should not be considered a universal rule.

DOUBLE NEGATIVES

Standard English allows **two negatives** only when a **positive** meaning is intended. (e.g., The team was *not displeased* with their performance.) Double negatives to emphasize negation are not used in standard English.

Negative modifiers (e.g., never, no, and not) should not be paired with other negative modifiers or negative words (e.g., none, nobody, nothing, or neither). The modifiers *hardly, barely*, and *scarcely* are also considered negatives in standard English, so they should not be used with other negatives.

PUNCTUATION
END PUNCTUATION
PERIODS

Use a period to end all sentences except direct questions and exclamations. Periods are also used for abbreviations.

Examples: 3 p.m. | 2 a.m. | Mr. Jones | Mrs. Stevens | Dr. Smith | Bill, Jr. | Pennsylvania Ave.

Note: An abbreviation is a shortened form of a word or phrase.

QUESTION MARKS

Question marks should be used following a **direct question**. A polite request can be followed by a period instead of a question mark.

Direct Question: What is for lunch today? | How are you? | Why is that the answer?

Polite Requests: Can you please send me the item tomorrow. | Will you please walk with me on the track.

> **Review Video: Question Marks**
> Visit mometrix.com/academy and enter code: 118471

EXCLAMATION MARKS

Exclamation marks are used after a word group or sentence that shows much feeling or has special importance. Exclamation marks should not be overused. They are saved for proper **exclamatory interjections**.

Example: We're going to the finals! | You have a beautiful car! | "That's crazy!" she yelled.

Review Video: Exclamation Points
Visit mometrix.com/academy and enter code: 199367

COMMAS

The comma is a punctuation mark that can help you understand connections in a sentence. Not every sentence needs a comma. However, if a sentence needs a comma, you need to put it in the right place. A comma in the wrong place (or an absent comma) will make a sentence's meaning unclear.

These are some of the rules for commas:

Use Case	Example
Before a **coordinating conjunction** joining independent clauses	Bob caught three fish, and I caught two fish.
After an **introductory phrase**	After the final out, we went to a restaurant to celebrate.
After an **adverbial clause**	Studying the stars, I was awed by the beauty of the sky.
Between **items in a series**	I will bring the turkey, the pie, and the coffee.
For **interjections**	Wow, you know how to play this game.
After *yes* and *no* responses	No, I cannot come tomorrow.
Separate **nonessential modifiers**	John Frank, who coaches the team, was promoted today.
Separate **nonessential appositives**	Thomas Edison, an American inventor, was born in Ohio.
Separate **nouns of direct address**	You, John, are my only hope in this moment.
Separate **interrogative tags**	This is the last time, correct?
Separate **contrasts**	You are my friend, not my enemy.
Writing **dates**	July 4, 1776, is an important date to remember.
Writing **addresses**	He is meeting me at 456 Delaware Avenue, Washington, D.C., tomorrow morning.
Writing **geographical names**	Paris, France, is my favorite city.
Writing **titles**	John Smith, PhD, will be visiting your class today.
Separate **expressions like *he said***	"You can start," she said, "with an apology."

A comma is also used **between coordinate adjectives** not joined with *and*. However, not all adjectives are coordinate (i.e., equal or parallel). To determine if your adjectives are coordinate, try connecting them with *and* or reversing their order. If it still sounds right, they are coordinate.

Incorrect: The kind, brown dog followed me home.

Correct: The kind, loyal dog followed me home.

Review Video: When to Use a Comma
Visit mometrix.com/academy and enter code: 786797

SEMICOLONS

The semicolon is used to join closely related independent clauses without the need for a coordinating conjunction. Semicolons are also used in place of commas to separate list elements that have internal commas. Some rules for semicolons include:

Use Case	Example
Between closely connected independent clauses **not connected with a coordinating conjunction**	You are right; we should go with your plan.
Between independent clauses **linked with a transitional word**	I think that we can agree on this; however, I am not sure about my friends.
Between items in a **series that has internal punctuation**	I have visited New York, New York; Augusta, Maine; and Baltimore, Maryland.

> **Review Video: How to Use Semicolons**
> Visit mometrix.com/academy and enter code: 370605

COLONS

The colon is used to call attention to the words that follow it. When used in a sentence, a colon should only come at the **end** of a **complete sentence**. The rules for colons are as follows:

Use Case	Example
After an independent clause to **make a list**	I want to learn many languages: Spanish, German, and Italian.
For **explanations**	There is one thing that stands out on your resume: responsibility.
To give a **quote**	He started with an idea: "We are able to do more than we imagine."
After the **greeting in a formal letter**	To Whom It May Concern:
Show **hours and minutes**	It is 3:14 p.m.
Separate a **title and subtitle**	The essay is titled "America: A Short Introduction to a Modern Country."

> **Review Video: Using Colons**
> Visit mometrix.com/academy and enter code: 868673

PARENTHESES

Parentheses are used for additional information. Also, they can be used to put labels for letters or numbers in a series. Parentheses should be not be used very often. If they are overused, parentheses can be a distraction instead of a help.

Examples:

> **Extra Information**: The rattlesnake (see Image 2) is a dangerous snake of North and South America.

> **Series**: Include in the email (1) your name, (2) your address, and (3) your question for the author.

> **Review Video: Parentheses**
> Visit mometrix.com/academy and enter code: 947743

81

QUOTATION MARKS

Use quotation marks to close off **direct quotations** of a person's spoken or written words. Do not use quotation marks around indirect quotations. An indirect quotation gives someone's message without using the person's exact words. Use **single quotation marks** to close off a quotation inside a quotation.

> **Direct Quote**: Nancy said, "I am waiting for Henry to arrive."

> **Indirect Quote**: Henry said that he is going to be late to the meeting.

> **Quote inside a Quote**: The teacher asked, "Has everyone read 'The Gift of the Magi'?"

Quotation marks should be used around the titles of **short works**: newspaper and magazine articles, poems, short stories, songs, television episodes, radio programs, and subdivisions of books or websites.

Examples:

> "Rip Van Winkle" (short story by Washington Irving)

> "O Captain! My Captain!" (poem by Walt Whitman)

Although it is not standard usage, quotation marks are sometimes used to highlight **irony** or the use of words to mean something other than their dictionary definition. This type of usage should be employed sparingly, if at all.

Examples:

The boss warned Frank that he was walking on "thin ice."	Frank is not walking on real ice. Instead, he is being warned to avoid mistakes.
The teacher thanked the young man for his "honesty."	The quotation marks around *honesty* show that the teacher does not believe the young man's explanation.

> **Review Video: Quotation Marks**
> Visit mometrix.com/academy and enter code: 884918

Periods and commas are put **inside** quotation marks. Colons and semicolons are put **outside** the quotation marks. Question marks and exclamation points are placed inside quotation marks when they are part of a quote. When the question or exclamation mark goes with the whole sentence, the mark is left outside of the quotation marks.

Examples:

Period and comma	We read "The Gift of the Magi," "The Skylight Room," and "The Cactus."
Semicolon	They watched "The Nutcracker"; then, they went home.
Exclamation mark that is a part of a quote	The crowd cheered, "Victory!"
Question mark that goes with the whole sentence	Is your favorite short story "The Tell-Tale Heart"?

82

APOSTROPHES

An apostrophe is used to show **possession** or the **deletion of letters in contractions**. An apostrophe is not needed with the possessive pronouns *his, hers, its, ours, theirs, whose*, and *yours*.

Singular Nouns: David's car | a book's theme | my brother's board game

Plural Nouns that end with -*s*: the scissors' handle | boys' basketball

Plural Nouns that end without -*s*: Men's department | the people's adventure

> **Review Video: When to Use an Apostrophe**
> Visit mometrix.com/academy and enter code: 213068
>
> **Review Video: Punctuation Errors in Possessive Pronouns**
> Visit mometrix.com/academy and enter code: 221438

HYPHENS

Hyphens are used to **separate compound words**. Use hyphens in the following cases:

Use Case	Example
Compound numbers from 21 to 99 when written out in words	This team needs twenty-five points to win the game.
Written-out fractions that are used as adjectives	The recipe says that we need a three-fourths cup of butter.
Compound adjectives that come before a noun	The well-fed dog took a nap.
Unusual compound words that would be hard to read or easily confused with other words	This is the best anti-itch cream on the market.

Note: This is not a complete set of the rules for hyphens. A dictionary is the best tool for knowing if a compound word needs a hyphen.

> **Review Video: Hyphens**
> Visit mometrix.com/academy and enter code: 981632

DASHES

Dashes are used to show a **break** or a **change in thought** in a sentence or to act as parentheses in a sentence. When typing, use two hyphens to make a dash. Do not put a space before or after the dash. The following are the functions of dashes:

Use Case	Example
Set off parenthetical statements or an **appositive with internal punctuation**	The three trees—oak, pine, and magnolia—are coming on a truck tomorrow.
Show a **break or change in tone or thought**	The first question—how silly of me—does not have a correct answer.

ELLIPSIS MARKS

The ellipsis mark has **three** periods (...) to show when **words have been removed** from a quotation. If a **full sentence or more** is removed from a quoted passage, you need to use **four** periods to show the removed text and the end punctuation mark. The ellipsis mark should not be used at the beginning of a quotation. The ellipsis mark should also not be used at the end of a quotation unless some words have been deleted from the end of the final quoted sentence.

Example:

"Then he picked up the groceries...paid for them...later he went home."

BRACKETS

There are two main reasons to use brackets:

Use Case	Example
Placing **parentheses inside of parentheses**	The hero of this story, Paul Revere (a silversmith and industrialist [see Ch. 4]), rode through towns of Massachusetts to warn of advancing British troops.
Adding **clarification or detail to a quotation** that is not part of the quotation	The father explained, "My children are planning to attend my alma mater [State University]."

> **Review Video: Brackets**
> Visit mometrix.com/academy and enter code: 727546

COMMON USAGE MISTAKES
WORD CONFUSION
WHICH, THAT, AND WHO

The words *which*, *that*, and *who* can act as **relative pronouns** to help clarify or describe a noun.

Which is used for things only.

Example: Andrew's car, *which is old and rusty,* broke down last week.

That is used for people or things. *That* is usually informal when used to describe people.

Example: Is this the only book *that Louis L'Amour wrote?*

Example: Is Louis L'Amour the author *that wrote Western novels?*

Who is used for people or for animals that have an identity or personality.

Example: Mozart was the composer *who wrote those operas.*

Example: John's dog, *who is called Max,* is large and fierce.

84

HOMOPHONES

Homophones are words that sound alike (or similar) but have different **spellings** and **definitions**. A homophone is a type of **homonym**, which is a pair or group of words that are pronounced or spelled the same, but do not mean the same thing.

TO, TOO, AND TWO

To can be an adverb or a preposition for showing direction, purpose, and relationship. See your dictionary for the many other ways to use *to* in a sentence.

Examples: I went to the store. | I want to go with you.

Too is an adverb that means *also, as well, very,* or *in excess.*

Examples: I can walk a mile too. | You have eaten too much.

Two is a number.

Example: You have two minutes left.

THERE, THEIR, AND THEY'RE

There can be an adjective, adverb, or pronoun. Often, *there* is used to show a place or to start a sentence.

Examples: I went there yesterday. | There is something in his pocket.

Their is a pronoun that is used to show ownership.

Examples: He is their father. | This is their fourth apology this week.

They're is a contraction of *they are.*

Example: Did you know that they're in town?

KNEW AND NEW

Knew is the past tense of *know.*

Example: I knew the answer.

New is an adjective that means something is current, has not been used, or is modern.

Example: This is my new phone.

THEN AND THAN

Then is an adverb that indicates sequence or order:

Example: I'm going to run to the library and then come home.

Than is special-purpose word used only for comparisons:

Example: Susie likes chips more than candy.

ITS AND IT'S

Its is a pronoun that shows ownership.

Example: The guitar is in its case.

It's is a contraction of *it is*.

> Example: It's an honor and a privilege to meet you.

Note: The *h* in honor is silent, so *honor* starts with the vowel sound *o*, which must have the article *an*.

YOUR AND YOU'RE
Your is a pronoun that shows ownership.

> Example: This is your moment to shine.

You're is a contraction of *you are*.

> Example: Yes, you're correct.

SAW AND SEEN
Saw is the past-tense form of *see*.

> Example: I saw a turtle on my walk this morning.

Seen is the past participle of *see*.

> Example: I have seen this movie before.

AFFECT AND EFFECT
There are two main reasons that *affect* and *effect* are so often confused: 1) both words can be used as either a noun or a verb, and 2) unlike most homophones, their usage and meanings are closely related to each other. Here is a quick rundown of the four usage options:

Affect (n): feeling, emotion, or mood that is displayed

> Example: The patient had a flat *affect*. (i.e., his face showed little or no emotion)

Affect (v): to alter, to change, to influence

> Example: The sunshine *affects* the plant's growth.

Effect (n): a result, a consequence

> Example: What *effect* will this weather have on our schedule?

Effect (v): to bring about, to cause to be

> Example: These new rules will *effect* order in the office.

The noun form of *affect* is rarely used outside of technical medical descriptions, so if a noun form is needed on the test, you can safely select *effect*. The verb form of *effect* is not as rare as the noun form of *affect*, but it's still not all that likely to show up on your test. If you need a verb and you can't decide which to use based on the definitions, choosing *affect* is your best bet.

HOMOGRAPHS
Homographs are words that share the same spelling, but have different meanings and sometimes different pronunciations. To figure out which meaning is being used, you should be looking for

context clues. The context clues give hints to the meaning of the word. For example, the word *spot* has many meanings. It can mean "a place" or "a stain or blot." In the sentence "After my lunch, I saw a spot on my shirt," the word *spot* means "a stain or blot." The context clues of "After my lunch" and "on my shirt" guide you to this decision. A homograph is another type of homonym.

BANK

> (noun): an establishment where money is held for savings or lending

> (verb): to collect or pile up

CONTENT

> (noun): the topics that will be addressed within a book

> (adjective): pleased or satisfied

> (verb): to make someone pleased or satisfied

FINE

> (noun): an amount of money that acts a penalty for an offense

> (adjective): very small or thin

> (adverb): in an acceptable way

> (verb): to make someone pay money as a punishment

INCENSE

> (noun): a material that is burned in religious settings and makes a pleasant aroma

> (verb): to frustrate or anger

LEAD

> (noun): the first or highest position

> (noun): a heavy metallic element

> (verb): to direct a person or group of followers

> (adjective): containing lead

OBJECT

> (noun): a lifeless item that can be held and observed

> (verb): to disagree

PRODUCE

> (noun): fruits and vegetables

> (verb): to make or create something

REFUSE

> (noun): garbage or debris that has been thrown away

> (verb): to not allow

SUBJECT

(noun): an area of study

(verb): to force or subdue

TEAR

(noun): a fluid secreted by the eyes

(verb): to separate or pull apart

COMMONLY MISUSED WORDS AND PHRASES

A LOT

The phrase *a lot* should always be written as two words; never as *alot*.

Correct: That's a lot of chocolate!

Incorrect: He does that alot.

CAN

The word *can* is used to describe things that are possible occurrences; the word *may* is used to described things that are allowed to happen.

Correct: May I have another piece of pie?

Correct: I can lift three of these bags of mulch at a time.

Incorrect: Mom said we can stay up thirty minutes later tonight.

COULD HAVE

The phrase *could of* is often incorrectly substituted for the phrase *could have*. Similarly, *could of*, *may of*, and *might of* are sometimes used in place of the correct phrases *could have*, *may have*, and *might have*.

Correct: If I had known, I would have helped out.

Incorrect: Well, that could of gone much worse than it did.

MYSELF

The word *myself* is a reflexive pronoun, often incorrectly used in place of *I* or *me*.

Correct: He let me do it myself.

Incorrect: The job was given to Dave and myself.

OFF

The phrase *off of* is a redundant expression that should be avoided. In most cases, it can be corrected simply by removing *of*.

Correct: My dog chased the squirrel off its perch on the fence.

Incorrect: He finally moved his plate off of the table.

SUPPOSED TO

The phrase *suppose to* is sometimes used incorrectly in place of the phrase *supposed to*.

Correct: I was supposed to go to the store this afternoon.

Incorrect: When are we suppose to get our grades?

TRY TO

The phrase *try and* is often used in informal writing and conversation to replace the correct phrase *try to*.

Correct: It's a good policy to try to satisfy every customer who walks in the door.

Incorrect: Don't try and do too much.

Expression of Ideas

OUTLINING AND ORGANIZING IDEAS
ESSAYS

Essays usually focus on one topic, subject, or goal. There are several types of essays, including informative, persuasive, and narrative. An essay's structure and level of formality depend on the type of essay and its goal. While narrative essays typically do not include outside sources, other types of essays often require some research and the integration of primary and secondary sources.

The basic format of an essay typically has three major parts: the introduction, the body, and the conclusion. The body is further divided into the writer's main points. Short and simple essays may have three main points, while essays covering broader ranges and going into more depth can have almost any number of main points, depending on length.

An essay's introduction should answer three questions:

1. What is the **subject** of the essay?

   If a student writes an essay about a book, the answer would include the title and author of the book and any additional information needed—such as the subject or argument of the book.

2. How does the essay **address** the subject?

   To answer this, the writer identifies the essay's organization by briefly summarizing main points and the evidence supporting them.

3. What will the essay **prove**?

   This is the thesis statement, usually the opening paragraph's last sentence, clearly stating the writer's message.

The body elaborates on all the main points related to the thesis, introducing one main point at a time, and includes supporting evidence with each main point. Each body paragraph should state the point in a topic sentence, which is usually the first sentence in the paragraph. The paragraph should then explain the point's meaning, support it with quotations or other evidence, and then explain how this point and the evidence are related to the thesis. The writer should then repeat this procedure in a new paragraph for each additional main point.

The conclusion reiterates the content of the introduction, including the thesis, to remind the reader of the essay's main argument or subject. The essay writer may also summarize the highlights of the argument or description contained in the body of the essay, following the same sequence originally used in the body. For example, a conclusion might look like: Point 1 + Point 2 + Point 3 = Thesis, or Point 1 → Point 2 → Point 3 → Thesis Proof. Good organization makes essays easier for writers to compose and provides a guide for readers to follow. Well-organized essays hold attention better and are more likely to get readers to accept their theses as valid.

Main Ideas, Supporting Details, and Outlining a Topic

A writer often begins the first paragraph of a paper by stating the **main idea** or point, also known as the **topic sentence**. The rest of the paragraph supplies particular details that develop and support the main point. One way to visualize the relationship between the main point and supporting information is by considering a table: the tabletop is the main point, and each of the table's legs is a supporting detail or group of details. Both professional authors and students can benefit from planning their writing by first making an outline of the topic. Outlines facilitate quick identification of the main point and supporting details without having to wade through the additional language that will exist in the fully developed essay, article, or paper. Outlining can also help readers to analyze a piece of existing writing for the same reason. The outline first summarizes the main idea in one sentence. Then, below that, it summarizes the supporting details in a numbered list. Writing the paper then consists of filling in the outline with detail, writing a paragraph for each supporting point, and adding an introduction and conclusion.

Introduction

The purpose of the introduction is to capture the reader's attention and announce the essay's main idea. Normally, the introduction contains 50-80 words, or 3-5 sentences. An introduction can begin with an interesting quote, a question, or a strong opinion—something that will **engage** the reader's interest and prompt them to keep reading. If you are writing your essay to a specific prompt, your introduction should include a **restatement or summarization** of the prompt so that the reader will have some context for your essay. Finally, your introduction should briefly state your **thesis or main idea**: the primary thing you hope to communicate to the reader through your essay. Don't try to include all of the details and nuances of your thesis, or all of your reasons for it, in the introduction. That's what the rest of the essay is for!

> **Review Video: Introduction**
> Visit mometrix.com/academy and enter code: 961328

Thesis Statement

The thesis is the main idea of the essay. A temporary thesis, or working thesis, should be established early in the writing process because it will serve to keep the writer focused as ideas develop. This temporary thesis is subject to change as you continue to write.

The temporary thesis has two parts: a **topic** (i.e., the focus of your essay based on the prompt) and a **comment**. The comment makes an important point about the topic. A temporary thesis should be interesting and specific. Also, you need to limit the topic to a manageable scope. These three questions are useful tools to measure the effectiveness of any temporary thesis:

- Does the focus of my essay have enough interest to hold an audience?
- Is the focus of my essay specific enough to generate interest?
- Is the focus of my essay manageable for the time limit? Too broad? Too narrow?

The thesis should be a generalization rather than a fact because the thesis prepares readers for facts and details that support the thesis. The process of bringing the thesis into sharp focus may help in outlining major sections of the work. Once the thesis and introduction are complete, you can address the body of the work.

> **Review Video: Thesis Statements**
> Visit mometrix.com/academy and enter code: 691033

SUPPORTING THE THESIS

Throughout your essay, the thesis should be **explained clearly and supported** adequately by additional arguments. The thesis sentence needs to contain a clear statement of the purpose of your essay and a comment about the thesis. With the thesis statement, you have an opportunity to state what is noteworthy of this particular treatment of the prompt. Each sentence and paragraph should build on and support the thesis.

When you respond to the prompt, use parts of the passage to support your argument or defend your position. Using supporting evidence from the passage strengths your argument because readers can see your attention to the entire passage and your response to the details and facts within the passage. You can use facts, details, statistics, and direct quotations from the passage to uphold your position. Be sure to point out which information comes from the original passage and base your argument around that evidence.

BODY

In an essay's introduction, the writer establishes the thesis and may indicate how the rest of the piece will be structured. In the body of the piece, the writer **elaborates** upon, **illustrates**, and **explains** the **thesis statement**. How writers arrange supporting details and their choices of paragraph types are development techniques. Writers may give examples of the concept introduced in the thesis statement. If the subject includes a cause-and-effect relationship, the author may explain its causality. A writer will explain or analyze the main idea of the piece throughout the body, often by presenting arguments for the veracity or credibility of the thesis statement. Writers may use development to define or clarify ambiguous terms. Paragraphs within the body may be organized using natural sequences, like space and time. Writers may employ **inductive reasoning**, using multiple details to establish a generalization or causal relationship, or **deductive reasoning**, proving a generalized hypothesis or proposition through a specific example or case.

> **Review Video: Drafting Body Paragraphs**
> Visit mometrix.com/academy and enter code: 724590

PARAGRAPHS

After the introduction of a passage, a series of body paragraphs will carry a message through to the conclusion. Each paragraph should be **unified around a main point**. Normally, a good topic sentence summarizes the paragraph's main point. A topic sentence is a general sentence that gives an introduction to the paragraph.

The sentences that follow support the topic sentence. However, though it is usually the first sentence, the topic sentence can come as the final sentence to the paragraph if the earlier sentences give a clear explanation of the paragraph's topic. This allows the topic sentence to function as a concluding sentence. Overall, the paragraphs need to stay true to the main point. This means that any unnecessary sentences that do not advance the main point should be removed.

The main point of a paragraph requires adequate development (i.e., a substantial paragraph that covers the main point). A paragraph of two or three sentences does not cover a main point. This is especially true when the main point of the paragraph gives strong support to the argument of the thesis. An occasional short paragraph is fine as a transitional device. However, a well-developed argument will have paragraphs with more than a few sentences.

METHODS OF DEVELOPING PARAGRAPHS

Common methods of adding substance to paragraphs include examples, illustrations, analogies, and cause and effect.

- **Examples** are supporting details to the main idea of a paragraph or a passage. When authors write about something that their audience may not understand, they can provide an example to show their point. When authors write about something that is not easily accepted, they can give examples to prove their point.
- **Illustrations** are extended examples that require several sentences. Well-selected illustrations can be a great way for authors to develop a point that may not be familiar to their audience.
- **Analogies** make comparisons between items that appear to have nothing in common. Analogies are employed by writers to provoke fresh thoughts about a subject. These comparisons may be used to explain the unfamiliar, to clarify an abstract point, or to argue a point. Although analogies are effective literary devices, they should be used carefully in arguments. Two things may be alike in some respects but completely different in others.
- **Cause and effect** is an excellent device to explain the connection between an action or situation and a particular result. One way that authors can use cause and effect is to state the effect in the topic sentence of a paragraph and add the causes in the body of the paragraph. This method can give an author's paragraphs structure, which always strengthens writing.

TYPES OF PARAGRAPHS

A **paragraph of narration** tells a story or a part of a story. Normally, the sentences are arranged in chronological order (i.e., the order that the events happened). However, flashbacks (i.e., an anecdote from an earlier time) can be included.

A **descriptive paragraph** makes a verbal portrait of a person, place, or thing. When specific details are used that appeal to one or more of the senses (i.e., sight, sound, smell, taste, and touch), authors give readers a sense of being present in the moment.

A **process paragraph** is related to time order (i.e., First, you open the bottle. Second, you pour the liquid, etc.). Usually, this describes a process or teaches readers how to perform a process.

Comparing two things draws attention to their similarities and indicates a number of differences. When authors contrast, they focus only on differences. Both comparing and contrasting may be done point-by-point, noting both the similarities and differences of each point, or in sequential paragraphs, where you discuss all the similarities and then all the differences, or vice versa.

BREAKING TEXT INTO PARAGRAPHS

For most forms of writing, you will need to use multiple paragraphs. As such, determining when to start a new paragraph is very important. Reasons for starting a new paragraph include:

- To mark off the introduction and concluding paragraphs
- To signal a shift to a new idea or topic
- To indicate an important shift in time or place
- To explain a point in additional detail
- To highlight a comparison, contrast, or cause and effect relationship

PARAGRAPH LENGTH

Most readers find that their comfort level for a paragraph is between 100 and 200 words. Shorter paragraphs cause too much starting and stopping and give a choppy effect. Paragraphs that are too long often test the attention span of readers. Two notable exceptions to this rule exist. In scientific or scholarly papers, longer paragraphs suggest seriousness and depth. In journalistic writing, constraints are placed on paragraph size by the narrow columns in a newspaper format.

The first and last paragraphs of a text will usually be the introduction and conclusion. These special-purpose paragraphs are likely to be shorter than paragraphs in the body of the work. Paragraphs in the body of the essay follow the subject's outline (e.g., one paragraph per point in short essays and a group of paragraphs per point in longer works). Some ideas require more development than others, so it is good for a writer to remain flexible. A paragraph of excessive length may be divided, and shorter ones may be combined.

CONCLUSION

Two important principles to consider when writing a conclusion are strength and closure. A strong conclusion gives the reader a sense that the author's main points are meaningful and important, and that the supporting facts and arguments are convincing, solid, and well developed. When a conclusion achieves closure, it gives the impression that the writer has stated all necessary information and points and completed the work, rather than simply stopping after a specified length. Some things to avoid when writing concluding paragraphs include:

- Introducing a completely new idea
- Beginning with obvious or unoriginal phrases like "In conclusion" or "To summarize"
- Apologizing for one's opinions or writing
- Repeating the thesis word for word rather than rephrasing it
- Believing that the conclusion must always summarize the piece

> **Review Video: Drafting Conclusions**
> Visit mometrix.com/academy and enter code: 209408

COHERENCE IN WRITING

COHERENT PARAGRAPHS

A smooth flow of sentences and paragraphs without gaps, shifts, or bumps will lead to paragraph **coherence**. Ties between old and new information can be smoothed using several methods:

- **Linking ideas clearly**, from the topic sentence to the body of the paragraph, is essential for a smooth transition. The topic sentence states the main point, and this should be followed by specific details, examples, and illustrations that support the topic sentence. The support may be direct or indirect. In **indirect support**, the illustrations and examples may support a sentence that in turn supports the topic directly.
- The **repetition of key words** adds coherence to a paragraph. To avoid dull language, variations of the key words may be used.
- **Parallel structures** are often used within sentences to emphasize the similarity of ideas and connect sentences giving similar information.
- Maintaining a **consistent verb tense** throughout the paragraph helps. Shifting tenses affects the smooth flow of words and can disrupt the coherence of the paragraph.

> **Review Video: How to Write a Good Paragraph**
> Visit mometrix.com/academy and enter code: 682127

SEQUENCE WORDS AND PHRASES

When a paragraph opens with the topic sentence, the second sentence may begin with a phrase like *first of all*, introducing the first supporting detail or example. The writer may introduce the second supporting item with words or phrases like *also*, *in addition*, and *besides*. The writer might introduce succeeding pieces of support with wording like, *another thing*, *moreover*, *furthermore*, or *not only that, but*. The writer may introduce the last piece of support with *lastly*, *finally*, or *last but not least*. Writers get off the point by presenting off-target items not supporting the main point. For example, a main point *my dog is not smart* is supported by the statement, *he's six years old and still doesn't answer to his name*. But *he cries when I leave for school* is not supportive, as it does not indicate lack of intelligence. Writers stay on point by presenting only supportive statements that are directly relevant to and illustrative of their main point.

> **Review Video: Sequence**
> Visit mometrix.com/academy and enter code: 489027

TRANSITIONS

Transitions between sentences and paragraphs guide readers from idea to idea and indicate relationships between sentences and paragraphs. Writers should be judicious in their use of transitions, inserting them sparingly. They should also be selected to fit the author's purpose—transitions can indicate time, comparison, and conclusion, among other purposes. Tone is also important to consider when using transitional phrases, varying the tone for different audiences. For example, in a scholarly essay, *in summary* would be preferable to the more informal *in short*.

When working with transitional words and phrases, writers usually find a natural flow that indicates when a transition is needed. In reading a draft of the text, it should become apparent where the flow is disrupted. At this point, the writer can add transitional elements during the revision process. Revising can also afford an opportunity to delete transitional devices that seem heavy handed or unnecessary.

TYPES OF TRANSITIONAL WORDS

Time	afterward, immediately, earlier, meanwhile, recently, lately, now, since, soon, when, then, until, before, etc.
Sequence	too, first, second, further, moreover, also, again, and, next, still, besides, finally
Comparison	similarly, in the same way, likewise, also, again, once more
Contrasting	but, although, despite, however, instead, nevertheless, on the one hand... on the other hand, regardless, yet, in contrast
Cause and Effect	because, consequently, thus, therefore, then, to this end, since, so, as a result, if... then, accordingly
Examples	for example, for instance, such as, to illustrate, indeed, in fact, specifically
Place	near, far, here, there, to the left/right, next to, above, below, beyond, opposite, beside
Concession	granted that, naturally, of course, it may appear, although it is true that
Repetition, Summary, or Conclusion	as mentioned earlier, as noted, in other words, in short, on the whole, to summarize, therefore, as a result, to conclude, in conclusion
Addition	and, also, furthermore, moreover
Generalization	in broad terms, broadly speaking, in general

WRITING STYLE AND FORM

WRITING STYLE AND LINGUISTIC FORM

Linguistic form encodes the literal meanings of words and sentences. It comes from the phonological, morphological, syntactic, and semantic parts of a language. **Writing style** consists of different ways of encoding the meaning and indicating figurative and stylistic meanings. An author's writing style can also be referred to as his or her **voice**.

Writers' stylistic choices accomplish three basic effects on their audiences:

- They **communicate meanings** beyond linguistically dictated meanings,
- They communicate the **author's attitude**, such as persuasive or argumentative effects accomplished through style, and
- They communicate or **express feelings**.

Within style, component areas include:

- Narrative structure
- Viewpoint
- Focus
- Sound patterns

- Meter and rhythm
- Lexical and syntactic repetition and parallelism
- Writing genre
- Representational, realistic, and mimetic effects
- Representation of thought and speech
- Meta-representation (representing representation)
- Irony
- Metaphor and other indirect meanings
- Representation and use of historical and dialectal variations
- Gender-specific and other group-specific speech styles, both real and fictitious
- Analysis of the processes for inferring meaning from writing

TONE

Tone may be defined as the writer's **attitude** toward the topic, and to the audience. This attitude is reflected in the language used in the writing. The tone of a work should be **appropriate to the topic** and to the intended audience. While it may be fine to use slang or jargon in some pieces, other texts should not contain such terms. Tone can range from humorous to serious and any level in between. It may be more or less formal, depending on the purpose of the writing and its intended audience. All these nuances in tone can flavor the entire writing and should be kept in mind as the work evolves.

WORD SELECTION

A writer's choice of words is a signature of their style. Careful thought about the use of words can improve a piece of writing. A passage can be an exciting piece to read when attention is given to the use of vivid or specific nouns rather than general ones.

Example:

General: His kindness will never be forgotten.

Specific: His thoughtful gifts and bear hugs will never be forgotten.

ACTIVE AND PASSIVE LANGUAGE

Attention should also be given to the kind of verbs that are used in sentences. Active verbs (e.g., run, swim) are about an action. Whenever possible, an **active verb should replace a linking verb** to provide clear examples for arguments and to strengthen a passage overall. When using an active verb, one should be sure that the verb is used in the active voice instead of the passive voice. Verbs are in the active voice when the subject is the one doing the action. A verb is in the passive voice when the subject is the recipient of an action.

Example:

Passive: The winners were called to the stage by the judges.

Active: The judges called the winners to the stage.

CONCISENESS

Conciseness is writing that communicates a message in the fewest words possible. Writing concisely is valuable because short, uncluttered messages allow the reader to understand the author's message more easily and efficiently. Planning is important in writing concise messages. If

96

you have in mind what you need to write beforehand, it will be easier to make a message short and to the point. Do not state the obvious.

Revising is also important. After the message is written, make sure you have effective, pithy sentences that efficiently get your point across. When reviewing the information, imagine a conversation taking place, and concise writing will likely result.

APPROPRIATE KINDS OF WRITING FOR DIFFERENT TASKS, PURPOSES, AND AUDIENCES

When preparing to write a composition, consider the audience and purpose to choose the best type of writing. Four common types of writing are persuasive, expository, and narrative. **Persuasive**, or argumentative writing, is used to convince the audience to take action or agree with the author's claims. **Expository** writing is meant to inform the audience of the author's observations or research on a topic. **Narrative** writing is used to tell the audience a story and often allows more room for creativity. **Descriptive** writing is when a writer provides a substantial amount of detail to the reader so he or she can visualize the topic. While task, purpose, and audience inform a writer's mode of writing, these factors also impact elements such as tone, vocabulary, and formality.

For example, students who are writing to persuade their parents to grant them some additional privilege, such as permission for a more independent activity, should use more sophisticated vocabulary and diction that sounds more mature and serious to appeal to the parental audience. However, students who are writing for younger children should use simpler vocabulary and sentence structure, as well as choose words that are more vivid and entertaining. They should treat their topics more lightly, and include humor when appropriate. Students who are writing for their classmates may use language that is more informal, as well as age-appropriate.

> **Review Video: Writing Purpose and Audience**
> Visit mometrix.com/academy and enter code: 146627

FORMALITY IN WRITING
LEVEL OF FORMALITY

The relationship between writer and reader is important in choosing a **level of formality** as most writing requires some degree of formality. **Formal writing** is for addressing a superior in a school or work environment. Business letters, textbooks, and newspapers use a moderate to high level of formality. **Informal writing** is appropriate for private letters, personal emails, and business correspondence between close associates.

For your exam, you will want to be aware of informal and formal writing. One way that this can be accomplished is to watch for shifts in point of view in the essay. For example, unless writers are using a personal example, they will rarely refer to themselves (e.g., "*I* think that *my* point is very clear.") to avoid being informal when they need to be formal.

Also, be mindful of an author who addresses his or her audience **directly** in their writing (e.g., "Readers, *like you*, will understand this argument.") as this can be a sign of informal writing. Good writers understand the need to be consistent with their level of formality. Shifts in levels of formality or point of view can confuse readers and cause them to discount the message.

CLICHÉS

Clichés are phrases that have been **overused** to the point that the phrase has no importance or has lost the original meaning. These phrases have no originality and add very little to a passage. Therefore, most writers will avoid the use of clichés. Another option is to make changes to a cliché so that it is not predictable and empty of meaning.

Examples:

> When life gives you lemons, make lemonade.

> Every cloud has a silver lining.

JARGON

Jargon is **specialized vocabulary** that is used among members of a certain trade or profession. Since jargon is understood by only a small audience, writers will use jargon in passages that will only be read by a specialized audience. For example, medical jargon should be used in a medical journal but not in a New York Times article. Jargon includes exaggerated language that tries to impress rather than inform. Sentences filled with jargon are not precise and are difficult to understand.

Examples:

> "He is going to *toenail* these frames for us." (Toenail is construction jargon for nailing at an angle.)

> "They brought in a *kip* of material today." (Kip refers to 1000 pounds in architecture and engineering.)

SLANG

Slang is an **informal** and sometimes private language that is understood by some individuals. Slang terms have some usefulness, but they can have a small audience. So, most formal writing will not include this kind of language.

Examples:

> "Yes, the event was a blast!" (In this sentence, *blast* means that the event was a great experience.)

> "That attempt was an epic fail." (By *epic fail*, the speaker means that his or her attempt was not a success.)

COLLOQUIALISM

A colloquialism is a word or phrase that is found in informal writing. Unlike slang, **colloquial language** will be familiar to a greater range of people. However, colloquialisms are still considered inappropriate for formal writing. Colloquial language can include some slang, but these are limited to contractions for the most part.

Examples:

> "Can *y'all* come back another time?" (Y'all is a contraction of "you all.")

> "Will you stop him from building this *castle in the air*?" (A "castle in the air" is an improbable or unlikely event.)

ACADEMIC LANGUAGE

In educational settings, students are often expected to use academic language in their schoolwork. Academic language is also commonly found in dissertations and theses, texts published by academic journals, and other forms of academic research. Academic language conventions may vary between fields, but general academic language is free of slang, regional terminology, and noticeable grammatical errors. Specific terms may also be used in academic language, and it is important to understand their proper usage. A writer's command of academic language impacts their ability to communicate in an academic or professional context. While it is acceptable to use colloquialisms, slang, improper grammar, or other forms of informal speech in social settings or at home, it is inappropriate to practice non-academic language in academic contexts.

COMMON TYPES OF WRITING

AUTOBIOGRAPHICAL NARRATIVES

Autobiographical narratives are narratives written by an author about an event or period in their life. Autobiographical narratives are written from one person's perspective, in first person, and often include the author's thoughts and feelings alongside their description of the event or period. Structure, style, or theme varies between different autobiographical narratives, since each narrative is personal and specific to its author and his or her experience.

REFLECTIVE ESSAY

A less common type of essay is the reflective essay. **Reflective essays** allow the author to reflect, or think back, on an experience and analyze what they recall. They should consider what they learned from the experience, what they could have done differently, what would have helped them during the experience, or anything else that they have realized from looking back on the experience. Reflection essays incorporate both objective reflection on one's own actions and subjective explanation of thoughts and feelings. These essays can be written for a number of experiences in a formal or informal context.

JOURNALS AND DIARIES

A **journal** is a personal account of events, experiences, feelings, and thoughts. Many people write journals to express their feelings and thoughts or to help them process experiences they have had. Since journals are **private documents** not meant to be shared with others, writers may not be concerned with grammar, spelling, or other mechanics. However, authors may write journals that they expect or hope to publish someday; in this case, they not only express their thoughts and feelings and process their experiences, but they also attend to their craft in writing them. Some authors compose journals to record a particular time period or a series of related events, such as a cancer diagnosis, treatment, surviving the disease, and how these experiences have changed or affected them. Other experiences someone might include in a journal are recovering from addiction, journeys of spiritual exploration and discovery, time spent in another country, or anything else someone wants to personally document. Journaling can also be therapeutic, as some people use journals to work through feelings of grief over loss or to wrestle with big decisions.

EXAMPLES OF DIARIES IN LITERATURE

The Diary of a Young Girl by Dutch Jew Anne Frank (1947) contains her life-affirming, nonfictional diary entries from 1942-1944 while her family hid in an attic from World War II's genocidal Nazis. *Go Ask Alice* (1971) by Beatrice Sparks is a cautionary, fictional novel in the form of diary entries by Alice, an unhappy, rebellious teen who takes LSD, runs away from home and lives with hippies, and eventually returns home. Frank's writing reveals an intelligent, sensitive, insightful girl, raised by intellectual European parents—a girl who believes in the goodness of human nature despite surrounding atrocities. Alice, influenced by early 1970s counterculture, becomes less optimistic. However, similarities can be found between them: Frank dies in a Nazi concentration camp while the fictitious Alice dies from a drug overdose. Both young women are also unable to escape their surroundings. Additionally, adolescent searches for personal identity are evident in both books.

LETTERS

Letters are messages written to other people. In addition to letters written between individuals, some writers compose letters to the editors of newspapers, magazines, and other publications, while some write "Open Letters" to be published and read by the general public. Open letters, while intended for everyone to read, may also identify a group of people or a single person whom the letter directly addresses. In everyday use, the most-used forms are business letters and personal or friendly letters. Both kinds share common elements: business or personal letterhead stationery; the writer's return address at the top; the addressee's address next; a salutation, such as "Dear [name]" or some similar opening greeting, followed by a colon in business letters or a comma in personal letters; the body of the letter, with paragraphs as indicated; and a closing, like "Sincerely/Cordially/Best regards/etc." or "Love," in intimate personal letters.

EARLY LETTERS

The Greek word for "letter" is *epistolē*, which became the English word "epistle." The earliest letters were called epistles, including the New Testament's epistles from the apostles to the Christians. In ancient Egypt, the writing curriculum in scribal schools included the epistolary genre. Epistolary novels frame a story in the form of letters. Examples of noteworthy epistolary novels include:

- *Pamela* (1740), by 18th-century English novelist Samuel Richardson
- *Shamela* (1741), Henry Fielding's satire of *Pamela* that mocked epistolary writing.
- *Lettres persanes* (1721) by French author Montesquieu
- *The Sorrows of Young Werther* (1774) by German author Johann Wolfgang von Goethe
- *The History of Emily Montague* (1769), the first Canadian novel, by Frances Brooke
- *Dracula* (1897) by Bram Stoker
- *Frankenstein* (1818) by Mary Shelley
- *The Color Purple* (1982) by Alice Walker

BLOGS

The word "blog" is derived from "weblog" and refers to writing done exclusively on the internet. Readers of reputable newspapers expect quality content and layouts that enable easy reading. These expectations also apply to blogs. For example, readers can easily move visually from line to line when columns are narrow, while overly wide columns cause readers to lose their places. Blogs must also be posted with layouts enabling online readers to follow them easily. However, because the way people read on computer, tablet, and smartphone screens differs from how they read print on paper, formatting and writing blog content is more complex than writing newspaper articles. Two major principles are the bases for blog-writing rules: The first is while readers of print articles skim to estimate their length, online they must scroll down to scan; therefore, blog layouts need more subheadings, graphics, and other indications of what information follows. The second is onscreen reading can be harder on the eyes than reading printed paper, so legibility is crucial in blogs.

RULES AND RATIONALES FOR WRITING BLOGS

1. Format all posts for smooth page layout and easy scanning.
2. Column width should not be too wide, as larger lines of text can be difficult to read

3. Headings and subheadings separate text visually, enable scanning or skimming, and encourage continued reading.
4. Bullet-pointed or numbered lists enable quick information location and scanning.
5. Punctuation is critical, so beginners should use shorter sentences until confident in their knowledge of punctuation rules.
6. Blog paragraphs should be far shorter—two to six sentences each—than paragraphs written on paper to enable "chunking" because reading onscreen is more difficult.
7. Sans-serif fonts are usually clearer than serif fonts, and larger font sizes are better.
8. Highlight important material and draw attention with **boldface**, but avoid overuse. Avoid hard-to-read *italics* and ALL CAPITALS.
9. Include enough blank spaces: overly busy blogs tire eyes and brains. Images not only break up text but also emphasize and enhance text and can attract initial reader attention.
10. Use background colors judiciously to avoid distracting the eye or making it difficult to read.
11. Be consistent throughout posts, since people read them in different orders.
12. Tell a story with a beginning, middle, and end.

SPECIALIZED TYPES OF WRITING
EDITORIALS

Editorials are articles in newspapers, magazines, and other serial publications. Editorials express an opinion or belief belonging to the majority of the publication's leadership. This opinion or belief generally refers to a specific issue, topic, or event. These articles are authored by a member, or a small number of members, of the publication's leadership and are often written to affect their readers, such as persuading them to adopt a stance or take a particular action.

RESUMES

Resumes are brief, but formal, documents that outline an individual's experience in a certain area. Resumes are most often used for job applications. Such resumes will list the applicant's work experience, certification, and achievements or qualifications related to the position. Resumes should only include the most pertinent information. They should also use strategic formatting to highlight the applicant's most impressive experiences and achievements, to ensure the document can be read quickly and easily, and to eliminate both visual clutter and excessive negative space.

REPORTS

Reports summarize the results of research, new methodology, or other developments in an academic or professional context. Reports often include details about methodology and outside influences and factors. However, a report should focus primarily on the results of the research or development. Reports are objective and deliver information efficiently, sacrificing style for clear and effective communication.

MEMORANDA

A memorandum, also called a memo, is a formal method of communication used in professional settings. Memoranda are printed documents that include a heading listing the sender and their job title, the recipient and their job title, the date, and a specific subject line. Memoranda often include an introductory section explaining the reason and context for the memorandum. Next, a memorandum includes a section with details relevant to the topic. Finally, the memorandum will conclude with a paragraph that politely and clearly defines the sender's expectations of the recipient.

Mometrix

CRITICAL READING SKILLS

OPINIONS, FACTS, AND FALLACIES

Critical thinking skills are mastered through understanding various types of writing and the different purposes of authors can have for writing different passages. Every author writes for a purpose. When you understand their purpose and how they accomplish their goal, you will be able to analyze their writing and determine whether or not you agree with their conclusions.

Readers must always be aware of the difference between fact and opinion. A **fact** can be subjected to analysis and proven to be true. An **opinion**, on the other hand, is the author's personal thoughts or feelings and may not be altered by research or evidence. If the author writes that the distance from New York City to Boston is about two hundred miles, then he or she is stating a fact. If the author writes that New York City is too crowded, then he or she is giving an opinion because there is no objective standard for overpopulation. Opinions are often supported by facts. For instance, an author might use a comparison between the population density of New York City and that of other major American cities as evidence of an overcrowded population. An opinion supported by facts tends to be more convincing. On the other hand, when authors support their opinions with other opinions, readers should employ critical thinking and approach the argument with skepticism.

> **Review Video: Distinguishing Fact and Opinion**
> Visit mometrix.com/academy and enter code: 870899

RELIABLE SOURCES

When you read an argumentative passage, you need to be sure that facts are presented to the reader from **reliable sources**. An opinion is what the author thinks about a given topic. An opinion is not common knowledge or proven by expert sources, instead the information is the personal beliefs and thoughts of the author. To distinguish between fact and opinion, a reader needs to consider the type of source that is presenting information, the information that backs-up a claim, and the author's motivation to have a certain point-of-view on a given topic. For example, if a panel of scientists has conducted multiple studies on the effectiveness of taking a certain vitamin, then the results are more likely to be factual than those of a company that is selling a vitamin and simply claims that taking the vitamin can produce positive effects. The company is motivated to sell their product, and the scientists are using the scientific method to prove a theory. Remember, if you find sentences that contain phrases such as "I think…", then the statement is an opinion.

BIASES

In their attempts to persuade, writers often make mistakes in their thought processes and writing choices. These processes and choices are important to understand so you can make an informed decision about the author's credibility. Every author has a point of view, but authors demonstrate a **bias** when they ignore reasonable counterarguments or distort opposing viewpoints. A bias is evident whenever the author's claims are presented in a way that is unfair or inaccurate. Bias can be intentional or unintentional, but readers should be skeptical of the author's argument in either case. Remember that a biased author may still be correct. However, the author will be correct in spite of, not because of, his or her bias.

A **stereotype** is a bias applied specifically to a group of people or a place. Stereotyping is considered to be particularly abhorrent because it promotes negative, misleading generalizations

102

Copyright © Mometrix Media. You have been licensed one copy of this document for personal use only. Any other reproduction or redistribution is strictly prohibited. All rights reserved. This content is provided for test preparation purposes only and does not imply an endorsement by Mometrix of any particular political, scientific, or religious point of view.

about people. Readers should be very cautious of authors who use stereotypes in their writing. These faulty assumptions typically reveal the author's ignorance and lack of curiosity.

PERSUASION AND RHETORIC

PERSUASIVE TECHNIQUES

To **appeal using reason**, writers present logical arguments, such as using "If... then... because" statements. To **appeal to emotions**, authors may ask readers how they would feel about something or to put themselves in another's place, present their argument as one that will make the audience feel good, or tell readers how they should feel. To **appeal to character**, **morality**, or **ethics**, authors present their points to readers as the right or most moral choices. Authors cite expert opinions to show readers that someone very knowledgeable about the subject or viewpoint agrees with the author's claims. **Testimonials**, usually via anecdotes or quotations regarding the author's subject, help build the audience's trust in an author's message through positive support from ordinary people. **Bandwagon appeals** claim that everybody else agrees with the author's argument and persuade readers to conform and agree, also. Authors **appeal to greed** by presenting their choice as cheaper, free, or more valuable for less cost. They **appeal to laziness** by presenting their views as more convenient, easy, or relaxing. Authors also anticipate potential objections and argue against them before audiences think of them, thereby depicting those objections as weak.

Authors can use **comparisons** like analogies, similes, and metaphors to persuade audiences. For example, a writer might represent excessive expenses as "hemorrhaging" money, which the author's recommended solution will stop. Authors can use negative word connotations to make some choices unappealing to readers, and positive word connotations to make others more appealing. Using **humor** can relax readers and garner their agreement. However, writers must take care: ridiculing opponents can be a successful strategy for appealing to readers who already agree with the author, but can backfire by angering other readers. **Rhetorical questions** need no answer, but create effect that can force agreement, such as asking the question, "Wouldn't you rather be paid more than less?" **Generalizations** persuade readers by being impossible to disagree with. Writers can easily make generalizations that appear to support their viewpoints, like saying, "We all want peace, not war" regarding more specific political arguments. **Transfer** and **association** persuade by example: if advertisements show attractive actors enjoying their products, audiences imagine they will experience the same. **Repetition** can also sometimes effectively persuade audiences.

CLASSICAL AUTHOR APPEALS

In his *On Rhetoric,* ancient Greek philosopher Aristotle defined three basic types of appeal used in writing, which he called *pathos, ethos,* and *logos. Pathos* means suffering or experience and refers to appeals to the emotions (the English word *pathetic* comes from this root). Writing that is meant to entertain audiences, by making them either happy, as with comedy, or sad, as with tragedy, uses *pathos.* Aristotle's *Poetics* states that evoking the emotions of terror and pity is one of the criteria for writing tragedy. *Ethos* means character and connotes ideology (the English word *ethics* comes from this root). Writing that appeals to credibility, based on academic, professional, or personal merit, uses *ethos. Logos* means "I say" and refers to a plea, opinion, expectation, word or speech, account, opinion, or reason (the English word *logic* comes from this root.) Aristotle used it to mean persuasion that appeals to the audience through reasoning and logic to influence their opinions.

RHETORICAL DEVICES

- An **anecdote** is a brief story authors may relate to their argument, which can illustrate their points in a more real and relatable way.
- **Aphorisms** concisely state common beliefs and may rhyme. For example, Benjamin Franklin's "Early to bed and early to rise / Makes a man healthy, wealthy, and wise" is an aphorism.
- **Allusions** refer to literary or historical figures to impart symbolism to a thing or person and to create reader resonance. In John Steinbeck's *Of Mice and Men,* protagonist George's last name is Milton. This alludes to John Milton, who wrote *Paradise Lost*, and symbolizes George's eventual loss of his dream.
- **Satire** exaggerates, ridicules, or pokes fun at human flaws or ideas, as in the works of Jonathan Swift and Mark Twain.
- A **parody** is a form of satire that imitates another work to ridicule its topic or style.
- A **paradox** is a statement that is true despite appearing contradictory.
- **Hyperbole** is overstatement using exaggerated language.
- An **oxymoron** combines seeming contradictions, such as "deafening silence."
- **Analogies** compare two things that share common elements.
- **Similes** (stated comparisons using the words *like* or *as*) and **metaphors** (stated comparisons that do not use *like* or *as*) are considered forms of analogy.
- When using logic to reason with audiences, **syllogism** refers either to deductive reasoning or a deceptive, very sophisticated, or subtle argument.
- **Deductive reasoning** moves from general to specific, **inductive reasoning** from specific to general.
- **Diction** is author word choice that establishes tone and effect.
- **Understatement** achieves effects like contrast or irony by downplaying or describing something more subtly than warranted.
- **Chiasmus** uses parallel clauses, the second reversing the order of the first. Examples include T. S. Eliot's "Has the Church failed mankind, or has mankind failed the Church?" and John F. Kennedy's "Ask not what your country can do for you; ask what you can do for your country."
- **Anaphora** regularly repeats a word or phrase at the beginnings of consecutive clauses or phrases to add emphasis to an idea. A classic example of anaphora was Winston Churchill's emphasis of determination: "[W]e shall fight on the beaches, we shall fight on the landing grounds, we shall fight in the fields and in the streets, we shall fight in the hills; we shall never surrender..."

READING ARGUMENTATIVE WRITING

AUTHOR'S ARGUMENT IN ARGUMENTATIVE WRITING

In argumentative writing, the argument is a belief, position, or opinion that the author wants to convince readers to believe as well. For the first step, readers should identify the **issue**. Some issues are controversial, meaning people disagree about them. Gun control, foreign policy, and the death penalty are all controversial issues. The next step is to determine the **author's position** on the issue. That position or viewpoint constitutes the author's argument. Readers should then identify the **author's assumptions**: things he or she accepts, believes, or takes for granted without needing proof. Inaccurate or illogical assumptions produce flawed arguments and can mislead readers. Readers should identify what kinds of **supporting evidence** the author offers, such as research

results, personal observations or experiences, case studies, facts, examples, expert testimony and opinions, and comparisons. Readers should decide how relevant this support is to the argument.

> **Review Video: Argumentative Writing**
> Visit mometrix.com/academy and enter code: 561544

EVALUATING AN AUTHOR'S ARGUMENT

The first three reader steps to **evaluate an author's argument** are to identify the **author's assumptions**, identify the **supporting evidence**, and decide **whether the evidence is relevant**. For example, if an author is not an expert on a particular topic, then that author's personal experience or opinion might not be relevant. The fourth step is to assess the **author's objectivity**. For example, consider whether the author introduces clear, understandable supporting evidence and facts to support the argument. The fifth step is evaluating whether the author's **argument is complete**. When authors give sufficient support for their arguments and also anticipate and respond effectively to opposing arguments or objections to their points, their arguments are complete. However, some authors omit information that could detract from their arguments. If instead they stated this information and refuted it, it would strengthen their arguments. The sixth step in evaluating an author's argumentative writing is to assess whether the **argument is valid**. Providing clear, logical reasoning makes an author's argument valid. Readers should ask themselves whether the author's points follow a sequence that makes sense, and whether each point leads to the next. The seventh step is to determine whether the author's **argument is credible**, meaning that it is convincing and believable. Arguments that are not valid are not credible, so step seven depends on step six. Readers should be mindful of their own biases as they evaluate and should not expect authors to conclusively prove their arguments, but rather to provide effective support and reason.

EVALUATING AN AUTHOR'S METHOD OF APPEAL

To evaluate the effectiveness of an appeal, it is important to consider the author's purpose for writing. Any appeals an author uses in their argument must be relevant to the argument's goal. For example, a writer that argues for the reclassification of Pluto, but primarily uses appeals to emotion, will not have an effective argument. This writer should focus on using appeals to logic and support their argument with provable facts. While most arguments should include appeals to logic, emotion, and credibility, some arguments only call for one or two of these types of appeal. Evidence can support an appeal, but the evidence must be relevant to truly strengthen the appeal's effectiveness. If the writer arguing for Pluto's reclassification uses the reasons for Jupiter's classification as evidence, their argument would be weak. This information may seem relevant because it is related to the classification of planets. However, this classification is highly dependent on the size of the celestial object, and Jupiter is significantly bigger than Pluto. This use of evidence is illogical and does not support the appeal. Even when appropriate evidence and appeals are used, appeals and arguments lose their effectiveness when they create logical fallacies.

EVIDENCE

The term **text evidence** refers to information that supports a main point or minor points and can help lead the reader to a conclusion about the text's credibility. Information used as text evidence is precise, descriptive, and factual. A main point is often followed by supporting details that provide evidence to back up a claim. For example, a passage may include the claim that winter occurs during opposite months in the Northern and Southern hemispheres. Text evidence for this claim may include examples of countries where winter occurs in opposite months. Stating that the tilt of the Earth as it rotates around the sun causes winter to occur at different times in separate hemispheres is another example of text evidence. Text evidence can come from common knowledge, but it is also valuable to include text evidence from credible, relevant outside sources.

Review Video: Textual Evidence
Visit mometrix.com/academy and enter code: 486236

Evidence that supports the thesis and additional arguments needs to be provided. Most arguments must be supported by facts or statistics. A fact is something that is known with certainty, has been verified by several independent individuals, and can be proven to be true. In addition to facts, examples and illustrations can support an argument by adding an emotional component. With this component, you persuade readers in ways that facts and statistics cannot. The emotional component is effective when used alongside objective information that can be confirmed.

CREDIBILITY

The text used to support an argument can be the argument's downfall if the text is not credible. A text is **credible**, or believable, when its author is knowledgeable and objective, or unbiased. The author's motivations for writing the text play a critical role in determining the credibility of the text and must be evaluated when assessing that credibility. Reports written about the ozone layer by an environmental scientist and a hairdresser will have a different level of credibility.

Review Video: Author Credibility
Visit mometrix.com/academy and enter code: 827257

APPEAL TO EMOTION

Sometimes, authors will appeal to the reader's emotion in an attempt to persuade or to distract the reader from the weakness of the argument. For instance, the author may try to inspire the pity of the reader by delivering a heart-rending story. An author also might use the bandwagon approach, in which he suggests that his opinion is correct because it is held by the majority. Some authors resort to name-calling, in which insults and harsh words are delivered to the opponent in an attempt to distract. In advertising, a common appeal is the celebrity testimonial, in which a famous person endorses a product. Of course, the fact that a famous person likes something should not really mean anything to the reader. These and other emotional appeals are usually evidence of poor reasoning and a weak argument.

Review Video: Emotional Language in Literature
Visit mometrix.com/academy and enter code: 759390

COUNTER ARGUMENTS

When authors give both sides to the argument, they build trust with their readers. As a reader, you should start with an undecided or neutral position. If an author presents only his or her side to the argument, then they are not exhibiting credibility and are weakening their argument.

Building common ground with readers can be effective for persuading neutral, skeptical, or opposed readers. Sharing values with undecided readers can allow people to switch positions without giving up what they feel is important. People who may oppose a position need to feel that they can change their minds without betraying who they are as a person. This appeal to having an open mind can be a powerful tool in arguing a position without antagonizing other views. Objections can be countered on a point-by-point basis or in a summary paragraph. Be mindful of how an author points out flaws in counter arguments. If they are unfair to the other side of the argument, then you should lose trust with the author.

Mathematics

Mathematics Test Overview

The math portion of the SAT consists of two 70-minute modules with 22 questions each. This gives you approximately 1.59 minutes to solve each problem.

CONCEPTS COVERED

SAT math questions fall into four categories:

- Algebra
- Advanced Math
- Problem-Solving and Data Analysis
- Geometry and Trigonometry

The table below gives a complete breakdown of questions:

Combined Modules	Number of Questions	% of Test
Total Questions	44	*100%*
Multiple Choice	28–32	75%
Student-Produced Response	8–12	25%
Content Categories		
Algebra	13–15	35%
Advanced Math	13–15	35%
Problem-Solving and Data Analysis	5–7	15%
Geometry and Trigonometry	5–7	15%

USE THE PRACTICE TESTS

The best thing you can do to prepare for the SAT is to take several practice tests and review all your wrong answers very carefully. Work back through those problems until you understand how the answer was derived and you are confident you could answer a similar problem on your own.

This guide includes 3 practice tests with answer keys and explanations. Examples are also available on the College Board website. If you feel uncertain about a particular concept or problem type, use these tests to practice.

Introductory Information

NUMBER BASICS

CLASSIFICATIONS OF NUMBERS

Numbers are the basic building blocks of mathematics. Specific features of numbers are identified by the following terms:

Integer – any positive or negative whole number, including zero. Integers do not include fractions $\left(\frac{1}{3}\right)$, decimals (0.56), or mixed numbers $\left(7\frac{3}{4}\right)$.

Prime number – any whole number greater than 1 that has only two factors, itself and 1; that is, a number that can be divided evenly only by 1 and itself.

Composite number – any whole number greater than 1 that has more than two different factors; in other words, any whole number that is not a prime number. For example: The composite number 8 has the factors of 1, 2, 4, and 8.

Even number – any integer that can be divided by 2 without leaving a remainder. For example: 2, 4, 6, 8, and so on.

Odd number – any integer that cannot be divided evenly by 2. For example: 3, 5, 7, 9, and so on.

Decimal number – any number that uses a decimal point to show the part of the number that is less than one. Example: 1.234.

Decimal point – a symbol used to separate the ones place from the tenths place in decimals or dollars from cents in currency.

Decimal place – the position of a number to the right of the decimal point. In the decimal 0.123, the 1 is in the first place to the right of the decimal point, indicating tenths; the 2 is in the second place, indicating hundredths; and the 3 is in the third place, indicating thousandths.

The **decimal**, or base 10, system is a number system that uses ten different digits (0, 1, 2, 3, 4, 5, 6, 7, 8, 9). An example of a number system that uses something other than ten digits is the **binary**, or base 2, number system, used by computers, which uses only the numbers 0 and 1. It is thought that the decimal system originated because people had only their 10 fingers for counting.

Rational numbers include all integers, decimals, and fractions. Any terminating or repeating decimal number is a rational number.

Irrational numbers cannot be written as fractions or decimals because the number of decimal places is infinite and there is no recurring pattern of digits within the number. For example, pi (π) begins with 3.141592 and continues without terminating or repeating, so pi is an irrational number.

Real numbers are the set of all rational and irrational numbers.

> **Review Video: Classification of Numbers**
> Visit mometrix.com/academy and enter code: 461071
>
> **Review Video: Prime and Composite Numbers**
> Visit mometrix.com/academy and enter code: 565581

NUMBERS IN WORD FORM AND PLACE VALUE

When writing numbers out in word form or translating word form to numbers, it is essential to understand how a place value system works. In the decimal or base-10 system, each digit of a number represents how many of the corresponding place value—a specific factor of 10—are contained in the number being represented. To make reading numbers easier, every three digits to the left of the decimal place is preceded by a comma. The following table demonstrates some of the place values:

Power of 10	10^3	10^2	10^1	10^0	10^{-1}	10^{-2}	10^{-3}
Value	1,000	100	10	1	0.1	0.01	0.001
Place	thousands	hundreds	tens	ones	tenths	hundredths	thousandths

For example, consider the number 4,546.09, which can be separated into each place value like this:

4: thousands
5: hundreds
4: tens
6: ones
0: tenths
9: hundredths

This number in word form would be *four thousand five hundred forty-six and nine hundredths*.

RATIONAL NUMBERS

The term **rational** means that the number can be expressed as a ratio or fraction. That is, a number, r, is rational if and only if it can be represented by a fraction $\frac{a}{b}$ where a and b are integers and b does not equal 0. The set of rational numbers includes integers and decimals. If there is no finite way to represent a value with a fraction of integers, then the number is **irrational**. Common examples of irrational numbers include: $\sqrt{5}$, $\left(1 + \sqrt{2}\right)$, and π.

NUMBER LINES

A number line is a graph to see the distance between numbers. Basically, this graph shows the relationship between numbers. So a number line may have a point for zero and may show negative numbers on the left side of the line. Any positive numbers are placed on the right side of the line. For example, consider the points labeled on the following number line:

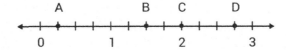

We can use the dashed lines on the number line to identify each point. Each dashed line between two whole numbers is $\frac{1}{4}$. The line halfway between two numbers is $\frac{1}{2}$.

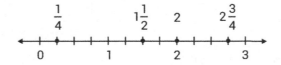

ABSOLUTE VALUE

A precursor to working with negative numbers is understanding what **absolute values** are. A number's absolute value is simply the distance away from zero a number is on the number line. The absolute value of a number is always positive and is written $|x|$. For example, the absolute value of 3, written as $|3|$, is 3 because the distance between 0 and 3 on a number line is three units. Likewise, the absolute value of –3, written as $|-3|$, is 3 because the distance between 0 and –3 on a number line is three units. So $|3| = |-3|$.

OPERATIONS

An **operation** is simply a mathematical process that takes some value(s) as input(s) and produces an output. Elementary operations are often written in the following form: *value operation value.* For instance, in the expression $1 + 2$ the values are 1 and 2 and the operation is addition. Performing the operation gives the output of 3. In this way we can say that $1 + 2$ and 3 are equal, or $1 + 2 = 3$.

ADDITION

Addition increases the value of one quantity by the value of another quantity (both called **addends**). Example: $2 + 4 = 6$ or $8 + 9 = 17$. The result is called the **sum**. With addition, the order does not matter, $4 + 2 = 2 + 4$.

When adding signed numbers, if the signs are the same simply add the absolute values of the addends and apply the original sign to the sum. For example, $(+4) + (+8) = +12$ and $(-4) + (-8) = -12$. When the original signs are different, take the absolute values of the addends and subtract the smaller value from the larger value, then apply the original sign of the larger value to the difference. Example: $(+4) + (-8) = -4$ and $(-4) + (+8) = +4$.

SUBTRACTION

Subtraction is the opposite operation to addition; it decreases the value of one quantity (the **minuend**) by the value of another quantity (the **subtrahend**). For example, $6 - 4 = 2$ or $17 - 8 = 9$. The result is called the **difference**. Note that with subtraction, the order does matter, $6 - 4 \neq 4 - 6$.

For subtracting signed numbers, change the sign of the subtrahend and then follow the same rules used for addition. Example: $(+4) - (+8) = (+4) + (-8) = -4$

MULTIPLICATION

Multiplication can be thought of as repeated addition. One number (the **multiplier**) indicates how many times to add the other number (the **multiplicand**) to itself. Example: $3 \times 2 = 2 + 2 + 2 = 6$. With multiplication, the order does not matter, $2 \times 3 = 3 \times 2$ or $3 + 3 = 2 + 2 + 2$, either way the result (the **product**) is the same.

If the signs are the same, the product is positive when multiplying signed numbers. Example: $(+4) \times (+8) = +32$ and $(-4) \times (-8) = +32$. If the signs are opposite, the product is negative. Example: $(+4) \times (-8) = -32$ and $(-4) \times (+8) = -32$. When more than two factors are multiplied together, the sign of the product is determined by how many negative factors are present. If there are an odd number of negative factors then the product is negative, whereas an even number of negative factors indicates a positive product. Example: $(+4) \times (-8) \times (-2) = +64$ and $(-4) \times (-8) \times (-2) = -64$.

DIVISION

Division is the opposite operation to multiplication; one number (the **divisor**) tells us how many parts to divide the other number (the **dividend**) into. The result of division is called the **quotient**. Example: $20 \div 4 = 5$. If 20 is split into 4 equal parts, each part is 5. With division, the order of the numbers does matter, $20 \div 4 \neq 4 \div 20$.

The rules for dividing signed numbers are similar to multiplying signed numbers. If the dividend and divisor have the same sign, the quotient is positive. If the dividend and divisor have opposite signs, the quotient is negative. Example: $(-4) \div (+8) = -0.5$.

> **Review Video: Mathematical Operations**
> Visit mometrix.com/academy and enter code: 208095

PARENTHESES

Parentheses are used to designate which operations should be done first when there are multiple operations. Example: $4 - (2 + 1) = 1$; the parentheses tell us that we must add 2 and 1, and then subtract the sum from 4, rather than subtracting 2 from 4 and then adding 1 (this would give us an answer of 3).

> **Review Video: Mathematical Parentheses**
> Visit mometrix.com/academy and enter code: 978600

EXPONENTS

An **exponent** is a superscript number placed next to another number at the top right. It indicates how many times the base number is to be multiplied by itself. Exponents provide a shorthand way to write what would be a longer mathematical expression, Example: $2^4 = 2 \times 2 \times 2 \times 2$. A number with an exponent of 2 is said to be "squared," while a number with an exponent of 3 is said to be "cubed." The value of a number raised to an exponent is called its power. So 8^4 is read as "8 to the 4th power," or "8 raised to the power of 4."

ROOTS

A **root**, such as a square root, is another way of writing a fractional exponent. Instead of using a superscript, roots use the radical symbol ($\sqrt{}$) to indicate the operation. A radical will have a number underneath the bar, and may sometimes have a number in the upper left: $\sqrt[n]{a}$, read as "the nth root of a." The relationship between radical notation and exponent notation can be described by this equation:

$$\sqrt[n]{a} = a^{\frac{1}{n}}$$

The two special cases of $n = 2$ and $n = 3$ are called square roots and cube roots. If there is no number to the upper left, the radical is understood to be a square root ($n = 2$). Nearly all of the roots you encounter will be square roots. A square root is the same as a number raised to the one-half power. When we say that a is the square root of b ($a = \sqrt{b}$), we mean that a multiplied by itself equals b: ($a \times a = b$).

A **perfect square** is a number that has an integer for its square root. There are 10 perfect squares from 1 to 100: 1, 4, 9, 16, 25, 36, 49, 64, 81, 100 (the squares of integers 1 through 10).

WORD PROBLEMS AND MATHEMATICAL SYMBOLS

When working on word problems, you must be able to translate verbal expressions or "math words" into math symbols. This chart contains several "math words" and their appropriate symbols:

Phrase	Symbol
equal, is, was, will be, has, costs, gets to, is the same as, becomes	$=$
times, of, multiplied by, product of, twice, doubles, halves, triples	$\times$
divided by, per, ratio of/to, out of	$\div$
plus, added to, sum, combined, and, more than, totals of	$+$
subtracted from, less than, decreased by, minus, difference between	$-$
what, how much, original value, how many, a number, a variable	x, n, etc.

EXAMPLES OF TRANSLATED MATHEMATICAL PHRASES

- The phrase four more than twice a number can be written algebraically as $2x + 4$.
- The phrase half a number decreased by six can be written algebraically as $\frac{1}{2}x - 6$.
- The phrase the sum of a number and the product of five and that number can be written algebraically as $x + 5x$.

- You may see a test question that says, "Olivia is constructing a bookcase from seven boards. Two of them are for vertical supports and five are for shelves. The height of the bookcase is twice the width of the bookcase. If the seven boards total 36 feet in length, what will be the height of Olivia's bookcase?" You would need to make a sketch and then create the equation to determine the width of the shelves. The height can be represented as double the width. (If x represents the width of the shelves in feet, then the height of the bookcase is $2x$. Since the seven boards total 36 feet, $2x + 2x + x + x + x + x + x = 36$ or $9x = 36$; $x = 4$. The height is twice the width, or 8 feet.)

SUBTRACTION WITH REGROUPING

A great way to make use of some of the features built into the decimal system would be regrouping when attempting longform subtraction operations. When subtracting within a place value, sometimes the minuend is smaller than the subtrahend, **regrouping** enables you to 'borrow' a unit from a place value to the left in order to get a positive difference. For example, consider subtracting 189 from 525 with regrouping.

First, set up the subtraction problem in vertical form:

$$
\begin{array}{r}
525 \\
- \ 189 \\
\hline
\end{array}
$$

Notice that the numbers in the ones and tens columns of 525 are smaller than the numbers in the ones and tens columns of 189. This means you will need to use regrouping to perform subtraction:

$$
\begin{array}{ccc}
5 & 2 & 5 \\
- \ 1 & 8 & 9 \\
\hline
\end{array}
$$

To subtract 9 from 5 in the ones column you will need to borrow from the 2 in the tens columns:

$$
\begin{array}{ccc}
5 & 1 & 15 \\
- \ 1 & 8 & 9 \\
\hline
 & & 6 \\
\end{array}
$$

Next, to subtract 8 from 1 in the tens column you will need to borrow from the 5 in the hundreds column:

$$
\begin{array}{ccc}
4 & 11 & 15 \\
- \ 1 & 8 & 9 \\
\hline
 & 3 & 6 \\
\end{array}
$$

Last, subtract the 1 from the 4 in the hundreds column:

$$
\begin{array}{ccc}
4 & 11 & 15 \\
- \ 1 & 8 & 9 \\
\hline
3 & 3 & 6 \\
\end{array}
$$

> **Review Video: Subtracting Large Numbers**
> Visit mometrix.com/academy and enter code: 603350

ORDER OF OPERATIONS

The **order of operations** is a set of rules that dictates the order in which we must perform each operation in an expression so that we will evaluate it accurately. If we have an expression that includes multiple different operations, the order of operations tells us which operations to do first. The most common mnemonic for the order of operations is **PEMDAS**, or "Please Excuse My Dear Aunt Sally." PEMDAS stands for parentheses, exponents, multiplication, division, addition, and subtraction. It is important to understand that multiplication and division have equal precedence, as do addition and subtraction, so those pairs of operations are simply worked from left to right in order.

For example, evaluating the expression $5 + 20 \div 4 \times (2 + 3)^2 - 6$ using the correct order of operations would be done like this:

- **P:** Perform the operations inside the parentheses: $(2 + 3) = 5$
- **E:** Simplify the exponents: $(5)^2 = 5 \times 5 = 25$
  - The expression now looks like this: $5 + 20 \div 4 \times 25 - 6$
- **MD:** Perform multiplication and division from left to right: $20 \div 4 = 5$; then $5 \times 25 = 125$
  - The expression now looks like this: $5 + 125 - 6$
- **AS:** Perform addition and subtraction from left to right: $5 + 125 = 130$; then $130 - 6 = 124$

> **Review Video: Order of Operations**
> Visit mometrix.com/academy and enter code: 259675

PROPERTIES OF EXPONENTS

The properties of exponents are as follows:

Property	Description
$a^1 = a$	Any number to the power of 1 is equal to itself
$1^n = 1$	The number 1 raised to any power is equal to 1
$a^0 = 1$	Any number raised to the power of 0 is equal to 1
$a^n \times a^m = a^{n+m}$	Add exponents to multiply powers of the same base number
$a^n \div a^m = a^{n-m}$	Subtract exponents to divide powers of the same base number
$(a^n)^m = a^{n \times m}$	When a power is raised to a power, the exponents are multiplied
$(a \times b)^n = a^n \times b^n$ $(a \div b)^n = a^n \div b^n$	Multiplication and division operations inside parentheses can be raised to a power. This is the same as each term being raised to that power.
$a^{-n} = \dfrac{1}{a^n}$	A negative exponent is the same as the reciprocal of a positive exponent

Note that exponents do not have to be integers. Fractional or decimal exponents follow all the rules above as well. Example: $5^{\frac{1}{4}} \times 5^{\frac{3}{4}} = 5^{\frac{1}{4}+\frac{3}{4}} = 5^1 = 5$.

> **Review Video: Properties of Exponents**
> Visit mometrix.com/academy and enter code: 532558

114

FACTORS AND MULTIPLES
FACTORS AND GREATEST COMMON FACTOR

Factors are numbers that are multiplied together to obtain a **product**. For example, in the equation $2 \times 3 = 6$, the numbers 2 and 3 are factors. A **prime number** has only two factors (1 and itself), but other numbers can have many factors.

A **common factor** is a number that divides exactly into two or more other numbers. For example, the factors of 12 are 1, 2, 3, 4, 6, and 12, while the factors of 15 are 1, 3, 5, and 15. The common factors of 12 and 15 are 1 and 3.

A **prime factor** is also a prime number. Therefore, the prime factors of 12 are 2 and 3. For 15, the prime factors are 3 and 5.

The **greatest common factor (GCF)** is the largest number that is a factor of two or more numbers. For example, the factors of 15 are 1, 3, 5, and 15; the factors of 35 are 1, 5, 7, and 35. Therefore, the greatest common factor of 15 and 35 is 5.

> **Review Video: <u>Factors</u>**
> Visit mometrix.com/academy and enter code: 920086
>
> **Review Video: <u>Prime Numbers and Factorization</u>**
> Visit mometrix.com/academy and enter code: 760669
>
> **Review Video: <u>Greatest Common Factor and Least Common Multiple</u>**
> Visit mometrix.com/academy and enter code: 838699

MULTIPLES AND LEAST COMMON MULTIPLE

Often listed out in multiplication tables, **multiples** are integer increments of a given factor. In other words, dividing a multiple by the factor will result in an integer. For example, the multiples of 7 include: $1 \times 7 = 7, 2 \times 7 = 14, 3 \times 7 = 21, 4 \times 7 = 28, 5 \times 7 = 35$. Dividing 7, 14, 21, 28, or 35 by 7 will result in the integers 1, 2, 3, 4, and 5, respectively.

The least common multiple (**LCM**) is the smallest number that is a multiple of two or more numbers. For example, the multiples of 3 include 3, 6, 9, 12, 15, etc.; the multiples of 5 include 5, 10, 15, 20, etc. Therefore, the least common multiple of 3 and 5 is 15.

> **Review Video: <u>Multiples</u>**
> Visit mometrix.com/academy and enter code: 626738

Algebra

SLOPE

On a graph with two points, (x_1, y_1) and (x_2, y_2), the **slope** is found with the formula $m = \frac{y_2 - y_1}{x_2 - x_1}$; where $x_1 \neq x_2$ and m stands for slope. If the value of the slope is **positive**, the line has an *upward direction* from left to right. If the value of the slope is **negative**, the line has a *downward direction* from left to right. Consider the following example:

A new book goes on sale in bookstores and online stores. In the first month, 5,000 copies of the book are sold. Over time, the book continues to grow in popularity. The data for the number of copies sold is in the table below.

# of Months on Sale	1	2	3	4	5
# of Copies Sold (In Thousands)	5	10	15	20	25

So, the number of copies that are sold and the time that the book is on sale is a proportional relationship. In this example, an equation can be used to show the data: $y = 5x$, where x is the number of months that the book is on sale. Also, y is the number of copies sold. So, the slope of the corresponding line is $\frac{\text{rise}}{\text{run}} = \frac{5}{1} = 5$.

> **Review Video: Finding the Slope of a Line**
> Visit mometrix.com/academy and enter code: 766664

LINEAR EQUATIONS

Equations that can be written as $ax + b = 0$, where $a \neq 0$, are referred to as **one variable linear equations**. A solution to such an equation is called a **root**. In the case where we have the equation $5x + 10 = 0$, if we solve for x we get a solution of $x = -2$. In other words, the root of the equation is –2. This is found by first subtracting 10 from both sides, which gives $5x = -10$. Next, simply divide both sides by the coefficient of the variable, in this case 5, to get $x = -2$. This can be checked by plugging –2 back into the original equation $(5)(-2) + 10 = -10 + 10 = 0$.

The **solution set** is the set of all solutions of an equation. In our example, the solution set would simply be –2. If there were more solutions (there usually are in multivariable equations) then they would also be included in the solution set. When an equation has no true solutions, it is referred to as an **empty set**. Equations with identical solution sets are **equivalent equations**. An **identity** is a term whose value or determinant is equal to 1.

Linear equations can be written many ways. Below is a list of some forms linear equations can take:

- **Standard Form**: $Ax + By = C$; the slope is $\frac{-A}{B}$ and the y-intercept is $\frac{C}{B}$
- **Slope Intercept Form**: $y = mx + b$, where m is the slope and b is the y-intercept
- **Point-Slope Form**: $y - y_1 = m(x - x_1)$, where m is the slope and (x_1, y_1) is a point on the line
- **Two-Point Form**: $\frac{y - y_1}{x - x_1} = \frac{y_2 - y_1}{x_2 - x_1}$, where (x_1, y_1) and (x_2, y_2) are two points on the given line
- **Intercept Form**: $\frac{x}{x_1} + \frac{y}{y_1} = 1$, where $(x_1, 0)$ is the point at which a line intersects the x-axis, and $(0, y_1)$ is the point at which the same line intersects the y-axis

> **Review Video: Slope-Intercept and Point-Slope Forms**
> Visit mometrix.com/academy and enter code: 113216
>
> **Review Video: Linear Equations Basics**
> Visit mometrix.com/academy and enter code: 793005

SOLVING EQUATIONS
SOLVING ONE-VARIABLE LINEAR EQUATIONS

Multiply all terms by the lowest common denominator to eliminate any fractions. Look for addition or subtraction to undo so you can isolate the variable on one side of the equal sign. Divide both sides by the coefficient of the variable. When you have a value for the variable, substitute this value into the original equation to make sure you have a true equation. Consider the following example:

Kim's savings are represented by the table below. Represent her savings, using an equation.

X (Months)	Y (Total Savings)
2	$1,300
5	$2,050
9	$3,050
11	$3,550
16	$4,800

The table shows a function with a constant rate of change, or slope, of 250. Given the points on the table, the slopes can be calculated as $\frac{(2,050-1300)}{(5-2)}$, $\frac{(3,050-2,050)}{(9-5)}$, $\frac{(3,550-3,050)}{(11-9)}$, and $\frac{(4,800-3,550)}{(16-11)}$, each of which equals 250. Thus, the table shows a constant rate of change, indicating a linear function. The slope-intercept form of a linear equation is written as $y = mx + b$, where m represents the slope and b represents the y-intercept. Substituting the slope into this form gives $y = 250x + b$. Substituting corresponding x- and y-values from any point into this equation will give the y-intercept, or b. Using the point, $(2, 1,300)$, gives $1,300 = 250(2) + b$, which simplifies as $b = 800$. Thus, her savings may be represented by the equation, $y = 250x + 800$.

RULES FOR MANIPULATING EQUATIONS
LIKE TERMS

Like terms are terms in an equation that have the same variable, regardless of whether or not they also have the same coefficient. This includes terms that *lack* a variable; all constants (i.e., numbers without variables) are considered like terms. If the equation involves terms with a variable raised to different powers, the like terms are those that have the variable raised to the same power.

For example, consider the equation $x^2 + 3x + 2 = 2x^2 + x - 7 + 2x$. In this equation, 2 and –7 are like terms; they are both constants. $3x$, x, and $2x$ are like terms, they all include the variable x raised to the first power. x^2 and $2x^2$ are like terms, they both include the variable x, raised to the second power. $2x$ and $2x^2$ are not like terms; although they both involve the variable x, the variable is not raised to the same power in both terms. The fact that they have the same coefficient, 2, is not relevant.

> **Review Video: Rules for Manipulating Equations**
> Visit mometrix.com/academy and enter code: 838871

CARRYING OUT THE SAME OPERATION ON BOTH SIDES OF AN EQUATION

When solving an equation, the general procedure is to carry out a series of operations on both sides of an equation, choosing operations that will tend to simplify the equation when doing so. The reason why the same operation must be carried out on both sides of the equation is because that leaves the meaning of the equation unchanged, and yields a result that is equivalent to the original equation. This would not be the case if we carried out an operation on one side of an equation and not the other. Consider what an equation means: it is a statement that two values or expressions are equal. If we carry out the same operation on both sides of the equation—add 3 to both sides, for example—then the two sides of the equation are changed in the same way, and so remain equal. If we do that to only one side of the equation—add 3 to one side but not the other—then that wouldn't be true; if we change one side of the equation but not the other then the two sides are no longer equal.

ADVANTAGE OF COMBINING LIKE TERMS

Combining like terms refers to adding or subtracting like terms—terms with the same variable— and therefore reducing sets of like terms to a single term. The main advantage of doing this is that it simplifies the equation. Often, combining like terms can be done as the first step in solving an equation, though it can also be done later, such as after distributing terms in a product.

For example, consider the equation $2(x + 3) + 3(2 + x + 3) = -4$. The 2 and the 3 in the second set of parentheses are like terms, and we can combine them, yielding $2(x + 3) + 3(x + 5) = -4$. Now we can carry out the multiplications implied by the parentheses, distributing the outer 2 and 3 accordingly: $2x + 6 + 3x + 15 = -4$. The $2x$ and the $3x$ are like terms, and we can add them together: $5x + 6 + 15 = -4$. Now, the constants 6, 15, and –4 are also like terms, and we can combine them as well: subtracting 6 and 15 from both sides of the equation, we get $5x = -4 - 6 - 15$, or $5x = -25$, which simplifies further to $x = -5$.

> **Review Video: Solving Equations by Combining Like Terms**
> Visit mometrix.com/academy and enter code: 668506

CANCELING TERMS ON OPPOSITE SIDES OF AN EQUATION

Two terms on opposite sides of an equation can be canceled if and only if they *exactly* match each other. They must have the same variable raised to the same power and the same coefficient. For example, in the equation $3x + 2x^2 + 6 = 2x^2 - 6$, $2x^2$ appears on both sides of the equation and can be canceled, leaving $3x + 6 = -6$. The 6 on each side of the equation *cannot* be canceled, because it is added on one side of the equation and subtracted on the other. While they cannot be canceled, however, the 6 and –6 are like terms and can be combined, yielding $3x = -12$, which simplifies further to $x = -4$.

It's also important to note that the terms to be canceled must be independent terms and cannot be part of a larger term. For example, consider the equation $2(x + 6) = 3(x + 4) + 1$. We cannot cancel the x's, because even though they match each other they are part of the larger terms $2(x + 6)$ and $3(x + 4)$. We must first distribute the 2 and 3, yielding $2x + 12 = 3x + 12 + 1$. Now we see that the terms with the x's do not match, but the 12s do, and can be canceled, leaving $2x = 3x + 1$, which simplifies to $x = -1$.

PROCESS FOR MANIPULATING EQUATIONS
ISOLATING VARIABLES

To **isolate a variable** means to manipulate the equation so that the variable appears by itself on one side of the equation, and does not appear at all on the other side. Generally, an equation or inequality is considered to be solved once the variable is isolated and the other side of the equation or inequality is simplified as much as possible. In the case of a two-variable equation or inequality, only one variable needs to be isolated; it will not usually be possible to simultaneously isolate both variables.

For a linear equation—an equation in which the variable only appears raised to the first power—isolating a variable can be done by first moving all the terms with the variable to one side of the equation and all other terms to the other side. (*Moving* a term really means adding the inverse of the term to both sides; when a term is *moved* to the other side of the equation its sign is flipped.) Then combine like terms on each side. Finally, divide both sides by the coefficient of the variable, if applicable. The steps need not necessarily be done in this order, but this order will always work.

> **Review Video: Solving One-Step Equations**
> Visit mometrix.com/academy and enter code: 777004

EQUATIONS WITH MORE THAN ONE SOLUTION

Some types of non-linear equations, such as equations involving squares of variables, may have more than one solution. For example, the equation $x^2 = 4$ has two solutions: 2 and –2. Equations with absolute values can also have multiple solutions: $|x| = 1$ has the solutions $x = 1$ and $x = -1$.

It is also possible for a linear equation to have more than one solution, but only if the equation is true regardless of the value of the variable. In this case, the equation is considered to have infinitely many solutions, because any possible value of the variable is a solution. We know a linear equation has infinitely many solutions if when we combine like terms the variables cancel, leaving a true statement. For example, consider the equation $2(3x + 5) = x + 5(x + 2)$. Distributing, we get $6x + 10 = x + 5x + 10$; combining like terms gives $6x + 10 = 6x + 10$, and the $6x$-terms cancel to leave $10 = 10$. This is clearly true, so the original equation is true for any value of x. We could also have canceled the 10s leaving $0 = 0$, but again this is clearly true—in general if both sides of the equation match exactly, it has infinitely many solutions.

EQUATIONS WITH NO SOLUTION

Some types of non-linear equations, such as equations involving squares of variables, may have no solution. For example, the equation $x^2 = -2$ has no solutions in the real numbers, because the square of any real number must be positive. Similarly, $|x| = -1$ has no solution, because the absolute value of a number is always positive.

It is also possible for an equation to have no solution even if does not involve any powers greater than one, absolute values, or other special functions. For example, the equation $2(x + 3) + x = 3x$ has no solution. We can see that if we try to solve it: first we distribute, leaving $2x + 6 + x = 3x$. But now if we try to combine all the terms with the variable, we find that they cancel: we have $3x$ on the left and $3x$ on the right, canceling to leave us with $6 = 0$. This is clearly false. In general, whenever the variable terms in an equation cancel leaving different constants on both sides, it means that the equation has no solution. (If we are left with the *same* constant on both sides, the equation has infinitely many solutions instead.)

FEATURES OF EQUATIONS THAT REQUIRE SPECIAL TREATMENT
LINEAR EQUATIONS

A linear equation is an equation in which variables only appear by themselves: not multiplied together, not with exponents other than one, and not inside absolute value signs or any other functions. For example, the equation $x + 1 - 3x = 5 - x$ is a linear equation; while x appears multiple times, it never appears with an exponent other than one, or inside any function. The two-variable equation $2x - 3y = 5 + 2x$ is also a linear equation. In contrast, the equation $x^2 - 5 = 3x$ is *not* a linear equation, because it involves the term x^2. $\sqrt{x} = 5$ is not a linear equation, because it involves a square root. $(x - 1)^2 = 4$ is not a linear equation because even though there's no exponent on the x directly, it appears as part of an expression that is squared. The two-variable equation $x + xy - y = 5$ is not a linear equation because it includes the term xy, where two variables are multiplied together.

Linear equations can always be solved (or shown to have no solution) by combining like terms and performing simple operations on both sides of the equation. Some non-linear equations can be solved by similar methods, but others may require more advanced methods of solution, if they can be solved analytically at all.

SOLVING EQUATIONS INVOLVING ROOTS

In an equation involving roots, the first step is to isolate the term with the root, if possible, and then raise both sides of the equation to the appropriate power to eliminate it. Consider an example equation, $2\sqrt{x + 1} - 1 = 3$. In this case, begin by adding 1 to both sides, yielding $2\sqrt{x + 1} = 4$, and then dividing both sides by 2, yielding $\sqrt{x + 1} = 2$. Now square both sides, yielding $x + 1 = 4$. Finally, subtracting 1 from both sides yields $x = 3$.

Squaring both sides of an equation may, however, yield a spurious solution—a solution to the squared equation that is *not* a solution of the original equation. It's therefore necessary to plug the solution back into the original equation to make sure it works. In this case, it does: $2\sqrt{3 + 1} - 1 = 2\sqrt{4} - 1 = 2(2) - 1 = 4 - 1 = 3$.

The same procedure applies for other roots as well. For example, given the equation $3 + \sqrt[3]{2x} = 5$, we can first subtract 3 from both sides, yielding $\sqrt[3]{2x} = 2$ and isolating the root. Raising both sides to the third power yields $2x = 2^3$; i.e., $2x = 8$. We can now divide both sides by 2 to get $x = 4$.

> **Review Video: Solving Equations Involving Roots**
> Visit mometrix.com/academy and enter code: 297670

SOLVING EQUATIONS WITH EXPONENTS

To solve an equation involving an exponent, the first step is to isolate the variable with the exponent. We can then take the appropriate root of both sides to eliminate the exponent. For instance, for the equation $2x^3 + 17 = 5x^3 - 7$, we can subtract $5x^3$ from both sides to get $-3x^3 + 17 = -7$, and then subtract 17 from both sides to get $-3x^3 = -24$. Finally, we can divide both sides by –3 to get $x^3 = 8$. Finally, we can take the cube root of both sides to get $x = \sqrt[3]{8} = 2$.

One important but often overlooked point is that equations with an exponent greater than 1 may have more than one answer. The solution to $x^2 = 9$ isn't simply $x = 3$; it's $x = \pm 3$ (that is, $x = 3$ or $x = -3$). For a slightly more complicated example, consider the equation $(x - 1)^2 - 1 = 3$. Adding 1 to both sides yields $(x - 1)^2 = 4$; taking the square root of both sides yields $x - 1 = 2$. We can then add 1 to both sides to get $x = 3$. However, there's a second solution. We also have the possibility that $x - 1 = -2$, in which case $x = -1$. Both $x = 3$ and $x = -1$ are valid solutions, as can be verified by substituting them both into the original equation.

> **Review Video: Solving Equations with Exponents**
> Visit mometrix.com/academy and enter code: 514557

SOLVING EQUATIONS WITH ABSOLUTE VALUES

When solving an equation with an absolute value, the first step is to isolate the absolute value term. We then consider two possibilities: when the expression inside the absolute value is positive or when it is negative. In the former case, the expression in the absolute value equals the expression on the other side of the equation; in the latter, it equals the additive inverse of that expression—the expression times negative one. We consider each case separately and finally check for spurious solutions.

For instance, consider solving $|2x - 1| + x = 5$ for x. We can first isolate the absolute value by moving the x to the other side: $|2x - 1| = -x + 5$. Now, we have two possibilities. First, that $2x - 1$ is positive, and hence $2x - 1 = -x + 5$. Rearranging and combining like terms yields $3x = 6$, and hence $x = 2$. The other possibility is that $2x - 1$ is negative, and hence $2x - 1 = -(-x + 5) = x - 5$. In this case, rearranging and combining like terms yields $x = -4$. Substituting $x = 2$ and $x = -4$ back into the original equation, we see that they are both valid solutions.

Note that the absolute value of a sum or difference applies to the sum or difference as a whole, not to the individual terms; in general, $|2x - 1|$ is not equal to $|2x + 1|$ or to $|2x| - 1$.

SPURIOUS SOLUTIONS

A **spurious solution** may arise when we square both sides of an equation as a step in solving it or under certain other operations on the equation. It is a solution to the squared or otherwise modified equation that is *not* a solution of the original equation. To identify a spurious solution, it's useful when you solve an equation involving roots or absolute values to plug the solution back into the original equation to make sure it's valid.

CHOOSING WHICH VARIABLE TO ISOLATE IN TWO-VARIABLE EQUATIONS

Similar to methods for a one-variable equation, solving a two-variable equation involves isolating a variable: manipulating the equation so that a variable appears by itself on one side of the equation, and not at all on the other side. However, in a two-variable equation, you will usually only be able to isolate one of the variables; the other variable may appear on the other side along with constant terms, or with exponents or other functions.

Often one variable will be much more easily isolated than the other, and therefore that's the variable you should choose. If one variable appears with various exponents, and the other is only raised to the first power, the latter variable is the one to isolate: given the equation $a^2 + 2b = a^3 + b + 3$, the b only appears to the first power, whereas a appears squared and cubed, so b is the variable that can be solved for: combining like terms and isolating the b on the left side of the equation, we get $b = a^3 - a^2 + 3$. If both variables are equally easy to isolate, then it's best to isolate the dependent variable, if one is defined; if the two variables are x and y, the convention is that y is the dependent variable.

> **Review Video: Solving Equations with Variables on Both Sides**
> Visit mometrix.com/academy and enter code: 402497

CROSS MULTIPLICATION
FINDING AN UNKNOWN IN EQUIVALENT EXPRESSIONS

It is often necessary to apply information given about a rate or proportion to a new scenario. For example, if you know that Jedha can run a marathon (26.2 miles) in 3 hours, how long would it take her to run 10 miles at the same pace? Start by setting up equivalent expressions:

$$\frac{26.2 \text{ mi}}{3 \text{ hr}} = \frac{10 \text{ mi}}{x \text{ hr}}$$

Now, cross multiply and solve for x:

$$26.2x = 30$$
$$x = \frac{30}{26.2} = \frac{15}{13.1}$$
$$x \approx 1.15 \text{ hrs } or \text{ 1 hr 9 min}$$

So, at this pace, Jedha could run 10 miles in about 1.15 hours or about 1 hour and 9 minutes.

> **Review Video: <u>Cross Multiplying Fractions</u>**
> Visit mometrix.com/academy and enter code: 893904

GRAPHING EQUATIONS
GRAPHICAL SOLUTIONS TO EQUATIONS

When equations are shown graphically, they are usually shown on a **Cartesian coordinate plane**. The Cartesian coordinate plane consists of two number lines placed perpendicular to each other and intersecting at the zero point, also known as the origin. The horizontal number line is known as the x-axis, with positive values to the right of the origin, and negative values to the left of the origin. The vertical number line is known as the y-axis, with positive values above the origin, and negative values below the origin. Any point on the plane can be identified by an ordered pair in the form (x, y), called coordinates. The x-value of the coordinate is called the abscissa, and the y-value of the coordinate is called the ordinate. The two number lines divide the plane into **four quadrants**: I, II, III, and IV.

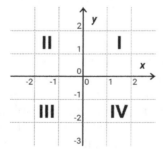

Note that in quadrant I $x > 0$ and $y > 0$, in quadrant II $x < 0$ and $y > 0$, in quadrant III $x < 0$ and $y < 0$, and in quadrant IV $x > 0$ and $y < 0$.

Recall that if the value of the slope of a line is positive, the line slopes upward from left to right. If the value of the slope is negative, the line slopes downward from left to right. If the y-coordinates are the same for two points on a line, the slope is 0 and the line is a **horizontal line**. If the x-coordinates are the same for two points on a line, there is no slope and the line is a **vertical line**. Two or more lines that have equivalent slopes are **parallel lines**. **Perpendicular lines** have slopes that are negative reciprocals of each other, such as $\frac{a}{b}$ and $\frac{-b}{a}$.

> **Review Video: <u>Cartesian Coordinate Plane and Graphing</u>**
> Visit mometrix.com/academy and enter code: 115173

GRAPHING EQUATIONS IN TWO VARIABLES

One way of graphing an equation in two variables is to plot enough points to get an idea for its shape and then draw the appropriate curve through those points. A point can be plotted by substituting in a value for one variable and solving for the other. If the equation is linear, we only need two points and can then draw a straight line between them.

For example, consider the equation $y = 2x - 1$. This is a linear equation—both variables only appear raised to the first power—so we only need two points. When $x = 0$, $y = 2(0) - 1 = -1$. When $x = 2$, $y = 2(2) - 1 = 3$. We can therefore choose the points $(0, -1)$ and $(2, 3)$, and draw a line between them:

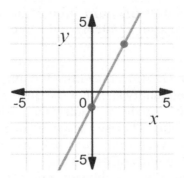

INEQUALITIES

WORKING WITH INEQUALITIES

Commonly in algebra and other upper-level fields of math you find yourself working with mathematical expressions that do not equal each other. The statement comparing such expressions with symbols such as $<$ (less than) or $>$ (greater than) is called an *inequality*. An example of an inequality is $7x > 5$. To solve for x, simply divide both sides by 7 and the solution is shown to be $x > \frac{5}{7}$. Graphs of the solution set of inequalities are represented on a number line. Open circles are used to show that an expression approaches a number but is never quite equal to that number.

> **Review Video: Solving Multi-Step Inequalities**
> Visit mometrix.com/academy and enter code: 347842
>
> **Review Video: Solving Inequalities Using All 4 Basic Operations**
> Visit mometrix.com/academy and enter code: 401111

Conditional inequalities are those with certain values for the variable that will make the condition true and other values for the variable where the condition will be false. **Absolute inequalities** can have any real number as the value for the variable to make the condition true, while there is no real number value for the variable that will make the condition false. Solving inequalities is done by following the same rules for solving equations with the exception that when multiplying or dividing by a negative number the direction of the inequality sign must be flipped or reversed. **Double inequalities** are situations where two inequality statements apply to the same variable expression. Example: $-c < ax + b < c$.

> **Review Video: Conditional and Absolute Inequalities**
> Visit mometrix.com/academy and enter code: 980164

DETERMINING SOLUTIONS TO INEQUALITIES

To determine whether a coordinate is a solution of an inequality, you can substitute the values of the coordinate into the inequality, simplify, and check whether the resulting statement holds true.

123

For instance, to determine whether $(-2,4)$ is a solution of the inequality $y \geq -2x + 3$, substitute the values into the inequality, $4 \geq -2(-2) + 3$. Simplify the right side of the inequality and the result is $4 \geq 7$, which is a false statement. Therefore, the coordinate is not a solution of the inequality. You can also use this method to determine which part of the graph of an inequality is shaded. The graph of $y \geq -2x + 3$ includes the solid line $y = -2x + 3$ and, since it excludes the point $(-2,4)$ to the left of the line, it is shaded to the right of the line.

Review Video: Graphing Linear Inequalities
Visit mometrix.com/academy and enter code: 439421

FLIPPING INEQUALITY SIGNS

When given an inequality, we can always turn the entire inequality around, swapping the two sides of the inequality and changing the inequality sign. For instance, $x + 2 > 2x - 3$ is equivalent to $2x - 3 < x + 2$. Aside from that, normally the inequality does not change if we carry out the same operation on both sides of the inequality. There is, however, one principal exception: if we *multiply* or *divide* both sides of the inequality by a *negative number*, the inequality is flipped. For example, if we take the inequality $-2x < 6$ and divide both sides by –2, the inequality flips and we are left with $x > -3$. This *only* applies to multiplication and division, and only with negative numbers. Multiplying or dividing both sides by a positive number, or adding or subtracting any number regardless of sign, does not flip the inequality. Another special case that flips the inequality sign is when reciprocals are used. For instance, $3 > 2$ but the relation of the reciprocals is $\frac{1}{2} < \frac{1}{3}$.

COMPOUND INEQUALITIES

A **compound inequality** is an equality that consists of two inequalities combined with *and* or *or*. The two components of a proper compound inequality must be of opposite type: that is, one must be greater than (or greater than or equal to), the other less than (or less than or equal to). For instance, "$x + 1 < 2$ or $x + 1 > 3$" is a compound inequality, as is "$2x \geq 4$ and $2x \leq 6$." An *and* inequality can be written more compactly by having one inequality on each side of the common part: "$2x \geq 1$ and $2x \leq 6$," can also be written as $1 \leq 2x \leq 6$.

In order for the compound inequality to be meaningful, the two parts of an *and* inequality must overlap; otherwise, no numbers satisfy the inequality. On the other hand, if the two parts of an *or* inequality overlap, then *all* numbers satisfy the inequality and as such the inequality is usually not meaningful.

Solving a compound inequality requires solving each part separately. For example, given the compound inequality "$x + 1 < 2$ or $x + 1 > 3$," the first inequality, $x + 1 < 2$, reduces to $x < 1$, and the second part, $x + 1 > 3$, reduces to $x > 2$, so the whole compound inequality can be written as "$x < 1$ or $x > 2$." Similarly, $1 \leq 2x \leq 6$ can be solved by dividing each term by 2, yielding $\frac{1}{2} \leq x \leq 3$.

Review Video: Compound Inequalities
Visit mometrix.com/academy and enter code: 786318

SOLVING INEQUALITIES INVOLVING ABSOLUTE VALUES

To solve an inequality involving an absolute value, first isolate the term with the absolute value. Then proceed to treat the two cases separately as with an absolute value equation, but flipping the inequality in the case where the expression in the absolute value is negative (since that essentially involves multiplying both sides by –1.) The two cases are then combined into a compound inequality; if the absolute value is on the greater side of the inequality, then it is an *or* compound inequality, if on the lesser side, then it's an *and*.

Consider the inequality $2 + |x - 1| \geq 3$. We can isolate the absolute value term by subtracting 2 from both sides: $|x - 1| \geq 1$. Now, we're left with the two cases $x - 1 \geq 1$ or $x - 1 \leq -1$: note that in the latter, negative case, the inequality is flipped. $x - 1 \geq 1$ reduces to $x \geq 2$, and $x - 1 \leq -1$ reduces to $x \leq 0$. Since in the inequality $|x - 1| \geq 1$ the absolute value is on the greater side, the two cases combine into an *or* compound inequality, so the final, solved inequality is "$x \leq 0$ or $x \geq 2$."

> **Review Video: <u>Solving Absolute Value Inequalities</u>**
> Visit mometrix.com/academy and enter code: 997008

SOLVING INEQUALITIES INVOLVING SQUARE ROOTS

Solving an inequality with a square root involves two parts. First, we solve the inequality as if it were an equation, isolating the square root and then squaring both sides of the equation. Second, we restrict the solution to the set of values of x for which the value inside the square root sign is non-negative.

For example, in the inequality, $\sqrt{x - 2} + 1 < 5$, we can isolate the square root by subtracting 1 from both sides, yielding $\sqrt{x - 2} < 4$. Squaring both sides of the inequality yields $x - 2 < 16$, so $x < 18$. Since we can't take the square root of a negative number, we also require the part inside the square root to be non-negative. In this case, that means $x - 2 \geq 0$. Adding 2 to both sides of the inequality yields $x \geq 2$. Our final answer is a compound inequality combining the two simple inequalities: $x \geq 2$ and $x < 18$, or $2 \leq x < 18$.

Note that we only get a compound inequality if the two simple inequalities are in opposite directions; otherwise, we take the one that is more restrictive.

The same technique can be used for other even roots, such as fourth roots. It is *not*, however, used for cube roots or other odd roots—negative numbers *do* have cube roots, so the condition that the quantity inside the root sign cannot be negative does not apply.

> **Review Video: <u>Solving Inequalities Involving Square Roots</u>**
> Visit mometrix.com/academy and enter code: 800288

SPECIAL CIRCUMSTANCES

Sometimes an inequality involving an absolute value or an even exponent is true for all values of x, and we don't need to do any further work to solve it. This is true if the inequality, once the absolute value or exponent term is isolated, says that term is greater than a negative number (or greater than or equal to zero). Since an absolute value or a number raised to an even exponent is *always* non-negative, this inequality is always true.

GRAPHICAL SOLUTIONS TO INEQUALITIES

GRAPHING SIMPLE INEQUALITIES

To graph a simple inequality, we first mark on the number line the value that signifies the end point of the inequality. If the inequality is strict (involves a less than or greater than), we use a hollow circle; if it is not strict (less than or equal to or greater than or equal to), we use a solid circle. We then fill in the part of the number line that satisfies the inequality: to the left of the marked point for less than (or less than or equal to), to the right for greater than (or greater than or equal to).

For example, we would graph the inequality $x < 5$ by putting a hollow circle at 5 and filling in the part of the line to the left:

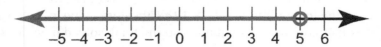

GRAPHING COMPOUND INEQUALITIES

To graph a compound inequality, we fill in both parts of the inequality for an *or* inequality, or the overlap between them for an *and* inequality. More specifically, we start by plotting the endpoints of each inequality on the number line. For an *or* inequality, we then fill in the appropriate side of the line for each inequality. Typically, the two component inequalities do not overlap, which means the shaded part is *outside* the two points. For an *and* inequality, we instead fill in the part of the line that meets both inequalities.

For the inequality "$x \le -3$ or $x > 4$," we first put a solid circle at –3 and a hollow circle at 4. We then fill the parts of the line *outside* these circles:

GRAPHING INEQUALITIES INCLUDING ABSOLUTE VALUES

An inequality with an absolute value can be converted to a compound inequality. To graph the inequality, first convert it to a compound inequality, and then graph that normally. If the absolute value is on the greater side of the inequality, we end up with an *or* inequality; we plot the endpoints of the inequality on the number line and fill in the part of the line *outside* those points. If the absolute value is on the smaller side of the inequality, we end up with an *and* inequality; we plot the endpoints of the inequality on the number line and fill in the part of the line *between* those points.

For example, the inequality $|x + 1| \ge 4$ can be rewritten as $x \ge 3$ or $x \le -5$. We place solid circles at the points 3 and –5 and fill in the part of the line *outside* them:

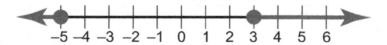

GRAPHING INEQUALITIES IN TWO VARIABLES

To graph an inequality in two variables, we first graph the border of the inequality. This means graphing the equation that we get if we replace the inequality sign with an equals sign. If the inequality is strict ($>$ or $<$), we graph the border with a dashed or dotted line; if it is not strict ($\ge$ or $\le$), we use a solid line. We can then test any point not on the border to see if it satisfies the inequality. If it does, we shade in that side of the border; if not, we shade in the other side. As an example, consider $y > 2x + 2$. To graph this inequality, we first graph the border, $y = 2x + 2$. Since it is a strict inequality, we use a dashed line. Then, we choose a test point. This can be any point not on the border; in this case, we will choose the origin, (0,0). (This makes the calculation easy and is generally a good choice unless the border passes through the origin.) Putting this into the original inequality, we get $0 > 2(0) + 2$, i.e., $0 > 2$. This is *not* true, so we shade in the side of the border that does *not* include the point $(0,0)$:

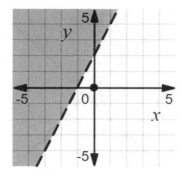

GRAPHING COMPOUND INEQUALITIES IN TWO VARIABLES

One way to graph a compound inequality in two variables is to first graph each of the component inequalities. For an *and* inequality, we then shade in only the parts where the two graphs overlap; for an *or* inequality, we shade in any region that pertains to either of the individual inequalities.

Consider the graph of "$y \geq x - 1$ and $y \leq -x$":

We first shade in the individual inequalities:

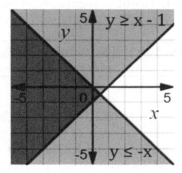

Now, since the compound inequality has an *and*, we only leave shaded the overlap—the part that pertains to *both* inequalities:

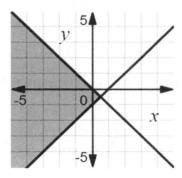

If instead the inequality had been "$y \geq x - 1$ or $y \leq -x$," our final graph would involve the *total* shaded area:

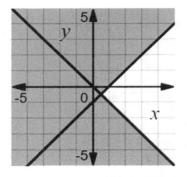

SYSTEMS OF EQUATIONS
SOLVING SYSTEMS OF EQUATIONS

A **system of equations** is a set of simultaneous equations that all use the same variables. A solution to a system of equations must be true for each equation in the system. **Consistent systems** are those with at least one solution. **Inconsistent systems** are systems of equations that have no solution.

SUBSTITUTION

To solve a system of linear equations by **substitution**, start with the easier equation and solve for one of the variables. Express this variable in terms of the other variable. Substitute this expression in the other equation and solve for the other variable. The solution should be expressed in the form (x, y). Substitute the values into both of the original equations to check your answer. Consider the following system of equations:

$$x + 6y = 15$$
$$3x - 12y = 18$$

Solving the first equation for x: $x = 15 - 6y$

Substitute this value in place of x in the second equation, and solve for y:

$$3(15 - 6y) - 12y = 18$$
$$45 - 18y - 12y = 18$$
$$30y = 27$$
$$y = \frac{27}{30} = \frac{9}{10} = 0.9$$

Plug this value for y back into the first equation to solve for x:

$$x = 15 - 6(0.9) = 15 - 5.4 = 9.6$$

Check both equations if you have time:

$$9.6 + 6(0.9) = 15 \qquad 3(9.6) - 12(0.9) = 18$$
$$9.6 + 5.4 = 15 \qquad 28.8 - 10.8 = 18$$
$$15 = 15 \qquad 18 = 18$$

Therefore, the solution is $(9.6, 0.9)$.

> **Review Video: The Substitution Method**
> Visit mometrix.com/academy and enter code: 565151
>
> **Review Video: Substitution and Elimination**
> Visit mometrix.com/academy and enter code: 958611

ELIMINATION

To solve a system of equations using **elimination**, begin by rewriting both equations in standard form $Ax + By = C$. Check to see if the coefficients of one pair of like variables add to zero. If not, multiply one or both of the equations by a non-zero number to make one set of like variables add to zero. Add the two equations to solve for one of the variables. Substitute this value into one of the original equations to solve for the other variable. Check your work by substituting into the other equation. Now, let's look at solving the following system using the elimination method:

$$5x + 6y = 4$$
$$x + 2y = 4$$

If we multiply the second equation by -3, we can eliminate the y-terms:

$$5x + 6y = 4$$
$$-3x - 6y = -12$$

Add the equations together and solve for x:

$$2x = -8$$
$$x = \frac{-8}{2} = -4$$

Plug the value for x back in to either of the original equations and solve for y:

$$-4 + 2y = 4$$
$$y = \frac{4+4}{2} = 4$$

Check both equations if you have time:

$$5(-4) + 6(4) = 4 \qquad -4 + 2(4) = 4$$
$$-20 + 24 = 4 \qquad -4 + 8 = 4$$
$$4 = 4 \qquad 4 = 4$$

129

Therefore, the solution is $(-4,4)$.

GRAPHICALLY

To solve a system of linear equations **graphically**, plot both equations on the same graph. The solution of the equations is the point where both lines cross. If the lines do not cross (are parallel), then there is **no solution**.

For example, consider the following system of equations:

$$y = 2x + 7$$
$$y = -x + 1$$

Since these equations are given in slope-intercept form, they are easy to graph; the y-intercepts of the lines are $(0,7)$ and $(0,1)$. The respective slopes are 2 and –1, thus the graphs look like this:

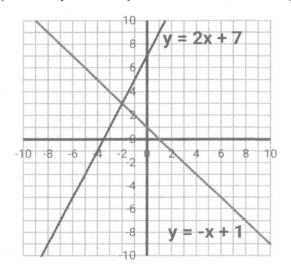

The two lines intersect at the point $(-2,3)$, thus this is the solution to the system of equations.

Solving a system graphically is generally only practical if both coordinates of the solution are integers; otherwise the intersection will lie between gridlines on the graph and the coordinates will be difficult or impossible to determine exactly. It also helps if, as in this example, the equations are in slope-intercept form or some other form that makes them easy to graph. Otherwise, another method of solution (by substitution or elimination) is likely to be more useful.

SOLVING SYSTEMS OF EQUATIONS USING THE TRACE FEATURE

Using the trace feature on a calculator requires that you rewrite each equation, isolating the y-variable on one side of the equal sign. Enter both equations in the graphing calculator and plot the graphs simultaneously. Use the trace cursor to find where the two lines cross. Use the zoom feature if necessary to obtain more accurate results. Always check your answer by substituting into the original equations. The trace method is likely to be less accurate than other methods due to the resolution of graphing calculators but is a useful tool to provide an approximate answer.

Advanced Math

LINEAR EXPRESSIONS
TERMS AND COEFFICIENTS

Mathematical expressions consist of a combination of one or more values arranged in terms that are added together. As such, an expression could be just a single number, including zero. A **variable term** is the product of a real number, also called a **coefficient**, and one or more variables, each of which may be raised to an exponent. Expressions may also include numbers without a variable, called **constants** or **constant terms**. The expression $6s^2$, for example, is a single term where the coefficient is the real number 6 and the variable term is s^2. Note that if a term is written as simply a variable to some exponent, like t^2, then the coefficient is 1, because $t^2 = 1t^2$.

LINEAR EXPRESSIONS

A **single variable linear expression** is the sum of a single variable term, where the variable has no exponent, and a constant, which may be zero. For instance, the expression $2w + 7$ has $2w$ as the variable term and 7 as the constant term. It is important to realize that terms are separated by addition or subtraction. Since an expression is a sum of terms, expressions such as $5x - 3$ can be written as $5x + (-3)$ to emphasize that the constant term is negative. A real-world example of a single variable linear expression is the perimeter of a square, four times the side length, often expressed: $4s$.

In general, a **linear expression** is the sum of any number of variable terms so long as none of the variables have an exponent. For example, $3m + 8n - \frac{1}{4}p + 5.5q - 1$ is a linear expression, but $3y^3$ is not. In the same way, the expression for the perimeter of a general triangle, the sum of the side lengths $(a + b + c)$ is considered to be linear, but the expression for the area of a square, the side length squared (s^2) is not.

ADVANCED SYSTEMS OF EQUATIONS
SOLVING A SYSTEM OF EQUATIONS CONSISTING OF A LINEAR EQUATION AND A QUADRATIC EQUATION
ALGEBRAICALLY

Generally, the simplest way to solve a system of equations consisting of a linear equation and a quadratic equation algebraically is through the method of substitution. One possible strategy is to solve the linear equation for y and then substitute that expression into the quadratic equation. After expansion and combining like terms, this will result in a new quadratic equation for x, which, like all quadratic equations, may have zero, one, or two solutions. Plugging each solution for x back into one of the original equations will then produce the corresponding value of y.

For example, consider the following system of equations:

$$x + y = 1$$
$$y = (x + 3)^2 - 2$$

131

We can solve the linear equation for y to yield $y = -x + 1$. Substituting this expression into the quadratic equation produces $-x + 1 = (x + 3)^2 - 2$. We can simplify this equation:

$$-x + 1 = (x + 3)^2 - 2$$
$$-x + 1 = x^2 + 6x + 9 - 2$$
$$-x + 1 = x^2 + 6x + 7$$
$$0 = x^2 + 7x + 6$$

This quadratic equation can be factored as $(x + 1)(x + 6) = 0$. It therefore has two solutions: $x_1 = -1$ and $x_2 = -6$. Plugging each of these back into the original linear equation yields $y_1 = -x_1 + 1 = -(-1) + 1 = 2$ and $y_2 = -x_2 + 1 = -(-6) + 1 = 7$. Thus, this system of equations has two solutions, $(-1,2)$ and $(-6,7)$.

It may help to check your work by putting each x- and y-value back into the original equations and verifying that they do provide a solution.

GRAPHICALLY

To solve a system of equations consisting of a linear equation and a quadratic equation graphically, plot both equations on the same graph. The linear equation will, of course, produce a straight line, while the quadratic equation will produce a parabola. These two graphs will intersect at zero, one, or two points; each point of intersection is a solution of the system.

For example, consider the following system of equations:

$$y = -2x + 2$$
$$y = -2x^2 + 4x + 2$$

The linear equation describes a line with a y-intercept of $(0,2)$ and a slope of -2.

To graph the quadratic equation, we can first find the vertex of the parabola: the x-coordinate of the vertex is $h = -\frac{b}{2a} = -\frac{4}{2(-2)} = 1$, and the y-coordinate is $k = -2(1)^2 + 4(1) + 2 = 4$. Thus, the vertex lies at $(1,4)$. To get a feel for the rest of the parabola, we can plug in a few more values of x to find more points; by putting in $x = 2$ and $x = 3$ in the quadratic equation, we find that the points

(2,2) and (3, −4) lie on the parabola; by symmetry, so must (0, 2) and (−1, −4). We can now plot both equations:

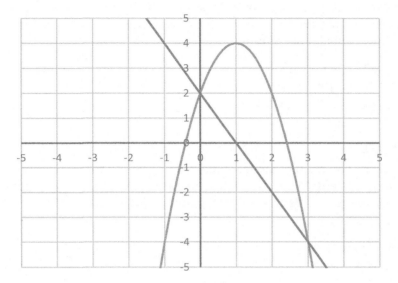

These two curves intersect at the points (0,2) and (3, −4), thus these are the solutions of the equation.

> **Review Video: Solving a System of Equations Consisting of a Linear Equation and Quadratic Equations**
> Visit mometrix.com/academy and enter code: 194870

POLYNOMIALS

MONOMIALS AND POLYNOMIALS

A **monomial** is a single constant, variable, or product of constants and variables, such as 7, x, $2x$, or x^3y. There will never be addition or subtraction symbols in a monomial. Like monomials have like variables, but they may have different coefficients. **Polynomials** are algebraic expressions that use addition and subtraction to combine two or more monomials. Two terms make a **binomial**, three terms make a **trinomial**, etc. The **degree of a monomial** is the sum of the exponents of the variables. The **degree of a polynomial** is the highest degree of any individual term.

> **Review Video: Polynomials**
> Visit mometrix.com/academy and enter code: 305005

SIMPLIFYING POLYNOMIALS

Simplifying polynomials requires combining like terms. The like terms in a polynomial expression are those that have the same variable raised to the same power. It is often helpful to connect the like terms with arrows or lines in order to separate them from the other monomials. Once you have determined the like terms, you can rearrange the polynomial by placing them together. Remember to include the sign that is in front of each term. Once the like terms are placed together, you can apply each operation and simplify. When adding and subtracting polynomials, only add and subtract the **coefficient**, or the number part; the variable and exponent stay the same.

ADD POLYNOMIALS

To add polynomials, you need to add like terms. These terms have the same variable part. An example is $4x^2$ and $3x^2$ have x^2 terms. To find the sum of like terms, find the sum of the coefficients. Then, keep the same variable part. You can use the distributive property to distribute the plus sign to each term of the polynomial. For example:

$(4x^2 - 5x + 7) + (3x^2 + 2x + 1) =$
$(4x^2 - 5x + 7) + 3x^2 + 2x + 1 =$
$(4x^2 + 3x^2) + (-5x + 2x) + (7 + 1) =$
$7x^2 - 3x + 8$

SUBTRACT POLYNOMIALS

To subtract polynomials, you need to subtract like terms. To find the difference of like terms, find the difference of the coefficients. Then, keep the same variable part. You can use the distributive property to distribute the minus sign to each term of the polynomial. For example:

$(-2x^2 - x + 5) - (3x^2 - 4x + 1) =$
$(-2x^2 - x + 5) - 3x^2 + 4x - 1 =$
$(-2x^2 - 3x^2) + (-x + 4x) + (5 - 1) =$
$-5x^2 + 3x + 4$

> **Review Video: Adding and Subtracting Polynomials**
> Visit mometrix.com/academy and enter code: 124088

MULTIPLYING POLYNOMIALS

In general, multiplying polynomials is done by multiplying each term in one polynomial by each term in the other and adding the results. In the specific case for multiplying binomials, there is a useful acronym, FOIL, that can help you make sure to cover each combination of terms. The **FOIL method** for $(Ax + By)(Cx + Dy)$ would be:

F	Multiply the *first* terms of each binomial	$(\overset{first}{Ax} + By)(\overset{first}{Cx} + Dy)$	ACx^2
O	Multiply the *outer* terms	$(\overset{outer}{Ax} + By)(Cx + \overset{outer}{Dy})$	$ADxy$
I	Multiply the *inner* terms	$(Ax + \overset{inner}{By})(\overset{inner}{Cx} + Dy)$	$BCxy$
L	Multiply the *last* terms of each binomial	$(Ax + \overset{last}{By})(Cx + \overset{last}{Dy})$	BDy^2

Then, add up the result of each and combine like terms: $ACx^2 + (AD + BC)xy + BDy^2$.

For example, using the FOIL method on binomials $(x + 2)$ and $(x - 3)$:

First: $(\boxed{x} + 2)(\boxed{x} + (-3)) \rightarrow (x)(x) = x^2$

Outer: $(\boxed{x} + 2)(x + \boxed{(-3)}) \rightarrow (x)(-3) = -3x$

Inner: $(x + \boxed{2})(\boxed{x} + (-3)) \rightarrow (2)(x) = 2x$

Last: $(x + \boxed{2})(x + \boxed{(-3)}) \rightarrow (2)(-3) = -6$

This results in: $(x^2) + (-3x) + (2x) + (-6)$

Combine like terms: $x^2 + (-3 + 2)x + (-6) = x^2 - x - 6$

> **Review Video: Multiplying Terms Using the FOIL Method**
> Visit mometrix.com/academy and enter code: 854792

DIVIDING POLYNOMIALS

Use long division to divide a polynomial by either a monomial or another polynomial of equal or lesser degree.

When **dividing by a monomial**, divide each term of the polynomial by the monomial.

When **dividing by a polynomial**, begin by arranging the terms of each polynomial in order of one variable. You may arrange in ascending or descending order, but be consistent with both polynomials. To get the first term of the quotient, divide the first term of the dividend by the first term of the divisor. Multiply the first term of the quotient by the entire divisor and subtract that product from the dividend. Repeat for the second and successive terms until you either get a remainder of zero or a remainder whose degree is less than the degree of the divisor. If the quotient has a remainder, write the answer as a mixed expression in the form:

$$\text{quotient} + \frac{\text{remainder}}{\text{divisor}}$$

For example, we can evaluate the following expression in the same way as long division:

$$\frac{x^3 - 3x^2 - 2x + 5}{x - 5}$$

$$
\begin{array}{r}
x^2 + 2x + 8 \\
x - 5 \overline{)\; x^3 - 3x^2 - 2x + 5} \\
-(x^3 - 5x^2) \\
\hline
2x^2 - 2x \\
-(2x^2 - 10x) \\
\hline
8x + 5 \\
-(8x - 40) \\
\hline
45
\end{array}
$$

$$\frac{x^3 - 3x^2 - 2x + 5}{x - 5} = x^2 + 2x + 8 + \frac{45}{x - 5}$$

When **factoring** a polynomial, first check for a common monomial factor, that is, look to see if each coefficient has a common factor or if each term has an x in it. If the factor is a trinomial but not a perfect trinomial square, look for a factorable form, such as one of these:

$$x^2 + (a + b)x + ab = (x + a)(x + b)$$
$$(ac)x^2 + (ad + bc)x + bd = (ax + b)(cx + d)$$

For factors with four terms, look for groups to factor. Once you have found the factors, write the original polynomial as the product of all the factors. Make sure all of the polynomial factors are

135

prime. Monomial factors may be *prime* or *composite*. Check your work by multiplying the factors to make sure you get the original polynomial.

Below are patterns of some special products to remember to help make factoring easier:

- Perfect trinomial squares: $x^2 + 2xy + y^2 = (x + y)^2$ or $x^2 - 2xy + y^2 = (x - y)^2$
- Difference between two squares: $x^2 - y^2 = (x + y)(x - y)$
- Sum of two cubes: $x^3 + y^3 = (x + y)(x^2 - xy + y^2)$
  - Note: the second factor is *not* the same as a perfect trinomial square, so do not try to factor it further.
- Difference between two cubes: $x^3 - y^3 = (x - y)(x^2 + xy + y^2)$
  - Again, the second factor is *not* the same as a perfect trinomial square.
- Perfect cubes: $x^3 + 3x^2y + 3xy^2 + y^3 = (x + y)^3$ and $x^3 - 3x^2y + 3xy^2 - y^3 = (x - y)^3$

RATIONAL EXPRESSIONS

Rational expressions are fractions with polynomials in both the numerator and the denominator; the value of the polynomial in the denominator cannot be equal to zero. Be sure to keep track of values that make the denominator of the original expression zero as the final result inherits the same restrictions. For example, a denominator of $x - 3$ indicates that the expression is not defined when $x = 3$ and, as such, regardless of any operations done to the expression, it remains undefined there.

To **add or subtract** rational expressions, first find the common denominator, then rewrite each fraction as an equivalent fraction with the common denominator. Finally, add or subtract the numerators to get the numerator of the answer, and keep the common denominator as the denominator of the answer.

When **multiplying** rational expressions, factor each polynomial and cancel like factors (a factor which appears in both the numerator and the denominator). Then, multiply all remaining factors in the numerator to get the numerator of the product, and multiply the remaining factors in the denominator to get the denominator of the product. Remember: cancel entire factors, not individual terms.

To **divide** rational expressions, take the reciprocal of the divisor (the rational expression you are dividing by) and multiply by the dividend.

> **Review Video: Rational Expressions**
> Visit mometrix.com/academy and enter code: 415183

SIMPLIFYING RATIONAL EXPRESSIONS

To simplify a rational expression, factor the numerator and denominator completely. Factors that are the same and appear in the numerator and denominator have a ratio of 1. For example, look at the following expression:

$$\frac{x - 1}{1 - x^2}$$

The denominator, $(1 - x^2)$, is a difference of squares. It can be factored as $(1 - x)(1 + x)$. The factor $1 - x$ and the numerator $x - 1$ are opposites and have a ratio of –1. Rewrite the numerator as $-1(1 - x)$. So, the rational expression can be simplified as follows:

$$\frac{x - 1}{1 - x^2} = \frac{-1(1 - x)}{(1 - x)(1 + x)} = \frac{-1}{1 + x}$$

Note that since the original expression is only defined for $x \neq \{-1, 1\}$, the simplified expression has the same restrictions.

QUADRATICS
SOLVING QUADRATIC EQUATIONS
Quadratic equations are a special set of trinomials of the form $y = ax^2 + bx + c$ that occur commonly in math and real-world applications. The **roots** of a quadratic equation are the solutions that satisfy the equation when $y = 0$; in other words, where the graph touches the x-axis. There are several ways to determine these solutions including using the quadratic formula, factoring, completing the square, and graphing the function.

QUADRATIC FORMULA
The **quadratic formula** is used to solve quadratic equations when other methods are more difficult. To use the quadratic formula to solve a quadratic equation, begin by rewriting the equation in standard form $ax^2 + bx + c = 0$, where a, b, and c are coefficients. Once you have identified the values of the coefficients, substitute those values into the quadratic formula

$$x = \frac{-b \pm \sqrt{b^2 - 4ac}}{2a}$$

Evaluate the equation and simplify the expression. Again, check each root by substituting into the original equation. In the quadratic formula, the portion of the formula under the radical ($b^2 - 4ac$) is called the **discriminant**. If the discriminant is zero, there is only one root: $-\frac{b}{2a}$. If the discriminant is positive, there are two different real roots. If the discriminant is negative, there are no real roots; you will instead find complex roots. Often these solutions don't make sense in context and are ignored.

FACTORING
To solve a quadratic equation by factoring, begin by rewriting the equation in standard form, $x^2 + bx + c = 0$. Remember that the goal of factoring is to find numbers f and g such that $(x + f)(x + g) = x^2 + (f + g)x + fg$, in other words $(f + g) = b$ and $fg = c$. This can be a really

useful method when b and c are integers. Determine the factors of c and look for pairs that could sum to b.

For example, consider finding the roots of $x^2 + 6x - 16 = 0$. The factors of -16 include, -4 and 4, -8 and 2, -2 and 8, -1 and 16, and 1 and -16. The factors that sum to 6 are -2 and 8. Write these factors as the product of two binomials, $0 = (x - 2)(x + 8)$. Finally, since these binomials multiply together to equal zero, set them each equal to zero and solve each for x. This results in $x - 2 = 0$, which simplifies to $x = 2$ and $x + 8 = 0$, which simplifies to $x = -8$. Therefore, the roots of the equation are 2 and -8.

Review Video: <u>Factoring Quadratic Equations</u>
Visit mometrix.com/academy and enter code: 336566

COMPLETING THE SQUARE

One way to find the roots of a quadratic equation is to find a way to manipulate it such that it follows the form of a perfect square $(x^2 + 2px + p^2)$ by adding and subtracting a constant. This process is called **completing the square**. In other words, if you are given a quadratic that is not a perfect square, $x^2 + bx + c = 0$, you can find a constant d that could be added in to make it a perfect square:

$$x^2 + bx + c + (d - d) = 0; \; \{\text{Let } b = 2p \text{ and } c + d = p^2\}$$

then:

$$x^2 + 2px + p^2 - d = 0 \text{ and } d = \frac{b^2}{4} - c$$

Once you have completed the square you can find the roots of the resulting equation:

$$x^2 + 2px + p^2 - d = 0$$
$$(x + p)^2 = d$$
$$x + p = \pm\sqrt{d}$$
$$x = -p \pm \sqrt{d}$$

It is worth noting that substituting the original expressions into this solution gives the same result as the quadratic formula where $a = 1$:

$$x = -p \pm \sqrt{d} = -\frac{b}{2} \pm \sqrt{\frac{b^2}{4} - c} = -\frac{b}{2} \pm \frac{\sqrt{b^2 - 4c}}{2} = \frac{-b \pm \sqrt{b^2 - 4c}}{2}$$

Completing the square can be seen as arranging block representations of each of the terms to be as close to a square as possible and then filling in the gaps. For example, consider the quadratic expression $x^2 + 6x + 2$:

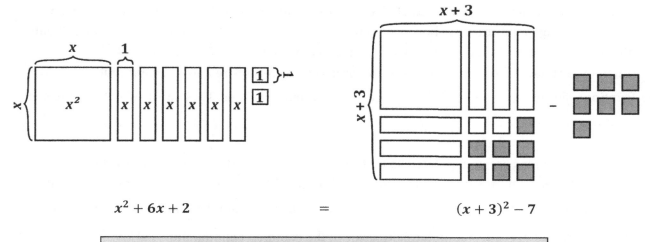

$$x^2 + 6x + 2 \qquad = \qquad (x + 3)^2 - 7$$

> **Review Video: Completing the Square**
> Visit mometrix.com/academy and enter code: 982479

USING GIVEN ROOTS TO FIND QUADRATIC EQUATION

One way to find the roots of a quadratic equation is to factor the equation and use the **zero product property**, setting each factor of the equation equal to zero to find the corresponding root. We can use this technique in reverse to find an equation given its roots. Each root corresponds to a linear equation which in turn corresponds to a factor of the quadratic equation.

For example, we can find a quadratic equation whose roots are $x = 2$ and $x = -1$. The root $x = 2$ corresponds to the equation $x - 2 = 0$, and the root $x = -1$ corresponds to the equation $x + 1 = 0$.

These two equations correspond to the factors $(x - 2)$ and $(x + 1)$, from which we can derive the equation $(x - 2)(x + 1) = 0$, or $x^2 - x - 2 = 0$.

Any integer multiple of this entire equation will also yield the same roots, as the integer will simply cancel out when the equation is factored. For example, $2x^2 - 2x - 4 = 0$ factors as $2(x - 2)(x + 1) = 0$.

Problem-Solving and Data Analysis

FRACTIONS, DECIMALS, AND PERCENTAGES

FRACTIONS

A **fraction** is a number that is expressed as one integer written above another integer, with a dividing line between them $\left(\frac{x}{y}\right)$. It represents the **quotient** of the two numbers "x divided by y." It can also be thought of as x out of y equal parts.

The top number of a fraction is called the **numerator**, and it represents the number of parts under consideration. The 1 in $\frac{1}{4}$ means that 1 part out of the whole is being considered in the calculation. The bottom number of a fraction is called the **denominator**, and it represents the total number of equal parts. The 4 in $\frac{1}{4}$ means that the whole consists of 4 equal parts. A fraction cannot have a denominator of zero; this is referred to as "*undefined.*"

Fractions can be manipulated, without changing the value of the fraction, by multiplying or dividing (but not adding or subtracting) both the numerator and denominator by the same number. If you divide both numbers by a common factor, you are **reducing** or simplifying the fraction. Two fractions that have the same value but are expressed differently are known as **equivalent fractions**. For example, $\frac{2}{10}, \frac{3}{15}, \frac{4}{20}$, and $\frac{5}{25}$ are all equivalent fractions. They can also all be reduced or simplified to $\frac{1}{5}$.

When two fractions are manipulated so that they have the same denominator, this is known as finding a **common denominator**. The number chosen to be that common denominator should be the least common multiple of the two original denominators. Example: $\frac{3}{4}$ and $\frac{5}{6}$; the least common multiple of 4 and 6 is 12. Manipulating to achieve the common denominator: $\frac{3}{4} = \frac{9}{12}; \frac{5}{6} = \frac{10}{12}$.

> **Review Video: Overview of Fractions**
> Visit mometrix.com/academy and enter code: 262335

PROPER FRACTIONS AND MIXED NUMBERS

A fraction whose denominator is greater than its numerator is known as a **proper fraction**, while a fraction whose numerator is greater than its denominator is known as an **improper fraction**. Proper fractions have values *less than one* and improper fractions have values *greater than one*.

A **mixed number** is a number that contains both an integer and a fraction. Any improper fraction can be rewritten as a mixed number. Example: $\frac{8}{3} = \frac{6}{3} + \frac{2}{3} = 2 + \frac{2}{3} = 2\frac{2}{3}$. Similarly, any mixed number can be rewritten as an improper fraction. Example: $1\frac{3}{5} = 1 + \frac{3}{5} = \frac{5}{5} + \frac{3}{5} = \frac{8}{5}$.

> **Review Video: Proper and Improper Fractions and Mixed Numbers**
> Visit mometrix.com/academy and enter code: 211077

ADDING AND SUBTRACTING FRACTIONS

If two fractions have a common denominator, they can be added or subtracted simply by adding or subtracting the two numerators and retaining the same denominator. If the two fractions do not already have the same denominator, one or both of them must be manipulated to achieve a common denominator before they can be added or subtracted. Example: $\frac{1}{2} + \frac{1}{4} = \frac{2}{4} + \frac{1}{4} = \frac{3}{4}$.

> **Review Video: Adding and Subtracting Fractions**
> Visit mometrix.com/academy and enter code: 378080

MULTIPLYING FRACTIONS

Two fractions can be multiplied by multiplying the two numerators to find the new numerator and the two denominators to find the new denominator. Example: $\frac{1}{3} \times \frac{2}{3} = \frac{1 \times 2}{3 \times 3} = \frac{2}{9}$.

DIVIDING FRACTIONS

Two fractions can be divided by flipping the numerator and denominator of the second fraction and then proceeding as though it were a multiplication problem. Example: $\frac{2}{3} \div \frac{3}{4} = \frac{2}{3} \times \frac{4}{3} = \frac{8}{9}$.

Review Video: <u>Multiplying and Dividing Fractions</u>
Visit mometrix.com/academy and enter code: 473632

MULTIPLYING A MIXED NUMBER BY A WHOLE NUMBER OR A DECIMAL

When multiplying a mixed number by something, it is usually best to convert it to an improper fraction first. Additionally, if the multiplicand is a decimal, it is most often simplest to convert it to a fraction. For instance, to multiply $4\frac{3}{8}$ by 3.5, begin by rewriting each quantity as a whole number plus a proper fraction. Remember, a mixed number is a fraction added to a whole number and a decimal is a representation of the sum of fractions, specifically tenths, hundredths, thousandths, and so on:

$$4\frac{3}{8} \times 3.5 = \left(4 + \frac{3}{8}\right) \times \left(3 + \frac{1}{2}\right)$$

Next, the quantities being added need to be expressed with the same denominator. This is achieved by multiplying and dividing the whole number by the denominator of the fraction. Recall that a whole number is equivalent to that number divided by 1:

$$= \left(\frac{4}{1} \times \frac{8}{8} + \frac{3}{8}\right) \times \left(\frac{3}{1} \times \frac{2}{2} + \frac{1}{2}\right)$$

When multiplying fractions, remember to multiply the numerators and denominators separately:

$$= \left(\frac{4 \times 8}{1 \times 8} + \frac{3}{8}\right) \times \left(\frac{3 \times 2}{1 \times 2} + \frac{1}{2}\right)$$
$$= \left(\frac{32}{8} + \frac{3}{8}\right) \times \left(\frac{6}{2} + \frac{1}{2}\right)$$

Now that the fractions have the same denominators, they can be added:

$$= \frac{35}{8} \times \frac{7}{2}$$

Finally, perform the last multiplication and then simplify:

$$= \frac{35 \times 7}{8 \times 2} = \frac{245}{16} = \frac{240}{16} + \frac{5}{16} = 15\frac{5}{16}$$

COMPARING FRACTIONS

It is important to master the ability to compare and order fractions. This skill is relevant to many real-world scenarios. For example, carpenters often compare fractional construction nail lengths when preparing for a project, and bakers often compare fractional measurements to have the correct ratio of ingredients. There are three commonly used strategies when comparing fractions.

These strategies are referred to as the common denominator approach, the decimal approach, and the cross-multiplication approach.

USING A COMMON DENOMINATOR TO COMPARE FRACTIONS

The fractions $\frac{2}{3}$ and $\frac{4}{7}$ have different denominators. $\frac{2}{3}$ has a denominator of 3, and $\frac{4}{7}$ has a denominator of 7. In order to precisely compare these two fractions, it is necessary to use a common denominator. A common denominator is a common multiple that is shared by both denominators. In this case, the denominators 3 and 7 share a multiple of 21. In general, it is most efficient to select the least common multiple for the two denominators.

Rewrite each fraction with the common denominator of 21. Then, calculate the new numerators as illustrated below.

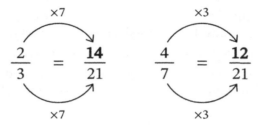

For $\frac{2}{3}$, multiply the numerator and denominator by 7. The result is $\frac{14}{21}$.

For $\frac{4}{7}$, multiply the numerator and denominator by 3. The result is $\frac{12}{21}$.

Now that both fractions have a denominator of 21, the fractions can accurately be compared by comparing the numerators. Since 14 is greater than 12, the fraction $\frac{14}{21}$ is greater than $\frac{12}{21}$. This means that $\frac{2}{3}$ is greater than $\frac{4}{7}$.

USING DECIMALS TO COMPARE FRACTIONS

Sometimes decimal values are easier to compare than fraction values. For example, $\frac{5}{8}$ is equivalent to 0.625 and $\frac{3}{5}$ is equivalent to 0.6. This means that the comparison of $\frac{5}{8}$ and $\frac{3}{5}$ can be determined by comparing the decimals 0.625 and 0.6. When both decimal values are extended to the thousandths place, they become 0.625 and 0.600, respectively. It becomes clear that 0.625 is greater than 0.600 because 625 thousandths is greater than 600 thousandths. In other words, $\frac{5}{8}$ is greater than $\frac{3}{5}$ because 0.625 is greater than 0.6.

USING CROSS-MULTIPLICATION TO COMPARE FRACTIONS

Cross-multiplication is an efficient strategy for comparing fractions. This is a shortcut for the common denominator strategy. Start by writing each fraction next to one another. Multiply the numerator of the fraction on the left by the denominator of the fraction on the right. Write down the result next to the fraction on the left. Now multiply the numerator of the fraction on the right by the denominator of the fraction on the left. Write down the result next to the fraction on the right. Compare both products. The fraction with the larger result is the larger fraction.

Consider the fractions $\frac{4}{7}$ and $\frac{5}{9}$.

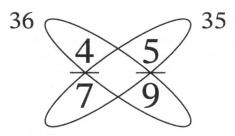

36 is greater than 35. Therefore, $\frac{4}{7}$ is greater than $\frac{5}{9}$.

DECIMALS

Decimals are one way to represent parts of a whole. Using the place value system, each digit to the right of a decimal point denotes the number of units of a corresponding *negative* power of ten. For example, consider the decimal 0.24. We can use a model to represent the decimal. Since a dime is worth one-tenth of a dollar and a penny is worth one-hundredth of a dollar, one possible model to represent this fraction is to have 2 dimes representing the 2 in the tenths place and 4 pennies representing the 4 in the hundredths place:

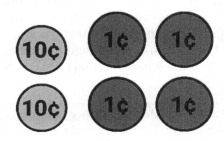

To write the decimal as a fraction, put the decimal in the numerator with 1 in the denominator. Multiply the numerator and denominator by tens until there are no more decimal places. Then simplify the fraction to lowest terms. For example, converting 0.24 to a fraction:

$$0.24 = \frac{0.24}{1} = \frac{0.24 \times 100}{1 \times 100} = \frac{24}{100} = \frac{6}{25}$$

> **Review Video: Decimals**
> Visit mometrix.com/academy and enter code: 837268

OPERATIONS WITH DECIMALS

ADDING AND SUBTRACTING DECIMALS

When adding and subtracting decimals, the decimal points must always be aligned. Adding decimals is just like adding regular whole numbers. Example: $4.5 + 2.0 = 6.5$.

If the problem-solver does not properly align the decimal points, an incorrect answer of 4.7 may result. An easy way to add decimals is to align all of the decimal points in a vertical column visually. This will allow you to see exactly where the decimal should be placed in the final answer. Begin adding from right to left. Add each column in turn, making sure to carry the number to the left if a column adds up to more than 9. The same rules apply to the subtraction of decimals.

> **Review Video: Adding and Subtracting Decimals**
> Visit mometrix.com/academy and enter code: 381101

MULTIPLYING DECIMALS

A simple multiplication problem has two components: a **multiplicand** and a **multiplier**. When multiplying decimals, work as though the numbers were whole rather than decimals. Once the final product is calculated, count the number of places to the right of the decimal in both the multiplicand and the multiplier. Then, count that number of places from the right of the product and place the decimal in that position.

For example, 12.3×2.56 has a total of three places to the right of the respective decimals. Multiply 123×256 to get 31,488. Now, beginning on the right, count three places to the left and insert the decimal. The final product will be 31.488.

> **Review Video: How to Multiply Decimals**
> Visit mometrix.com/academy and enter code: 731574

DIVIDING DECIMALS

Every division problem has a **divisor** and a **dividend**. The dividend is the number that is being divided. In the problem $14 \div 7$, 14 is the dividend and 7 is the divisor. In a division problem with decimals, the divisor must be converted into a whole number. Begin by moving the decimal in the divisor to the right until a whole number is created. Next, move the decimal in the dividend the same number of spaces to the right. For example, 4.9 into 24.5 would become 49 into 245. The decimal was moved one space to the right to create a whole number in the divisor, and then the same was done for the dividend. Once the whole numbers are created, the problem is carried out normally: $245 \div 49 = 5$.

> **Review Video: Dividing Decimals**
> Visit mometrix.com/academy and enter code: 560690
>
> **Review Video: Dividing Decimals by Whole Numbers**
> Visit mometrix.com/academy and enter code: 535669

PERCENTAGES

Percentages can be thought of as fractions that are based on a whole of 100; that is, one whole is equal to 100%. The word **percent** means "per hundred." Percentage problems are often presented in three main ways:

- Find what percentage of some number another number is.
  - Example: What percentage of 40 is 8?
- Find what number is some percentage of a given number.
  - Example: What number is 20% of 40?
- Find what number another number is a given percentage of.
  - Example: What number is 8 20% of?

There are three components in each of these cases: a **whole** (W), a **part** (P), and a **percentage** (%). These are related by the equation: $P = W \times \%$. This can easily be rearranged into other forms that may suit different questions better: $\% = \frac{P}{W}$ and $W = \frac{P}{\%}$. Percentage problems are often also word problems. As such, a large part of solving them is figuring out which quantities are what. For example, consider the following word problem:

In a school cafeteria, 7 students choose pizza, 9 choose hamburgers, and 4 choose tacos. What percentage of student choose tacos?

To find the whole, you must first add all of the parts: $7 + 9 + 4 = 20$. The percentage can then be found by dividing the part by the whole $\left(\% = \frac{P}{W}\right)$: $\frac{4}{20} = \frac{20}{100} = 20\%$.

Review Video: <u>Computation with Percentages</u>
Visit mometrix.com/academy and enter code: 693099

CONVERTING BETWEEN PERCENTAGES, FRACTIONS, AND DECIMALS

Converting decimals to percentages and percentages to decimals is as simple as moving the decimal point. To *convert from a decimal to a percentage*, move the decimal point **two places to the right**. To *convert from a percentage to a decimal*, move it **two places to the left**. It may be helpful to remember that the percentage number will always be larger than the equivalent decimal number. Example:

$$0.23 = 23\% \quad 5.34 = 534\% \quad 0.007 = 0.7\%$$
$$700\% = 7.00 \quad 86\% = 0.86 \quad 0.15\% = 0.0015$$

To convert a fraction to a decimal, simply divide the numerator by the denominator in the fraction. To convert a decimal to a fraction, put the decimal in the numerator with 1 in the denominator. Multiply the numerator and denominator by tens until there are no more decimal places. Then simplify the fraction to lowest terms. For example, converting 0.24 to a fraction:

$$0.24 = \frac{0.24}{1} = \frac{0.24 \times 100}{1 \times 100} = \frac{24}{100} = \frac{6}{25}$$

Fractions can be converted to a percentage by finding equivalent fractions with a denominator of 100. Example:

$$\frac{7}{10} = \frac{70}{100} = 70\% \quad \frac{1}{4} = \frac{25}{100} = 25\%$$

To convert a percentage to a fraction, divide the percentage number by 100 and reduce the fraction to its simplest possible terms. Example:

$$60\% = \frac{60}{100} = \frac{3}{5} \quad 96\% = \frac{96}{100} = \frac{24}{25}$$

Review Video: <u>Converting Fractions to Percentages and Decimals</u>
Visit mometrix.com/academy and enter code: 306233

Review Video: <u>Converting Percentages to Decimals and Fractions</u>
Visit mometrix.com/academy and enter code: 287297

Review Video: <u>Converting Decimals to Fractions and Percentages</u>
Visit mometrix.com/academy and enter code: 986765

PROPORTIONS AND RATIOS

PROPORTIONS

A proportion is a relationship between two quantities that dictates how one changes when the other changes. A **direct proportion** describes a relationship in which a quantity increases by a set amount for every increase in the other quantity, or decreases by that same amount for every decrease in the other quantity. Example: Assuming a constant driving speed, the time required for a car trip increases as the distance of the trip increases. The distance to be traveled and the time required to travel are directly proportional.

An **inverse proportion** is a relationship in which an increase in one quantity is accompanied by a decrease in the other, or vice versa. Example: the time required for a car trip decreases as the speed increases and increases as the speed decreases, so the time required is inversely proportional to the speed of the car.

RATIOS

A **ratio** is a comparison of two quantities in a particular order. Example: If there are 14 computers in a lab, and the class has 20 students, there is a student to computer ratio of 20 to 14, commonly written as 20: 14. Ratios are normally reduced to their smallest whole number representation, so 20: 14 would be reduced to 10: 7 by dividing both sides by 2.

CONSTANT OF PROPORTIONALITY

When two quantities have a proportional relationship, there exists a **constant of proportionality** between the quantities. The product of this constant and one of the quantities is equal to the other quantity. For example, if one lemon costs $0.25, two lemons cost $0.50, and three lemons cost $0.75, there is a proportional relationship between the total cost of lemons and the number of lemons purchased. The constant of proportionality is the **unit price**, namely $0.25/lemon. Notice that the total price of lemons, t, can be found by multiplying the unit price of lemons, p, and the number of lemons, n: $t = pn$.

WORK/UNIT RATE

Unit rate expresses a quantity of one thing in terms of one unit of another. For example, if you travel 30 miles every two hours, a unit rate expresses this comparison in terms of one hour: in one hour you travel 15 miles, so your unit rate is 15 miles per hour. Other examples are how much one ounce of food costs (price per ounce) or figuring out how much one egg costs out of the dozen (price per 1 egg, instead of price per 12 eggs). The denominator of a unit rate is always 1. Unit rates are used to compare different situations to solve problems. For example, to make sure you get the best deal when deciding which kind of soda to buy, you can find the unit rate of each. If soda #1 costs $1.50 for a 1-liter bottle, and soda #2 costs $2.75 for a 2-liter bottle, it would be a better deal to buy soda #2, because its unit rate is only $1.375 per 1-liter, which is cheaper than soda #1. Unit rates can also help determine the length of time a given event will take. For example, if you can paint 2 rooms in 4.5 hours, you can determine how long it will take you to paint 5 rooms by solving for the unit rate per room and then multiplying that by 5.

> **Review Video: Rates and Unit Rates**
> Visit mometrix.com/academy and enter code: 185363

METRIC AND CUSTOMARY MEASUREMENTS
METRIC MEASUREMENT PREFIXES

Giga-	One billion	1 *giga*watt is one billion watts
Mega-	One million	1 *mega*hertz is one million hertz
Kilo-	One thousand	1 *kilo*gram is one thousand grams
Deci-	One-tenth	1 *deci*meter is one-tenth of a meter
Centi-	One-hundredth	1 *centi*meter is one-hundredth of a meter
Milli-	One-thousandth	1 *milli*liter is one-thousandth of a liter
Micro-	One-millionth	1 *micro*gram is one-millionth of a gram

> **Review Video: Metric System Conversion - How the Metric System Works**
> Visit mometrix.com/academy and enter code: 163709

MEASUREMENT CONVERSION

When converting between units, the goal is to maintain the same meaning but change the way it is displayed. In order to go from a larger unit to a smaller unit, multiply the number of the known amount by the equivalent amount. When going from a smaller unit to a larger unit, divide the number of the known amount by the equivalent amount.

For complicated conversions, it may be helpful to set up conversion fractions. In these fractions, one fraction is the **conversion factor**. The other fraction has the unknown amount in the numerator. So, the known value is placed in the denominator. Sometimes, the second fraction has the known value from the problem in the numerator and the unknown in the denominator. Multiply the two fractions to get the converted measurement. Note that since the numerator and the denominator of the factor are equivalent, the value of the fraction is 1. That is why we can say that the result in the new units is equal to the result in the old units even though they have different numbers.

It can often be necessary to chain known conversion factors together. As an example, consider converting 512 square inches to square meters. We know that there are 2.54 centimeters in an inch and 100 centimeters in a meter, and we know we will need to square each of these factors to achieve the conversion we are looking for.

$$\frac{512 \text{ in}^2}{1} \times \left(\frac{2.54 \text{ cm}}{1 \text{ in}}\right)^2 \times \left(\frac{1 \text{ m}}{100 \text{ cm}}\right)^2 = \frac{512 \text{ in}^2}{1} \times \left(\frac{6.4516 \text{ cm}^2}{1 \text{ in}^2}\right) \times \left(\frac{1 \text{ m}^2}{10,000 \text{ cm}^2}\right) = 0.330 \text{ m}^2$$

> **Review Video: Measurement Conversions**
> Visit mometrix.com/academy and enter code: 316703

COMMON UNITS AND EQUIVALENTS
METRIC EQUIVALENTS

1000 µg (microgram)	1 mg
1000 mg (milligram)	1 g
1000 g (gram)	1 kg
1000 kg (kilogram)	1 metric ton
1000 mL (milliliter)	1 L
1000 µm (micrometer)	1 mm
1000 mm (millimeter)	1 m
100 cm (centimeter)	1 m
1000 m (meter)	1 km

DISTANCE AND AREA MEASUREMENT

Unit	Abbreviation	US equivalent	Metric equivalent
Inch	in	1 inch	2.54 centimeters
Foot	ft	12 inches	0.305 meters
Yard	yd	3 feet	0.914 meters
Mile	mi	5280 feet	1.609 kilometers
Acre	ac	4840 square yards	0.405 hectares
Square Mile	sq. mi. or mi.^{2}	640 acres	2.590 square kilometers

CAPACITY MEASUREMENTS

Unit	Abbreviation	US equivalent	Metric equivalent
Fluid Ounce	fl oz	8 fluid drams	29.573 milliliters
Cup	c	8 fluid ounces	0.237 liter
Pint	pt.	16 fluid ounces	0.473 liter
Quart	qt.	2 pints	0.946 liter
Gallon	gal.	4 quarts	3.785 liters
Teaspoon	t or tsp.	1 fluid dram	5 milliliters
Tablespoon	T or tbsp.	4 fluid drams	15 or 16 milliliters
Cubic Centimeter	cc or cm^3	0.271 drams	1 milliliter

WEIGHT MEASUREMENTS

Unit	Abbreviation	US equivalent	Metric equivalent
Ounce	oz	16 drams	28.35 grams
Pound	lb	16 ounces	453.6 grams
Ton	tn.	2,000 pounds	907.2 kilograms

VOLUME AND WEIGHT MEASUREMENT CLARIFICATIONS

Always be careful when using ounces and fluid ounces. They are not equivalent.

1 pint = 16 fluid ounces	1 fluid ounce ≠ 1 ounce
1 pound = 16 ounces	1 pint ≠ 1 pound

Having one pint of something does not mean you have one pound of it. In the same way, just because something weighs one pound does not mean that its volume is one pint.

In the United States, the word "ton" by itself refers to a short ton or a net ton. Do not confuse this with a long ton (also called a gross ton) or a metric ton (also spelled *tonne*), which have different measurement equivalents.

$$1 \text{ US ton} = 2000 \text{ pounds} \qquad \neq \qquad 1 \text{ metric ton} = 1000 \text{ kilograms}$$

PROBABILITY

Probability is the likelihood of a certain outcome occurring for a given event. An **event** is any situation that produces a result. It could be something as simple as flipping a coin or as complex as launching a rocket. Determining the probability of an outcome for an event can be equally simple or complex. As such, there are specific terms used in the study of probability that need to be understood:

- **Compound event**—an event that involves two or more independent events (rolling a pair of dice and taking the sum)
- **Desired outcome** (or success)—an outcome that meets a particular set of criteria (a roll of 1 or 2 if we are looking for numbers less than 3)
- **Independent events**—two or more events whose outcomes do not affect one another (two coins tossed at the same time)
- **Dependent events**—two or more events whose outcomes affect one another (two cards drawn consecutively from the same deck)
- **Certain outcome**—probability of outcome is 100% or 1
- **Impossible outcome**—probability of outcome is 0% or 0
- **Mutually exclusive outcomes**—two or more outcomes whose criteria cannot all be satisfied in a single event (a coin coming up heads and tails on the same toss)
- **Random variable**—refers to all possible outcomes of a single event which may be discrete or continuous.

> **Review Video: Intro to Probability**
> Visit mometrix.com/academy and enter code: 212374

SAMPLE SPACE

The total set of all possible results of a test or experiment is called a **sample space**, or sometimes a universal sample space. The sample space, represented by one of the variables S, Ω, or U (for universal sample space) has individual elements called outcomes. Other terms for outcome that may be used interchangeably include elementary outcome, simple event, or sample point. The number of outcomes in a given sample space could be infinite or finite, and some tests may yield multiple unique sample sets. For example, tests conducted by drawing playing cards from a standard deck would have one sample space of the card values, another sample space of the card suits, and a third sample space of suit-denomination combinations. For most tests, the sample spaces considered will be finite.

An **event**, represented by the variable E, is a portion of a sample space. It may be one outcome or a group of outcomes from the same sample space. If an event occurs, then the test or experiment will generate an outcome that satisfies the requirement of that event. For example, given a standard deck of 52 playing cards as the sample space, and defining the event as the collection of face cards, then the event will occur if the card drawn is a *J*, *Q*, or *K*. If any other card is drawn, the event is said to have not occurred.

For every sample space, each possible outcome has a specific likelihood, or probability, that it will occur. The probability measure, also called the **distribution**, is a function that assigns a real number probability, from zero to one, to each outcome. For a probability measure to be accurate, every outcome must have a real number probability measure that is greater than or equal to zero and less than or equal to one. Also, the probability measure of the sample space must equal one, and the probability measure of the union of multiple outcomes must equal the sum of the individual probability measures.

Probabilities of events are expressed as real numbers from zero to one. They give a numerical value to the chance that a particular event will occur. The probability of an event occurring is the sum of the probabilities of the individual elements of that event. For example, in a standard deck of 52 playing cards as the sample space and the collection of face cards as the event, the probability of drawing a specific face card is $\frac{1}{52} = 0.019$, but the probability of drawing any one of the twelve face cards is $12(0.019) = 0.228$. Note that rounding of numbers can generate different results. If you multiplied 12 by the fraction $\frac{1}{52}$ before converting to a decimal, you would get the answer $\frac{12}{52} = 0.231$.

THEORETICAL AND EXPERIMENTAL PROBABILITY

Theoretical probability can usually be determined without actually performing the event. The likelihood of an outcome occurring, or the probability of an outcome occurring, is given by the formula:

$$P(A) = \frac{\text{Number of acceptable outcomes}}{\text{Number of possible outcomes}}$$

Note that $P(A)$ is the probability of an outcome *A* occurring, and each outcome is just as likely to occur as any other outcome. If each outcome has the same probability of occurring as every other possible outcome, the outcomes are said to be equally likely to occur. The total number of acceptable outcomes must be less than or equal to the total number of possible outcomes. If the two are equal, then the outcome is certain to occur and the probability is 1. If the number of acceptable outcomes is zero, then the outcome is impossible and the probability is 0. For example, if there are 20 marbles in a bag and 5 are red, then the theoretical probability of randomly selecting a red marble is 5 out of 20, $\left(\frac{5}{20} = \frac{1}{4}, 0.25, \text{ or } 25\%\right)$.

If the theoretical probability is unknown or too complicated to calculate, it can be estimated by an experimental probability. **Experimental probability**, also called empirical probability, is an estimate of the likelihood of a certain outcome based on repeated experiments or collected data. In other words, while theoretical probability is based on what *should* happen, experimental probability is based on what *has* happened. Experimental probability is calculated in the same way as theoretical probability, except that actual outcomes are used instead of possible outcomes. The more experiments performed or datapoints gathered, the better the estimate should be.

Theoretical and experimental probability do not always line up with one another. Theoretical probability says that out of 20 coin-tosses, 10 should be heads. However, if we were actually to toss 20 coins, we might record just 5 heads. This doesn't mean that our theoretical probability is incorrect; it just means that this particular experiment had results that were different from what was predicted. A practical application of empirical probability is the insurance industry. There are no set functions that define lifespan, health, or safety. Insurance companies look at factors from hundreds of thousands of individuals to find patterns that they then use to set the formulas for insurance premiums.

> **Review Video: Empirical Probability**
> Visit mometrix.com/academy and enter code: 513468

OBJECTIVE AND SUBJECTIVE PROBABILITY

Objective probability is based on mathematical formulas and documented evidence. Examples of objective probability include raffles or lottery drawings where there is a pre-determined number of possible outcomes and a predetermined number of outcomes that correspond to an event. Other cases of objective probability include probabilities of rolling dice, flipping coins, or drawing cards. Most gambling games are based on objective probability.

In contrast, **subjective probability** is based on personal or professional feelings and judgments. Often, there is a lot of guesswork following extensive research. Areas where subjective probability is applicable include sales trends and business expenses. Attractions set admission prices based on subjective probabilities of attendance based on varying admission rates in an effort to maximize their profit.

COMPLEMENT OF AN EVENT

Sometimes it may be easier to calculate the possibility of something not happening, or the **complement of an event**. Represented by the symbol $\bar{A}$, the complement of A is the probability that event A does not happen. When you know the probability of event A occurring, you can use the formula $P(\bar{A}) = 1 - P(A)$, where $P(\bar{A})$ is the probability of event A not occurring, and $P(A)$ is the probability of event A occurring.

ADDITION RULE

The **addition rule** for probability is used for finding the probability of a compound event. Use the formula $P(A \cup B) = P(A) + P(B) - P(A \cap B)$, where $P(A \cap B)$ is the probability of both events occurring to find the probability of a compound event. The probability of both events occurring at the same time must be subtracted to eliminate any overlap in the first two probabilities.

CONDITIONAL PROBABILITY

Given two events A and B, the **conditional probability** $P(A|B)$ is the probability that event A will occur, given that event B has occurred. The conditional probability cannot be calculated simply from $P(A)$ and $P(B)$; these probabilities alone do not give sufficient information to determine the conditional probability. It can, however, be determined if you are also given the probability of the intersection of events A and B, $P(A \cap B)$, the probability that events A and B both occur. Specifically, $P(A|B) = \frac{P(A \cap B)}{P(B)}$. For instance, suppose you have a jar containing two red marbles and two blue marbles, and you draw two marbles at random. Consider event A being the event that the first marble drawn is red, and event B being the event that the second marble drawn is blue. If we want to find the probability that B occurs given that A occurred, $P(B|A)$, then we can compute it using the fact that $P(A)$ is $\frac{1}{2}$, and $P(A \cap B)$ is $\frac{1}{3}$. (The latter may not be obvious, but may be determined by finding the product of $\frac{1}{2}$ and $\frac{2}{3}$). Therefore $P(B|A) = \frac{P(A \cap B)}{P(A)} = \frac{1/3}{1/2} = \frac{2}{3}$.

CONDITIONAL PROBABILITY IN EVERYDAY SITUATIONS

Conditional probability often arises in everyday situations in, for example, estimating the risk or benefit of certain activities. The conditional probability of having a heart attack given that you exercise daily may be smaller than the overall probability of having a heart attack. The conditional probability of having lung cancer given that you are a smoker is larger than the overall probability of having lung cancer. Note that changing the order of the conditional probability changes the meaning: the conditional probability of having lung cancer given that you are a smoker is a very different thing from the probability of being a smoker given that you have lung cancer. In an extreme case, suppose that a certain rare disease is caused only by eating a certain food, but even then, it is unlikely. Then the conditional probability of having that disease given that you eat the dangerous food is nonzero but low, but the conditional probability of having eaten that food given that you have the disease is 100%!

> **Review Video: Conditional Probability**
> Visit mometrix.com/academy and enter code: 397924

INDEPENDENCE

The conditional probability $P(A|B)$ is the probability that event A will occur given that event B occurs. If the two events are independent, we do not expect that whether or not event B occurs should have any effect on whether or not event A occurs. In other words, we expect $P(A|B) = P(A)$.

This can be proven using the usual equations for conditional probability and the joint probability of independent events. The conditional probability $P(A|B) = \frac{P(A \cap B)}{P(B)}$. If A and B are independent, then $P(A \cap B) = P(A)P(B)$. So $P(A|B) = \frac{P(A)P(B)}{P(B)} = P(A)$. By similar reasoning, if A and B are independent then $P(B|A) = P(B)$.

MULTIPLICATION RULE

The **multiplication rule** can be used to find the probability of two independent events occurring using the formula $P(A \cap B) = P(A) \times P(B)$, where $P(A \cap B)$ is the probability of two independent events occurring, $P(A)$ is the probability of the first event occurring, and $P(B)$ is the probability of the second event occurring.

The multiplication rule can also be used to find the probability of two dependent events occurring using the formula $P(A \cap B) = P(A) \times P(B|A)$, where $P(A \cap B)$ is the probability of two dependent events occurring and $P(B|A)$ is the probability of the second event occurring after the first event has already occurred.

Use a **combination of the multiplication** rule and the rule of complements to find the probability that at least one outcome of the element will occur. This is given by the general formula $P(\text{at least one event occurring}) = 1 - P(\text{no outcomes occurring})$. For example, to find the probability that at least one even number will show when a pair of dice is rolled, find the probability that two odd numbers will be rolled (no even numbers) and subtract from one. You can always use a tree diagram or make a chart to list the possible outcomes when the sample space is small, such as in the dice-rolling example, but in most cases it will be much faster to use the multiplication and complement formulas.

> **Review Video: Multiplication Rule**
> Visit mometrix.com/academy and enter code: 782598

UNION AND INTERSECTION OF TWO SETS OF OUTCOMES

If A and B are each a set of elements or outcomes from an experiment, then the **union** (symbol $\cup$) of the two sets is the set of elements found in set A or set B. For example, if $A = \{2, 3, 4\}$ and $B = \{3, 4, 5\}$, $A \cup B = \{2, 3, 4, 5\}$. Note that the outcomes 3 and 4 appear only once in the union. For statistical events, the union is equivalent to "or"; $P(A \cup B)$ is the same thing as $P(A \text{ or } B)$. The **intersection** (symbol $\cap$) of two sets is the set of outcomes common to both sets. For the above sets A and B, $A \cap B = \{3, 4\}$. For statistical events, the intersection is equivalent to "and"; $P(A \cap B)$ is the same thing as $P(A \text{ and } B)$. It is important to note that union and intersection operations commute. That is:

$$A \cup B = B \cup A \text{ and } A \cap B = B \cap A$$

TREE DIAGRAMS

For a simple sample space, possible outcomes may be determined by using a **tree diagram** or an organized chart. In either case, you can easily draw or list out the possible outcomes. For example, to determine all the possible ways three objects can be ordered, you can draw a tree diagram:

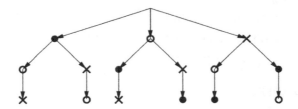

Review Video: Tree Diagrams
Visit mometrix.com/academy and enter code: 829158

You can also make a chart to list all the possibilities:

First object	Second object	Third object
●	X	O
●	O	X
O	●	X
O	X	●
X	●	O
X	O	●

Either way, you can easily see there are six possible ways the three objects can be ordered.

If two events have no outcomes in common, they are said to be **mutually exclusive**. For example, in a standard deck of 52 playing cards, the event of all card suits is mutually exclusive to the event of all card values. If two events have no bearing on each other so that one event occurring has no influence on the probability of another event occurring, the two events are said to be independent. For example, rolling a standard six-sided die multiple times does not change that probability that a particular number will be rolled from one roll to the next. If the outcome of one event does affect the probability of the second event, the two events are said to be dependent. For example, if cards are drawn from a deck, the probability of drawing an ace after an ace has been drawn is different than the probability of drawing an ace if no ace (or no other card, for that matter) has been drawn.

In probability, the **odds in favor of an event** are the number of times the event will occur compared to the number of times the event will not occur. To calculate the odds in favor of an event, use the formula $\frac{P(A)}{1-P(A)}$, where $P(A)$ is the probability that the event will occur. Many times, odds in favor is given as a ratio in the form $\frac{a}{b}$ or $a: b$, where a is the probability of the event occurring and b is the complement of the event, the probability of the event not occurring. If the odds in favor are given as 2:5, that means that you can expect the event to occur two times for every 5 times that it does not occur. In other words, the probability that the event will occur is $\frac{2}{2+5} = \frac{2}{7}$.

In probability, the **odds against an event** are the number of times the event will not occur compared to the number of times the event will occur. To calculate the odds against an event, use the formula $\frac{1-P(A)}{P(A)}$, where $P(A)$ is the probability that the event will occur. Many times, odds against is given as a ratio in the form $\frac{b}{a}$ or $b: a$, where b is the probability the event will not occur (the complement of the event) and a is the probability the event will occur. If the odds against an event are given as 3:1, that means that you can expect the event to not occur 3 times for every one time it does occur. In other words, 3 out of every 4 trials will fail.

TWO-WAY FREQUENCY TABLES

If we have a two-way frequency table, it is generally a straightforward matter to read off the probabilities of any two events A and B, as well as the joint probability of both events occurring, $P(A \cap B)$. We can then find the conditional probability $P(A|B)$ by calculating $P(A|B) = \frac{P(A \cap B)}{P(B)}$. We could also check whether or not events are independent by verifying whether $P(A)P(B) = P(A \cap B)$.

For example, a certain store's recent T-shirt sales:

	Small	Medium	Large	Total
Blue	25	40	35	100
White	27	25	22	74
Black	8	23	15	46
Total	60	88	72	220

Suppose we want to find the conditional probability that a customer buys a black shirt (event A), given that the shirt he buys is size small (event B). From the table, the probability $P(B)$ that a customer buys a small shirt is $\frac{60}{220} = \frac{3}{11}$. The probability $P(A \cap B)$ that he buys a small, black shirt is $\frac{8}{220} = \frac{2}{55}$. The conditional probability $P(A|B)$ that he buys a black shirt, given that he buys a small shirt, is therefore $P(A|B) = \frac{2/55}{3/11} = \frac{2}{15}$.

Similarly, if we want to check whether the event a customer buys a blue shirt, A, is independent of the event that a customer buys a medium shirt, B. From the table, $P(A) = \frac{100}{220} = \frac{5}{11}$ and

$P(B) = \frac{88}{220} = \frac{4}{10}$. Also, $P(A \cap B) = \frac{40}{220} = \frac{2}{11}$. Since $\left(\frac{5}{11}\right)\left(\frac{4}{10}\right) = \frac{20}{110} = \frac{2}{11}$, $P(A)P(B) = P(A \cap B)$ and these two events are indeed independent.

INTRODUCTION TO STATISTICS

Statistics is the branch of mathematics that deals with collecting, recording, interpreting, illustrating, and analyzing large amounts of **data**. The following terms are often used in the discussion of data and **statistics**:

- **Data** – the collective name for pieces of information (singular is datum)
- **Quantitative data** – measurements (such as length, mass, and speed) that provide information about quantities in numbers
- **Qualitative data** – information (such as colors, scents, tastes, and shapes) that cannot be measured using numbers
- **Discrete data** – information that can be expressed only by a specific value, such as whole or half numbers. (e.g., since people can be counted only in whole numbers, a population count would be discrete data.)
- **Continuous data** – information (such as time and temperature) that can be expressed by any value within a given range
- **Primary data** – information that has been collected directly from a survey, investigation, or experiment, such as a questionnaire or the recording of daily temperatures. (Primary data that has not yet been organized or analyzed is called **raw data**.)
- **Secondary data** – information that has been collected, sorted, and processed by the researcher
- **Ordinal data** – information that can be placed in numerical order, such as age or weight
- **Nominal data** – information that *cannot* be placed in numerical order, such as names or places

DATA COLLECTION

POPULATION

In statistics, the **population** is the entire collection of people, plants, etc., that data can be collected from. For example, a study to determine how well students in local schools perform on a standardized test would have a population of all the students enrolled in those schools, although a study may include just a small sample of students from each school. A **parameter** is a numerical value that gives information about the population, such as the mean, median, mode, or standard deviation. Remember that the symbol for the mean of a population is μ and the symbol for the standard deviation of a population is σ.

SAMPLE

A **sample** is a portion of the entire population. Whereas a parameter helped describe the population, a **statistic** is a numerical value that gives information about the sample, such as mean, median, mode, or standard deviation. Keep in mind that the symbols for mean and standard deviation are different when they are referring to a sample rather than the entire population. For a sample, the symbol for mean is $\bar{x}$ and the symbol for standard deviation is s. The mean and standard deviation of a sample may or may not be identical to that of the entire population due to a sample only being a subset of the population. However, if the sample is random and large enough, statistically significant values can be attained. Samples are generally used when the population is too large to justify including every element or when acquiring data for the entire population is impossible.

INFERENTIAL STATISTICS

Inferential statistics is the branch of statistics that uses samples to make predictions about an entire population. This type of statistic is often seen in political polls, where a sample of the population is questioned about a particular topic or politician to gain an understanding of the attitudes of the entire population of the country. Often, exit polls are conducted on election days using this method. Inferential statistics can have a large margin of error if you do not have a valid sample.

SAMPLING DISTRIBUTION

Statistical values calculated from various samples of the same size make up the **sampling distribution**. For example, if several samples of identical size are randomly selected from a large population and then the mean of each sample is calculated, the distribution of values of the means would be a sampling distribution.

The **sampling distribution of the mean** is the distribution of the sample mean, $\bar{x}$, derived from random samples of a given size. It has three important characteristics. First, the mean of the sampling distribution of the mean is equal to the mean of the population that was sampled. Second, assuming the standard deviation is non-zero, the standard deviation of the sampling distribution of the mean equals the standard deviation of the sampled population divided by the square root of the sample size. This is sometimes called the standard error. Finally, as the sample size gets larger, the sampling distribution of the mean gets closer to a normal distribution via the central limit theorem.

SURVEY STUDY

A **survey study** is a method of gathering information from a small group in an attempt to gain enough information to make accurate general assumptions about the population. Once a survey study is completed, the results are then put into a summary report.

Survey studies are generally in the format of surveys, interviews, or questionnaires as part of an effort to find opinions of a particular group or to find facts about a group.

It is important to note that the findings from a survey study are only as accurate as the sample chosen from the population.

CORRELATIONAL STUDIES

Correlational studies seek to determine how much one variable is affected by changes in a second variable. For example, correlational studies may look for a relationship between the amount of time a student spends studying for a test and the grade that student earned on the test or between student scores on college admissions tests and student grades in college.

It is important to note that correlational studies cannot show a cause and effect, but rather can show only that two variables are or are not potentially correlated.

EXPERIMENTAL STUDIES

Experimental studies take correlational studies one step farther, in that they attempt to prove or disprove a cause-and-effect relationship. These studies are performed by conducting a series of experiments to test the hypothesis. For a study to be scientifically accurate, it must have both an experimental group that receives the specified treatment and a control group that does not get the treatment. This is the type of study pharmaceutical companies do as part of drug trials for new medications. Experimental studies are only valid when the proper scientific method has been followed. In other words, the experiment must be well-planned and executed without bias in the

testing process, all subjects must be selected at random, and the process of determining which subject is in which of the two groups must also be completely random.

OBSERVATIONAL STUDIES

Observational studies are the opposite of experimental studies. In observational studies, the tester cannot change or in any way control all of the variables in the test. For example, a study to determine which gender does better in math classes in school is strictly observational. You cannot change a person's gender, and you cannot change the subject being studied. The big downfall of observational studies is that you have no way of proving a cause-and-effect relationship because you cannot control outside influences. Events outside of school can influence a student's performance in school, and observational studies cannot take that into consideration.

RANDOM SAMPLES

For most studies, a **random sample** is necessary to produce valid results. Random samples should not have any particular influence to cause sampled subjects to behave one way or another. The goal is for the random sample to be a **representative sample**, or a sample whose characteristics give an accurate picture of the characteristics of the entire population. To accomplish this, you must make sure you have a proper **sample size**, or an appropriate number of elements in the sample.

BIASES

In statistical studies, biases must be avoided. **Bias** is an error that causes the study to favor one set of results over another. For example, if a survey to determine how the country views the president's job performance only speaks to registered voters in the president's party, the results will be skewed because a disproportionately large number of responders would tend to show approval, while a disproportionately large number of people in the opposite party would tend to express disapproval. **Extraneous variables** are, as the name implies, outside influences that can affect the outcome of a study. They are not always avoidable but could trigger bias in the result.

DATA ANALYSIS

DISPERSION

A **measure of dispersion** is a single value that helps to "interpret" the measure of central tendency by providing more information about how the data values in the set are distributed about the measure of central tendency. The measure of dispersion helps to eliminate or reduce the disadvantages of using the mean, median, or mode as a single measure of central tendency, and give a more accurate picture of the dataset as a whole. To have a measure of dispersion, you must know or calculate the range, standard deviation, or variance of the data set.

RANGE

The **range** of a set of data is the difference between the greatest and lowest values of the data in the set. To calculate the range, you must first make sure the units for all data values are the same, and then identify the greatest and lowest values. If there are multiple data values that are equal for the highest or lowest, just use one of the values in the formula. Write the answer with the same units as the data values you used to do the calculations.

> **Review Video: Statistical Range**
> Visit mometrix.com/academy and enter code: 778541

SAMPLE STANDARD DEVIATION

Standard deviation is a measure of dispersion that compares all the data values in the set to the mean of the set to give a more accurate picture. To find the **standard deviation of a sample**, use the formula

$$s = \sqrt{\frac{\sum_{i=1}^{n}(x_i - \bar{x})^2}{n-1}}$$

Note that s is the standard deviation of a sample, x_i represents the individual values in the data set, $\bar{x}$ is the mean of the data values in the set, and n is the number of data values in the set. The higher the value of the standard deviation is, the greater the variance of the data values from the mean. The units associated with the standard deviation are the same as the units of the data values.

> **Review Video: Standard Deviation**
> Visit mometrix.com/academy and enter code: 419469

SAMPLE VARIANCE

The **variance of a sample** is the square of the sample standard deviation (denoted s^2). While the mean of a set of data gives the average of the set and gives information about where a specific data value lies in relation to the average, the variance of the sample gives information about the degree to which the data values are spread out and tells you how close an individual value is to the average compared to the other values. The units associated with variance are the same as the units of the data values squared.

PERCENTILE

Percentiles and quartiles are other methods of describing data within a set. **Percentiles** tell what percentage of the data in the set fall below a specific point. For example, achievement test scores are often given in percentiles. A score at the 80th percentile is one which is equal to or higher than 80 percent of the scores in the set. In other words, 80 percent of the scores were lower than that score.

Quartiles are percentile groups that make up quarter sections of the data set. The first quartile is the 25th percentile. The second quartile is the 50th percentile; this is also the median of the dataset. The third quartile is the 75th percentile.

SKEWNESS

Skewness is a way to describe the symmetry or asymmetry of the distribution of values in a dataset. If the distribution of values is symmetrical, there is no skew. In general the closer the mean of a data set is to the median of the data set, the less skew there is. Generally, if the mean is to the right of the median, the data set is *positively skewed*, or right-skewed, and if the mean is to the left of the median, the data set is *negatively skewed*, or left-skewed. However, this rule of thumb is not infallible. When the data values are graphed on a curve, a set with no skew will be a perfect bell curve.

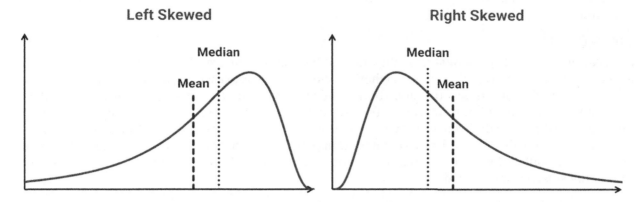

To estimate skew, use the formula:

$$\text{skew} = \frac{\sqrt{n(n-1)}}{n-2}\left(\frac{\frac{1}{n}\sum_{i=1}^{n}(x_i-\bar{x})^3}{\left(\frac{1}{n}\sum_{i=1}^{n}(x_i-\bar{x})^2\right)^{\frac{3}{2}}}\right)$$

Note that n is the datapoints in the set, x_i is the ith value in the set, and $\bar{x}$ is the mean of the set.

> **Review Video: Skew**
> Visit mometrix.com/academy and enter code: 661486

UNIMODAL VS. BIMODAL

If a distribution has a single peak, it would be considered **unimodal**. If it has two discernible peaks it would be considered **bimodal**. Bimodal distributions may be an indication that the set of data being considered is actually the combination of two sets of data with significant differences. A **uniform distribution** is a distribution in which there is *no distinct peak or variation* in the data. No values or ranges are particularly more common than any other values or ranges.

OUTLIER

An outlier is an extremely high or extremely low value in the data set. It may be the result of measurement error, in which case, the outlier is not a valid member of the data set. However, it may also be a valid member of the distribution. Unless a measurement error is identified, the experimenter cannot know for certain if an outlier is or is not a member of the distribution. There are arbitrary methods that can be employed to designate an extreme value as an outlier. One method designates an outlier (or possible outlier) to be any value less than $Q_1 - 1.5(IQR)$ or any value greater than $Q_3 + 1.5(IQR)$.

DATA ANALYSIS
SIMPLE REGRESSION

In statistics, **simple regression** is using an equation to represent a relation between independent and dependent variables. The independent variable is also referred to as the explanatory variable or the predictor and is generally represented by the variable x in the equation. The dependent variable, usually represented by the variable y, is also referred to as the response variable. The

159

equation may be any type of function – linear, quadratic, exponential, etc. The best way to handle this task is to use the regression feature of your graphing calculator. This will easily give you the curve of best fit and provide you with the coefficients and other information you need to derive an equation.

LINE OF BEST FIT

In a scatter plot, the **line of best fit** is the line that best shows the trends of the data. The line of best fit is given by the equation $\hat{y} = ax + b$, where a and b are the regression coefficients. The regression coefficient a is also the slope of the line of best fit, and b is also the y-coordinate of the point at which the line of best fit crosses the y-axis. Not every point on the scatter plot will be on the line of best fit. The differences between the y-values of the points in the scatter plot and the corresponding y-values according to the equation of the line of best fit are the residuals. The line of best fit is also called the least-squares regression line because it is also the line that has the lowest sum of the squares of the residuals.

CORRELATION COEFFICIENT

The **correlation coefficient** is the numerical value that indicates how strong the relationship is between the two variables of a linear regression equation. A correlation coefficient of –1 is a perfect negative correlation. A correlation coefficient of +1 is a perfect positive correlation. Correlation coefficients close to –1 or +1 are very strong correlations. A correlation coefficient equal to zero indicates there is no correlation between the two variables. This test is a good indicator of whether or not the equation for the line of best fit is accurate. The formula for the correlation coefficient is

$$r = \frac{\sum_{i=1}^{n}(x_i - \bar{x})(y_i - \bar{y})}{\sqrt{\sum_{i=1}^{n}(x_i - \bar{x})^2}\sqrt{\sum_{i=1}^{n}(y_i - \bar{y})^2}}$$

where r is the correlation coefficient, n is the number of data values in the set, (x_i, y_i) is a point in the set, and $\bar{x}$ and $\bar{y}$ are the means.

Z-SCORE

A **z-score** is an indication of how many standard deviations a given value falls from the sample mean. To calculate a z-score, use the formula:

$$\frac{x - \bar{x}}{\sigma}$$

In this formula x is the data value, $\bar{x}$ is the mean of the sample data, and σ is the standard deviation of the population. If the z-score is positive, the data value lies above the mean. If the z-score is negative, the data value falls below the mean. These scores are useful in interpreting data such as standardized test scores, where every piece of data in the set has been counted, rather than just a small random sample. In cases where standard deviations are calculated from a random sample of the set, the z-scores will not be as accurate.

CENTRAL LIMIT THEOREM

According to the **central limit theorem**, regardless of what the original distribution of a sample is, the distribution of the means tends to get closer and closer to a normal distribution as the sample size gets larger and larger (this is necessary because the sample is becoming more all-encompassing of the elements of the population). As the sample size gets larger, the distribution of the sample mean will approach a normal distribution with a mean of the population mean and a variance of the population variance divided by the sample size.

MEASURES OF CENTRAL TENDENCY

A **measure of central tendency** is a statistical value that gives a reasonable estimate for the center of a group of data. There are several different ways of describing the measure of central tendency. Each one has a unique way it is calculated, and each one gives a slightly different perspective on the data set. Whenever you give a measure of central tendency, always make sure the units are the same. If the data has different units, such as hours, minutes, and seconds, convert all the data to the same unit, and use the same unit in the measure of central tendency. If no units are given in the data, do not give units for the measure of central tendency.

MEAN

The **statistical mean** of a group of data is the same as the arithmetic average of that group. To find the mean of a set of data, first convert each value to the same units, if necessary. Then find the sum of all the values, and count the total number of data values, making sure you take into consideration each individual value. If a value appears more than once, count it more than once. Divide the sum of the values by the total number of values and apply the units, if any. Note that the mean does not have to be one of the data values in the set, and may not divide evenly.

$$\text{mean} = \frac{\text{sum of the data values}}{\text{quantity of data values}}$$

For instance, the mean of the data set {88, 72, 61, 90, 97, 68, 88, 79, 86, 93, 97, 71, 80, 84, 89} would be the sum of the fifteen numbers divided by 15:

$$\frac{88 + 72 + 61 + 90 + 97 + 68 + 88 + 79 + 86 + 93 + 97 + 71 + 80 + 84 + 89}{15} = \frac{1242}{15} = 82.8$$

While the mean is relatively easy to calculate and averages are understood by most people, the mean can be very misleading if it is used as the sole measure of central tendency. If the data set has outliers (data values that are unusually high or unusually low compared to the rest of the data values), the mean can be very distorted, especially if the data set has a small number of values. If unusually high values are countered with unusually low values, the mean is not affected as much. For example, if five of twenty students in a class get a 100 on a test, but the other 15 students have an average of 60 on the same test, the class average would appear as 70. Whenever the mean is skewed by outliers, it is always a good idea to include the median as an alternate measure of central tendency.

A **weighted mean**, or weighted average, is a mean that uses "weighted" values. The formula is weighted mean $= \frac{w_1 x_1 + w_2 x_2 + w_3 x_3 \dots + w_n x_n}{w_1 + w_2 + w_3 + \dots + w_n}$. Weighted values, such as $w_1, w_2, w_3, \dots w_n$ are assigned to each member of the set $x_1, x_2, x_3, \dots x_n$. When calculating the weighted mean, make sure a weight value for each member of the set is used.

Review Video: All About Averages
Visit mometrix.com/academy and enter code: 176521

MEDIAN

The **statistical median** is the value in the middle of the set of data. To find the median, list all data values in order from smallest to largest or from largest to smallest. Any value that is repeated in the set must be listed the number of times it appears. If there are an odd number of data values, the median is the value in the middle of the list. If there is an even number of data values, the median is the arithmetic mean of the two middle values.

For example, the median of the data set {88, 72, 61, 90, 97, 68, 88, 79, 86, 93, 97, 71, 80, 84, 88} is 86 since the ordered set is {61, 68, 71, 72, 79, 80, 84, **86**, 88, 88, 88, 90, 93, 97, 97}.

The big disadvantage of using the median as a measure of central tendency is that is relies solely on a value's relative size as compared to the other values in the set. When the individual values in a set of data are evenly dispersed, the median can be an accurate tool. However, if there is a group of rather large values or a group of rather small values that are not offset by a different group of values, the information that can be inferred from the median may not be accurate because the distribution of values is skewed.

MODE

The **statistical mode** is the data value that occurs the greatest number of times in the data set. It is possible to have exactly one mode, more than one mode, or no mode. To find the mode of a set of data, arrange the data like you do to find the median (all values in order, listing all multiples of data values). Count the number of times each value appears in the data set. If all values appear an equal number of times, there is no mode. If one value appears more than any other value, that value is the mode. If two or more values appear the same number of times, but there are other values that appear fewer times and no values that appear more times, all of those values are the modes.

For example, the mode of the data set {**88**, 72, 61, 90, 97, 68, **88**, 79, 86, 93, 97, 71, 80, 84, **88**} is 88.

The main disadvantage of the mode is that the values of the other data in the set have no bearing on the mode. The mode may be the largest value, the smallest value, or a value anywhere in between in the set. The mode only tells which value or values, if any, occurred the greatest number of times. It does not give any suggestions about the remaining values in the set.

> **Review Video: Mean, Median, and Mode**
> Visit mometrix.com/academy and enter code: 286207

STANDARD DEVIATION

The **standard deviation** (σ) of a data set measures variation, or how spread out the values are. To calculate it, first find the mean of the data set. Then find the difference of each value and the mean and square the differences. Find the **variance** (σ^2) by adding each of these squared differences together and dividing by one less than the number of values. Finally, take the root of the variance and you have the standard deviation.

> **Review Video: Standard Deviation**
> Visit mometrix.com/academy and enter code: 419469

EXAMPLE

For the following data set (4, 8, 2, 7, 11, 13, 6, 5, 7), we first find the mean:

$$\frac{4 + 8 + 2 + 7 + 11 + 13 + 6 + 5 + 7}{9} = 7$$

Then we find the difference of each value and the mean, square and add them, and divide by one less than the number of data points:

$$\sigma^2 = \frac{(7-4)^2 + (7-8)^2 + (7-2)^2 + (7-7)^2 + (7-11)^2 + (7-13)^2 + (7-6)^2 + (7-5)^2 + (7-7)^2}{9-1}$$

$$= \frac{9 + 1 + 25 + 0 + 16 + 36 + 1 + 4 + 0}{8}$$

$$= \frac{92}{8}$$

$$= 11.5$$

So the variance is 11.5, and we take the root to find the standard deviation: $\sigma = \sqrt{11.5} \approx 3.39$.

DISTRIBUTIONS

NORMAL DISTRIBUTIONS

If a distribution is **normal**, this means that the variables are mostly symmetrical about the mean. Approximately half of the values are below the mean and half are above. Most values are clustered closely about the mean, with approximately 68% within one standard deviation, 95% within two standard deviations, and 99.7% within three standard deviations. Anything beyond this is an **outlier**.

EXAMPLE

If the height of freshman women at a university is normally distributed with a mean of 66" and a standard deviation of 1.5", we can calculate the percentage of women in various height brackets. Since the standard deviation is 1.5" and 68% of values in a normal distribution fall within one distribution, we can say that approximately 68% of the freshman women are between 64.5" and 67.5", 95% are between 63" and 69", and 99.7% within 61.5" and 70.5". Anyone shorter than 61.5" or taller than 70.5" is an outlier.

UNIFORM DISTRIBUTIONS

In a **uniform distribution**, every outcome is equally likely. For instance, in flipping a fair coin or rolling a die, each outcome is as likely as any of the others. A random generator is another example, since each number within the parameters has an equal chance of being selected.

EXAMPLE

Suppose a collection of songs has a range of anywhere from 4 to 11 notes, inclusive, and they are distributed uniformly. We could find the probability that a given song has six or fewer notes. There are eight possibilities (from 4 to 11) and three of them have six or fewer notes (4, 5, 6). So the probability is $\frac{3}{8}$ or 0.375.

BINOMIAL DISTRIBUTIONS

A binomial distribution has two possible outcomes, like flipping a coin or a true/false quiz. It is typically used on a series of trials (like flipping a coin 50 times). None of the trials impact the others, so the probability of success or failure is the same on each, but the number of trials can affect overall probability. For example, flipping a coin 20 times gives a much higher probability of getting at least one heads than flipping it once, even though the probability for each individual flip is the same. The formula for **binomial distribution** is $P_x = \binom{n}{x} p^x q^{n-x}$, where P is the probability, n is the number of trials, x is the number of times of the desired outcome, p is the probability of success on any trial, and q is the probability of failure on any trial.

EXAMPLE

Suppose a jar has 20 marbles, 10 red and 10 blue. If Lea draws a marble 10 times, replacing it after each draw, there is a 50% chance on each draw of getting red, and a 50% chance of getting blue, so this is a binomial distribution. The probability of getting three reds can be calculated:

$$P_3 = \binom{10}{3}\left(\frac{1}{2}\right)^3 \left(\frac{1}{2}\right)^7 = \frac{10!}{3!\,7!}(0.5)^3(0.5)^7 = \frac{10 \times 9 \times 8 \times 7 \times 6 \times 5 \times 4 \times 3 \times 2 \times 1}{7 \times 6 \times 5 \times 4 \times 3 \times 2 \times 1 \times 3 \times 2 \times 1}\left(\frac{1}{2}\right)^{10} = \frac{15}{128}$$

DISPLAYING INFORMATION

FREQUENCY TABLES

Frequency tables show how frequently each unique value appears in a set. A **relative frequency table** is one that shows the proportions of each unique value compared to the entire set. Relative frequencies are given as percentages; however, the total percent for a relative frequency table will not necessarily equal 100 percent due to rounding. An example of a frequency table with relative frequencies is below.

Favorite Color	Frequency	Relative Frequency
Blue	4	13%
Red	7	22%
Green	3	9%
Purple	6	19%
Cyan	12	38%

> **Review Video: Data Interpretation of Graphs**
> Visit mometrix.com/academy and enter code: 200439

CIRCLE GRAPHS

Circle graphs, also known as *pie charts*, provide a visual depiction of the relationship of each type of data compared to the whole set of data. The circle graph is divided into sections by drawing radii to create central angles whose percentage of the circle is equal to the individual data's percentage of the whole set. Each 1% of data is equal to 3.6° in the circle graph. Therefore, data represented by a 90° section of the circle graph makes up 25% of the whole. When complete, a circle graph often looks like a pie cut into uneven wedges. The pie chart below shows the data from the frequency table referenced earlier where people were asked their favorite color.

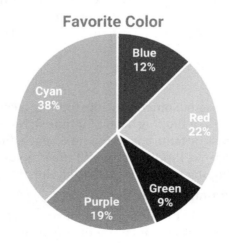

Favorite Color

164

PICTOGRAPHS

A **pictograph** is a graph, generally in the horizontal orientation, that uses pictures or symbols to represent the data. Each pictograph must have a key that defines the picture or symbol and gives the quantity each picture or symbol represents. Pictures or symbols on a pictograph are not always shown as whole elements. In this case, the fraction of the picture or symbol shown represents the same fraction of the quantity a whole picture or symbol stands for. For example, a row with $3\frac{1}{2}$ ears of corn, where each ear of corn represents 100 stalks of corn in a field, would equal $3\frac{1}{2} \times 100 = 350$ stalks of corn in the field.

Name	Number of ears of corn eaten	Field	Number of stalks of corn
Michael	🌽🌽🌽🌽🌽	Field 1	🌽🌽🌽🌽🌽
Tara	🌽🌽	Field 2	🌽🌽🌽
John	🌽🌽🌽🌽	Field 3	🌽🌽🌽🌽
Sara	🌽	Field 4	🌽
Jacob	🌽🌽🌽	Field 5	🌽🌽🌽🌽

Each 🌽 represents 1 ear of corn eaten. Each 🌽 represents 100 stalks of corn.

Review Video: Pictographs
Visit mometrix.com/academy and enter code: 147860

LINE GRAPHS

Line graphs have one or more lines of varying styles (solid or broken) to show the different values for a set of data. The individual data are represented as ordered pairs, much like on a Cartesian plane. In this case, the x- and y-axes are defined in terms of their units, such as dollars or time. The individual plotted points are joined by line segments to show whether the value of the data is increasing (line sloping upward), decreasing (line sloping downward), or staying the same (horizontal line). Multiple sets of data can be graphed on the same line graph to give an easy visual comparison. An example of this would be graphing achievement test scores for different groups of students over the same time period to see which group had the greatest increase or decrease in performance from year to year (as shown below).

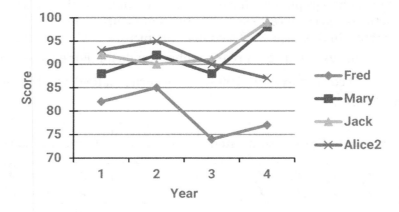

LINE PLOTS

A **line plot**, also known as a *dot plot*, has plotted points that are not connected by line segments. In this graph, the horizontal axis lists the different possible values for the data, and the vertical axis lists the number of times the individual value occurs. A single dot is graphed for each value to show the number of times it occurs. This graph is more closely related to a bar graph than a line graph. Do not connect the dots in a line plot or it will misrepresent the data.

STEM AND LEAF PLOTS

A **stem and leaf plot** is useful for depicting groups of data that fall into a range of values. Each piece of data is separated into two parts: the first, or left, part is called the stem; the second, or right, part is called the leaf. Each stem is listed in a column from smallest to largest. Each leaf that has the common stem is listed in that stem's row from smallest to largest. For example, in a set of two-digit numbers, the digit in the tens place is the stem, and the digit in the ones place is the leaf. With a stem and leaf plot, you can easily see which subset of numbers (10s, 20s, 30s, etc.) is the largest. This information is also readily available by looking at a histogram, but a stem and leaf plot also allows you to look closer and see exactly which values fall in that range. Using a sample set of test scores (82, 88, 92, 93, 85, 90, 92, 95, 74, 88, 90, 91, 78, 87, 98, 99), we can assemble a stem and leaf plot like the one below.

Test Scores

7	4	8						
8	2	5	7	8	8			
9	0	0	1	2	2	3	5	8	9

BAR GRAPHS

A **bar graph** is one of the few graphs that can be drawn correctly in two different configurations – both horizontally and vertically. A bar graph is similar to a line plot in the way the data is organized on the graph. Both axes must have their categories defined for the graph to be useful. Rather than placing a single dot to mark the point of the data's value, a bar, or thick line, is drawn from zero to the exact value of the data, whether it is a number, percentage, or other numerical value. Longer bar lengths correspond to greater data values. To read a bar graph, read the labels for the axes to find the units being reported. Then, look where the bars end in relation to the scale given on the corresponding axis and determine the associated value.

The bar chart below represents the responses from our favorite-color survey.

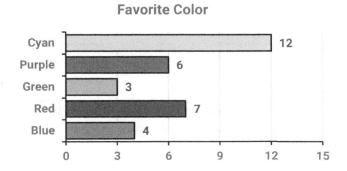

HISTOGRAMS

At first glance, a **histogram** looks like a vertical bar graph. The difference is that a bar graph has a separate bar for each piece of data and a histogram has one continuous bar for each *range* of data. For example, a histogram may have one bar for the range 0–9, one bar for 10–19, etc. While a bar graph has numerical values on one axis, a histogram has numerical values on both axes. Each range is of equal size, and they are ordered left to right from lowest to highest. The height of each column on a histogram represents the number of data values within that range. Like a stem and leaf plot, a histogram makes it easy to glance at the graph and quickly determine which range has the greatest quantity of values. A simple example of a histogram is below.

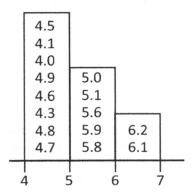

5-NUMBER SUMMARY

The **5-number summary** of a set of data gives a very informative picture of the set. The five numbers in the summary include the minimum value, maximum value, and the three quartiles. This information gives the reader the range and median of the set, as well as an indication of how the data is spread about the median.

BOX AND WHISKER PLOTS

A **box-and-whiskers plot** is a graphical representation of the 5-number summary. To draw a box-and-whiskers plot, plot the points of the 5-number summary on a number line. Draw a box whose ends are through the points for the first and third quartiles. Draw a vertical line in the box through the median to divide the box in half. Draw a line segment from the first quartile point to the minimum value, and from the third quartile point to the maximum value.

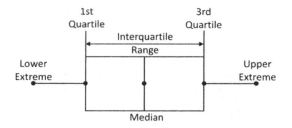

> ### Review Video: Box and Whisker Plots
> Visit mometrix.com/academy and enter code: 810817

EXAMPLE

Given the following data (32, 28, 29, 26, 35, 27, 30, 31, 27, 32), we first sort it into numerical order: 26, 27, 27, 28, 29, 30, 31, 32, 32, 35. We can then find the median. Since there are ten values, we take the average of the 5th and 6th values to get 29.5. We find the lower quartile by taking the median of the data smaller than the median. Since there are five values, we take the 3rd value, which is 27. We find the upper quartile by taking the median of the data larger than the overall median, which is 32. Finally, we note our minimum and maximum, which are simply the smallest and largest values in the set: 26 and 35, respectively. Now we can create our box plot:

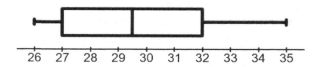

This plot is fairly "long" on the right whisker, showing one or more unusually high values (but not quite outliers). The other quartiles are similar in length, showing a fairly even distribution of data.

INTERQUARTILE RANGE

The **interquartile range, or IQR**, is the difference between the upper and lower quartiles. It measures how the data is dispersed: a high IQR means that the data is more spread out, while a low IQR means that the data is clustered more tightly around the median. To find the IQR, subtract the lower quartile value (Q_1) from the upper quartile value (Q_3).

EXAMPLE

To find the upper and lower quartiles, we first find the median and then take the median of all values above it and all values below it. In the following data set (16, 18, 13, 24, 16, 51, 32, 21, 27, 39), we first rearrange the values in numerical order: 13, 16, 16, 18, 21, 24, 27, 32, 39, 51. There are

10 values, so the median is the average of the 5th and 6th: $\frac{21+24}{2} = \frac{45}{2} = 22.5$. We do not actually need this value to find the upper and lower quartiles. We look at the set of numbers below the median: 13, 16, 16, 18, 21. There are five values, so the 3rd is the median (16), or the value of the lower quartile (Q_1). Then we look at the numbers above the median: 24, 27, 32, 39, 51. Again there are five values, so the 3rd is the median (32), or the value of the upper quartile (Q_3). We find the IQR by subtracting Q_1 from Q_3: $32 - 16 = 16$.

68-95-99.7 RULE

The **68–95–99.7 rule** describes how a normal distribution of data should appear when compared to the mean. This is also a description of a normal bell curve. According to this rule, 68 percent of the data values in a normally distributed set should fall within one standard deviation of the mean (34 percent above and 34 percent below the mean), 95 percent of the data values should fall within two standard deviations of the mean (47.5 percent above and 47.5 percent below the mean), and 99.7 percent of the data values should fall within three standard deviations of the mean, again, equally distributed on either side of the mean. This means that only 0.3 percent of all data values should fall more than three standard deviations from the mean. On the graph below, the normal curve is centered on the y-axis. The x-axis labels are how many standard deviations away from the center you are. Therefore, it is easy to see how the 68-95-99.7 rule can apply.

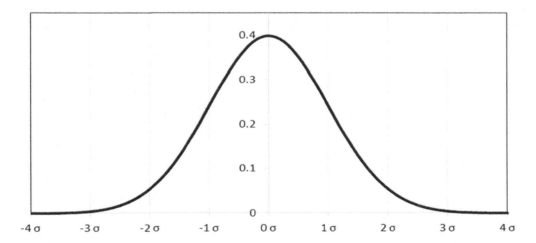

SCATTER PLOTS
BIVARIATE DATA

Bivariate data is simply data from two different variables. (The prefix *bi-* means *two*.) In a *scatter plot*, each value in the set of data is plotted on a grid similar to a Cartesian plane, where each axis represents one of the two variables. By looking at the pattern formed by the points on the grid, you can often determine whether or not there is a relationship between the two variables, and what that relationship is, if it exists. The variables may be directly proportionate, inversely proportionate, or show no proportion at all. It may also be possible to determine if the data is linear, and if so, to find an equation to relate the two variables. The following scatter plot shows the relationship between preference for brand "A" and the age of the consumers surveyed.

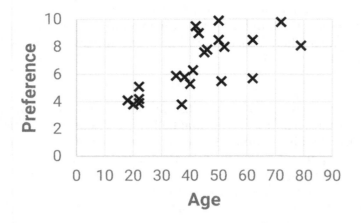

SCATTER PLOTS

Scatter plots are also useful in determining the type of function represented by the data and finding the simple regression. Linear scatter plots may be positive or negative. Nonlinear scatter plots are generally exponential or quadratic. Below are some common types of scatter plots:

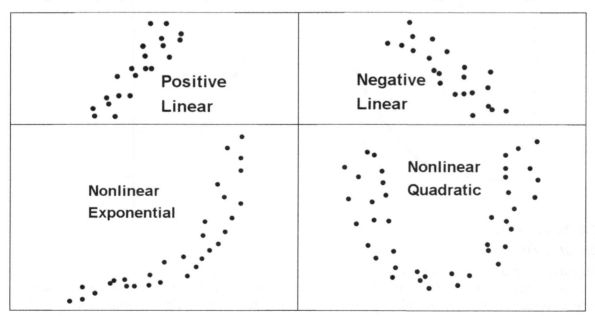

Review Video: What is a Scatter Plot?
Visit mometrix.com/academy and enter code: 596526

Geometry and Trigonometry

POINTS, LINES, AND PLANES

POINTS AND LINES

A **point** is a fixed location in space, has no size or dimensions, and is commonly represented by a dot. A **line** is a set of points that extends infinitely in two opposite directions. It has length, but no width or depth. A line can be defined by any two distinct points that it contains. A **line segment** is a portion of a line that has definite endpoints. A **ray** is a portion of a line that extends from a single point on that line in one direction along the line. It has a definite beginning, but no ending.

INTERACTIONS BETWEEN LINES

Intersecting lines are lines that have exactly one point in common. **Concurrent lines** are multiple lines that intersect at a single point. **Perpendicular lines** are lines that intersect at right angles. They are represented by the symbol ⊥. The shortest distance from a line to a point not on the line is a perpendicular segment from the point to the line. **Parallel lines** are lines in the same plane that have no points in common and never meet. It is possible for lines to be in different planes, have no points in common, and never meet, but they are not parallel because they are in different planes.

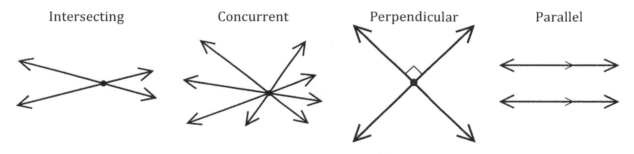

Review Video: Parallel and Perpendicular Lines
Visit mometrix.com/academy and enter code: 815923

A **transversal** is a line that intersects at least two other lines, which may or may not be parallel to one another. A transversal that intersects parallel lines is a common occurrence in geometry. A **bisector** is a line or line segment that divides another line segment into two equal lengths. A **perpendicular bisector** of a line segment is composed of points that are equidistant from the endpoints of the segment it is dividing.

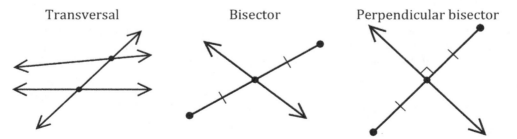

The **projection of a point on a line** is the point at which a perpendicular line drawn from the given point to the given line intersects the line. This is also the shortest distance from the given point to

171

the line. The **projection of a segment on a line** is a segment whose endpoints are the points formed when perpendicular lines are drawn from the endpoints of the given segment to the given line. This is similar to the length a diagonal line appears to be when viewed from above.

Projection of a point on a line   Projection of a segment on a line

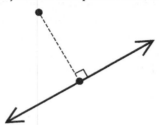 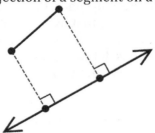

PLANES

A **plane** is a two-dimensional flat surface defined by three non-collinear points. A plane extends an infinite distance in all directions in those two dimensions. It contains an infinite number of points, parallel lines and segments, intersecting lines and segments, as well as parallel or intersecting rays. A plane will never contain a three-dimensional figure or skew lines, which are lines that don't intersect and are not parallel. Two given planes are either parallel or they intersect at a line. A plane may intersect a circular conic surface to form **conic sections**, such as a parabola, hyperbola, circle or ellipse.

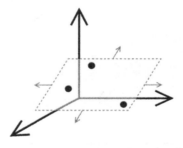

Review Video: Lines and Planes
Visit mometrix.com/academy and enter code: 554267

ANGLES
ANGLES AND VERTICES

An **angle** is formed when two lines or line segments meet at a common point. It may be a common starting point for a pair of segments or rays, or it may be the intersection of lines. Angles are represented by the symbol ∠.

The **vertex** is the point at which two segments or rays meet to form an angle. If the angle is formed by intersecting rays, lines, and/or line segments, the vertex is the point at which four angles are formed. The pairs of angles opposite one another are called vertical angles, and their measures are equal.

- An **acute** angle is an angle with a degree measure less than 90°.
- A **right** angle is an angle with a degree measure of exactly 90°.
- An **obtuse** angle is an angle with a degree measure greater than 90° but less than 180°.

- A **straight angle** is an angle with a degree measure of exactly 180°. This is also a semicircle.
- A **reflex angle** is an angle with a degree measure greater than 180° but less than 360°.
- A **full angle** is an angle with a degree measure of exactly 360°. This is also a circle.

Review Video: Angles
Visit mometrix.com/academy and enter code: 264624

RELATIONSHIPS BETWEEN ANGLES

Two angles whose sum is exactly 90° are said to be **complementary**. The two angles may or may not be adjacent. In a right triangle, the two acute angles are complementary.

Two angles whose sum is exactly 180° are said to be **supplementary**. The two angles may or may not be adjacent. Two intersecting lines always form two pairs of supplementary angles. Adjacent supplementary angles will always form a straight line.

Two angles that have the same vertex and share a side are said to be **adjacent**. Vertical angles are not adjacent because they share a vertex but no common side.

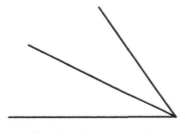

Adjacent
Share vertex and side

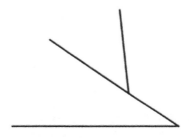

Not adjacent
Share part of a side, but not vertex

When two parallel lines are cut by a transversal, the angles that are between the two parallel lines are **interior angles**. In the diagram below, angles 3, 4, 5, and 6 are interior angles.

When two parallel lines are cut by a transversal, the angles that are outside the parallel lines are **exterior angles**. In the diagram below, angles 1, 2, 7, and 8 are exterior angles.

When two parallel lines are cut by a transversal, the angles that are in the same position relative to the transversal and a parallel line are **corresponding angles**. The diagram below has four pairs of corresponding angles: angles 1 and 5, angles 2 and 6, angles 3 and 7, and angles 4 and 8. Corresponding angles formed by parallel lines are congruent.

When two parallel lines are cut by a transversal, the two interior angles that are on opposite sides of the transversal are called **alternate interior angles**. In the diagram below, there are two pairs of alternate interior angles: angles 3 and 6, and angles 4 and 5. Alternate interior angles formed by parallel lines are congruent.

When two parallel lines are cut by a transversal, the two exterior angles that are on opposite sides of the transversal are called **alternate exterior angles**.

In the diagram below, there are two pairs of alternate exterior angles: angles 1 and 8, and angles 2 and 7. Alternate exterior angles formed by parallel lines are congruent.

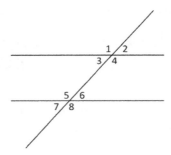

When two lines intersect, four angles are formed. The non-adjacent angles at this vertex are called vertical angles. Vertical angles are congruent. In the diagram, $\angle ABD \cong \angle CBE$ and $\angle ABC \cong \angle DBE$. The other pairs of angles, $(\angle ABC, \angle CBE)$ and $(\angle ABD, \angle DBE)$, are supplementary, meaning the pairs sum to $180°$.

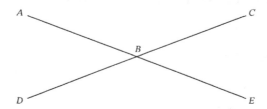

POLYGONS

A **polygon** is a closed, two-dimensional figure with three or more straight line segments called **sides**. The point at which two sides of a polygon intersect is called the **vertex**. In a polygon, the number of sides is always equal to the number of vertices. A polygon with all sides congruent and all angles equal is called a **regular polygon**. Common polygons are:

Triangle = 3 sides
Quadrilateral = 4 sides
Pentagon = 5 sides
Hexagon = 6 sides
Heptagon = 7 sides
Octagon = 8 sides
Nonagon = 9 sides
Decagon = 10 sides
Dodecagon = 12 sides

More generally, an n-gon is a polygon that has n angles and n sides.

> **Review Video: Intro to Polygons**
> Visit mometrix.com/academy and enter code: 271869

The sum of the interior angles of an n-sided polygon is $(n - 2) \times 180°$. For example, in a triangle $n = 3$. So the sum of the interior angles is $(3 - 2) \times 180° = 180°$. In a quadrilateral, $n = 4$, and the sum of the angles is $(4 - 2) \times 180° = 360°$.

> **Review Video: Sum of Interior Angles**
> Visit mometrix.com/academy and enter code: 984991

CONVEX AND CONCAVE POLYGONS

A **convex polygon** is a polygon whose diagonals all lie within the interior of the polygon. A **concave polygon** is a polygon with a least one diagonal that is outside the polygon. In the diagram below, quadrilateral $ABCD$ is concave because diagonal $\overline{AC}$ lies outside the polygon and quadrilateral $EFGH$ is convex because both diagonals lie inside the polygon.

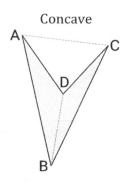

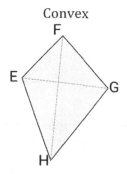

CONGRUENCE AND SIMILARITY

Congruent figures are geometric figures that have the same size and shape. All corresponding angles are equal, and all corresponding sides are equal. Congruence is indicated by the symbol ≅.

Congruent polygons

Similar figures are geometric figures that have the same shape, but do not necessarily have the same size. All corresponding angles are equal, and all corresponding sides are proportional, but they do not have to be equal. It is indicated by the symbol ~.

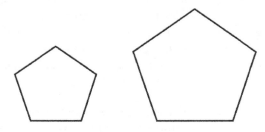

Similar polygons

Note that all congruent figures are also similar, but not all similar figures are congruent.

Review Video: Congruent Shapes
Visit mometrix.com/academy and enter code: 492281

TRIANGLES

A triangle is a three-sided figure with the sum of its interior angles being 180°. The **perimeter of any triangle** is found by summing the three side lengths; $P = a + b + c$. For an equilateral triangle, this is the same as $P = 3a$, where a is any side length, since all three sides are the same length.

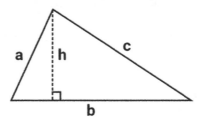

The **area of any triangle** can be found by taking half the product of one side length referred to as the base, often given the variable b and the perpendicular distance from that side to the opposite vertex called the altitude or height and given the variable h. In equation form that is $A = \frac{1}{2}bh$. Another formula that works for any triangle is $A = \sqrt{s(s-a)(s-b)(s-c)}$, where s is the semiperimeter: $\frac{a+b+c}{2}$, and a, b, and c are the lengths of the three sides. Special cases include isosceles triangles, $A = \frac{1}{2}b\sqrt{a^2 - \frac{b^2}{4}}$, where b is the unique side and a is the length of one of the two congruent sides, and equilateral triangles, $A = \frac{\sqrt{3}}{4}a^2$, where a is the length of a side.

PARTS OF A TRIANGLE

An **altitude** of a triangle is a line segment drawn from one vertex perpendicular to the opposite side. In the diagram that follows, $\overline{BE}$, $\overline{AD}$, and $\overline{CF}$ are altitudes. The length of an altitude is also called the height of the triangle. The three altitudes in a triangle are always concurrent. The point of concurrency of the altitudes of a triangle, O, is called the **orthocenter**. Note that in an obtuse triangle, the orthocenter will be outside the triangle, and in a right triangle, the orthocenter is the vertex of the right angle.

A **median** of a triangle is a line segment drawn from one vertex to the midpoint of the opposite side. In the diagram that follows, $\overline{BH}$, $\overline{AG}$, and $\overline{CI}$ are medians. This is not the same as the altitude, except the altitude to the base of an isosceles triangle and all three altitudes of an equilateral triangle. The point of concurrency of the medians of a triangle, T, is called the **centroid**. This is the same point as the orthocenter only in an equilateral triangle. Unlike the orthocenter, the centroid is always inside the triangle. The centroid can also be considered the exact center of the triangle. Any shape triangle can be perfectly balanced on a tip placed at the centroid. The centroid is also the point that is two-thirds the distance from the vertex to the opposite side.

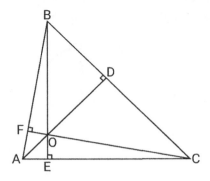 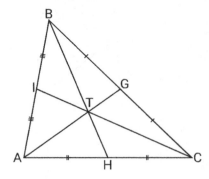

TRIANGLE PROPERTIES
CLASSIFICATIONS OF TRIANGLES

A **scalene triangle** is a triangle with no congruent sides. A scalene triangle will also have three angles of different measures. The angle with the largest measure is opposite the longest side, and the angle with the smallest measure is opposite the shortest side. An **acute triangle** is a triangle whose three angles are all less than 90°. If two of the angles are equal, the acute triangle is also an **isosceles triangle**. An isosceles triangle will also have two congruent angles opposite the two congruent sides. If the three angles are all equal, the acute triangle is also an **equilateral triangle**. An equilateral triangle will also have three congruent angles, each 60°. All equilateral triangles are also acute triangles. An **obtuse triangle** is a triangle with exactly one angle greater than 90°. The other two angles may or may not be equal. If the two remaining angles are equal, the obtuse triangle is also an isosceles triangle. A **right triangle** is a triangle with exactly one angle equal to 90°. All right triangles follow the Pythagorean theorem. A right triangle can never be acute or obtuse.

The table below illustrates how each descriptor places a different restriction on the triangle:

Sides \ Angles	Acute: All angles < 90°	Obtuse: One angle > 90°	Right: One angle = 90°
Scalene: No equal side lengths	$90° > \angle a > \angle b > \angle c$ $x > y > z$	$\angle a > 90° > \angle b > \angle c$ $x > y > z$	$90° = \angle a > \angle b > \angle c$ $x > y > z$
Isosceles: Two equal side lengths	$90° > \angle a, \angle b, or \angle c$ $\angle b = \angle c, \qquad y = z$	$\angle a > 90° > \angle b = \angle c$ $x > y = z$	$\angle a = 90°$ $\angle b = \angle c = 45°$ $x > y = z$
Equilateral: Three equal side lengths	$60° = \angle a = \angle b = \angle c$ $x = y = z$		

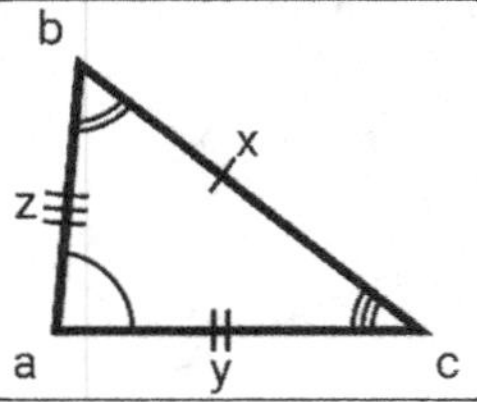

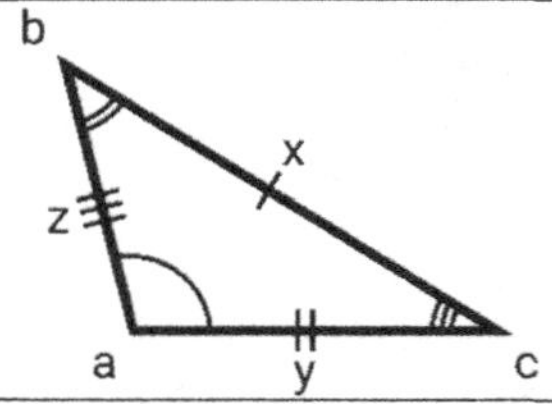

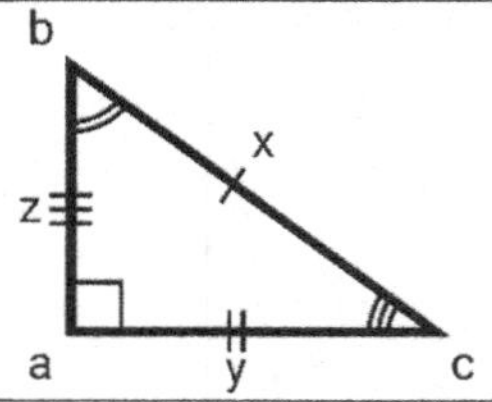

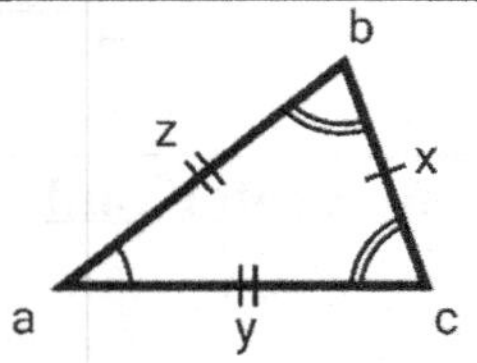

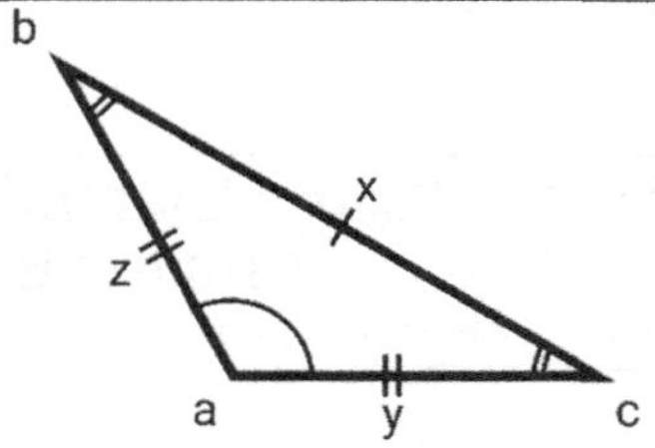

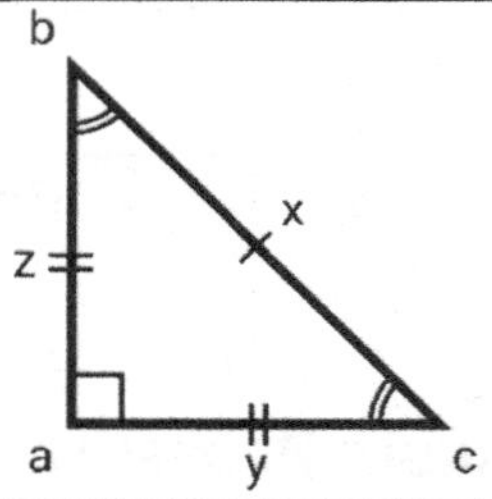

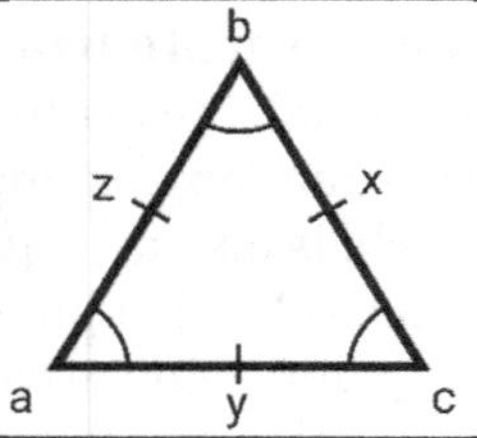

Review Video: Introduction to Types of Triangles
Visit mometrix.com/academy and enter code: 511711

GENERAL RULES FOR TRIANGLES

The **triangle inequality theorem** states that the sum of the measures of any two sides of a triangle is always greater than the measure of the third side. If the sum of the measures of two sides were equal to the third side, a triangle would be impossible because the two sides would lie flat across the third side and there would be no vertex. If the sum of the measures of two of the sides was less than the third side, a closed figure would be impossible because the two shortest sides would never meet. In other words, for a triangle with sides lengths A, B, and C: $A + B > C$, $B + C > A$, and $A + C > B$.

The sum of the measures of the interior angles of a triangle is always 180°. Therefore, a triangle can never have more than one angle greater than or equal to 90°.

In any triangle, the angles opposite congruent sides are congruent, and the sides opposite congruent angles are congruent. The largest angle is always opposite the longest side, and the smallest angle is always opposite the shortest side.

The line segment that joins the midpoints of any two sides of a triangle is always parallel to the third side and exactly half the length of the third side.

> **Review Video: General Rules (Triangle Inequality Theorem)**
> Visit mometrix.com/academy and enter code: 166488

SIMILARITY AND CONGRUENCE RULES

Similar triangles are triangles whose corresponding angles are equal and whose corresponding sides are proportional. Represented by AAA. Similar triangles whose corresponding sides are congruent are also congruent triangles.

Triangles can be shown to be **congruent** in 5 ways:

- **SSS**: Three sides of one triangle are congruent to the three corresponding sides of the second triangle.
- **SAS**: Two sides and the included angle (the angle formed by those two sides) of one triangle are congruent to the corresponding two sides and included angle of the second triangle.
- **ASA**: Two angles and the included side (the side that joins the two angles) of one triangle are congruent to the corresponding two angles and included side of the second triangle.
- **AAS**: Two angles and a non-included side of one triangle are congruent to the corresponding two angles and non-included side of the second triangle.
- **HL**: The hypotenuse and leg of one right triangle are congruent to the corresponding hypotenuse and leg of the second right triangle.

> **Review Video: Similar Triangles**
> Visit mometrix.com/academy and enter code: 398538

TRANSFORMATIONS
ROTATION

A **rotation** is a transformation that turns a figure around a point called the **center of rotation**, which can lie anywhere in the plane. If a line is drawn from a point on a figure to the center of rotation, and another line is drawn from the center to the rotated image of that point, the angle between the two lines is the **angle of rotation**. The vertex of the angle of rotation is the center of rotation.

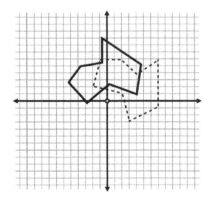

TRANSLATION AND DILATION

A **translation** is a transformation which slides a figure from one position in the plane to another position in the plane. The original figure and the translated figure have the same size, shape, and orientation. A **dilation** is a transformation which proportionally stretches or shrinks a figure by a **scale factor**. The dilated image is the same shape and orientation as the original image but a different size. A polygon and its dilated image are similar.

Translation

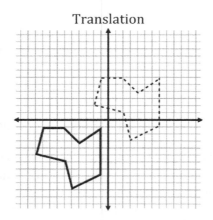

Dilation

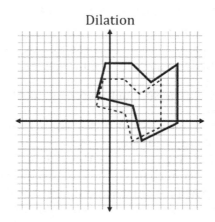

A **reflection of a figure over a line** (a "flip") creates a congruent image that is the same distance from the line as the original figure but on the opposite side. The **line of reflection** is the perpendicular bisector of any line segment drawn from a point on the original figure to its reflected image (unless the point and its reflected image happen to be the same point, which happens when a figure is reflected over one of its own sides). A **reflection of a figure over a point** (an inversion) in two dimensions is the same as the rotation of the figure 180° about that point. The image of the figure is congruent to the original figure. The **point of reflection** is the midpoint of a line segment which connects a point in the figure to its image (unless the point and its reflected image happen to be the same point, which happens when a figure is reflected in one of its own points).

Reflection of a figure over a line

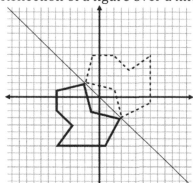

Reflection of a figure over a point

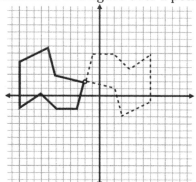

> **Review Video: Reflection**
> Visit mometrix.com/academy and enter code: 955068

PYTHAGOREAN THEOREM

The side of a triangle opposite the right angle is called the **hypotenuse**. The other two sides are called the legs. The Pythagorean theorem states a relationship among the legs and hypotenuse of a right triangle: $(a^2 + b^2 = c^2)$, where a and b are the lengths of the legs of a right triangle, and c is the length of the hypotenuse. Note that this formula will only work with right triangles.

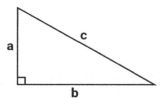

> **Review Video: Pythagorean Theorem**
> Visit mometrix.com/academy and enter code: 906576

TRIGONOMETRIC FORMULAS

In the diagram below, angle C is the right angle, and side c is the hypotenuse. Side a is the side opposite to angle A and side b is the side opposite to angle B. Using ratios of side lengths as a means to calculate the sine, cosine, and tangent of an acute angle only works for right triangles.

$$\sin A = \frac{\text{opposite side}}{\text{hypotenuse}} = \frac{a}{c} \qquad \csc A = \frac{1}{\sin A} = \frac{\text{hypotenuse}}{\text{opposite side}} = \frac{c}{a}$$

$$\cos A = \frac{\text{adjacent side}}{\text{hypotenuse}} = \frac{b}{c} \qquad \sec A = \frac{1}{\cos A} = \frac{\text{hypotenuse}}{\text{adjacent side}} = \frac{c}{b}$$

$$\tan A = \frac{\text{opposite side}}{\text{adjacent side}} = \frac{a}{b} \qquad \cot A = \frac{1}{\tan A} = \frac{\text{adjacent side}}{\text{opposite side}} = \frac{b}{a}$$

LAWS OF SINES AND COSINES

The **law of sines** states that $\frac{\sin A}{a} = \frac{\sin B}{b} = \frac{\sin C}{c}$, where A, B, and C are the angles of a triangle, and a, b, and c are the sides opposite their respective angles. This formula will work with all triangles, not just right triangles.

The **law of cosines** is given by the formula $c^2 = a^2 + b^2 - 2ab(\cos C)$, where a, b, and c are the sides of a triangle, and C is the angle opposite side c. This is a generalized form of the Pythagorean theorem that can be used on any triangle.

> **Review Video: <u>Upper Level Trig: Law of Sines</u>**
> Visit mometrix.com/academy and enter code: 206844
>
> **Review Video: <u>Upper Level Trig: Law of Cosines</u>**
> Visit mometrix.com/academy and enter code: 158911

QUADRILATERALS

A **quadrilateral** is a closed two-dimensional geometric figure that has four straight sides. The sum of the interior angles of any quadrilateral is 360°.

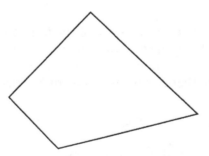

> **Review Video: <u>Diagonals of Parallelograms, Rectangles, and Rhombi</u>**
> Visit mometrix.com/academy and enter code: 320040

KITE

A **kite** is a quadrilateral with two pairs of adjacent sides that are congruent. A result of this is perpendicular diagonals. A kite can be concave or convex and has one line of symmetry.

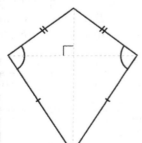
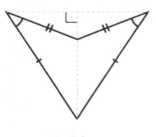

TRAPEZOID

Trapezoid: A trapezoid is defined as a quadrilateral that has at least one pair of parallel sides. There are no rules for the second pair of sides. So, there are no rules for the diagonals and no lines of symmetry for a trapezoid.

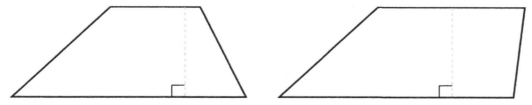

The **area of a trapezoid** is found by the formula $A = \frac{1}{2}h(b_1 + b_2)$, where h is the height (segment joining and perpendicular to the parallel bases), and b_1 and b_2 are the two parallel sides (bases). Do not use one of the other two sides as the height unless that side is also perpendicular to the parallel bases.

The **perimeter of a trapezoid** is found by the formula $P = a + b_1 + c + b_2$, where a, b_1, c, and b_2 are the four sides of the trapezoid.

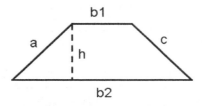

> **Review Video: Area and Perimeter of a Trapezoid**
> Visit mometrix.com/academy and enter code: 587523

Isosceles trapezoid: A trapezoid with equal base angles. This gives rise to other properties including: the two nonparallel sides have the same length, the two non-base angles are also equal, and there is one line of symmetry through the midpoints of the parallel sides.

PARALLELOGRAM

A **parallelogram** is a quadrilateral that has two pairs of opposite parallel sides. As such it is a special type of trapezoid. The sides that are parallel are also congruent. The opposite interior angles are always congruent, and the consecutive interior angles are supplementary. The diagonals of a parallelogram divide each other. Each diagonal divides the parallelogram into two congruent triangles. A parallelogram has no line of symmetry, but does have 180-degree rotational symmetry about the midpoint.

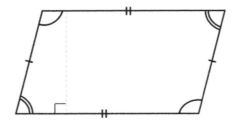

The **area of a parallelogram** is found by the formula $A = bh$, where b is the length of the base, and h is the height. Note that the base and height correspond to the length and width in a rectangle, so this formula would apply to rectangles as well. Do not confuse the height of a parallelogram with the length of the second side. The two are only the same measure in the case of a rectangle.

The **perimeter of a parallelogram** is found by the formula $P = 2a + 2b$ or $P = 2(a + b)$, where a and b are the lengths of the two sides.

> **Review Video: <u>How to Find the Area and Perimeter of a Parallelogram</u>**
> Visit mometrix.com/academy and enter code: 718313

RECTANGLE

A **rectangle** is a quadrilateral with four right angles. All rectangles are parallelograms and trapezoids, but not all parallelograms or trapezoids are rectangles. The diagonals of a rectangle are congruent. Rectangles have two lines of symmetry (through each pair of opposing midpoints) and 180-degree rotational symmetry about the midpoint.

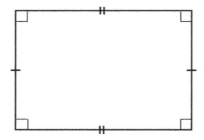

The **area of a rectangle** is found by the formula $A = lw$, where A is the area of the rectangle, l is the length (usually considered to be the longer side) and w is the width (usually considered to be the shorter side). The numbers for l and w are interchangeable.

The **perimeter of a rectangle** is found by the formula $P = 2l + 2w$ or $P = 2(l + w)$, where l is the length, and w is the width. It may be easier to add the length and width first and then double the result, as in the second formula.

RHOMBUS

A **rhombus** is a quadrilateral with four congruent sides. All rhombuses are parallelograms and kites; thus, they inherit all the properties of both types of quadrilaterals. The diagonals of a rhombus are perpendicular to each other. Rhombi have two lines of symmetry (along each of the diagonals) and 180° rotational symmetry. The **area of a rhombus** is half the product of the diagonals: $A = \frac{d_1 d_2}{2}$ and the perimeter of a rhombus is: $P = 2\sqrt{(d_1)^2 + (d_2)^2}$.

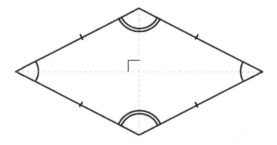

SQUARE

A **square** is a quadrilateral with four right angles and four congruent sides. Squares satisfy the criteria of all other types of quadrilaterals. The diagonals of a square are congruent and perpendicular to each other. Squares have four lines of symmetry (through each pair of opposing midpoints and along each of the diagonals) as well as 90° rotational symmetry about the midpoint.

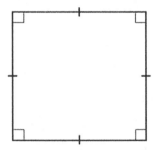

The **area of a square** is found by using the formula $A = s^2$, where s is the length of one side. The **perimeter of a square** is found by using the formula $P = 4s$, where s is the length of one side. Because all four sides are equal in a square, it is faster to multiply the length of one side by 4 than to add the same number four times. You could use the formulas for rectangles and get the same answer.

> **Review Video: Area and Perimeter of Rectangles and Squares**
> Visit mometrix.com/academy and enter code: 428109

HIERARCHY OF QUADRILATERALS

The hierarchy of quadrilaterals is as follows:

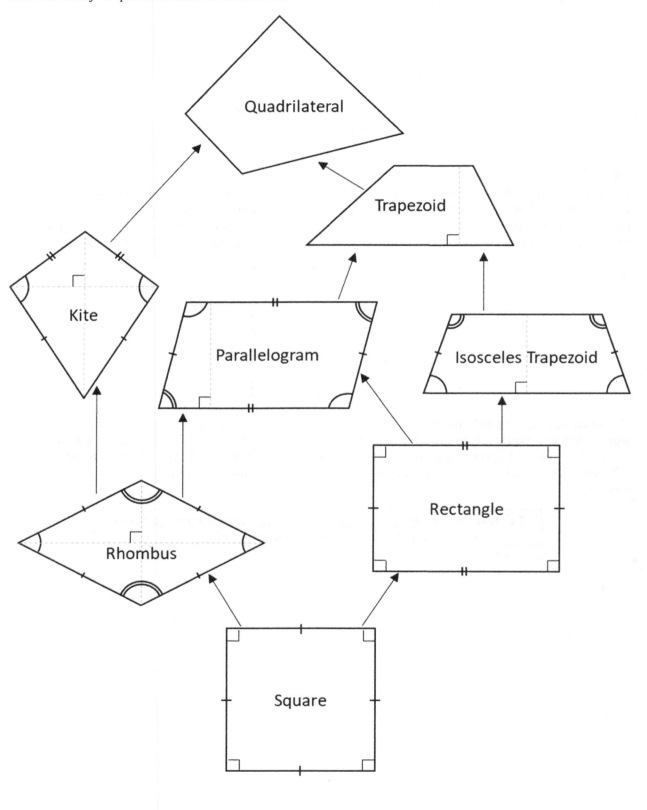

CIRCLES

The **center** of a circle is the single point from which every point on the circle is **equidistant**. The **radius** is a line segment that joins the center of the circle and any one point on the circle. All radii of a circle are equal. Circles that have the same center but not the same length of radii are **concentric**. The **diameter** is a line segment that passes through the center of the circle and has both endpoints on the circle. The length of the diameter is exactly twice the length of the radius. Point O in the diagram below is the center of the circle, segments $\overline{OX}$, $\overline{OY}$, and $\overline{OZ}$ are radii; and segment $\overline{XZ}$ is a diameter.

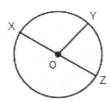

> **Review Video: Points of a Circle**
> Visit mometrix.com/academy and enter code: 420746
>
> **Review Video: The Diameter, Radius, and Circumference of Circles**
> Visit mometrix.com/academy and enter code: 448988

The **area of a circle** is found by the formula $A = \pi r^2$, where r is the length of the radius. If the diameter of the circle is given, remember to divide it in half to get the length of the radius before proceeding.

The **circumference** of a circle is found by the formula $C = 2\pi r$, where r is the radius. Again, remember to convert the diameter if you are given that measure rather than the radius.

> **Review Video: Area and Circumference of a Circle**
> Visit mometrix.com/academy and enter code: 243015

INSCRIBED AND CIRCUMSCRIBED FIGURES

These terms can both be used to describe a given arrangement of figures, depending on perspective. If each of the vertices of figure A lie on figure B, then it can be said that figure A is **inscribed** in figure B, but it can also be said that figure B is **circumscribed** about figure A. The following table and examples help to illustrate the concept. Note that the figures cannot both be circles, as they would be completely overlapping and neither would be inscribed or circumscribed.

Given	Description	Equivalent Description	Figures
Each of the sides of a pentagon is tangent to a circle	The circle is inscribed in the pentagon	The pentagon is circumscribed about the circle	
Each of the vertices of a pentagon lie on a circle	The pentagon is inscribed in the circle	The circle is circumscribed about the pentagon	

CIRCLE PROPERTIES
ARCS

An **arc** is a portion of a circle. Specifically, an arc is the set of points between and including two points on a circle. An arc does not contain any points inside the circle. When a segment is drawn from the endpoints of an arc to the center of the circle, a sector is formed. A **minor arc** is an arc that has a measure less than 180°. A **major arc** is an arc that has a measure of at least 180°. Every minor arc has a corresponding major arc that can be found by subtracting the measure of the minor arc from 360°. A **semicircle** is an arc whose endpoints are the endpoints of the diameter of a circle. A semicircle is exactly half of a circle.

Arc length is the length of that portion of the circumference between two points on the circle. The formula for arc length is $s = \frac{\pi r \theta}{180°}$, where s is the arc length, r is the length of the radius, and θ is the angular measure of the arc in degrees, or $s = r\theta$, where θ is the angular measure of the arc in radians (2π radians = 360 degrees).

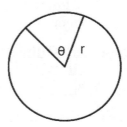

ANGLES OF CIRCLES

A **central angle** is an angle whose vertex is the center of a circle and whose legs intercept an arc of the circle. The measure of a central angle is equal to the measure of the minor arc it intercepts.

An **inscribed angle** is an angle whose vertex lies on a circle and whose legs contain chords of that circle. The portion of the circle intercepted by the legs of the angle is called the intercepted arc. The measure of the intercepted arc is exactly twice the measure of the inscribed angle. In the following diagram, angle ABC is an inscribed angle. $\overset{\frown}{AC} = 2(\text{m}\angle ABC)$.

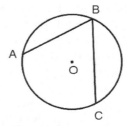

Any angle inscribed in a semicircle is a right angle. The intercepted arc is 180°, making the inscribed angle half that, or 90°. In the diagram below, angle ABC is inscribed in semicircle ABC, making angle ABC equal to 90°.

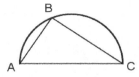

SECANTS, CHORDS, AND TANGENTS

A **secant** is a line that intersects a circle in two points. The segment of a secant line that is contained within the circle is called a **chord**. Two secants may intersect inside the circle, on the circle, or outside the circle. When the two secants intersect on the circle, an inscribed angle is formed. When two secants intersect inside a circle, the measure of each of two vertical angles is equal to half the sum of the two intercepted arcs. Consider the following diagram where m$\angle AEB = \frac{1}{2}(\widehat{AB} + \widehat{CD})$ and m$\angle BEC = \frac{1}{2}(\widehat{BC} + \widehat{AD})$.

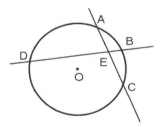

When two secants intersect outside a circle, the measure of the angle formed is equal to half the difference of the two arcs that lie between the two secants. In the diagram below, m$\angle AEB = \frac{1}{2}(\widehat{AB} - \widehat{CD})$.

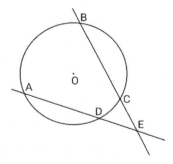

A **tangent** is a line in the same plane as a circle that touches the circle in exactly one point. The point at which a tangent touches a circle is called the **point of tangency**. While a line segment can be tangent to a circle as part of a line that is tangent, it is improper to say a tangent can be simply a line segment that touches the circle in exactly one point.

189

In the diagram below, $\overleftrightarrow{EB}$ is a secant and contains chord $\overline{EB}$, and $\overleftrightarrow{CD}$ is tangent to circle A. Notice that $\overline{FB}$ is not tangent to the circle. $\overline{FB}$ is a line segment that touches the circle in exactly one point, but if the segment were extended, it would touch the circle in a second point. In the diagram below, point B is the point of tangency.

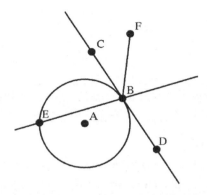

SECTORS

A **sector** is the portion of a circle formed by two radii and their intercepted arc. While the arc length is exclusively the points that are also on the circumference of the circle, the sector is the entire area bounded by the arc and the two radii.

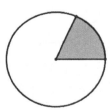

The **area of a sector** of a circle is found by the formula, $A = \frac{\theta r^2}{2}$, where A is the area, θ is the measure of the central angle in radians, and r is the radius. To find the area with the central angle in degrees, use the formula, $A = \frac{\theta \pi r^2}{360}$, where θ is the measure of the central angle and r is the radius.

3D SHAPES

SOLIDS

The **surface area of a solid object** is the area of all sides or exterior surfaces. For objects such as prisms and pyramids, a further distinction is made between base surface area (B) and lateral surface area (LA). For a prism, the total surface area (SA) is $SA = LA + 2B$. For a pyramid or cone, the total surface area is $SA = LA + B$.

The **surface area of a sphere** can be found by the formula $A = 4\pi r^2$, where r is the radius. The volume is given by the formula $V = \frac{4}{3}\pi r^3$, where r is the radius. Both quantities are generally given in terms of π.

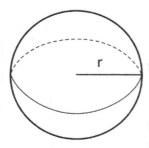

The **volume of any prism** is found by the formula $V = Bh$, where B is the area of the base, and h is the height (perpendicular distance between the bases). The surface area of any prism is the sum of the areas of both bases and all sides. It can be calculated as $SA = 2B + Ph$, where P is the perimeter of the base.

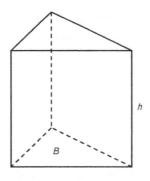

For a **rectangular prism**, the volume can be found by the formula $V = lwh$, where V is the volume, l is the length, w is the width, and h is the height. The surface area can be calculated as $SA = 2lw + 2hl + 2wh$ or $SA = 2(lw + hl + wh)$.

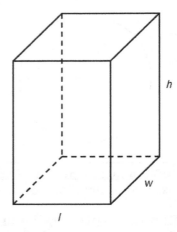

The **volume of a cube** can be found by the formula $V = s^3$, where s is the length of a side. The surface area of a cube is calculated as $SA = 6s^2$, where SA is the total surface area and s is the length of a side. These formulas are the same as the ones used for the volume and surface area of a rectangular prism, but simplified since all three quantities (length, width, and height) are the same.

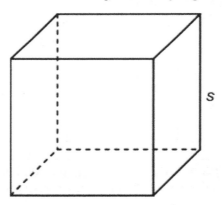

The **volume of a cylinder** can be calculated by the formula $V = \pi r^2 h$, where r is the radius, and h is the height. The surface area of a cylinder can be found by the formula $SA = 2\pi r^2 + 2\pi rh$. The first term is the base area multiplied by two, and the second term is the perimeter of the base multiplied by the height.

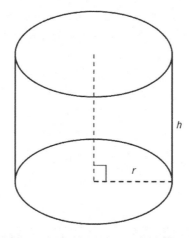

The **volume of a pyramid** is found by the formula $V = \frac{1}{3}Bh$, where B is the area of the base, and h is the height (perpendicular distance from the vertex to the base). Notice this formula is the same as $\frac{1}{3}$ times the volume of a prism. Like a prism, the base of a pyramid can be any shape.

Finding the **surface area of a pyramid** is not as simple as the other shapes we've looked at thus far. If the pyramid is a right pyramid, meaning the base is a regular polygon and the vertex is directly over the center of that polygon, the surface area can be calculated as $SA = B + \frac{1}{2}Ph_s$, where P is the perimeter of the base, and h_s is the slant height (distance from the vertex to the midpoint of one side of the base). If the pyramid is irregular, the area of each triangle side must be calculated individually and then summed, along with the base.

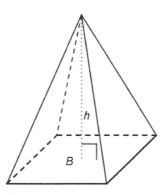

The **volume of a cone** is found by the formula $V = \frac{1}{3}\pi r^2 h$, where r is the radius, and h is the height. Notice this is the same as $\frac{1}{3}$ times the volume of a cylinder. The surface area can be calculated as $SA = \pi r^2 + \pi rs$, where s is the slant height. The slant height can be calculated using the Pythagorean theorem to be $\sqrt{r^2 + h^2}$, so the surface area formula can also be written as $SA = \pi r^2 + \pi r\sqrt{r^2 + h^2}$.

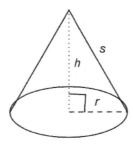

> **Review Video: Volume and Surface Area of a Right Circular Cone**
> Visit mometrix.com/academy and enter code: 573574

THE UNIT CIRCLE
DEGREES, RADIANS, AND THE UNIT CIRCLE

It is important to understand the deep connection between trigonometry and circles. Specifically, the two main units, **degrees** (°) and **radians** (rad), that are used to measure angles are related this way: 360° in one full circle and 2π radians in one full circle: (360° = 2π rad). The conversion factor relating the two is often stated as $\frac{180°}{\pi}$. For example, to convert $\frac{3\pi}{2}$ radians to degrees, multiply by the conversion factor: $\frac{3\pi}{2} \times \frac{180°}{\pi} = 270°$. As another example, to convert 60° to radians, divide by the conversion factor or multiply by the reciprocal: $60° \times \frac{\pi}{180°} = \frac{\pi}{3}$ radians.

Recall that the standard equation for a circle is $(x - h)^2 + (y - k)^2 = r^2$. A **unit circle** is a circle with a radius of 1 ($r = 1$) that has its center at the origin ($h = 0, k = 0$). Thus, the equation for the unit circle simplifies from the standard equation down to $x^2 + y^2 = 1$.

Standard position is the position of an angle of measure θ whose vertex is at the origin, the initial side crosses the unit circle at the point $(1, 0)$, and the terminal side crosses the unit circle at some other point (a, b). In the standard position, $\sin \theta = b$, $\cos \theta = a$, and $\tan \theta = \frac{b}{a}$.

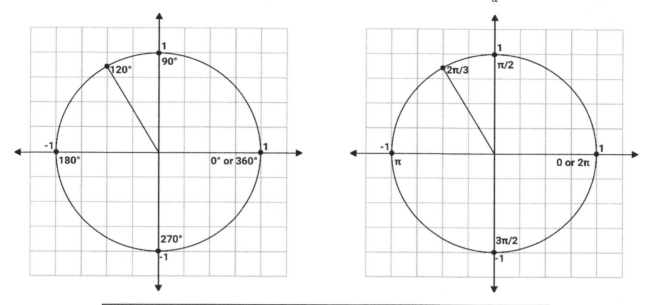

Review Video: Upper Level Trig: Unit Circle
Visit mometrix.com/academy and enter code: 333922

TABLE OF COMMONLY ENCOUNTERED ANGLES

$0° = 0$ radians, $30° = \frac{\pi}{6}$ radians, $45° = \frac{\pi}{4}$ radians, $60° = \frac{\pi}{3}$ radians, and $90° = \frac{\pi}{2}$ radians

$\sin 0° = 0$	$\cos 0° = 1$	$\tan 0° = 0$
$\sin 30° = \dfrac{1}{2}$	$\cos 30° = \dfrac{\sqrt{3}}{2}$	$\tan 30° = \dfrac{\sqrt{3}}{3}$
$\sin 45° = \dfrac{\sqrt{2}}{2}$	$\cos 45° = \dfrac{\sqrt{2}}{2}$	$\tan 45° = 1$
$\sin 60° = \dfrac{\sqrt{3}}{2}$	$\cos 60° = \dfrac{1}{2}$	$\tan 60° = \sqrt{3}$
$\sin 90° = 1$	$\cos 90° = 0$	$\tan 90° = \text{undefined}$
$\csc 0° = \text{undefined}$	$\sec 0° = 1$	$\cot 0° = \text{undefined}$
$\csc 30° = 2$	$\sec 30° = \dfrac{2\sqrt{3}}{3}$	$\cot 30° = \sqrt{3}$
$\csc 45° = \sqrt{2}$	$\sec 45° = \sqrt{2}$	$\cot 45° = 1$
$\csc 60° = \dfrac{2\sqrt{3}}{3}$	$\sec 60° = 2$	$\cot 60° = \dfrac{\sqrt{3}}{3}$
$\csc 90° = 1$	$\sec 90° = \text{undefined}$	$\cot 90° = 0$

The values in the upper half of this table are values you should have memorized or be able to find quickly and those in the lower half can easily be determined as the reciprocal of the corresponding function.

SAT Practice Test #1

Want to take this practice test in an online interactive format?
Check out the bonus page, which includes interactive practice questions and
much more: **mometrix.com/bonus948/sat**

Reading and Writing—Module 1

1. Which choice completes the text so that it conforms to the conventions of Standard English?

The field of astronomy has made significant strides in recent years, thanks to advancements in technology and the development of powerful telescopes. These innovations have enabled astronomers to observe distant galaxies, study the formation of stars, and even detect exoplanets orbiting other stars. These discoveries _____.

A) that expand our knowledge of the universe
B) and expand our knowledge of the universe
C) have expanded our knowledge of the universe
D) expanding our knowledge of the universe

2. Which choice completes the text with the most logical and precise word or phrase?

The concept of community-based participatory research has gained prominence as a means of fostering collaborative efforts between indigenous communities and academic institutions. An illuminating example of such a partnership can be found in the collaboration between the Navajo Nation and the University of Arizona, which serves as a beacon of success in this field. Navajo citizens actively participated in the formulation of research methodologies, and they continue to play an integral role in data collection. This model of cooperation effectively _____ the principles of community-based participatory research.

A) circumvents
B) eclipses
C) fabricates
D) exemplifies

3. Which quotation from the passage most effectively illustrates the claim?

A student claims that the humanities are fundamental to human understanding, encompassing history, literature, philosophy, and the arts.

He offers the following as support for his claim:

The humanities, encompassing the study of history, literature, philosophy, and the arts, play a vital role in shaping our understanding of the human experience. It is through the lens of the humanities that we delve into human history, exploring the triumphs and tribulations of civilizations long past. Literature, with its profound narratives, allows us to walk in the shoes of characters from different times and cultures, expanding our empathy and perspective. Philosophy challenges us to ponder life's most profound questions, encouraging critical thinking and ethical reflection. The arts, whether in the form of paintings, sculptures, music, or dance, provide avenues for self-expression and the exploration of beauty and meaning. The humanities are not merely academic disciplines; they are the very essence of what it means to be human, offering insights into our past, shaping our present, and guiding our future.

A) "The humanities are not merely academic disciplines; they are the very essence of what it means to be human."
B) "Literature, with its profound narratives, allows us to walk in the shoes of characters from different times and cultures."
C) "It is through the lens of the humanities that we delve into human history."
D) "Philosophy challenges us to ponder life's most profound questions, encouraging critical thinking and ethical reflection."

4. What does the order of the steps in the scientific method in this passage primarily serve to do?

The scientific method is a systematic approach to solving problems and answering questions. The first step is making careful observations of the natural world. By observing phenomena and gathering data, scientists can identify patterns or anomalies that pique their curiosity. These observations lead to the formation of hypotheses, which are educated guesses about the underlying explanations for what is observed. Subsequently, scientists design experiments to test these hypotheses and collect further data. Finally, they analyze the data to draw conclusions and advance our understanding of the natural world. The initial step of making observations is crucial, as it provides the foundation for scientific inquiry.

A) To provide a chronological account of scientific discoveries
B) To persuade readers to engage in scientific research
C) To emphasize the importance of making observations
D) To explain the process of conducting experiments

5. Which choice best characterizes the purpose of Sarah's statement, "Believe me, Alex, your excuses won't cut it this time"?

In a bustling cafe on a rainy afternoon, Sarah and Alex found themselves in a tense conversation. Sarah's eyes narrowed as she leaned in, her voice dripping with disdain.

"Believe me, Alex, your excuses won't cut it this time."

Alex, taken aback, responded firmly, "I stand by my decisions, Sarah."

It was a showdown neither of them had expected.

A) It reflects Sarah's admiration for Alex's decisions.
B) It signifies Sarah's understanding of Alex's predicament.
C) It conveys Sarah's skepticism and criticism of Alex's explanations.
D) It demonstrates Sarah's eagerness to collaborate with Alex.

6. Which finding, if true, would most directly support the notion that the leafcutter ants have evolved specialized adaptations for efficient farming of their fungus gardens?

In the heart of the Amazon rainforest, the remarkable leafcutter ant colonies thrive and display complex social structures with a sophisticated division of labor. The ants are particularly renowned for their ability to harvest leaves and carry them back to their underground nests where they use the leaves to cultivate a fungus garden. The fungus serves as their primary food source, and the leafcutter ants have evolved specialized adaptations to make this farming process efficient and productive.

A) Leafcutter ants have been observed using leaves from a wide variety of plant species for their fungus gardens.
B) The fungus cultivated by leafcutter ants has been found to be a unique, previously undiscovered species.
C) Leafcutter ant colonies located deeper in the rainforest are less efficient at harvesting leaves than those near the forest edge.
D) Leafcutter ants possess a specialized enzyme that enhances the growth of the fungus they cultivate.

7. The student wants to emphasize the uniqueness of periods. Which choice most effectively uses relevant information from the notes to accomplish this goal?

While researching a topic, a student has taken the following notes:

- Ancient Greek philosophers emphasized the pursuit of knowledge and wisdom.
- Renaissance art celebrated humanism and individualism.
- The Enlightenment promoted reason, science, and skepticism.
- Romantic literature valued emotions, nature, and imagination.
- Postmodernism challenged traditional narratives and embraced diversity.

A) Ancient Greeks and The Enlightenment valued knowledge and wisdom.
B) The Enlightenment's focus on reason, science, and skepticism was common among many historical eras.
C) Romantic literature valued imagination and nature, setting it apart from other historical periods.
D) Like many other eras, the Renaissance shared a celebration of humanism and individualism.

8. According to the text, what can be inferred about Mr. Johnson's character?

> In the bustling city of Eldertown, Mr. Johnson was known for his remarkable skills as a baker. He tirelessly worked long hours, crafting delicious pastries and bread that left the townsfolk eagerly waiting in line at his bakery. Despite the demands of his profession, Mr. Johnson always found time to donate fresh loaves of bread to the local shelter, ensuring that those less fortunate could enjoy a warm meal.

A) Mr. Johnson rarely had time to bake due to his busy schedule.
B) The townsfolk of Eldertown disliked Mr. Johnson's pastries.
C) Mr. Johnson was known for his generosity toward the local shelter.
D) Mr. Johnson only baked for those who could afford his pastries.

9. What is the main purpose of this passage?

> As an author, I have always believed that literature holds the power to transport readers to different worlds and illuminate aspects of the human experience. Through storytelling, we can explore complex themes, create vivid characters, and share our perspectives on society, culture, and the human condition. Writing allows us to convey our thoughts, emotions, and ideas in a way that resonates with readers on a profound level.

A) To describe the history of literature as an art form
B) To persuade readers to become authors themselves
C) To compare different literary genres and their impact
D) To reflect on the author's belief in the significance of literature

10. What does the passage primarily emphasize?

> Artistic movements have shaped the course of human history, with each reflecting the values and cultural context of its time. The Renaissance, for example, celebrated humanism, scientific exploration, and classical aesthetics, while Romanticism embraced emotion, individualism, and the sublime. Understanding these movements allows us to appreciate the diverse ways in which art has mirrored and influenced society.

A) The influence of scientific exploration on artistic movements
B) The values and cultural context reflected in artistic movements
C) The celebration of emotion and individualism in Romanticism
D) The appreciation of classical aesthetics in the Renaissance

11. Which choice completes the text with the most logical and precise word or phrase?

> Given the intricate relationships in the coral reef ecosystem, it's not surprising that the impact of climate change has lacked _____ explanation. Marine biologists have conducted extensive research, and Dr. Olivia Chang's recent findings offer hope for the preservation of these fragile ecosystems.

A) an intricate
B) an elusive
C) a conclusive
D) a clear

12. Which choice most logically completes the text?

Space exploration has captured the imagination of humanity for decades. In recent years, NASA and other space agencies have made significant strides in exploring the cosmos. The Mars rovers, for instance, have provided valuable insights into the Martian surface and collected evidence of the presence of water in the planet's past. Beyond Mars, ambitious missions aim to send astronauts back to the Moon. These endeavors pave the way for future exploration of Mars and deeper into the solar system. They represent humanity's _____.

A) Pursuit of earthly riches
B) Desire to conquer other worlds
C) Instinctive curiosity
D) Commitment to environmental conservation

13. Which sentence in the passage contains a verb tense error?

Shakespeare's works are revered for their enduring relevance and insight into the human condition. His plays, such as *Hamlet* and *Romeo and Juliet*, explore timeless themes like love, ambition, and the complexities of human relationships. Even today, his words resonate with audiences, reminded us of the universality of human experiences. Shakespeare's writings have a unique ability to transport readers to different eras.

A) "Shakespeare's works are revered for their enduring relevance and insight into the human condition."
B) "His plays, such as *Hamlet* and *Romeo and Juliet*, explore timeless themes like love, ambition, and the complexities of human relationships."
C) "Even today, his words resonate with audiences, reminded us of the universality of human experiences."
D) "Shakespeare's writings have a unique ability to transport readers to different eras."

14. Which of the following statements most effectively compares the roles of Daisy Buchanan and Jordan Baker in *The Great Gatsby*?

While researching a topic, a student has taken the following notes:

Daisy Buchanan - The Alluring Socialite:
- Daisy Buchanan is portrayed as a captivating socialite in the novel.
- She represents the allure of wealth and status during the Roaring Twenties.
- Daisy's presence at Gatsby's extravagant parties adds to their appeal and opulence.
- Her character embodies the shallowness and materialism of the era.

Jordan Baker - The Confident Athlete:
- Jordan Baker is a professional golfer and a friend of Daisy Buchanan.
- She stands out as a confident and poised individual, in contrast to the excesses of the time.
- Jordan's cool demeanor and independence make her a compelling figure in the story.
- Her romantic involvement with Nick Carraway, the novel's narrator, adds depth to her character.

A) Daisy Buchanan's character reflects the disillusionment and emptiness of the wealthy elite, while Jordan Baker represents a more independent and self-reliant woman.

B) Daisy Buchanan's allure stems from her mysterious past, while Jordan Baker's confidence and athleticism make her a unique and memorable character.

C) Both Daisy Buchanan and Jordan Baker symbolize the pursuit of the American Dream during the Roaring Twenties, but they have different approaches and outcomes.

D) Daisy Buchanan and Jordan Baker are both socialites in the story, contributing equally to the lavish parties thrown by Jay Gatsby.

15. **Based on the data in the table, which fertilizer type resulted in the largest increase in average plant height compared to the height with no fertilizer (None)?**

Plant Growth and Fertilizer Application

Fertilizer Type	Shortest Plant Height (cm)	Tallest Plant Height (cm)
None	20	35
Type A	30	35
Type B	20	40
Type C	40	45
Type D	45	50

Researchers conducted a plant growth experiment with various types of fertilizers to determine their effects on plant height.

A) Type A
B) Type B
C) Type C
D) Type D

16. **Which choice completes the text with the most logical transition?**

The field of chemistry encompasses the study of a wide range of substances and reactions, including acids and bases. Acids donate protons (H+) to solutions. _____ bases accept protons. Some substances exhibit neutral properties on the pH scale, neither donating nor accepting protons, and this neutrality is also a significant aspect of their chemical behavior.

A) Consequently
B) Furthermore
C) Conversely
D) Nonetheless

202

17. Which choice completes the text so that it conforms to the conventions of Standard English?

The Scarlet Letter by Nathaniel Hawthorne

"The _____ attire, on the other hand, was distinguished by a fanciful, or, we might rather say, a fantastic ingenuity, which served, indeed, to heighten the airy charm that early began to develop itself in the little girl, but which appeared to have also a deeper meaning."

A) child
B) children's
C) child's
D) childs'

18. Which choice completes the text with the most logical and precise word or phrase?

Jane Austen's novels are celebrated for their keen social judgment, and her witty observations provide readers with an insightful _____ on the society and manners of her time.

A) endorsement
B) perspective
C) commentary
D) refusal

19. Which choice completes the text with the most logical transition?

The Renaissance, characterized by a revival of art and learning, saw the emergence of remarkable individuals who left an indelible mark on history. Leonardo da Vinci, _____ his mastery of various fields, including painting, anatomy, and engineering, is often considered a quintessential Renaissance polymath. His famous painting *Mona Lisa* continues to captivate viewers with its enigmatic smile and detailed craftsmanship.

A) and
B) because of
C) but
D) so

20. Which choice most effectively uses relevant information from the notes to accomplish the goal of explaining the role of enzymes?

While researching a scientific topic, a student has taken the following notes:

- Enzymes are biological catalysts that increase the speed of chemical reactions in living organisms without being consumed in the process.
- Each enzyme is highly specific to its substrate, meaning it works with a particular molecule or group of molecules, which ensures precise control over biochemical reactions.
- Enzyme activity can be regulated by factors such as temperature, pH levels, and the presence of cofactors or inhibitors, allowing cells to fine-tune metabolic pathways.
- Enzymes play a crucial role in fundamental biological processes, including digestion, cellular respiration, DNA replication, and protein synthesis, making them essential for life.

A) Enzymes are consumed during the chemical reactions they catalyze, which is why they need to be continuously produced in cells to maintain vital processes.

B) Enzymes are universal molecules that can work with any substrate, making them indispensable for a wide range of biological reactions.

C) Enzymes are specialized proteins that help speed up chemical reactions in living organisms, contributing to various essential processes like digestion, cellular respiration, DNA replication, and protein synthesis.

D) Enzymes primarily regulate temperature and pH levels in cells, ensuring that biochemical reactions occur at an optimal rate.

21. Which choice completes the text so that it conforms to the conventions of Standard English?

The concept of black holes in astrophysics has intrigued scientists and the general public alike. A black hole is formed when a massive star collapses under its own gravity, creating an incredibly dense region where the escape velocity exceeds the speed of light. This phenomenon has profound implications for our understanding of space and time _____.

A) - and it challenges the known laws of physics

B) , which challenges the known laws of physics

C) ; that challenges the known laws of physics

D) , challenging the known laws of physics

22. Which choice completes the text so that it conforms to the conventions of Standard English?

Photosynthesis is a vital process in nature. It involves the conversion of carbon dioxide, a greenhouse gas, into oxygen, _____ is essential for the survival of many organisms.

A) where

B) which

C) when

D) whom

23. Which choice completes the blank so that it conforms to the conventions of Standard English?

> The philosophies of thinkers like Socrates, Confucius, and Simone de Beauvoir challenge us to ponder the fundamental questions of existence, ethics, and morality. _____ ideas have left an indelible mark on our collective consciousness, influencing the way we view the world and our place within it.

A) They're
B) It's
C) Their
D) Its

24. Which choice most logically completes the text?

> In the heart of the ancient forest, a sense of tranquility enveloped the weary travelers as they ventured deeper into the woods. The towering trees formed a natural canopy above, casting dappled shadows on the forest floor. The air was thick with the earthy scent of moss and fallen leaves, and the gentle rustling of leaves in the breeze created a soothing symphony. It was a place where time seemed to stand still, where one could almost hear the whispers of the past in the rustling leaves. Immediately, _____.

A) a feeling of unease settled in
B) they began to feel lost
C) they felt an overwhelming sense of wonder
D) their pace quickened

25. How would Maya Angelou likely respond to Mark Twain's use of dialects and portrayal of race in *The Adventures of Huckleberry Finn*, as described in Passage 1?

> Passage 1:
> Mark Twain's *The Adventures of Huckleberry Finn* is a classic American novel that has been both celebrated and criticized for its portrayal of race. Twain's use of dialects and vernacular language was groundbreaking at the time, but it has also sparked debates about racial stereotypes in literature.

> Passage 2:
> Maya Angelou, known for her powerful memoir *I Know Why the Caged Bird Sings*, emphasized the importance of literature as a tool for empowerment and social change. Angelou believed that literature could be a means of breaking down racial barriers and promoting an understanding among people of different backgrounds.

A) Angelou would praise Twain for his sensitive portrayal of race in the novel.
B) Angelou would criticize Twain for perpetuating racial stereotypes in his work.
C) Angelou would view Twain's approach as unrelated to her own beliefs about literature.
D) Angelou would suggest that Twain's use of dialects is necessary for authenticity in storytelling.

Reading and Writing—Module 2

1. What is the central idea of the passage?

In the field of astronomy, the Hubble Space Telescope has revolutionized our understanding of the universe. Orbiting above Earth's atmosphere, Hubble captures breathtaking images of distant galaxies, stars, and nebulae. Its observations have revealed the vastness of the cosmos and provided crucial data for numerous scientific discoveries.

A) Hubble's observations have revolutionized astronomy.
B) Hubble captures images of galaxies and stars.
C) The Hubble Space Telescope orbits Earth's atmosphere.
D) The universe is vast and unexplored.

2. Which choice completes the text so that it conforms to the conventions of Standard English?

Jane Austen's novels continue to captivate readers with their keen observations of human nature and social intricacies. Austen's works, including *Pride and Prejudice* and *Sense and Sensibility*, provide a window into the manners and mores of early 19th-century England. Her characters often grapple with societal expectations and the pursuit of happiness.

One of Austen's recurring themes is the importance of individual integrity and moral character. She believed that true virtue lay in "the sincerity of one's actions and the genuineness of one's sentiments." Austen emphasized that societal conformity should not overshadow the integrity of the _____ all individuals to hold dear their inner values.

A) heart, reminding
B) heart: reminding
C) heart; reminding
D) heart. Reminding

3. The student wants to provide an explanation and example of Rosa Parks' significance in the Civil Rights Movement. Which choice most effectively uses relevant information from the notes to accomplish this goal?

While researching a topic, a student has taken the following notes on Rosa Parks:

- Rosa Parks was a prominent civil rights activist in the United States.
- She is best known for her pivotal role in the Montgomery Bus Boycott of 1955-1956 sparked by her refusal to give up her bus seat to a white passenger.
- Parks' act of civil disobedience and her subsequent arrest became a symbol of the Civil Rights Movement.
- Her actions and the boycott ultimately led to a US Supreme Court ruling that segregation on public buses was unconstitutional, which was a significant milestone in the struggle for civil rights.

A) Rosa Parks was a civil rights activist known for her refusal to give up her bus seat, which became a symbol of the Civil Rights Movement.
B) Rosa Parks' act of civil disobedience on the bus prompted immediate changes in segregation laws across the United States, eliminating racial discrimination on all forms of public transportation.
C) Rosa Parks' refusal to give up her bus seat in the Montgomery Bus Boycott led to the Supreme Court ending all segregation in the United States.
D) Rosa Parks was primarily known for her boycott of public transportation, which led the city of Montgomery to end segregation on its buses.

4. Which choice completes the text with the most logical transition?

"Alice started to her feet, for it flashed across her mind that she had never before seen a rabbit with either a waistcoat-pocket, or a watch to take out of it, and burning with curiosity, she ran across the field after it, and _____ was just in time to see it pop down a large rabbit-hole under the hedge." From Lewis Carroll's *Alice's Adventures in Wonderland*

A) fortunately
B) therefore
C) unexpectedly
D) nevertheless

5. Which choice completes the text with the most logical transition?

The Romantic era in literature and art celebrated the beauty of nature and the emotions of the individual. William Wordsworth, a prominent Romantic poet, composed verses that reflected his deep connection to the natural world. In his poem "I Wandered Lonely as a Cloud," he vividly described the sight of daffodils dancing in the breeze. _____, Wordsworth's work, with its vivid portrayal of nature's beauty, epitomizes the Romantic movement's emphasis on the sublime in nature.

A) In contrast
B) In conclusion
C) Consequently
D) On the other hand

6. Which choice most effectively uses relevant information from the notes to accomplish the goal of explaining the role of the atmosphere in regulating Earth's temperature?

While researching a scientific topic, a student has taken the following notes:

- The Earth's atmosphere contains primarily nitrogen (approximately 78%) and oxygen (about 21%).
- The greenhouse effect is caused by the trapping of heat in the atmosphere due to certain gases like carbon dioxide and methane.
- The ozone layer in the stratosphere plays a critical role in absorbing harmful ultraviolet (UV) radiation from the sun.
- Photosynthesis is the process by which plants convert carbon dioxide and water into glucose and oxygen.

A) The Earth's atmosphere is primarily composed of nitrogen and oxygen, and the greenhouse effect is caused by gases like carbon dioxide and methane that trap heat, regulating the planet's temperature.

B) The greenhouse effect, caused by gases like carbon dioxide and methane, plays a crucial role in maintaining the Earth's temperature. Additionally, the ozone layer in the stratosphere absorbs harmful UV radiation from the sun.

C) The atmosphere, comprising mainly nitrogen and oxygen, is responsible for regulating Earth's temperature through processes like photosynthesis, which converts carbon dioxide into glucose and oxygen.

D) The ozone layer in the stratosphere absorbs harmful UV radiation from the sun, while the atmosphere's composition of nitrogen and oxygen helps to control temperature and support photosynthesis.

7. Which choice most logically completes the text?

Photosynthesis is an intricate biochemical reaction in which plants and some microorganisms convert sunlight, carbon dioxide, and water into glucose and oxygen. Organisms that use this process produce approximately 20% of the world's oxygen supply. Photosynthesis also serves as a fundamental mechanism for capturing and storing solar energy. This stored energy can then be used by organisms throughout the food chain. This process is essential for _____.

A) Sustaining life on Earth
B) Supporting the growth of plants
C) Maintaining the Earth's magnetic field
D) Regulating ocean tides

8. Which choice completes the text with the most logical and precise word or phrase?

William Shakespeare is a timeless figure whose writings have left a lasting impact. His amazing skill in creating characters with complex personalities and deep emotions has made storytelling an art form. Every character in his plays is carefully crafted, and their dialogue in his stories reflects what it's like to be human. Shakespeare's work doesn't just entertain; it also beautifully _____ the depth of human life.

A) avoids
B) captures
C) mirrors
D) diminishes

9. What is the structural purpose of using Scout as the narrator in this novel?

In Harper Lee's novel *To Kill a Mockingbird*, readers are introduced to the story through the eyes of Scout Finch, a young girl. Scout serves as the primary narrator, offering a distinctive lens through which we experience the events of the novel. Her narration immerses us in the small Southern town of Maycomb, a place marked by complex societal dynamics and deep-rooted prejudices.

A) To provide a detailed analysis of the novel's themes
B) To create a sense of mystery about the story's events
C) To emphasize the innocence of childhood in contrast to adult viewpoints
D) To explore the lives of various characters in the novel

10. Which word in the passage represents a plural possessive form of a noun?

Art history enthusiasts often explore the concept of artistic movements, which are marked by distinctive forms and styles that emerged during specific periods. One such movement, Impressionism, originated in the late 19th century and sought to capture the fleeting effects of light and color. Impressionism's artists include Claude Monet and Pierre-Auguste Renoir. The artists' loose brushstrokes and vivid palettes convey impressions of landscapes and everyday life rather than carefully posed portraits. This movement had a profound impact on the art world, challenging traditional artistic conventions and influencing subsequent generations of painters.

A) movements
B) Impressionism's
C) artists'
D) enthusiasts

11. Which choice completes the text with the most logical and precise word or phrase?

Critics have debated the ____ nature of the protagonist in this novel, with some viewing the character as a symbol of hope and others as a representation of despair.

A) complex
B) one-dimensional
C) unambiguous
D) predictable

12. Which choice completes the text so that it conforms to the conventions of Standard English?

The Adventures of Huckleberry Finn by Mark Twain

"Tom's voice _____ whilst he was reading them, and he most broke down. When he got done he couldn't no way make up his mind which one for Jim to scrabble on to the wall, they was all so good; but at last he allowed he would let him scrabble them all on."

A) tremble
B) trembles
C) trembled
D) trembling

13. Which choice best states the main purpose of the text?

Amidst the tranquil forest, the old oak stood tall and wise, its branches swaying in the gentle breeze. Beneath its shade, a traveler found solace, a moment of respite from the world's chaos.

A) To describe the traveler's journey through the forest
B) To highlight the strength of the old oak tree
C) To depict the peaceful ambiance of the forest
D) To narrate a traveler's encounter with a talking tree

14. Which choice most logically completes the text?

The Renaissance period, known for its revival of art and intellectual pursuits, marked a significant shift in human history. During this time, artists like Leonardo da Vinci, Michelangelo, and Raphael produced iconic works that continue to inspire awe and admiration. In addition to art, the Renaissance also fostered an environment of _____.

A) Scientific inquiry and innovation
B) Political turmoil and conflict
C) Isolation and social stagnation
D) Environmental conservation and awareness

15. Which choice completes the text so that it conforms to the conventions of Standard English?

Climate change is a pressing global issue, with the increase in greenhouse gas emissions being a major contributor to rising temperatures. The effects of climate change are far-reaching, including more frequent and severe weather events, rising sea levels, and disruptions to ecosystems. Addressing this crisis _____.

A) requires concerted efforts at the global level
B) requiring concerted efforts at the global level
C) and requiring concerted efforts at the global level
D) it requires concerted efforts at the global level

16. How would Dr. Johnson likely respond to Dr. Smith's argument about the primary driver of climate change, as described in Passage 1?

Passage 1:
In his research paper, Dr. Smith argues that climate change is primarily driven by human activities, especially the burning of fossil fuels. He presents data on rising carbon dioxide levels and global temperatures as evidence of this phenomenon.

Passage 2:
In her research article, Dr. Johnson acknowledges the impact of human activities on climate change but emphasizes the natural factors influencing climate as well. She argues that volcanic eruptions and solar variations also play significant roles in shaping our planet's climate.

A) Dr. Johnson would agree with Dr. Smith's assessment of human activities as the main driver of climate change.
B) Dr. Johnson would disagree with Dr. Smith and argue that natural factors are the dominant contributors to climate change.
C) Dr. Johnson would view Dr. Smith's research as unrelated to her own work on climate variability.
D) Dr. Johnson would suggest that both human activities and natural factors must be considered in climate research.

17. Which choice completes the text with the most logical and precise word or phrase?

The remarkable ability of chameleons to change the color of their skin has long puzzled scientists. Recent findings by Dr. Michel Milinkovitch and his team suggest that chameleons achieve their color-changing magic by controlling the arrangement of nanocrystals in their skin cells. This enables them to achieve perfect _____ with their surroundings.

A) prediction
B) moderation
C) synchronization
D) hibernation

18. Which choice most effectively uses data from the table to complete the example?

Solar System Planets' Characteristics

Planet	Average Distance from Sun (Million km)	Surface Temperature (°C)
Mercury	57.9	427
Venus	108.2	467
Earth	149.6	15
Mars	227.9	-65
Jupiter	778.3	-145
Saturn	1,427	-178
Uranus	2,869.6	-224
Neptune	4,496.3	-218

When we explore our solar system, we encounter a diverse range of planets with unique characteristics. One interesting difference is the surface temperature of these planets. For example, while Venus is the closest planet to Earth in terms of distance from the Sun, it has an extremely high surface temperature of 467 °C, making it the hottest planet. Mars, which is farther from the Sun, has a lower surface temperature of -65 °C. To complete the example, let's consider Neptune, the farthest planet from the Sun, which has a surface temperature of -218 °C.

A) Neptune has a surface temperature lower than both Venus and Mars.
B) Neptune has the highest surface temperature among all the planets.
C) Venus has a cooler surface temperature compared to Mars and Earth.
D) Mars has the highest surface temperature among all planets.

19. What is the main role of literature, as described in the passage?

Throughout history, literature has served as a mirror to society, reflecting its joys, struggles, and complexities. Novels like *To Kill a Mockingbird* by Harper Lee shed light on issues of racial injustice, while George Orwell's *1984* explores the dangers of totalitarianism. These literary works continue to provide valuable insights into the human condition.

A) To entertain readers with fictional stories
B) To provide a glimpse into historical events
C) To reflect societal issues and human experiences
D) To promote the study of totalitarianism

20. How would Mary Shelley likely respond to John Keats' view on Romanticism, as expressed in Passage 1?

Passage 1:
In his essay on Romanticism, John Keats extolled the movement's embrace of emotion, individualism, and the sublime. Keats argued that Romanticism's emphasis on nature and emotion offered a profound departure from the rationalism of the Enlightenment, championing a deeper connection between the individual and the natural world.

Passage 2:
Mary Shelley's novel *Frankenstein* is often seen as a product of Romanticism. The novel explores themes of individuality, the power of nature, and the consequences of unchecked scientific experimentation. Shelley's work reflects the Romantic era's fascination with the boundaries of the human experience and the unknown.

A) Shelley would agree with Keats and expand on the importance of emotion in literature.
B) Shelley would disagree with Keats and argue that Romanticism stifles individual creativity.
C) Shelley would see Keats' perspective as unrelated to her own work in *Frankenstein*.
D) Shelley would agree with Keats but assert that the Enlightenment had its merits as well.

21. Which choice completes the text so that it conforms to the conventions of Standard English?

As an experienced chef, I have prepared countless dishes over the years. When crafting a culinary masterpiece, it's crucial to choose the finest ingredients and combine _____ thoughtfully. Each ingredient contributes its unique flavor and texture, making the dish a harmonious blend of tastes.

A) them
B) one
C) you
D) it

22. Which finding, if true, would most directly support the student's claim?

In a recent class discussion, a student passionately argued that literature has a profound impact on society and individuals. The student claimed that literature not only reflects societal values and challenges but also actively shapes our perceptions, beliefs, and behaviors. To support this assertion, the student highlighted the power of literature to evoke empathy, provide diverse perspectives, and spark critical thinking. The student contended that literature serves as a mirror in which we see ourselves and as a window through which we explore the world. However, some of the student's peers questioned this perspective, suggesting that literature may have a limited influence in the modern digital age. To resolve the debate, the class decided to investigate whether there is empirical evidence linking literature to societal attitudes and behaviors.

A) Modern society places a greater emphasis on visual media, making literature less influential in shaping public opinion.
B) Studies have shown that individuals who read literature featuring diverse characters and experiences exhibit increased empathy and tolerance in their attitudes.
C) Literary classics from different time periods consistently receive lower readership and engagement compared to contemporary literature.
D) There is no substantial correlation between the type of literature individuals read and their beliefs or actions.

23. Which choice completes the text so that it conforms to the conventions of Standard English?

The traditional Japanese tea ceremony, known as *chanoyu* or *sado*, is a highly ritualized practice that dates back centuries. During this ceremony, participants engage in a series of precise, choreographed movements and interactions. These rituals emphasize mindfulness, simplicity, and the appreciation of the beauty in everyday objects. They _____ the deep connection between Japanese culture and the philosophy of Zen Buddhism.

A) representing
B) represent
C) represent a
D) represents

24. Which choice completes the text with the most logical transition?

The study of electromagnetism in the field of physics has not only revolutionized technology but has also deepened our understanding of the natural world. Electromagnetic waves, such as radio waves, microwaves, and visible light, serve as the foundation for various applications, including communication, energy transmission, and our exploration of the universe through telescopes. _____, the knowledge of these waves has paved the way for the development of numerous devices and technologies that harness different segments of the electromagnetic spectrum.

A) For example,
B) In conclusion,
C) As a result,
D) In other words,

25. Which choice completes the text so that it conforms to the conventions of Standard English?

The human brain is a complex organ, and its functions are still not fully understood. However, neuroscientists have made significant progress in recent years, and ongoing research is shedding light on the intricacies of brain function. These discoveries are crucial for advancing our knowledge of neuroscience _____ treatments for neurological disorders.

A) ; and developing
B) and for developing
C) , with developing
D) - developing

Mathematics—Module 1

1. An apple falls from a high branch. The height of the apple is modeled by the function $f(x) = -x^2 - 2x + 7$, where $f(x)$ represents the height of the apple and x represents the number of seconds since the fall. After how many seconds will the apple reach the ground?

A) 1.8
B) 2.1
C) 2.3
D) 2.6

2. If $2x + 6 = -2$, what is the value of $10x + 11$?

A) −4
B) −8
C) −29
D) −51

3. Expand the following expression: $(x + 2)(x - 3)$

A) $x^2 - 1$
B) $x^2 - 6$
C) $x^2 - x - 6$
D) $x^2 - 5x - 1$

Refer to the following for question 4:

The table below represents the test scores on a chemistry final, as well as the lab grades for the semester.

Final Exam	78	85	91	77	94	83	87
Lab Grade	84	86	98	90	97	85	90

4. What is the difference of the mean and median of the lab grades?

A) 0
B) 1.5
C) 3
D) 4.5

5. The graph of $y = 2x^2 + 3x$ intersects the graph of $y = -x$ at $(0,0)$ and (a, b). What is the value of b?

6. A population of bacteria tripled every day. After 5 days, there were 2,430 bacteria. How many were there originally?

Refer to the following for question 7:

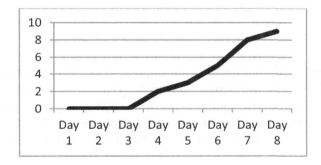

Beth plants a number of sunflower seeds and checks daily to see if any have sprouted. The graph above shows how many seedlings are growing each day when she checks.

7. Which day did the first seedling appear?

A) Day 1
B) Day 2
C) Day 3
D) Day 4

8. Kasie is filling glasses with water. Each glass is cylindrical with a radius of 1.25 inches and a height of 6 inches. If she fills them to a height of 5 inches, how many glasses can she fill with 3 quarts of water (1 gallon = 231 cubic inches)? Use 3.14 for π.

A) 3
B) 5
C) 7
D) 9

9. Mandy can buy 4 containers of yogurt and 3 boxes of crackers for $9.55. She can buy 2 containers of yogurt and 2 boxes of crackers for $5.90. How much does one box of crackers cost?

   A) $1.75
   B) $2.00
   C) $2.25
   D) $2.50

10. A researcher surveyed 350 people at a grocery store, offering them a sample of a well-known juice along with a new brand of juice. 85% of those who tasted the two juices preferred the new brand. Which of the following inferences is a logical conclusion?

   A) 85% of shoppers will prefer the new brand of juice.
   B) 15% of shoppers will prefer the new brand of juice.
   C) Most shoppers will prefer the new brand of juice.
   D) Most shoppers will prefer the well-known juice.

11. If the solution for the system of equations below is (x, y), what is the value of $x^2 - 3y$?
$$5x - 6y = 12$$
$$-2x + 3y = -5$$

   A) −3
   B) −1
   C) 3
   D) 5

12. A colony of *Escherichia coli* is inoculated from a Petri dish into a test tube containing 50 mL of nutrient broth. The test tube is placed in a 37 °C incubator and agitator. After one hour, the number of bacteria in the test tube is determined to be 8×10^6. Given that the doubling time of *Escherichia coli* is 20 minutes with agitation at 37 °C, approximately how many bacteria should the test tube contain after eight hours of growth?

   A) 2.56×10^8
   B) 2.05×10^9
   C) 1.7×10^{14}
   D) 1.7×10^{13}

13. If $3x - 4 = -1$, what is the value of $12x + 3$?

   A) 18
   B) 15
   C) 6
   D) 1

14. Evaluate the expression $4\sqrt{6} + 8\sqrt{6}$. Simplify your answer as much as possible.

   A) $12\sqrt{12}$
   B) 72
   C) $12\sqrt{6}$
   D) $24\sqrt{3}$

15. In the figure below (not drawn to scale), $\triangle ABC$ is similar to $\triangle EDC$. What is the length of AB?

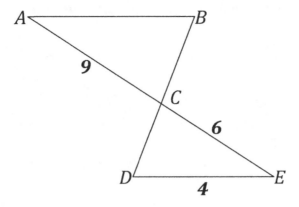

16. The equation of a circle is shown below. What is the circle's diameter?

$$x^2 + y^2 - 4x + 2y = 4$$

A) 2
B) 3
C) 5
D) 6

17. If $4a + 3 \leq 1$, what is the greatest possible value of $6a - 2$?

A) -5
B) -3
C) $-\frac{1}{2}$
D) 1

18. In the equations below, i refers to the amount of money (in dollars) invested in production of x products and p refers to the profits. What is the "break even" number of products, where investments are equal to profits?

$$i = 15,200 + 0.75x$$
$$p = 5.5x$$

A) 2,432
B) 3,075
C) 3,200
D) 17,600

19. The scatterplot below shows Julio's time (in hours) on the y-axis spent practicing his trumpet on the days (x-axis) leading up to a band concert. What is the difference in the amount of time he spent on the final day versus the amount predicted by the line of best fit?

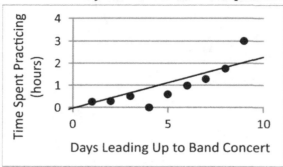

A) 0.5 hours
B) 1 hour
C) 2 hours
D) 3 hours

20. The formula for finding the volume of a cone is $V = \frac{1}{3}\pi r^2 h$. Which of the following equations is correctly solved for r?

A) $r = \frac{1}{3}\pi h$

B) $r = \sqrt{\frac{3V}{\pi h}}$

C) $r = \frac{3V}{\pi h}$

D) $r = V - \frac{1}{3}\pi h$

21. Jan has six pairs of socks for every pair of shoes she owns. If she has 12 pairs of shoes and s pairs of socks, which of the following equations is true?

A) $12s = 6$
B) $6s = 12$
C) $\frac{s}{6} = 12$
D) $s + 6 = 12$

22. If $x^{-\frac{1}{2}} = m$, what is x?

A) m^2
B) $1 - m^2$
C) $\frac{1}{m^2}$
D) $\frac{1}{m}$

Mathematics—Module 2

1. In the figures below (not drawn to scale), right triangle △*ABC* is similar to △*EFG*. What is the ratio of the area of △*ABC* to the area of △*EFG*?

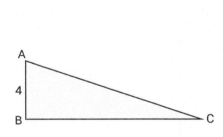
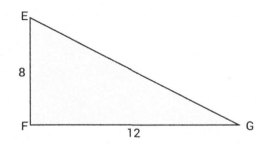

2. The function *f* is defined by a polynomial. The table below gives values for x and $f(x)$. Which of the following must be a factor of $f(x)$?

x	$f(x)$
0	4
1	2
2	0

A) x
B) $x - 1$
C) $x + 2$
D) $x - 2$

3. In the system of equations below, *a* is a constant and *x* and *y* are variables. For which of the following values of *a* will the system have no solution?

$$x + 3y = -7$$
$$ax - 2y = 6$$

A) $-\frac{2}{3}$
B) $-\frac{1}{3}$
C) 0
D) $\frac{7}{3}$

4. What is the sum of all values of *x* that satisfy the following equation?

$$5x^2 - 30x - 32 = 3$$

A) −1
B) 0
C) 6
D) 7

5. In right triangle MNP below, angle M measures $a°$ and $\cos a° = \frac{3}{5}$. What is $\cos(90 - a°)$?

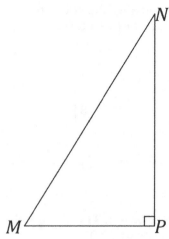

6. If 52% of 25 people polled in a coffee survey preferred Brand A and 48% preferred Brand B, which of the following inferences is a logical conclusion?
   A) At least 52% of shoppers will prefer Brand A over Brand B.
   B) The majority of shoppers will prefer Brand A over Brand B.
   C) The majority of shoppers will prefer Brand B over Brand A.
   D) The number of shoppers who prefer Brand A may be similar to the number of shoppers who prefer Brand B.

7. Ben bought a bag of assorted rubber balls and measured each one. Each had a diameter between 1.2 and 1.5 inches. What is a possible volume, rounded to the nearest cubic inch, of one of the balls? Use 3.14 for π.

8. How many gallon jugs of water should Julia buy to completely fill a container in the shape of a rectangular prism if the length is 8 feet, the width is 4 feet, and the height is 3 feet (1 gallon $= 231$ cubic inches)?
   A) 5
   B) 718
   C) 719
   D) 165,888

9. Subtract the polynomials: $(2x^2 + 3x + 2) - (x^2 + 2x - 3)$
   A) $x^2 + x + 5$
   B) $x^2 + x - 1$
   C) $x^2 + 5x + 5$
   D) $x^2 + 5x - 1$

10. The table below shows the breakdown of orders at a frozen yogurt shop. There were two flavors of yogurt (strawberry and lemon) and two sizes (small and large). If a person among those who ordered frozen yogurt is chosen at random, what is the probability that this person ordered a small serving of lemon yogurt?

	Strawberry	Lemon	Total
Small	12	9	21
Large	20	16	36
Total	32	25	57

A) $\frac{9}{25}$

B) $\frac{3}{7}$

C) $\frac{7}{19}$

D) $\frac{3}{19}$

11. If (x, y) is the solution to the following system of equations, what is the value of $x + y$?

$$3x + y = -2$$
$$y = -x$$

A) -1

B) 0

C) 1

D) 2

Refer to the following for questions 12 - 13:

Elise, Max, and Rylie are each offering lawn care services. Their prices for each service are listed in the table below. Prices are per square foot.

	Elise	Max	Rylie
Mowing	$0.0025	$0.002	$0.003
Edging	$0.0015	$0.0015	$0.002
Weeding	$0.055	$0.065	$0.05

12. Rylie was asked to mow and edge a lawn as well as weed a 1,000 square foot garden. If she will spend $12 on gas and other overhead costs, how large of a lawn does she need to be able to make a $75 profit?

A) 2,600 ft^2

B) 5,000 ft^2

C) 6,875 ft^2

D) 7,400 ft^2

13. Ms. Lin wants to have her 7,500 square foot lawn mowed and edged. She also has a flower bed of x square feet to be weeded. Which of the following inequalities represents x if Elise's services are a better deal than Max's?

A) $x < 250$

B) $x < 375$

C) $x > 250$

D) $x > 375$

14. A number of cash prizes were awarded for the top salespeople at ABC Communications, each in the amount of $100, $200, or $400. If the prizes totaled $1,600 and there were 7 total prizes awarded, what is the greatest possible number of $100 prizes awarded?

15. The graph of the system of inequalities $y \leq \frac{2}{3}x - \frac{3}{2}$ and $y \geq -2x - \frac{5}{2}$ has solutions in which quadrants on the xy-plane below?

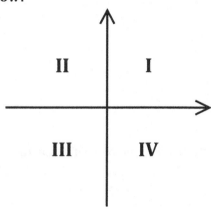

A) Quadrants I and IV
B) Quadrants II and III
C) Quadrants I, II, and IV
D) Quadrants I, III, and IV

16. The equation below is used to solve for the distance, d (meters), that an object travels in a certain amount of time, t (seconds), with an initial velocity of v meters per second. Which of the following equations gives a in terms of d, v, and t?

$$d = vt + \frac{1}{2}at^2$$

A) $\frac{2d - 2vt}{t}$

B) $\frac{2dvt}{t^2}$

C) $\frac{2d}{t^2} - \frac{2v}{t}$

D) $\frac{2d}{t^2} - 2vt$

17. The function f is defined by a polynomial. The table below gives values for x and $f(x)$. Which of the following must be a factor of $f(x)$?

x	$f(x)$
−5	14
−3	0
−1	−6

A) $x + 3$
B) $x - 3$
C) $x + 5$
D) $x - 5$

222

18. Simplify the following expression.

$$(3x + 5)(4x - 6)$$

A) $12x^2 - 38x - 30$
B) $12x^2 + 2x - 30$
C) $12x^2 - 2x - 1$
D) $12x^2 + 2x + 30$

19. If (x, y) is the solution to the following system of equations, what is the value of $x - y$?

$$4x - y = 11$$
$$x = 3y$$

A) 0
B) 1
C) 2
D) 3

20. The equation below is used to calculate the period of a pendulum (i.e., the time it takes a pendulum to make one full oscillation). If T refers to the time in seconds, L is the length of the pendulum in meters, and g is the acceleration due to gravity in meters per second squared, which of the following equations gives L in terms of T, g, and π?

$$T = 2\pi\sqrt{\frac{L}{g}}$$

A) $(T - 2\pi)^2 g$
B) $g\sqrt{\dfrac{T}{2\pi}}$
C) $\dfrac{T^2 g}{4\pi^2}$
D) $\dfrac{4\pi^2}{T^2 g}$

21. If $x > 0$ and $x^2 - 4x = 12$, what is the value of x?

22. In the function below, b is a constant. If $f(2) = 0$, what is the value of $f(-1)$?

$$f(x) = \frac{3}{2}x + b$$

A) $-\dfrac{9}{2}$
B) -3
C) $-\dfrac{3}{2}$
D) $\dfrac{3}{2}$

Answer Key and Explanations

Reading and Writing—Module 1

1. C: In this passage, the sentence is in the present perfect tense, indicating that these innovations and discoveries have already occurred and continue to be relevant. The phrase "have expanded" in choice C correctly indicates a past action with ongoing implications. These innovations and discoveries, initiated in the past, have contributed to expanding our knowledge of the universe, and this expansion is ongoing.

2. D: *Exemplifies* is the correct choice because it means to serve as a typical or model example of something, which aligns perfectly with the passage's description of the collaboration between the Navajo Nation and the University of Arizona as a shining model demonstrating the principles of community-based participatory research. In contrast, Choice A (*circumvents*) implies avoidance or bypassing, directly contradicting the portrayal of the successful partnership in the passage. Choice B (*eclipses*) suggests complete overshadowing, which does not capture the collaborative essence intended by *exemplifies*. Choice C (*fabricates*) denotes a false creation, a concept that contradicts the genuine nature of the collaboration portrayed in the passage.

3. A: This quotation effectively illustrates the claim made in the passage about the role and significance of the humanities. It conveys the central idea that the humanities are not just academic subjects but are deeply connected to the essence of humanity itself. It emphasizes that the humanities are integral to our understanding of the human experience and our identity as human beings.

4. C: In this passage, the order of the steps in the scientific method serves primarily to emphasize the importance of making observations. The passage outlines the steps of the scientific method sequentially and highlights that it starts with making observations. This structure emphasizes the foundational role of observation in the scientific process. While the scientific method does involve forming hypotheses, conducting experiments, and analyzing data, the passage's primary focus is on the initial step of making observations and how it contributes to scientific progress.

5. C: In the provided passage, Sarah's statement, "Believe me, Alex, your excuses won't cut it this time," is marked by her narrowed eyes and disdainful tone. This expression suggests a strong sense of skepticism and criticism. She is clearly not supportive of Alex's explanations and is questioning their validity. Therefore, choice C, which characterizes Sarah's statement as conveying skepticism and criticism, best aligns with the purpose of her statement in the context of the passage.

6. D: The passage discusses how leafcutter ants have evolved specialized adaptations for efficiently farming their fungus gardens. In this context, the presence of a specialized enzyme that enhances the growth of the cultivated fungus directly supports the idea that they have evolved specific mechanisms to optimize their farming process.

7. C: Choice C effectively highlights the uniqueness of Romantic literature by emphasizing its distinctive focus on imagination and nature. This choice directly addresses the student's goal of emphasizing each period's uniqueness.

8. C: The passage mentions that despite his busy schedule as a baker, Mr. Johnson always found time to donate fresh loaves of bread to the local shelter. This act of generosity indicates that he is known for his charitable actions and kindness toward those in need.

9. D: The passage primarily serves as a reflection on the author's personal belief in the power and significance of literature. It discusses the author's perspective on literature as a means of conveying ideas and emotions. While it mentions various aspects of literature, the central focus is on the author's viewpoint and belief.

10. B: The passage primarily emphasizes the values and cultural contexts reflected in artistic movements throughout history. It discusses how movements like the Renaissance and Romanticism celebrated and represented certain values and cultural aspects of their respective times. The passage does not specifically focus on the influence of scientific exploration, the celebration of emotion and individualism in Romanticism, or the appreciation of classical aesthetics in the Renaissance, although these topics are mentioned as part of the broader context.

11. C: The passage suggests that the impact of climate change on coral reefs has been challenging to understand due to intricate relationships. However, Dr. Olivia Chang's recent findings offer hope for preservation, indicating a more definitive, or *conclusive*, explanation. The other options do not fit as well: *an intricate* implies complexity; *an elusive* suggests difficulty in understanding; and *a clear* does not capture the idea of a definitive explanation.

12. C: This choice logically completes the text by emphasizing the underlying motivation for space exploration: scientific curiosity. While there are various objectives in space exploration, the primary driver is our innate curiosity to learn more about the cosmos. This choice aligns with the main theme of the passage.

13. C: The sentence starts in the present tense with "Even today, his words resonate," but then it suddenly switches to the past tense with "reminded us." This inconsistency in verb tense disrupts the flow and meaning of the sentence. To correct this error, the past tense *reminded* should be changed to the present participle *reminding* to maintain consistent verb tense throughout the sentence.

14. A: Choice A effectively compares the roles of Daisy Buchanan and Jordan Baker by highlighting their contrasting characteristics and the roles they play in the novel. It accurately describes Daisy as reflecting the disillusionment and emptiness of the wealthy elite, which aligns with her portrayal in the novel, and it correctly characterizes Jordan as a more independent and self-reliant woman, which is also consistent with her character.

15. D: Plants treated with Type D fertilizer achieved an average height of 47.5 cm, which is 20 cm higher than the average of the plants without fertilizer.

16. C: *Conversely*, is the most appropriate transition in this context. It helps to establish a contrast or counterpoint to the previous statement. The passage discusses the properties of acids (donating) and bases (accepting).

17. C: In the sentence, we are describing attire that belongs to the little girl, an individual child. To indicate possession in this context, we need to use a possessive form of *child*. The correct possessive form for a singular noun like *child* is *child's*.

18. B: Choice B, *perspective*, is the most appropriate selection, as it accurately conveys how Jane Austen's novels provide readers with a distinctive and insightful lens through which to view the society and manners of her time. Choice A, *endorsement*, doesn't align with the context of the sentence, as it suggests approval or support rather than the insightful perspective on society and manners that Austen's novels offer. Likewise, Choice C, *commentary*, pertains to providing opinions or explanations but doesn't quite capture the essence of offering a unique viewpoint or deep insight

225

into the subject at hand, which is the primary focus of the sentence. Lastly, Choice D, *refusal*, is entirely unrelated to the context of the sentence and lacks relevance.

19. B: *Because of* is the most suitable choice in this context because it indicates a causal relationship. It explains why Leonardo da Vinci is considered a quintessential Renaissance polymath: he had mastered numerous fields. This transition helps connect the introductory statement about the Renaissance to da Vinci's significance.

20. C: Choice C effectively utilizes relevant information from the notes to explain the role of enzymes. It begins by highlighting that enzymes are specialized proteins, setting the stage for understanding their essential function in living organisms. By stating that enzymes "speed up chemical reactions in living organisms," it directly addresses their catalytic role, clarifying that they act as biological catalysts. The option then goes on to provide specific examples of how enzymes contribute to various crucial biological processes, such as digestion, cellular respiration, DNA replication, and protein synthesis. This detailed information demonstrates that enzymes play a central role in these fundamental processes, emphasizing their significance in biological systems.

21. D: This choice effectively uses a non-restrictive participial phrase, "challenging the known laws of physics," set off by commas to provide additional information about the concept of black holes without making it essential to understanding the sentence. The use of commas correctly indicates that this information is supplemental but not necessary for the core meaning of the sentence, enhancing clarity and readability.

22. B: The word *which* is a relative pronoun that correctly connects the two clauses. It refers to *oxygen* and helps to provide additional information about it.

23. C: In this sentence, the blank refers to the ideas of multiple thinkers: Socrates, Confucius, and Simone de Beauvoir. Therefore, a plural pronoun is needed to agree with the plural noun *ideas*. *Their* is a plural possessive pronoun that correctly indicates that the ideas belong to the thinkers mentioned.

24. C: This choice provides a logical and fitting completion to the sentence in the passage. The previous descriptions in the passage convey a serene and awe-inspiring atmosphere in the forest. The phrase "they felt an overwhelming sense of wonder" aligns with the tranquil and captivating nature of the forest setting, making it the most suitable choice to complete the sentence.

25. B: In Passage 2, it's mentioned that Maya Angelou emphasized the importance of literature as a tool for empowerment and social change, with a specific focus on breaking down racial barriers and promoting an understanding among people of different backgrounds. Given this perspective, it's likely that Angelou would be critical of Twain's portrayal of race in *The Adventures of Huckleberry Finn*, which has sparked debates about racial stereotypes in literature.

Reading and Writing—Module 2

1. A: The passage highlights the significant impact of the Hubble Space Telescope in the field of astronomy. It mentions that Hubble has revolutionized our understanding of the universe, capturing images of distant galaxies, stars, and nebulae. The central idea revolves around the transformative role of Hubble's observations in the field of astronomy.

2. A: In this sentence, the use of a comma after *heart* is appropriate because it creates a pause that helps to clarify the structure of the sentence. The comma sets off the phrase "reminding all individuals to hold dear their inner values" as an appositive, providing additional information about *heart*.

3. A: This answer effectively and correctly provides an explanation of Rosa Parks' significance in the Civil Rights Movement by highlighting her act of civil disobedience and her refusal to give up her bus seat as a symbol of the movement. It directly addresses the student's goal of explaining and providing an example of Rosa Parks' significance based on the information from the notes.

4. A: In the sentence, *fortunately* is used as a transition word to indicate a fortunate or positive outcome of the situation. It logically connects the action of Alice running after the rabbit to the result of her being just in time to see it go down the rabbit-hole. The other options, such as *therefore*, *unexpectedly*, and *nevertheless*, do not provide a suitable transition in this context and would not convey the intended meaning.

5. B: The transitional phrase *In conclusion* is the most appropriate choice here because it indicates a final statement summarizing the passage.

6. B: Choice B combines information about the greenhouse effect and the ozone layer to provide a comprehensive explanation of how the atmosphere regulates Earth's temperature.

Choice A provides relevant information about the atmosphere's composition and the greenhouse effect but doesn't mention the ozone layer's role in UV radiation absorption, making it less comprehensive. Choice C mentions the atmosphere's composition and photosynthesis but doesn't directly explain the role in regulating temperature, making it less effective. Choice D provides information about the ozone layer and the atmosphere's composition but doesn't directly explain the greenhouse effect and its role in temperature regulation, making it less comprehensive.

7. A: The passage discusses the importance of photosynthesis, particularly in terms of providing oxygen and capturing solar energy. Given this context, the most logical completion for the text is to emphasize that photosynthesis is essential for sustaining life on Earth.

8. B: Choice B aligns best with the passage's emphasis on Shakespeare's beautiful representation of human life, making it the most logical and precise word. Choice A contradicts the passage by suggesting it *avoids* depth. Choice C, while similar to *captures*, implies direct copying, not creative representation. Choice D, *diminishes*, contradicts the passage's praise for enhancing human life's depth.

9. C: The passage highlights that Scout serves as the primary narrator. She immerses readers in Maycomb, a town marked by complex societal dynamics and prejudices. This emphasis on Scout as the narrator, along with the reference to her being a young girl, suggests that her role is primarily to provide a contrast between the innocence of childhood and the often biased and prejudiced viewpoints of adults.

10. C: A plural possessive form is used to indicate that something belongs to or is associated with a plural noun. In this passage, the word *artists'* is the only word that represents a plural possessive form. The phrase "The artists' loose brushstrokes and vivid palettes" indicates that the artists used their painting style and color selection to create their desired impression.

11. A: *Complex* is the most fitting word to complete the sentence. The sentence describes critics debating the nature of the protagonist in a novel, with some seeing the character as a symbol of hope and others as a representation of despair. This suggests that there is a diversity of opinions regarding the character's attributes. The other choices, *one-dimensional*, *unambiguous*, and *predictable*, do not align with the sentence's context.

12. C: In this sentence, the verb should be in the past tense to match the past tense context of the sentence. "Tom's voice" and "he was reading them" both indicate actions that occurred in the past. Therefore, the past tense form of the verb, *trembled*, is appropriate.

13. C: The main purpose of the passage is to paint a vivid picture of the forest's serene and tranquil atmosphere, with the old oak tree serving as a symbol of wisdom and solace. The passage doesn't primarily focus on describing the traveler's journey, emphasizing the strength of the tree, or suggesting an interaction with a talking tree. Instead, it aims to convey the calming and peaceful ambiance of the forest, making choice C the most suitable description of its purpose.

14. A: "Scientific inquiry and innovation" best fits this description, as the Renaissance was a time of great scientific advancement and exploration, with figures like those mentioned above making significant contributions to the understanding of the natural world.

15. A: In this passage, the sentence is discussing a necessity in the present tense, which requires the use of *requires* in choice A. Choices B and C use *requiring*, which is in the present participle form and doesn't fit the context. Choice D is grammatically incorrect as it adds *it* before *requires*, which is unnecessary in this sentence structure.

16. D: In Passage 2, Dr. Johnson acknowledges the impact of human activities on climate change but emphasizes the role of natural factors like volcanic eruptions and solar variations in shaping the Earth's climate as well. This suggests that Dr. Johnson's perspective aligns with the idea that both human activities and natural factors are significant contributors to climate change.

17. C: In the passage, it's mentioned that chameleons have the remarkable ability to change the color of their skin. The word *synchronization* is the most appropriate word in this context because it implies that chameleons synchronize, or match, their skin color with the environment, making them virtually invisible to predators or prey. The other choices, *prediction*, *moderation*, and *hibernation*, do not convey the same sense of matching or alignment with the surroundings and are not logical in this context.

18. A: The passage provides information about the surface temperatures of planets. To complete the example using data from the table, the planets' surface temperatures need to be noted and compared to each other. Choice A correctly states that Neptune has a lower surface temperature than Venus and Mars.

19. C: The main role of literature, as described in the passage, is to reflect societal issues and human experiences. The passage discusses how literature serves as a mirror to society, shedding light on issues such as racial injustice and totalitarianism. It emphasizes that literary works like *To Kill a Mockingbird* and *1984* provide valuable insights into the human condition by addressing and reflecting upon these societal issues and human experiences. While literature can certainly entertain and provide glimpses into historical events, the primary focus in this passage is on its role as a reflection of broader societal and human concerns.

20. A: Both passages highlight aspects of Romanticism. John Keats, in Passage 1, praises Romanticism for its emphasis on emotion, individualism, and a deeper connection with nature, which aligns with many of the themes in Mary Shelley's *Frankenstein* described in Passage 2. Shelley's novel, often considered a product of the Romantic era, explores themes of individuality and the power of nature. Given these shared themes, it's likely that Shelley would agree with Keats and expand on the importance of emotion in literature, as it resonates with the emotional depth and exploration in *Frankenstein*.

21. A: To ensure grammatical agreement and clarity, the pronoun *them* is the most suitable choice. *Them* refers to the plural noun *finest ingredients*, maintaining consistency in both subject and pronoun.

22. B: This finding, if true, most directly supports the student's claim that literature has a profound impact on society and individuals. It provides empirical evidence that reading literature with diverse characters and experiences can lead to increased empathy and tolerance in individuals, demonstrating how literature can shape attitudes and behaviors. This aligns with the student's argument that literature can evoke empathy and influence perceptions.

23. B: In the sentence, "They represent the deep connection between Japanese culture and the philosophy of Zen Buddhism," the verb tense should match the context of the passage. The passage primarily uses present tense verbs to describe the traditional Japanese tea ceremony and its characteristics. *Represent* maintains the present tense and is in agreement with the surrounding context.

24. C: Choice C is the most appropriate transition in this context because it effectively connects the preceding information about the role of electromagnetic waves to the consequence, which is the development of various devices and technologies. It logically shows the cause-and-effect relationship between the study of electromagnetism and the resulting technological advancements.

25. B: Choice B correctly uses the coordinating conjunction *and* to connect the independent and dependent clauses in the sentence. This maintains proper sentence structure and conveys the intended meaning effectively, indicating that these discoveries are important for advancing our knowledge of neuroscience and developing treatments for neurological disorders.

Mathematics—Module 1

1. A: To find when the apple reaches the ground, set the function $f(x)$ equal to 0 and solve for x.

$$0 = -x^2 - 2x + 7$$

This quadratic can't be easily factored, so use the quadratic formula to solve.

$$x = \frac{-b \pm \sqrt{b^2 - 4ac}}{2a}$$

$$x = \frac{-(-2) \pm \sqrt{(-2)^2 - 4(-1)(7)}}{2(-1)}$$

$$x = \frac{2 \pm \sqrt{4 + 28}}{-2}$$

$$x = \frac{2 \pm \sqrt{32}}{-2}$$

$$x = \frac{2 \pm 4\sqrt{2}}{-2}$$

229

$$x = -1 \pm 2\sqrt{2}$$

$$x \approx 1.8, -3.8$$

In this scenario, time can only be a positive value, so it took about 1.8 seconds for the apple to reach the ground.

2. C: First, solve for x in the first equation.

$$2x + 6 = -2$$

Subtract 6 from each side.

$$2x = -8$$

Then, divide each side by 2.

$$x = -4$$

Now we can plug this value of x into the second expression.

$$10(-4) + 11 = -40 + 11 = -29$$

3. C: A method commonly taught to multiply binomials is the FOIL method, an acronym for *first, outer, inner, last*: multiply the first terms of each factor, then the outer terms, then the inner terms, and finally, the last terms.

$$(x + 2)(x - 3)$$

$$(x)(x) + (x)(-3) + (2)(x) + (2)(-3)$$

From here, simplify and combine like terms.

$$x^2 - 3x + 2x - 6$$

$$x^2 - x - 6$$

4. A: We first find the mean, or average, of the lab grades by adding them and dividing by the number of grades.

$$\frac{84 + 86 + 98 + 90 + 97 + 85 + 90}{7} = \frac{630}{7} = 90$$

Then we find the median by arranging the grades in increasing order and finding the middle value: 84, 85, 86, 90, 90, 97, 98. The middle number is 90. So, the difference of the mean and median is $90 - 90 = 0$.

5. 2: We can find the points of intersection by setting the two equations equal to each other.

$$2x^2 + 3x = -x$$

Add x to each side and combine like terms.

$$2x^2 + 4x = 0$$

230

Factor the left side.

$$(2x)(x + 2) = 0$$

Setting the first term equal to 0 yields $2x = 0$. Thus, $x = 0$. This corresponds with the point we were given, $(0,0)$. Now we set the second term equal to 0: $x + 2 = 0$. We subtract 2 from each side to yield $x = -2$. This is a. To find b, we plug in –2 for x to either of the two equations and solve for y. Using the second equation: $y = -(-2)$, or $y = 2$. So, our point is $(-2,2)$ and $b = 2$.

6. 10: Since the population is multiplied by 3 for 5 days, we can write $x(3^5) = 2{,}430$, where x is the original population. Calculate 3^5 and simplify the equation.

$$243x = 2{,}430$$

Divide each side by 243.

$$x = 10$$

So, the original population was 10.

7. D: For Days 1, 2, and 3 (choices A, B, and C) on the chart, the number of seedlings is 0. Day 4 is the first time we see the line move away from 0, showing that 2 seedlings sprouted that day.

8. C: We first need to find the volume of water that Kasie is putting in each glass. The volume of a cylinder is $V = \pi r^2 h$. Since we know the radius is 1.25 and the height is 5 (ignore the actual height of the glass since it is not filled to the brim), we can write the following equation.

$$V = (3.14)(1.25)^2(5)$$

$$V \approx 24.53 \text{ in}^3$$

Now we need to find the number of cubic inches in 3 quarts.

$$\left(\frac{3 \text{ qt}}{1}\right)\left(\frac{1 \text{ gal}}{4 \text{ qt}}\right)\left(\frac{231 \text{ in}^3}{1 \text{ gal}}\right) = 173.25 \text{ in}^3$$

Finally, we divide 173.25 by 24.53 to find that Kasie could fill 7.06 glasses. In other words, she could completely fill 7 glasses.

9. C: The situation may be modeled by this system of equations:

$$\begin{cases} 4y + 3c = 9.55 \\ 2y + 2c = 5.90 \end{cases}$$

Multiplying the bottom equation by –2 gives:

$$\begin{cases} 4y + 3c = 9.55 \\ -4y - 4c = -11.80 \end{cases}$$

Adding the two equations gives $-c = -2.25$, or $c = 2.25$. Thus, one box of crackers costs \$2.25.

10. C: If 85% of the sample group prefer the new brand of juice, we can infer that most shoppers will likely prefer it. We cannot say that 85% of all shoppers will prefer it (choice A), because that would require testing all shoppers, but we can make a generalization that most shoppers seem to prefer the new brand. Choice B is incorrect because 15% is the number of the surveyed shoppers who did not prefer the new brand. Choice D is incorrect because it implies the opposite of the correct answer.

11. D: We solve for x and y by using elimination. We can multiply the second equation by 2 and then add the two equations to eliminate the y-terms.

$$5x - 6y = 12$$
$$\underline{+(-4x + 6y = -10)}$$
$$x = 2$$

If $x = 2$, we can solve for y by plugging the x-value back into one of the equations. For example, use the second equation.

$$-2(2) + 3y = -5$$

Simplify and add 4 to each side.

$$3y = -1$$

Divide each side by 3.

$$y = -\frac{1}{3}$$

So, the solution is $\left(2, -\frac{1}{3}\right)$. Now we can use these values to find $x^2 - 3y$.

$$(2)^2 - 3\left(-\frac{1}{3}\right) = 4 + 1 = 5$$

12. D: Bacterial growth is exponential. Let x be the number of times the population doubles, a be the number of bacteria in the colony originally transferred into the broth, and y be the number of bacteria in the broth after x doubling times. After 1 hour, the population would have doubled three times:

$$a(2)^x = y$$
$$a(2^3) = 8 \times 10^6$$
$$8a = 8 \times 10^6$$
$$a = 10^6$$

So, the number of bacteria originally transferred into the petri dish was 10^6. The equation for determining the number of bacteria is $y = (2^x) \times 10^6$. Since the bacteria double every twenty minutes, they go through three doubling times every hour. So, when the bacteria are allowed to grow for eight hours, they will have gone through $8 \times 3 = 24$ doubling times. When $x = 24$, $y = (2^{24}) \times 10^6 = 16,777,216 \times 10^6$, which is approximately 1.7×10^{13}.

13. B: We first solve for x in the first equation.

$$3x - 4 = -1$$

Add 4 to each side.

$$3x = 3$$

232

Then, divide each side by 3.

$$x = 1$$

Be careful not to mistakenly select answer choice D rather than finishing the problem. The final step is to plug this value of x into the second expression.

$$12(1) + 3 = 12 + 3 = 15$$

14. C: Because the radicals are the same, we can add the coefficients in front of the radicals and keep the radical the same.

$$4\sqrt{6} + 8\sqrt{6} = (4 + 8)\sqrt{6} = 12\sqrt{6}$$

Since the radicand, 6, has no perfect square factor, we cannot simplify this expression further.

15. 6: If the two triangles are similar, corresponding sides are also similar. Set up a ratio.

$$\frac{AB}{4} = \frac{9}{6}$$

Then, cross-multiply.

$$6AB = 9(4)$$
$$6AB = 36$$

Divide both sides by 6.

$$AB = 6$$

16. D: The equation of a circle is $(x - h)^2 + (y - k)^2 = r^2$, where r is the radius. We need to put the equation in this form to solve for r. First, we separate the x- and y-terms and then we complete the square.

$$(x^2 - 4x) + (y^2 + 2y) = 4$$
$$(x^2 - 4x + 4) - 4 + (y^2 + 2y + 1) - 1 = 4$$
$$(x - 2)^2 + (y + 1)^2 - 5 = 4$$
$$(x - 2)^2 + (y + 1)^2 = 9$$
$$(x - 2)^2 + (y + 1)^2 = 3^2$$

Thus, we can see that the radius is 3 (be careful not to mistakenly choose answer choice B). Since the diameter is twice the radius, we multiply 3 by 2 to obtain 6.

17. A: We begin by solving the inequality for a.

$$4x + 3 \leq 1$$

First, subtract 3 from each side.

$$4a \leq -2$$

Then, divide each side by 4 and reduce.

$$a \leq -\frac{1}{2}$$

So, $-\frac{1}{2}$ is the greatest possible value for a. We plug this value into $6a - 2$

$$6\left(-\frac{1}{2}\right) - 2 = -3 - 2 = -5$$

18. C: We need to find the point at which i is equal to p, so we set the two equations equal to each other.

$$5.5x = 15,200 + 0.75x$$

Subtract $0.75x$ from each side.

$$4.75x = 15,200$$

Divide each side by 4.75.

$$x = 3,200$$

Therefore, the "break even" number of products is 3,200.

19. B: The point marked on the scatterplot for the final day shows that Julio practiced for 3 hours, while the line of best fit crosses the 2-hour mark on the same day. The difference between 3 hours and 2 hours is 1 hour.

20. B: Dividing both sides of the equation by $\frac{1}{3}\pi h$ gives $r^2 = \frac{V}{\frac{1}{3}\pi h} = \frac{3V}{\pi h}$. We can then solve for r by taking the square root of both sides, which gives us $r = \sqrt{\frac{3V}{\pi h}}$.

21. C: If Jan has 6 pairs of socks for each pair of shoes, we can write that socks = 6(shoes). We can then substitute 12 for the shoes and s for the socks: $s = 6(12)$. We look through the answer choices to see which matches this. Answer choice A can be rewritten as $s = \frac{6}{12}$. Answer choice B can be rewritten as $s = \frac{12}{6}$. Answer choice C can be rewritten as $s = 6(12)$. Answer choice D can be rewritten as $s = 12 - 6$. So only answer choice C matches.

22. C: To solve, we raise each side to the –2 power. This yields $\left(x^{-\frac{1}{2}}\right)^{-2} = m^{-2}$. We can simplify to $x = \frac{1}{m^2}$. Answer choice A is incorrect because it raises m to the power of 2, not –2. Answer choice B is incorrect because it adds in a constant (1) and does not raise m to the power of –2. Answer choice D is incorrect because it raises m to the power of –1, not –2.

Mathematics—Module 2

1. 0.25: If the two triangles are similar, corresponding sides are also similar. We can set up a ratio: $\frac{AB}{EF} = \frac{4}{8} = \frac{1}{2}$, or 0.5. If the ratio of each side of $\triangle ABC$ to each side of $\triangle EFG$ is $\frac{1}{2}$, the ratio of the areas is $\left(\frac{1}{2}\right)^2 = \frac{1}{4}$, or 0.25. Alternatively, we could find the actual area of each right triangle. We can find side BC by multiplying side FG by $\frac{1}{2}$: $12 \times \frac{1}{2} = 6$. So the area of $\triangle ABC$ is $\frac{1}{2} \times 4 \times 6 = 12$. The area of $\triangle EFG$ is $\frac{1}{2} \times 8 \times 12 = 48$. Thus, the ratio of the areas is $\frac{\triangle ABC}{\triangle EFG} = \frac{12}{48} = \frac{1}{4}$, or 0.25.

2. D: We look for a value at which $f(x) = 0$ to determine a factor, because the graph of the equation crosses the x-axis at this point. The table shows that $f(x) = 0$ when $x = 2$, so the point is (2,0). This means that if we were to factor the original equation, one of the factors would be $(x - 2)$, as $y = x - 2$ goes through the point (2,0).

3. A: The solution(s) to a system of equations is the point or points at which the graphs of the two equations cross. If a system has no solution, this means that the graphs never cross. In other words, the two graphs are parallel. In the system here, we know the lines will be parallel if the slopes are identical. We can look at the first equation to find the slope by moving the x-value to the right and solving for y.

$$y = -\frac{1}{3}x - \frac{7}{3}$$

Thus, the slope of the second equation needs to also be $-\frac{1}{3}$. We again move the x-value to the right and solve for y.

$$y = \frac{-a}{-2}x + \frac{6}{-2}$$

$$y = \frac{a}{2} - 3$$

Therefore, the slope here is $\frac{a}{2}$. We can set the slopes equal to each other to solve for a.

$$\frac{a}{2} = -\frac{1}{3}$$

Then we cross-multiply.

$$3a = -2$$

Finally, we divide both sides by 3.

$$a = -\frac{2}{3}$$

4. C: We need to simplify the equation so we can factor it. First, we subtract 3 from each side.

$$5x^2 - 30x - 35 = 0$$

Then we can divide each term by 5.

235

$$x^2 - 6x - 7 = 0$$

Finally, we can factor.

$$(x + 1)(x - 7) = 0$$

Setting each factored term equal to 0 yields $x + 1 = 0$ and $x - 7 = 0$, or $x = -1$ and $x = 7$. The sum of –1 and 7 is 6.

5. 0.8: The cosine of an angle can be calculated as the adjacent Dside (3) divided by the hypotenuse (5). If angle M measures $a°$, then angle N measures $(90 - a)°$, so we are looking for the cosine of angle N. We begin by solving for the remaining side of the triangle. If the hypotenuse of a right triangle is 5 and one leg is 3, the other leg can be found with the Pythagorean theorem:

$$3^2 + NP^2 = 5^2$$
$$9 + NP^2 = 25$$

$$NP^2 = 16$$

$$NP = 4$$

So, we can find the cosine of angle N by taking the adjacent side (4) and dividing by the hypotenuse (5). So the answer is $\frac{4}{5}$ or 0.8.

6. D: If 52% of the sample group prefer Brand A, this is very close to half, and it is not logical to claim that either brand has a majority (answer choices B and C) when only 25 people were polled and results are fairly inconclusive (we can calculate that 13 liked Brand A and 12 liked Brand B). We cannot presume that 52% or more of all shoppers will prefer it (answer choice A), because there can be margin of error in either direction.

7. 1 or 2: We can choose any value between 1.2 and 1.5 to use as our diameter. The formula for volume of a sphere is $V = \frac{4}{3}\pi r^3$, so the first step is to find the radius, dividing the diameter by 2. If we choose the smallest value, our diameter is $1.2 \div 2 = 0.6$. We then can calculate volume.

$$V = \frac{4}{3}(3.14)(0.6)^3$$

$$V \approx 0.90$$

Rounding to the nearest cubic inch gives us 1 in^3.

If we choose the largest value, our diameter is $1.5 \div 2 = 0.75$. We then can calculate volume.

$$V = \frac{4}{3}(3.14)(0.75)^3$$

$$V \approx 2.4$$

Rounding to the nearest cubic inch gives us 2 in^3. Since any possible answer will be between these two values, either 1 or 2 is a correct answer.

8. C: We first need to find the volume of the container. Since we will need to know the volume in cubic inches to convert to gallons, we convert each measurement from feet to inches by multiplying each by 12. Thus, the length is $8 \times 12 = 96$ inches, the width is $4 \times 12 = 48$ inches, and the height is $3 \times 12 = 36$ inches. The volume of a rectangular prism is $V = lwh$, so we can calculate the container's volume.

$$V = 96 \times 48 \times 36 = 165{,}888 \text{ in}^3$$

Now we need to find the number of gallons needed to fill this container.

$$\left(\frac{165{,}888 \text{ in}^3}{1}\right)\left(\frac{1 \text{ gal}}{231 \text{ in}^3}\right) = 718.13 \text{ gallons}$$

Since the problem is asking for the number of gallon jugs to completely fill the container, we need to round up. Buying 718 jugs will almost completely fill the container, but a little water will be needed from jug 719.

Choice A is incorrect because it only multiplies the volume in feet by 12 to convert to inches, rather than multiplying each dimension. Choice B is incorrect because it rounds down instead of up. Choice D is incorrect because it is the volume in cubic inches rather than gallons.

9. A: Note that $(2x^2 + 3x + 2) - (x^2 + 2x - 3) = (2x^2 + 3x + 2) + (-1)(x^2 + 2x - 3)$. Distribute the -1 to remove the parentheses: $2x^2 + 3x + 2 - x^2 - 2x + 3$. Next, combine like terms.

$$(2x^2 - x^2) + (3x - 2x) + (2 + 3) = x^2 + x + 5$$

10. D: We can see from the table that 9 people ordered a small serving of lemon yogurt and that a total of 57 orders were placed. So, the probability is 9 out of 57, or $\frac{9}{57}$. We can divide both the numerator and denominator by 3 to reduce the fraction to $\frac{3}{19}$. Choice A is the probability of choosing a small serving given that lemon yogurt was selected (not the overall probability). Choice B is the probability of choosing lemon given that a small serving was selected ($\frac{9}{21}$ reduces to $\frac{3}{7}$). Choice C is the probability of choosing a small serving ($\frac{21}{57}$ reduces to $\frac{7}{19}$).

11. B: We can solve the system of equations by using substitution. We can plug in $-x$ for y in the top equation.

$$3x + (-x) = -2$$

This simplifies to $2x = -2$, and dividing each side by 2 yields $x = -1$. Then we can solve for y with the bottom equation.

$$y = -(-1) = 1$$

Finally, we can calculate $x + y = -1 + 1 = 0$. Choice A is incorrect because it is the value of x. Choice C is incorrect because it is the value of y. Choice D is incorrect because it is the value of $(y - x)$.

12. D: For Rylie to make \$75 in profit, she needs to earn $\$75 + \$12 = \$87$ to compensate for her overhead costs. We can calculate the amount she will earn by weeding the garden: $0.05(1{,}000) = \$50$. We subtract this from \$87 to find that she needs to earn an additional \$37 from mowing and edging the lawn. Letting the size of the lawn be x, we can write out our equation.

$$0.003x + 0.002x = 37$$

Simplify by combining like terms on the left side.

$$0.005x = 37$$

Next, divide each side by 0.005.

$$x = 7,400$$

So, the lawn needs to be at least 7,400 square feet.

13. D: Start by calculating the cost of each person's mowing and edging.

Elise's cost: $0.0025(7,500) + 0.0015(7,500) = 18.75 + 11.25 = \$30$

Max's cost: $0.002(7,500) + 0.0015(7,500) = 15 + 11.25 = \$26.25$

Now we can set up an inequality, letting x be the size of the flower bed. For Elise's services to be a better deal, they must cost less than Max's.

$$30 + 0.055x < 26.25 + 0.065x$$

Solve for x by subtracting $0.055x$ from both sides.

$$30 < 26.25 + 0.01x$$

Now, subtract 26.25 from each side.

$$3.75 < 0.01x$$

We rewrite this as $0.01x > 3.75$ and divide each side by 0.01 to obtain $x > 375$. It is important to remember to reverse the inequality sign when we move the x to the left so we don't end up with $x < 375$ (answer choice B).

14. 4: Since the total is an even number of hundreds (16) and the $100 prize is the only prize that is an odd number of hundreds, we can conclude that there must be an even number of $100 prizes awarded. Since we are looking for the greatest number, we should begin at the top and check each number to see if it is possible.

If there are six $100 prizes awarded, this leaves only one other prize to make up the difference.

$$\$1,600 - 6(\$100) = \$1,600 - \$600 = \$1,000$$

Since there is not a $1,000 prize, there cannot be six $100 prizes.

If there are four $100 prizes awarded, this leaves three other prizes to make up the difference.

$$\$1,600 - 4(\$100) = \$1,600 - \$400 = \$1,200$$

Note that $1,200 divided by 3 is $400, so a combination of four $100 prizes and three $400 prizes satisfies all the parameters.

15. D: We can graph the two lines on a coordinate plane by plotting the y-intercept and then finding another point based on the slope. For the first equation, the y-intercept is $-\frac{3}{2}$, so we plot the point $\left(0, -\frac{3}{2}\right)$. Then we use the slope $\left(\frac{2}{3}\right)$ to plot another point by moving up 2 and 3 to the right, to $\left(3, \frac{1}{2}\right)$.

Now we can draw a line passing through the two points. It is a solid line because the solution is less than or equal to the equation. Next, we graph the second line. The y-intercept is $-\frac{5}{2}$, so we plot the point $\left(0, -\frac{5}{2}\right)$. Then we use the slope (−2) to plot another point by moving down 2 and over 1, to $\left(1, -\frac{9}{2}\right)$. Now we can draw a line passing through the two points. It is also a solid line because the solution is greater than or equal to the equation. We shade the area that is both below the graph of the first line and above the graph of the second line. When we do this, we can see that the overlap of the shaded area in Quadrants I, III, and IV.

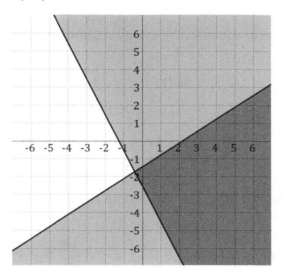

16. C: Solve for a by rearranging the equation to isolate a.

$$d = vt + \frac{1}{2}at^2$$

Subtract vt from both sides.

$$d - vt = \frac{1}{2}at^2$$

Then, multiply each side by $\frac{2}{t^2}$.

$$a = \frac{2d - 2vt}{t^2}$$

Finally, break it into two fractions and simplify.

$$\frac{2d}{t^2} - \frac{2v}{t}$$

Choice A is incorrect because it is missing one t in the denominator. Choice B is incorrect because it multiples the d and vt terms instead of subtracting them. Choice D is incorrect because it leaves off the denominator of t^2 in the second term.

17. A: We look for a value at which $f(x) = 0$ to determine a factor, because the graph of the equation crosses the x-axis at this point. The table shows that $f(x) = 0$ when $x = -3$, so the point is $(-3,0)$. This means that if we were to factor the original equation, one of the factors would be $(x + 3)$, as $y = x + 3$ goes through the point $(-3,0)$.

18. B: Use the FOIL method (first, outside, inside, and last) to expand the polynomial multiplication.

$$12x^2 - 18x + 20x - 30$$

Then, combine like terms to simplify the expression.

$$12x^2 + 2x - 30$$

19. C: We can solve the system of equations by using substitution. Plug in $3y$ for x in the top equation, and solve for y.

$$4(3y) - y = 11$$

$$12y - y = 11$$

$$11y = 11$$

$$y = 1$$

Then, solve for x by substituting 1 in for y in the bottom equation.

$$x = 3y = 3(1) = 3$$

Finally, we can calculate the final expression.

$$x - y = 3 - 1 = 2$$

20. C: Solve for L by rearranging the equation to isolate it. First, divide 2π from both sides.

$$\frac{T}{2\pi} = \sqrt{\frac{L}{g}}$$

Then, square each side to eliminate the radical.

$$\left(\frac{T}{2\pi}\right)^2 = \left(\sqrt{\frac{L}{g}}\right)^2$$

$$\frac{T^2}{4\pi^2} = \frac{L}{g}$$

Finally, multiply both sides by g.

$$\frac{T^2 g}{4\pi^2} = L$$

Choice A is incorrect because it subtracts 2π instead of dividing it. Choice B is incorrect because it takes the square root when it should have squared the fraction. Choice D is incorrect because it is the reciprocal of the correct answer.

21. 6: Solve for x in the equation by first subtracting 12 from each side.

$$x^2 - 4x - 12 = 0$$

Then, factor the left side.

$$(x + 2)(x - 6) = 0$$

Solving yields $x = -2$ or $x = 6$, and since the problem specifies that $x > 0$, this means that $x = 6$.

22. A: First, solve for the constant by using the ordered pair $(2,0)$.

$$0 = \frac{3}{2}(2) + b$$

Multiply on the right side.

$$0 = 3 + b$$

Then, solve for b by subtracting 3 from each side.

$$-3 = b$$

Now the equation can be rewritten with the value of b plugged in.

$$f(x) = \frac{3}{2}x - 3$$

Finally, plug in –1 for x and solve.

$$f(-1) = \frac{3}{2}(-1) - 3 = -\frac{3}{2} - \frac{6}{2} = -\frac{9}{2}$$

Answer choice B is incorrect because it is the value of b rather than the function required. Choice C is incorrect because it uses 1 for x rather than –1. Choice D is incorrect because it adds 3 rather than subtracting.

SAT Practice Test #2

Reading and Writing—Module 1

1. Which choice most logically completes the text?

The study of genetics has unlocked numerous secrets of heredity and evolution. Genetics is the branch of biology that delves into the inheritance of traits and the role of genes in shaping living organisms. By understanding the genetic code and the mechanisms of inheritance, scientists have made remarkable strides in medicine. For example, breakthroughs in medical genetics have led to the development of innovative treatments, such as gene therapies for inherited diseases like cystic fibrosis. These treatments address the root causes of genetic disorders by modifying or replacing faulty genes, marking a significant advancement in medical science. Ongoing genetics research is continually revealing connections between genes and various diseases, suggesting _____.

A) potential approaches for genetic engineering and cloning
B) promising avenues for the prevention and treatment of illnesses
C) a diminishing role of genetics in modern science
D) limitations in our current understanding of genetics and heredity

2. The student wants to emphasize the uniqueness of Emily Dickinson's contribution to literature. Which choice most effectively uses relevant information from the notes to accomplish this goal?

While researching a significant figure in literature, a student has collected the following information:

- Emily Dickinson, an American poet, is known for her unconventional style and reclusive life.
- She wrote nearly 1,800 poems, most of which were not published during her lifetime.
- Her work was published posthumously, and her poems garnered critical acclaim.
- Emily Dickinson's poetry is recognized for its unique use of punctuation, dashes, and enigmatic themes.
- Her work is often associated with themes of death, nature, and the human condition.

A) Emily Dickinson, the American poet, had an unconventional style and wrote nearly 1,800 poems, most of which remained unpublished during her lifetime.
B) Emily Dickinson's unconventional style, marked by innovative punctuation and enigmatic themes in her nearly 1,800 poems, distinguishes her as a unique and remarkable literary figure.
C) Emily Dickinson's work is often associated with themes of death, nature, and the human condition, making her contributions to literature unique and profound
D) Her extensive body of work, nearly 1,800 poems, often delves into themes of death, nature, and the human condition, setting her apart as a truly unique literary voice.

3. Which choice completes the text with the most logical and precise word or phrase?

The balcony scene in William Shakespeare's *Romeo and Juliet*, is one of the most iconic moments in literature. As Romeo stands in the Capulets' garden, he overhears Juliet confessing her love for him. The scene is _____ exploration of the intensity of young love as Romeo and Juliet declare their feelings for each other in poetic language. The balcony scene captures the passion, secrecy, and longing that define the love story of Romeo and Juliet, making it a cornerstone of Shakespearean tragedy.

A) an evocative
B) an emotional
C) a mundane
D) a superficial

4. Which findings about the calming effect of music and its ability to enhance concentration, if true, would most directly support the claim that music positively impacts mental health and productivity?

Music has long been celebrated for its profound impact on human emotions and well-being. From the stirring melodies of classical symphonies to the foot-tapping rhythms of rock and pop, music's influence on our moods and feelings is undeniable. Research in the field of music psychology has unearthed intriguing findings about the connection between music and various aspects of human life. It's been noted that listening to music can have a calming effect, reducing stress and anxiety. Moreover, certain types of music have the potential to enhance concentration and productivity, making it a useful tool for work or study. Beyond the individual experience, music also plays a pivotal role in building cultural identity and fostering a sense of community. Shared musical experiences, such as concerts and festivals, have the power to bring people together, fostering a sense of unity and belonging.

A) Some experimental data suggests that the impact of music on concentration and productivity varies, leaving room for debate on its role in improving mental health.
B) A certain genre of music known as "chaotic noise music" is found to increase stress and anxiety levels in individuals who listen to it during work or study.
C) Recent studies have revealed that background instrumental music during work or study can lead to improved focus and productivity.
D) Listening to jazz music has a mixed impact on concentration, sometimes enhancing it and sometimes distracting from tasks.

5. Which choice completes the text so that it conforms to the conventions of Standard English?

Hockey is more than just a sport; it's a fast-paced and thrilling journey that captivates _____ alike. Whether it's ice hockey or field hockey, this game has a way of uniting people through its sheer intensity and excitement.

A) the player and the fan
B) players and fans
C) the players and the fans
D) player and fan

6. Which choice completes the text so that it conforms to the conventions of Standard English?

The Asch Conformity Experiments, conducted by psychologist Solomon Asch in the 1950s, are renowned for shedding light on the powerful influence of social conformity. In these experiments, participants were shown a series of lines and asked to identify the one that matched a reference line in length. What made these studies fascinating was that a majority of participants would conform to the incorrect answers provided by their fellow group members, even when the correct answer was glaringly obvious. The findings illustrated the potency of social pressure and the human tendency to go along with the group, even if it meant disregarding their own judgment. Asch's work significantly contributed to our understanding of how social norms and peer pressure can shape individual behavior and

_____.

A) continues to be a pivotal reference in the study of conformity and group dynamics
B) will continue to be a pivotal reference in the study of conformity and group dynamics
C) continued to be a pivotal reference in the study of conformity and group dynamics
D) continuing to be a pivotal reference in the study of conformity and group dynamics

7. Based on the texts, both authors would most likely agree with which statement?

Passage 1: The Role of Folktales in Preserving Cultural Heritage
Folktales have long served as a means of preserving cultural heritage and passing down the values and traditions of a society from one generation to the next. These stories, often orally transmitted, contain moral lessons, historical narratives, and the collective wisdom of a community. For instance, in the folktales of many indigenous peoples, stories of ancestral spirits, nature, and bravery are shared to instill a sense of identity and connection to the land.

Passage 2: Literature as a Reflection of Societal Change
Throughout history, literature has reflected the shifts and changes in society. Novels, poems, and plays often capture the zeitgeist of their time, offering insights into the societal norms, values, and challenges. For instance, the works of Charles Dickens during the Industrial Revolution provide a vivid depiction of the social disparities and hardships faced by the working class.

A) Folktales are more effective than literature in preserving cultural heritage.
B) Both folktales and literature serve as means of preserving cultural heritage.
C) Folktales serve exclusively as historical records, while literature serves as a form of artistic expression.
D) Folktales are less effective than literature in reflecting societal change.

8. Which choice completes the text so that it conforms to the conventions of Standard English?

Dr. Sandra Faber's experiments have taken her into the depths of the _____ her approach is far from conventional. In her innovative work with gravitational lensing, she not only deepens our understanding of the universe but also challenges traditional perspectives. Gravitational lensing has allowed her to unveil cosmic phenomena that were previously hidden from view. These experiments have revealed the intricacies of the cosmos. It is not just her pioneering techniques that set her apart; it's the boundless curiosity and determination she brings to each exploration of the universe.

A) cosmos. But,
B) cosmos; however,
C) cosmos, however,
D) cosmos: but,

9. Which choice completes the text with the most logical and precise word or phrase?

Literature, as a cornerstone of the humanities, often serves as a reflection of society's values, beliefs, and cultural norms. Classic works of literature like George Orwell's *1984* or Harper Lee's *To Kill a Mockingbird* delve into complex social and moral issues. These novels not only entertain but also challenge readers to _____ ethical dilemmas, justice, and human nature. The humanities, through the study of literature and other artistic forms, provide us with a deeper understanding of the human experience and the complexities of the world around us.

A) obfuscate
B) contemplate
C) elude
D) resolve

10. Which choice best describes data from the table that support the researchers' claim?

Name	Temperature Increase (°C)	Sea Level Rise (cm)
Pacific Ocean	0.1	1.2
Atlantic Ocean	0.2	2.5
Indian Ocean	0.15	9.3
Arctic Ocean	0.5	11.5
Southern Ocean	0.08	0.1

A group of climate scientists from various research institutions collaborated on a comprehensive study to understand the factors influencing the increase in global sea levels over the past century. Their research claims that the primary contributors to rising sea levels are the thermal expansion of seawater due to global warming and the melting of glaciers and polar ice caps.

A) Among the five oceans in the table, the ocean with the highest temperature increase also has the highest rise in sea level.
B) The ocean with the highest temperature increase also exhibits the lowest rise in sea level.
C) The ocean with the highest rise in sea level had the smallest increase in temperature.
D) There was no correlation between ocean temperature increase and rise in sea level.

11. Which choice completes the text with the most logical transition?

Carlsbad Caverns, a world-renowned natural wonder located in New Mexico, is celebrated for its immense underground chambers and spectacular limestone formations. Explorers are greeted by a breathtaking descent into a subterranean realm filled with awe-inspiring stalactites and stalagmites. _____, the cave system is home to a unique ecosystem with diverse species adapted to the darkness, including thousands of Mexican free-tailed bats, making it a destination of both geological and biological significance.

A) Additionally
B) Therefore
C) For instance
D) Specifically

12. Which choice completes the text so that it conforms to the conventions of Standard English?

Gabriel Garcia Márquez, the celebrated Colombian author, is a literary icon whose works have left an indelible mark on the world of literature. His magical realism _____ readers to the enchanting and mystical realms of Latin America, where reality and fantasy intertwine seamlessly.

A) has transported
B) is transporting
C) will transport
D) transported

13. Which choice completes the text so that it conforms to the conventions of Standard English?

While the San Andreas Fault has been the subject of extensive research, one particular study conducted by scientists at the United States Geological Survey (USGS) involves the use of a comprehensive seismic hazard model for the Southern San Andreas Fault. This research _____ on estimating the probability of various levels of ground shaking in Southern California over specific time periods.

A) focused
B) focuses
C) focusing
D) focus

14. Which choice completes the text so that it conforms to the conventions of Standard English?

The Maasai Mara, a renowned wildlife reserve in southwestern _____ land of rolling grasslands, acacia-studded plains, and meandering rivers. It is famous for the annual wildebeest migration, a staggering spectacle where hundreds of thousands of wildebeest and zebras cross the Mara River, attracting predators like lions and crocodiles. This reserve also offers a glimpse into the rich culture of the Maasai people, known for their vibrant attire, intricate beadwork, and traditional ceremonies. The Maasai Mara is a paradise for nature enthusiasts and photographers where the grandeur of nature and the human spirit converge in a remarkable journey.

A) Kenya, a
B) Kenya; is a
C) Kenya, is a
D) Kenya: a

15. Which choice completes the text with the most logical transition?

Geckos, known for their remarkable climbing abilities, possess tiny, adhesive hairs on their toes called spatulae. These spatulae create attractive forces that allow geckos to cling to various surfaces, even upside down. _____, geckos are known for their remarkable agility, making them adept hunters and climbers in their natural habitats.

A) Similarly
B) However
C) Moreover
D) To illustrate

16. The student wants to emphasize the impact of Tesla's inventions on the electrical engineering field. Which choice most effectively uses relevant information from the notes to accomplish this goal?

While conducting research on a significant inventor, a student has gathered the following notes:

- Nikola Tesla, a Serbian American inventor, is renowned for his contributions to electrical engineering.
- He developed the alternating current (AC) electrical system, which revolutionized the power industry.

- Tesla held numerous patents related to electrical and mechanical devices.
- His famous Tesla coil is a key invention that demonstrated wireless transmission of electricity.
- Tesla's work laid the foundation for many modern electrical technologies.

A) Tesla developed the alternating current (AC) electrical system and the Tesla coil, which are breakthroughs that left a lasting mark on the electrical engineering field.
B) Tesla's numerous patents for mechanical devices show his significant impact on the field of electrical engineering
C) Tesla was known for his work with the Tesla coil, which is a famous invention that displayed some interesting scientific phenomena.
D) Tesla's Serbian American heritage and his numerous patents on both electrical and mechanical devices make him an interesting historical figure.

17. Which choice best states the main idea of the text?

"The Yellow Wallpaper" by Charlotte Perkins Stetson

We have been here two weeks, and I haven't felt like writing before, since that first day.

I am sitting by the window now, up in this atrocious nursery, and there is nothing to hinder my writing as much as I please, save lack of strength.

John is away all day, and even some nights when his cases are serious.

I am glad my case is not serious!

But these nervous troubles are dreadfully depressing.

John does not know how much I really suffer. He knows there is no reason to suffer, and that satisfies him.

Of course it is only nervousness. It does weigh on me so not to do my duty in any way!

I meant to be such a help to John, such a real rest and comfort, and here I am a comparative burden already!

Nobody would believe what an effort it is to do what little I am able—to dress and entertain, and order things.

It is fortunate Mary is so good with the baby. Such a dear baby!

And yet I cannot be with him, it makes me so nervous.

I suppose John never was nervous in his life. He laughs at me so about this wallpaper!

At first he meant to repaper the room, but afterwards he said that I was letting it get the better of me, and that nothing was worse for a nervous patient than to give way to such fancies.

A) The protagonist is facing challenges in her role as a wife and mother due to her nervous condition.
B) The protagonist is feeling overwhelmed by her duties and responsibilities, particularly in dealing with her baby.
C) The protagonist is obsessed with the room's wallpaper and is seeking to have it changed to alleviate her nervousness.
D) The protagonist is suffering from nervous troubles and is struggling with her husband's dismissive attitude towards her condition.

18. Which discoveries about dark matter, if true, would most directly support the claim that the collaborative efforts of scientists from various disciplines are essential in the pursuit of understanding dark matter's nature and role in the universe?

In the pursuit of understanding the enigmatic dark matter, scientists from diverse disciplines have joined forces. Astrophysicists, like Dr. Sarah Johnson, employ telescopes to study its gravitational effects on galaxies, while particle physicists, such as Dr. James Chen, conduct experiments to detect potential dark matter particles. Cosmologists, like Dr. Maria Rodriguez, explore the cosmic microwave background radiation for insights into the early universe and dark matter's distribution. Theoretical physicists, including Dr. Michael Turner, work on mathematical models guiding experimental and observational scientists in their shared mission to unveil the nature of dark matter. This collaborative effort brings us closer to unraveling the mysteries of the universe and expanding our understanding of its fundamental components.

A) The recent discovery of a new type of telescope technology that can observe dark matter with unprecedented accuracy
B) A breakthrough in particle physics research showing direct evidence of dark matter particles
C) A study highlighting the importance of individual astrophysicists in understanding dark matter
D) A theoretical model suggesting that dark matter is not significant in the structure and evolution of the universe

19. Which choice most logically completes the text?

In *The Little Friend* by Donna Tartt, the narrative unfolds in a small Southern town during the 1970s. This novel weaves a tale of mystery, revenge, and moral awakening through the experiences of Harriet, a young girl determined to solve her brother Robin's murder, which happened when she was just a baby. Harriett becomes obsessed with uncovering the truth behind her brother's death, and as she delves deeper into the secrets of her town and her own family, she embarks on a journey of self-discovery and unearthing hidden truths. While not as widely celebrated as some other literary classics, *The Little Friend* captivates audiences with its compelling storytelling and memorable characters. It remains an undiscovered gem that has the potential to _____.

A) motivate people to explore themes of childhood, innocence, and the importance of growing up
B) promote discussions on the importance of sibling relationships and family dynamics
C) encourage further exploration of Southern culture and regional identity
D) spark conversations about the complexities of human relationships and the nature of justice

20. Which choice best states the main purpose of the text?

The Adventures of Sherlock Holmes by Arthur Conan Doyle:

Life is infinitely stranger than anything which the mind of man could invent. We would not dare to conceive the things which are really mere commonplaces of existence. If we could fly out of that window hand in hand, hover over this great city, gently remove the roofs, and peep in at the queer things which are going on, the strange coincidences, the plannings, the cross-purposes, the wonderful chains of events, working through generations, and leading to the most outre results, it would make all fiction with its conventionalities and foreseen conclusions most stale and unprofitable.

A) To emphasize the predictability and conventional nature of real-life events
B) To suggest that human imagination can always outdo real-life occurrences in terms of strangeness
C) To highlight the extraordinary and unpredictable nature of real-life events in contrast to fiction
D) To advocate for the importance of adhering to traditional storytelling conventions in fiction

21. The student wants to compare the main spans of these two iconic bridges. Which choice most effectively uses relevant information from the notes to accomplish this goal?

While studying world-famous bridges, a student has gathered the following information:

- The Golden Gate Bridge is located in San Francisco, California.
- It spans the Golden Gate Strait, connecting San Francisco to Marin County.
- The main span of the bridge measures approximately 4,200 feet.
- The Akashi Kaikyō Bridge is situated in Japan.
- It crosses the Akashi Strait, connecting Awaji Island to the city of Kobe.
- The main span of the bridge is approximately 6,500 feet.

A) Some of the world's famous bridges, including one in San Francisco, have main spans that are several thousand feet long.
B) The Golden Gate Bridge has a main span of approximately 4,200 feet, while the Akashi Kaikyō Bridge boasts a longer main span of about 6,500 feet.
C) The Akashi Kaikyō Bridge, situated in Japan, connects Awaji Island to Kobe and features a main span of around 6,500 feet.
D) Both the Golden Gate Bridge in San Francisco and the Akashi Kaikyō Bridge in Japan are renowned examples of iconic bridge structures.

22. Which choice best states the main purpose of the text?

In the early 20th century, Marie Curie's groundbreaking work led to the discovery of radium, a remarkable element. Radium's unique properties, including its mesmerizing glow, challenged scientific understanding, and research on these properties significantly advanced our knowledge of atomic structure and subatomic particles. Curie's dedication to scientific inquiry resulted in two Nobel Prizes, and her research also revolutionized medical science. Her contributions continue to inspire scientists and impact the fields of physics, chemistry, and medicine.

A) Marie Curie's tireless research efforts and her remarkable discovery of radium.
B) The impact of radium on the fields of physics, chemistry, and medicine, thanks to Marie Curie's pioneering work.
C) The mysterious properties of radium and its effect on the scientific community.
D) Marie Curie's pursuit of two Nobel Prizes and her dedication to scientific truth.

23. Which choice best states the main idea of the text?

Machu Picchu, perched high in the Andes Mountains of Peru, is one of the world's most iconic archaeological sites and a testament to the remarkable achievements of the Inca civilization. This ancient city, often referred to as the "Lost City of the Incas," was constructed in the 15th century during the reign of the Inca emperor Pachacuti. Its exact purpose remains a subject of scholarly debate, but it is believed to have served as a royal estate or a ceremonial retreat. The site's remarkable architecture includes precisely cut stones that fit together without the use of mortar, which is a testament to the Incas' advanced engineering skills. In the 16th century, Machu Picchu was abandoned during the Spanish Conquest, keeping it hidden from the outside world until its rediscovery by American historian and explorer Hiram Bingham in 1911. Today, it stands as a UNESCO World Heritage Site and a symbol of Inca ingenuity and the enduring allure of ancient civilizations.

A) To provide an overview of the history of Machu Picchu
B) To discuss the life of Hiram Bingham, the American explorer
C) To analyze the historical context of the Spanish Conquest
D) To explore the geological formation of the Andes Mountains

24. Which choice best describes the function of the underlined sentence in the text as a whole?

Maya Angelou, a literary giant of the 20th century, left an indelible mark with her words and wisdom. <u>Her autobiographical masterpiece, *I Know Why the Caged Bird Sings*, illuminated the struggles of her youth in the segregated South, while her poetry resonated with themes of identity and resilience</u>. Beyond her literary prowess, Angelou was a civil rights activist whose life's journey, from adversity to triumph, continues to inspire and remind us of the enduring power of the human spirit. Maya Angelou's legacy is a testament to the transformative potential of literature and the importance of advocating for justice and equality.

A) To celebrate Maya Angelou's accomplishments in the literary world
B) To express admiration for Maya Angelou's poetic talents
C) To provide examples that enrich the reader's understanding of Maya Angelou's impact
D) To summarize the major themes of Maya Angelou's autobiographical masterpiece

25. Which choice completes the text with the most logical and precise word or phrase?

Rising ocean temperatures due to climate change pose a significant threat to coral reefs. As temperatures increase, corals undergo coral bleaching, expelling vital algae called zooxanthellae that provide nutrients and color to the corals. This process weakens the corals, making them more susceptible to disease and putting marine ecosystems at risk. Scientists are alarmed by the increasing frequency of coral bleaching events and _____ the urgent need for global efforts to reduce carbon emissions and protect these critical ecosystems.

A) marginalize
B) overlook
C) emphasize
D) trivialize

Reading and Writing—Module 2

1. Which quote from *Metamorphosis* by Franz Kafka most effectively illustrates the claim that individuals living in modern society can experience isolation and dehumanization?

Metamorphosis by Franz Kafka

Metamorphosis, written by Franz Kafka and first published in 1915, is a seminal work of 20th-century literature. This novella delves into the surreal and nightmarish world of its protagonist, Gregor Samsa, who undergoes a bizarre transformation into a gigantic insect. Set against a backdrop of alienation and existential absurdity, Kafka's work explores themes of identity, isolation, and the dehumanizing effects of modern society. *Metamorphosis* remains a thought-provoking and enduring exploration of the human condition, and it has left a lasting impact on literature and existential philosophy.

A) "Calm —indeed the calmest— reflection might be better than the most confused decisions"
B) "I only fear danger where I want to fear it."
C) "One morning, upon awakening from agitated dreams, Gregor Samsa found himself, in his bed, transformed into a monstrous vermin."
D) "The door could not be heard slamming; they had probably left it open, as is the custom in homes where a great misfortune has occurred."

2. Based on the texts, what would the author of text 1 most likely say about the experiments described in text 2?

Passage 1: The Impact of Environmental Pollution on Ecosystems
Our environment faces a grave threat from pollution, with various harmful substances like heavy metals, pesticides, and industrial chemicals contaminating our air, water, and soil. These pollutants are causing widespread damage, leading to the decline or extinction of many species and affecting their ability to reproduce and thrive. Pollutants like lead, DDT, and mercury are some of the culprits behind these adverse effects, and it's imperative that we delve into how they harm our ecosystems to find effective ways to protect them.

Passage 2: Research in Bioremediation Techniques
Scientists are hard at work running experiments to combat pollution. They're using specific microorganisms, like Pseudomonas bacteria and mycorrhizal fungi, to clean up contaminated environments, especially those polluted by substances like petroleum hydrocarbons, chlorinated solvents, and heavy metals. These microorganisms can break down and metabolize these specific pollutants, which helps our ecosystems heal and regain their natural balance.

A) The experiments in text 2 provide valuable insights into the potential solutions for addressing environmental pollution.

B) The experiments in text 2 are unrelated to the topic of environmental pollution and its effects on ecosystems as discussed in text 1.

C) The experiments in text 2 contradict the claims made in text 1, presenting conflicting data regarding the impact of pollutants on ecosystems.

D) The experiments in text 2 primarily focus on the use of specific microorganisms without any practical application for ecological restoration.

3. How might Author 2 from Passage 2 respond to Author 1 from Passage 1 regarding their respective topics?

Passage 1: Cultural Significance of Traditional Clothing
Traditional clothing holds a profound significance in representing identity, heritage, and values in various cultures. These garments often incorporate intricate designs and colors that convey historical narratives and social roles. For example, in many Native American communities, regalia worn during powwows features intricate beadwork and symbolism, reflecting the cultural history and spiritual beliefs of the wearers. Similarly, the vibrant, handwoven fabrics of West African clothing tell stories of tribal origins and social standing.

Passage 2: Art and Social Movements
Artistic expression has been a powerful tool in promoting social change and challenging the status quo. Street art, in particular, has gained prominence as a means of addressing societal issues. Graffiti artists, like Banksy, have used their work to draw attention to political injustices and inequalities. These artworks can serve as a form of protest and commentary, much like music in the civil rights movement.

A) Author 2 would argue that street art is a more effective means of cultural representation than traditional clothing.
B) Author 2 would suggest that the cultural significance of traditional clothing extends to street art.
C) Author 2 would emphasize that both traditional clothing and street art convey historical narratives.
D) Author 2 would likely concur that traditional clothing and street art are unrelated in their cultural significance.

4. Which choice completes the text with the most logical transition?

Lighthouses, with their towering structures and guiding beacons, hold profound symbolism in the maritime world. Serving as literal beacons, these iconic structures guide ships safely through treacherous waters. The significance of lighthouses extends beyond the maritime realm. _____, lighthouses are often used in poetry as a metaphor for safety and comfort. They convey a timeless message of resilience and human ingenuity, offering a broader representation of strength and reliability and guiding the way to safety in challenging circumstances.

A) Therefore
B) Nonetheless
C) In contrast
D) For example

5. What does the text most strongly suggest about the importance of iPhones?

iPhones, produced by Apple Inc., are iconic smartphones that have fundamentally transformed modern life. With their sleek design and cutting-edge technology, iPhones are celebrated for their user-friendly interfaces and continuous innovation. These devices serve as more than just phones, functioning as digital assistants, entertainment centers, and productivity tools. The iPhone's integrated ecosystem, including the App Store and a commitment to privacy and security, has made it a central part of daily life, symbolizing innovation, quality, and style in the digital age.

A) iPhones are primarily used as basic communication devices.
B) iPhones prioritize third-party apps.
C) iPhones offer innovation, functionality, and style.
D) iPhones serve as digital assistants and entertainment hubs.

6. Which choice completes the text so that it conforms to the conventions of Standard English?

Dance is a universal language that transcends boundaries and cultures. It's a form of artistic expression that has been a part of human history for centuries, evolving in countless ways. From classical ballet to contemporary hip-hop, dance encompasses a wide range of styles and techniques. Dancers use their bodies as instruments to convey emotions, tell stories, and communicate without words. The physical and mental benefits of dance are numerous, promoting physical fitness, flexibility, and emotional well-being. But how can we further encourage dance as an accessible and inclusive art form, _____

A) by providing opportunities for all to experience its joys and benefits.
B) by providing opportunities for all to experience its joys and benefits?
C) providing opportunities for all to experience its joys and benefits.
D) providing opportunities for all to experience its joys and benefits?

7. Which choice completes the text with the most logical and precise word or phrase?

The Industrial Revolution, a transformative period in the 18th and 19th centuries, had far-reaching implications for the humanities. Mechanization and urbanization fundamentally reshaped the fabric of society, triggering tumultuous changes that reverberated across all aspects of life. In response, artists and writers endeavored to capture the human experience within this transformation. Visionaries like J.M.W. Turner, sought to portray the stark beauty and chaos of industrial landscapes through their art, while authors such as Charles Dickens delved into the heart of the social and moral challenges faced by the working class. These creative works not only documented the era's _____ but also raised questions about the impact of industrialization on humanity's relationship with nature, labor, and society.

A) insignificance
B) stagnation
C) upheaval
D) tranquility

8. Which choice completes the text so that it conforms to the conventions of Standard English?

Volcanic infrasound, low-frequency sound waves produced by volcanoes, is invaluable for studying volcanic activity. _____, detected by specialized instruments, reveal insights into volcanic processes like magma movement, gas emissions, and potential eruptions. This research aids in volcano monitoring and early warning systems, enhancing our understanding of volcanic behavior and risk reduction.

A) These infrasound waves
B) This infrasound wave
C) It's infrasound waves
D) Their infrasound waves

9. Which choice completes the text so that it conforms to the conventions of Standard English?

War and Peace by Leo Tolstoy

"Never, never marry, my dear fellow! That's my _____ marry till you can say to yourself that you have done all you are capable of, and until you have ceased to love the woman of your choice and have seen her plainly as she is, or else you will make a cruel and irrevocable mistake."

A) advice, never
B) advice. Never
C) advice: never
D) advice; never

10. The student wants to provide an explanation and example of Picasso's involvement in the Cubist movement. Which choice most effectively uses relevant information from the notes to accomplish this goal?

While researching a well-known artist's career, a student has gathered the following notes:

- The Spanish artist Pablo Picasso is famous for his contributions to the art world.
- He co-founded the Cubist movement, a groundbreaking art style.
- *Les Demoiselles d'Avignon* is one of Picasso's iconic paintings.
- This painting is considered a masterpiece of the Cubist style.
- Juan Gris, a prominent figure in the Cubist movement, was known for his analytical and synthetic Cubism, which explored different facets of the style.
- Picasso's art in the Rose Period featured *Family of Saltimbanques* and *The Acrobat*.

A) Pablo Picasso, a renowned Spanish artist, is celebrated for co-founding the innovative Cubist movement, with *Les Demoiselles d'Avignon* as one of the iconic masterpieces that exemplifies this style.

B) Juan Gris's artistic contributions include his co-founding of the Cubist movement, with *Les Demoiselles d'Avignon* being a prime illustration of this revolutionary style.

C) The Cubist movement by Pablo Picasso left an enduring mark on the art world. During his Rose Period, Picasso created notable works like *Family of Saltimbanques* and *The Acrobat*.

D) Spanish artist Pablo Picasso played a pivotal role in the formation of the groundbreaking Cubist movement, where prominent figures like Juan Gris explored various facets of the style in paintings like *Les Demoiselles d'Avignon*.

11. Which choice completes the text so that it conforms to the conventions of Standard English?

Soldiers, sailors, airmen, and marines undergo rigorous training to develop the skills and mental fortitude required for their roles. They learn to operate complex machinery, execute strategic maneuvers, and adapt to challenging environments _____ upholding the core values of honor, duty, and integrity.

A) all the while
B) while
C) all while
D) while still

12. Which choice completes the text with the most logical and precise word or phrase?

The human brain's intricacies in memory formation and retrieval are subjects of intense research. Memories begin with encoding in the hippocampus, which converts short-term memories into long-term ones. These memories are stored in different brain regions based on their type. Episodic memories _____ in the prefrontal cortex, while procedural memories are stored in the cerebellum. Memory retrieval involves reactivating specific neural pathways, which are influenced by factors like emotions and environmental cues. This research holds promise for treating memory-related disorders and enhancing memory function.

A) disintegrate
B) formulate
C) annihilate
D) reside

13. Which choice completes the text so that it conforms to the conventions of Standard English?

In the heart of town, a quaint park provided a serene retreat, complete with a fountain at its center and well-tended flowerbeds. _____ was a place where friends gathered, children played, and artists found inspiration in the surroundings.

A) It
B) They're
C) Their
D) It's

14. Which choice best describes data from the table that support the researchers' claim?

Star Name	Luminosity	Temperature	Size
Star A	High	Hot	Large
Star B	Low	Cool	Small
Star C	Medium	Warm	Medium
Star D	High	Hot	Large
Star E	Low	Cool	Small

A team of astronomers, spanning observatories across the Northern and Southern Hemispheres, embarked on a groundbreaking study to investigate the characteristics of various types of stars in our galaxy. Their research revealed that while stars differ significantly in terms of their luminosity, temperature, and size, there is a remarkable consistency in the underlying physical processes driving their energy production. As a result, they claim that a star's luminosity and temperature affect its size.

A) Among the five stars in the table, stars with low luminosity (e.g., Star B and Star E) also tend to have low temperatures and small sizes.

B) Star C has a temperature similar to that of Star D but a much larger size, indicating that temperature alone doesn't necessarily correlate with star size.

C) Stars with high luminosity (e.g., Star A and Star D) do not always exhibit high temperatures or result in the largest sizes, contradicting the assumption that luminosity directly determines star size.

D) Star B and Star E share low luminosity and low temperatures but have different sizes, highlighting that temperature and luminosity alone do not solely determine star size.

15. Which choice completes the text so that it conforms to the conventions of Standard English?

The Great Depression was a period of profound economic hardship that gripped the United States and much of the world in the 1930s. It was a time of immense suffering, marked by widespread unemployment, poverty, and despair. The causes of the Great Depression were multifaceted, stemming from a stock market crash in 1929, a banking crisis, and a severe drought that devastated American agriculture. These events set off a chain reaction, _____ to a massive economic downturn.

A) leading
B) leaded
C) leads
D) which leads

16. According to the text, what is true about Mother?

Peter Pan by J. M. Barrie:

Of course they lived at 14, and until Wendy came her mother was the chief one. She was a lovely lady, with a romantic mind and such a sweet mocking mouth. Her romantic mind was like the tiny boxes, one within the other, that come from the puzzling East, however many you discover there is always one more; and her sweet mocking mouth had one kiss on it that Wendy could never get, though there it was, perfectly conspicuous in the right-hand corner.

A) She was a strict and overbearing parent.
B) She was a brilliant mathematician.
C) She had a delightful personality with a mind full of imagination and a playful demeanor.
D) She had a romantic mind, and her kiss was always easily attainable.

17. Which choice completes the text with the most logical transition?

Famous authors like William Shakespeare, Jane Austen, and Mark Twain have gained international acclaim for their literary contributions, leaving an indelible mark on the world of literature. _____, lesser-recognized but equally talented writers like Zora Neale Hurston, Kazuo Ishiguro, and Octavia Butler have produced exceptional works that are sometimes hidden in the shadows of their more celebrated counterparts. While the literary canon often highlights a select few, there is an abundance of hidden gems waiting to be discovered by avid readers.

A) Similarly
B) For instance
C) In particular
D) On the other hand

18. The student wants to provide an explanation and an example of oceanomics. Which choice most effectively uses relevant information from the notes to accomplish this goal?

While researching a topic, a student has taken the following notes:

- Dr. Lisa Patel is a marine biologist based in Miami.
- She coined the term *oceanomics* to describe her research approach, combining oceanography and genomics.
- Oceanomics aims to study the genetic diversity of marine life and its connection to ocean ecosystems.
- Her study "Coral Genomes" is a notable example of oceanomics.

A) Dr. Lisa Patel, a marine biologist in Miami, introduced the term *oceanomics* to describe her research approach, which combines oceanography and genomics.
B) Oceanomics, a research approach by Dr. Lisa Patel, explores the genetic diversity of marine life and its relationship to ocean ecosystems.
C) Dr. Lisa Patel's "Coral Genomes" study is a prominent example of oceanomics, a term she coined for her research blending oceanography and genomics.
D) In Miami, Dr. Lisa Patel practices oceanomics, a research approach that explores the connection between marine genetic diversity and ocean ecosystems, which she named herself.

19. Which choice completes the text with the most logical transition?

The study of genetics has revolutionized our understanding of heredity and inheritance. Prior to the discovery of DNA's structure, scientists had limited knowledge of how traits were passed from one generation to the next. _____ the elucidation of the DNA's double helix structure by James Watson and Francis Crick in 1953, genetics research advanced significantly, as this breakthrough enabled scientists to delve into the molecular underpinnings of genetics and explore the mechanisms behind trait inheritance.

A) In contrast to
B) Before
C) As a result of
D) Despite

20. Which choice most logically completes the text?

In a recent study on the effects of daily meditation, researchers found that participants who meditated for at least 20 minutes a day reported significant reductions in stress and anxiety levels. The study collected data from a diverse group of individuals, and the results indicate a strong correlation between the frequency of meditation and improved mental well-being. Participants also reported better sleep quality and enhanced emotional regulation as secondary benefits of their meditation practice. This study _____.

A) conclusively proves that meditation is the ultimate solution to all mental health issues
B) reveals that daily meditation can improve your mental health and well-being
C) shows that the results should be completely disregarded, as they lack scientific validity and rigor
D) indicates that benefits were found to be highly dependent on the individual's level of meditation experience

21. Which choice best states the main purpose of the text?

A Tale of Two Cities by Charles Dickens:

For you, and for any dear to you, I would do anything. If my career were of that better kind that there was any opportunity or capacity of sacrifice in it, I would embrace any sacrifice for you and for those dear to you. Try to hold me in your mind, at some quiet times, as ardent and sincere in this one thing. The time will come, the time will not be long in coming, when new ties will be formed about you-- ties that will bind you yet more tenderly and strongly to the home you so adorn--the dearest ties that will ever grace and gladden you. O Miss Manette, when the little picture of a happy father's face looks up in yours, when you see your own bright beauty springing up anew at your feet, think now and then that there is a man who would give his life, to keep a life you love beside you!

A) To provide a detailed description of Miss Manette's appearance and personality
B) To express deep love and devotion to Miss Manette and a willingness to make sacrifices for her
C) To express concerns about Miss Manette's choices and actions, highlighting potential consequences
D) To reflect on the complexities of life and the challenges of forming new bonds in the future

22. Which choice most logically completes the text?

Throughout history, empires and dynasties have risen and fallen, leaving their indelible marks on the world. These powerful entities have shaped societies, cultures, and economies in significant ways, often leaving legacies that persist for centuries. The rise of the Roman Empire, for instance, was marked by its remarkable engineering feats, governance systems, and widespread influence over vast territories. Similarly, the Ming Dynasty in China, known for its cultural achievements, introduced innovations such as the printing press and expeditions of maritime exploration that had a lasting impact. The annals of history are replete with examples of these transformative periods, providing invaluable insights into human civilization's development because _____.

A) they prove that empires and dynasties are the only driving forces behind human civilization's development

B) they reveal the insignificance of empires and dynasties in shaping human civilization

C) they offer valuable lessons and insights into the progression of human civilization over time

D) they illustrate the enduring effects of past civilizations on our world today

23. Which choice completes the text so that it conforms to the conventions of Standard English?

A dedicated team from the MARUM - Center for Marine Environmental Sciences at the University of Bremen recently embarked on a remarkable journey. Through ingenious flume-tank experiments, they sought to uncover how currents sculpt the ocean floor and dictate sediment patterns, a key to understanding our marine history. Recently unveiled in the journal *Communications Earth & Environment*, their discoveries shed light on contourites, sediment deposits shaped by near-bottom currents that harbor valuable clues about past climate conditions. Henriette Wilckens, the lead scientist, carefully crafted a miniature ocean floor in a large tank at the University of Utrecht. She uses this tank to mimic the currents and sediment flow of a real ocean floor, creating tiny sandcastles to decode the mysteries of the deep. This groundbreaking research opens up a brand-new chapter in ocean exploration, one that is not just academic but also _____ it is helping us understand and care for our planet's most mysterious realms.

A) practical, as
B) practical. As
C) practical; as
D) practical: as

24. According to the text, Starry Night was on display where in 1926?

Starry Night by Vincent van Gogh, one of the most iconic and beloved paintings in the world, has had a journey that is as fascinating as the artwork itself. Painted in 1889 during the artist's stay at the Saint-Paul-de-Mausole asylum in Saint-Rémy-de-Provence, France, the masterpiece began its odyssey in the possession of Vincent's brother, Theo van Gogh, after the artist's tragic death in 1890.

Upon Theo's passing in 1891, the painting then passed to his widow, Johanna van Gogh-Bonger, who worked tirelessly to promote her brother-in-law's work, ensuring that the world would come to appreciate his genius. In 1900, *Starry Night* found a new home in the Galerie Bernheim-Jeune in Paris.

It was only in 1941 that the painting found its permanent residence at the Museum of Modern Art (MoMA) in New York City. Industrialist and art collector Stephen C. Clark acquired it and generously donated it to the museum. Since then, *Starry Night* has become a centerpiece of MoMA's collection, captivating visitors from around the world with its swirling stars and evocative landscape. Its journey through time and ownership has made it a symbol of artistic transcendence, and it is now celebrated as an integral part of the rich tapestry of art history.

A) Galerie Bernheim-Jeune in Paris
B) Museum of Modern Art (MoMA) in New York City
C) Saint-Paul-de-Mausole asylum in Saint-Rémy-de-Provence, France
D) The Louvre Museum in Paris, France

25. Which choice completes the text with the most logical and precise word or phrase?

In Nathaniel Hawthorne's *The Scarlet Letter*, the Puritan society of 17th-century New England serves as _____ backdrop for the story of Hester Prynne, a woman condemned for adultery. Hawthorne's novel delves into themes of sin, guilt, and redemption as Hester grapples with the consequences of her actions. The scarlet letter "A" she is forced to wear becomes a symbol of her defiance in the face of societal judgment.

A) an inconsequential
B) a traditional
C) an indifferent
D) a somber

Mathematics—Module 1

1. The ratio of new car sales to used car sales at the car lot is 3 : 5. If the total car sales were $287,400 last month, what was the total of the used car sales?

2. A company has been asked to design a building for an athletic event. The building is in the shape of a square pyramid. The pyramid has a height of 481 feet, and the length of each side of the base is 756 feet. What is the approximate volume of the pyramid?

A) 1.21×10^5 ft³
B) 4.85×10^5 ft³
C) 9.16×10^7 ft³
D) 2.75×10^8 ft³

3. Simplify the following expression: $(2x^2 + 3x + 2) - (x^2 + 2x - 3)$

A) $x^2 + x + 5$
B) $x^2 + x - 1$
C) $x^2 + 5x + 5$
D) $x^2 + 5x - 1$

4. Simplify the following: $\frac{x^2}{y^2} + \frac{x}{y^3}$

A) $\frac{x^3 + x}{y^3}$
B) $\frac{x^2 + xy}{y^3}$
C) $\frac{x^2 y + xy}{y^3}$
D) $\frac{x^2 y + x}{y^3}$

5. The graph of $y = -x^2 + 5x$ intersects the graph of $y = 2x$ at $(0, 0)$ and (a, b). What is the value of b?

6. Max reads three books averaging 360 pages. Lucy reads five books averaging 200 pages. What is the average length of all the books that Max and Lucy read?

A) 212 pages
B) 232 pages
C) 260 pages
D) 295 pages

7. Solve: $7x^2 + 6x = -2$.

A) $x = \frac{-3 \pm \sqrt{23}}{7}$
B) $x = \pm i\sqrt{5}$
C) $x = \pm \frac{2i\sqrt{2}}{7}$
D) $x = \frac{-3 \pm i\sqrt{5}}{7}$

8. Ride Service A charges a flat rate of $10 for the first 10 miles, plus 25 cents per mile for anything over 10 miles. Ride Service B charges 40 cents per mile. Both services charge the same for a trip that is how long?

  A) 40 miles
  B) 45 miles
  C) 50 miles
  D) 55 miles

9. What is the perimeter of a 45-45-90 triangle if the hypotenuse is 4 inches?

  A) 4 inches
  B) 8 inches
  C) $4 + 4\sqrt{2}$ inches
  D) $4 + 2\sqrt{2}$ inches

10. Which of the following is equivalent to $x^2 + 3 > 2x + 2$?

  A) $x < -1$
  B) $x \neq 1$
  C) $x > 1$
  D) $x < -1$ or $x > 1$

11. In the system of equations below, n is a constant and x and y are variables. For which of the following values of n will the system have no solution?

$$3x - y = 2$$
$$nx + 3y = -5$$

  A) $-\frac{1}{3}$
  B) 3
  C) $-\frac{5}{3}$
  D) -9

12. Gillian is deciding between two data plans for her cellphone. Plan A provides 2.5 GB of data for a flat rate of $20/month and charges $15 per GB for any extra use. Plan B provides unlimited data for $50/month. What amount of data would Gillian have to use in a month for both plans to cost the same amount?

  A) 2 GB
  B) 3.5 GB
  C) 3.75 GB
  D) 4.5 GB

13. Every person attending a meeting hands out a business card to every other person at the meeting. If a total of 30 cards are handed out, how many people are at the meeting?

  A) 5 people
  B) 6 people
  C) 10 people
  D) 15 people

Mometrix

14. Which of the following is a solution to the inequality $4x - 12 < 4$?

A) 7
B) 6
C) 4
D) 3

15. The table below shows the breakdown of soup orders at a restaurant. There were two kinds of soup (chicken and veggie) and two sizes (cup and bowl). If a person among those who ordered soup is chosen at random, what is the probability that this person ordered a cup of veggie soup?

	Chicken	Veggie	Total
Cup	7	8	15
Bowl	15	12	27
Total	22	20	42

A) $\frac{8}{15}$
B) $\frac{1}{6}$
C) $\frac{2}{5}$
D) $\frac{4}{21}$

16. Jamal plants a white petunia for every three red petunias in the flowerbed. If he plants 8 white petunias and r red petunias, which of the following equations is true?

A) $3r = 8$
B) $8r = 3$
C) $\frac{r}{3} = 8$
D) $r + 3 = 8$

17. Solve $\sqrt{2x} - 3 = \sqrt{2x - 15}$.

A) $x = 0$
B) $x = 4$
C) $x = 8$
D) $x = 10$

18. What is the solution to the equation: $4\sqrt{x} + 8 = 24$?

A) $x = 2$
B) $x = 4$
C) $x = 12$
D) $x = 16$

19. What is the sum of all values of x that satisfy the following equation?
$$3x^2 - 3x - 34 = 2$$

A) –3
B) 0
C) 1
D) 4

266

20. The rectangle below has an area of 245 inches^2. What is the length of the longest side of the rectangle?

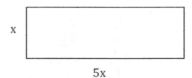

5x

A) 25 inches
B) 30 inches
C) 35 inches
D) 40 inches

21. The variables x and y have a linear relationship. The table below shows a few sample values. Which of the following graphs correctly represents the linear equation relating x and y?

x	y
−2	−11
−1	−8
0	−5
1	−2
2	1

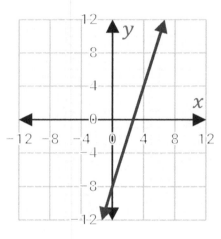

A.

B.

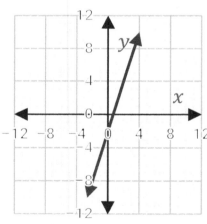

C.

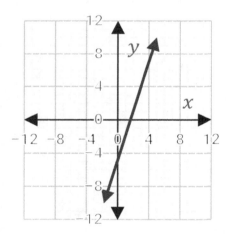

D.

22. Roxana walks x meters west and $x + 20$ meters south to get to her friend's house. On a neighborhood map which has a scale of 1 cm: 10 m, the direct distance between Roxana's house and her friend's house is 10 cm. How far did Roxana walk to her friend's house?

Mathematics—Module 2

1. If $\frac{1}{\sqrt[3]{x}} = a$, **what is** x?

A) a^3

B) $1 - a^3$

C) $\frac{1}{a^2}$

D) $\frac{1}{a^3}$

2. The graph of the system of inequalities $y \leq \frac{1}{4}x - 2$ **and** $y > 3x - \frac{7}{5}$ **has solutions in which quadrants on the** xy**-plane below?**

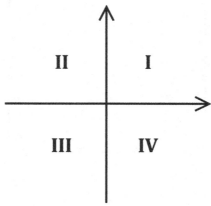

A) Quadrant III only

B) Quadrants II and III

C) Quadrants III and IV

D) Quadrants II, III, and IV

Refer to the following for questions 3 - 4:

Nurseries A, B, and C offer various plants for sale, as well as landscaping services to plant the trees and bushes. Prices are listed in the table below.

	A	B	C
Trees	$25	$30	$20
Bushes	$15	$20	$15
Landscaping (per hour)	$45	$55	$50

3. Nursery B was hired to plant 100 trees and 100 bushes. If their overhead cost of the plants, equipment, and personnel is $5,500, how many hours will they have to work to make a profit of $820?

A) 15 hours

B) 21.5 hours

C) 24 hours

D) 32.5 hours

269

4. Isabella plans to hire one of the companies to plant 10 trees and 8 bushes. This project will take x hours. Which of the following inequalities represents x if Nursery A offers a better deal than Nursery C?

A) $x < 5$
B) $x < 10$
C) $x > 5$
D) $x > 10$

5. A circle is inscribed within a square, as shown. What is the difference between the area of the square and that of the circle, where r is the radius of the circle?

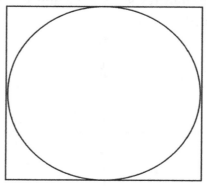

A) 2π
B) $\frac{4}{3}\pi r^3$
C) $r^2(4 - \pi)$
D) $2\pi r$

6. The equation below shows Emma's savings plan. She set aside an initial lump sum and adds to it on a monthly basis. If i is the total investment in cents and m is the number of months since she began, how much does she save each month?

$$i = 50,000 + 4,500m$$

A) $45
B) $500
C) $4,500
D) $50,000

7. Solve for n in the equation: $4n - p = 3r$

A) $\frac{3r}{4} - p$
B) $p + 3r$
C) $p - 3r$
D) $\frac{3r}{4} + \frac{p}{4}$

8. If the solution for the system of equations below is (x, y), what is the value of $2x^2 - y$?

$$3x - 2y = 0$$
$$-2x + 4y = -8$$

A) –3
B) –2
C) 5
D) 11

9. What is the y-coordinate of the center of the circle defined in the equation below?

$$x^2 + y^2 - y - 6x = -\frac{21}{4}$$

10. Riley has several $5 bills, $10 bills, and $20 bills. If she has a total of 9 bills that add up to $80, what is the greatest number of $5 bills she could have?

11. Which of the following represents the factored form of the expression $x^2 - 3x - 40$?

A) $(x - 8)(x + 5)$
B) $(x - 7)(x + 4)$
C) $(x + 10)(x - 4)$
D) $(x + 6)(x - 9)$

12. A new business is calculating the amount of products that must sell to break even (so that investments equal profits). If d dollars are invested to produce a products that can be sold for p profit, how much investment is required, according to the equations below?

$$d = 9,660 + 1.2a$$
$$p = 4a$$

A) $3,450
B) $4,140
C) $11,260
D) $13,800

13. If 3 times the square of a positive number is 48, what is the result when twice the number is subtracted from 15?

A) –7
B) 4
C) 7
D) 11

14. The scatterplot below shows Zac's time (in hours) on the y-axis spent working on his science project on the days (x-axis) leading up to the due date. Approximately how much longer did he spend on Day 8 than the amount predicted by the line of best fit?

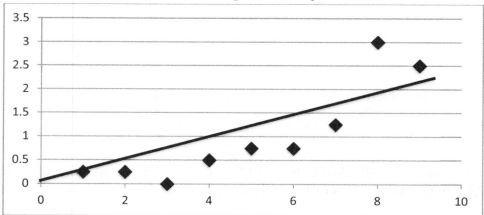

A) 0.5 hours
B) 1 hour
C) 2 hours
D) 3 hours

15. If $x > 0$ and $x^2 - 7 = 9$, what is the value of x?

16. If $\frac{3}{7}q = -6$, what is the value of q?

A) -14
B) $-\frac{18}{7}$
C) $-\frac{45}{7}$
D) -42

17. What is the expanded form of $(x + 6)(x - 6)$?

A) $x^2 - 12x - 36$
B) $x^2 + 12x - 36$
C) $x^2 + 12x + 36$
D) $x^2 - 36$

Refer to the following for questions 18 - 19:

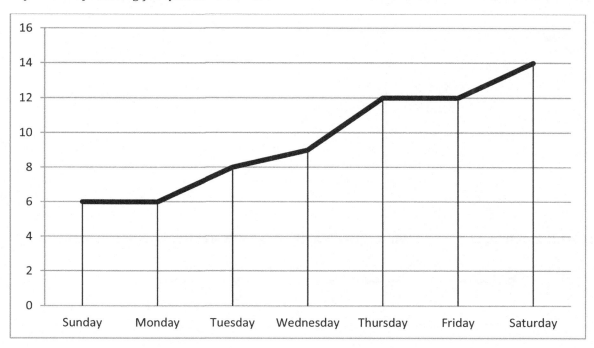

Every time Miguel gets quarters in change, he puts them in a jar. The chart above shows how many quarters he has in the jar at the end of each day during a particular week.

18. How many quarters did Miguel add on Monday?

   A) 0
   B) 1
   C) 3
   D) 6

19. Which day did Miguel add the most quarters to the jar?

   A) Monday
   B) Tuesday
   C) Thursday
   D) Saturday

20. The half-life of caffeine in the human body is 5 hours. If Rafe drinks a cup of coffee at 7:00 a.m., what percentage of the caffeine is still in his system at 2:00 p.m.? Round your answer to the nearest whole percent.

21. In right triangle $\triangle XYZ$ below, angle Z measures $z°$ and $\sin z° = \frac{4}{5}$. What is $\cos(90 - z)°$?

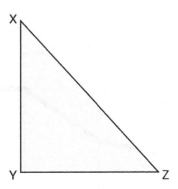

22. On line WZ below, $WX = XZ$. What is the length of WY? (Note: figure not drawn to scale)

$$a + 9 \qquad 4a - 9 \qquad 2a + 3$$

W   X   Y   Z

Answer Key and Explanations

Reading and Writing—Module 1

1. B: In the context of the passage, it is clear that genetics research has been highly beneficial in medicine. The passage emphasizes how genetics has led to innovative treatments and its connections with diseases. Therefore, the logical completion of the passage should suggest that ongoing genetics research is indicating promising avenues for the prevention and treatment of illnesses, aligning with the positive impact of genetics research in the medical field.

2. B: This option directly highlights her unconventional style, characterized by innovative punctuation and enigmatic themes in her vast body of work, consisting of nearly 1,800 poems. By underlining the distinctive nature of her style, it successfully distinguishes her as a unique and remarkable figure in the world of literature. This aligns with the student's goal to accentuate what makes Emily Dickinson's literary contributions stand out.

3. A: The word *evocative* is the most logical and precise choice to describe the nature of the balcony scene in *Romeo and Juliet*. While *emotional* is a valid choice, *evocative* is a more precise and fitting word for describing the balcony scene's impact and the way it captures the intensity of young love through its poetic language and imagery.

4. C: Choice C directly supports the passage's assertion that music has the potential to enhance concentration and productivity. It introduces new information about recent studies showing that background instrumental music can improve focus and productivity, which aligns with the passage's claim about the benefits of music in these contexts. This finding strengthens the argument that music positively impacts mental health and productivity.

5. B: The passage discusses how hockey captivates both the players and the fans. To maintain proper subject-verb agreement and convey the intended meaning, the plural form *players* and *fans* should be used.

6. A: The present tense *continues* is appropriate because it indicates that Asch's work is an ongoing and enduring reference. The other options, *will continue*, *continued*, and *continuing*, either introduce an unnecessary future tense or past tense, which don't align with the context.

7. B: In Passage 1, it is emphasized that folktales serve as a means of preserving cultural heritage and passing down values and traditions. In Passage 2, it is discussed that literature captures the zeitgeist of its time and reflects societal changes. Both passages highlight the role of their respective forms of storytelling (folktales and literature) in preserving cultural heritage.

8. B: In this passage, the context calls for a transitional word (*however*) to indicate a contrast or shift in the sentence's direction. A semicolon is appropriate to connect two related independent clauses, and it should be followed by *however* with a comma for proper punctuation.

9. B: To *contemplate* means to think deeply or consider something carefully. In the context of the passage, the word *contemplate* fits because it conveys the idea that literature encourages readers to think deeply and critically about complex issues. It aligns with the passage's message that literature serves as a reflection of society's values and beliefs and encourages readers to engage with these topics on a thoughtful level.

10. A: The data in the table show that the Arctic Ocean had both the greatest increase in temperature, 0.5 °C, and the highest rise in sea level, 11.5 cm. This reflects a connection between high ocean temperatures and an increase in sea level, which aligns with the researchers' claim about the influence of temperature and global warming on rising sea levels.

11. A: *Additionally* is the appropriate choice, as it smoothly introduces the idea of providing extra information about the cave's ecosystem, particularly the bats. It maintains a logical flow in the text, highlighting the connection between the geological features and the biological significance of the cave system.

12. A: The passage discusses Gabriel Garcia Márquez's impact on literature, and it's describing past actions that are still ongoing. To convey this sense of a past action with continuing relevance, the present perfect tense *has transported* is appropriate. The present perfect tense is used to show that an action started in the past and has relevance or implications in the present.

13. B: It is appropriate to use the present tense *focuses* here to maintain grammatical consistency. This verb tense indicates that the study is currently ongoing or was recently conducted, and the study is focusing on estimating the probability of ground shaking.

14. C: Using a comma and the word *is* provides the necessary clarity and proper punctuation to make it clear that the Maasai Mara is located in Kenya and can be described as "a land of rolling grasslands, acacia-studded plains, and meandering rivers." Excluding the word *is* would change the meaning of the sentence to describe all of Kenya as "a land of rolling grasslands, acacia-studded plains, and meandering rivers," which is not accurate because Kenya has other landscapes as well.

15. C: *Moreover* is the appropriate choice because it signals that additional information or a related point is about to be presented. In this case, it introduces the fact that geckos are known for their agility and proficiency as hunters and climbers, expanding on their remarkable climbing abilities discussed in the first sentence.

16. A: This choice directly highlights the development of the AC electrical system as well as his invention of the Tesla coil, thereby emphasizing Tesla's significance in the field of electrical engineering.

17. D: The main idea of the text revolves around the protagonist's emotional and psychological struggles as she battles nervous troubles. She also feels that her husband, John, does not understand the severity of her condition and dismisses her concerns. This is the central theme of the passage, making D the best choice. Choices A, B, and C touch on various aspects mentioned in the text but do not capture the core theme as effectively.

18. B: The passage emphasizes the collaborative efforts of scientists from various disciplines in understanding dark matter. Answer choice B directly supports the claim that collaboration is essential by indicating that a discovery in particle physics research, which is one of the mentioned disciplines, provides direct evidence of dark matter particles. This demonstrates the significance of various scientific fields working together.

19. D: The passage discusses how *The Little Friend* weaves a tale of mystery, revenge, and moral awakening. Choice D most logically completes the text by indicating that the book could spark conversations about the complexities of human relationships and the nature of justice, which aligns with the themes and content described in the passage.

20. C: The text emphasizes the idea that real-life events are stranger and more complex than anything one could invent, and it contrasts this unpredictability with the predictability of conventional fiction. The text encourages the reader to appreciate the richness and unpredictability of real-life events.

21. B: This is the most effective choice because it directly and clearly compares the main spans of the two bridges, the Golden Gate Bridge and the Akashi Kaikyō Bridge. It provides the relevant information from the notes, stating that the Golden Gate Bridge has a main span of approximately 4,200 feet, while the Akashi Kaikyō Bridge has a longer main span of about 6,500 feet.

22. B: The main idea of the passage is to convey the significant impact of radium on various scientific fields, including physics, chemistry, and medicine, due to Marie Curie's groundbreaking work. The passage discusses how Curie's discovery of radium challenged scientific understanding, advanced knowledge of atomic structure and subatomic particles, and ultimately influenced medical science.

23. A: The passage primarily focuses on the historical and archaeological significance of Machu Picchu, discussing its construction, purpose, architecture, abandonment, and rediscovery.

24. C: This sentence provides specific examples of Maya Angelou's work and its impact. It mentions her autobiographical masterpiece and poetry, illustrating how her writing addressed important themes. Although it mentions themes, it does not provide a comprehensive summary of the major themes of the autobiographical masterpiece. The primary purpose of the sentence is to give examples of Maya Angelou's work and its impact rather than summarizing the book's themes in detail.

25. C: The word *emphasize* aligns well with the sense of concern and urgency expressed by the scientists in the passage. It implies that they are stressing, or highlighting, the importance of taking action to protect these critical ecosystems.

Reading and Writing—Module 2

1. C: This quote serves as the opening sentence of the novella, setting the tone for the entire work. Gregor Samsa's transformation into an insect is a central element of the story, and it symbolizes the themes of identity, isolation, and the dehumanizing effects of modern society as described in the claim.

2. A: The experiments in text 2, which focus on bioremediation techniques using specific microorganisms, provide valuable insights into potential solutions for addressing environmental pollution, especially in the context of the specific pollutants mentioned in text 1.

3. C: This choice reflects the idea that even though they are different mediums, both artistic forms of expression are means by which historical narratives and cultural significance are conveyed. It highlights the shared element of historical storytelling and cultural representation between the two passages.

4. D: *For example* is the most suitable choice because the sentence describes one use of lighthouses as a symbol rather than their real-world use to guide ships.

5. C: The passage strongly suggests that iPhones are more than basic communication devices and highlights their importance by emphasizing their sleek design, cutting-edge technology, user-friendly interfaces, continuous innovation, and their role as digital assistants, entertainment centers, and productivity tools. The passage also mentions their commitment to privacy and security, which adds to their importance and quality.

6. D: Choice D is constructed as a declarative sentence with a question mark at the end. The declarative part of the sentence states, "providing opportunities for all to experience its joys and benefits," and the question mark at the end makes it clear that it is intended as a question.

7. C: The passage discusses how the Industrial Revolution brought significant changes to society that reshaped the world in profound ways. Artists and writers responded to these changes by capturing the human experience during this period. *Upheaval* accurately reflects the tumultuous and transformative nature of the Industrial Revolution. It implies a state of disruption, change, and instability, which aligns with the context described in the passage.

8. A: This choice maintains proper subject-verb agreement and clarity. The use of *These* in "These infrasound waves" correctly refers to the plural nature of the low-frequency sound waves generated by volcanoes.

9. C: The passage presents a thought from the speaker advising against marriage until certain conditions are met. The colon in choice C is used to introduce and continue the thought in a manner where the second part expands on or explains the first part.

10. A: Choice A is the most effective choice, as it concisely provides an explanation of Picasso's involvement in the Cubist movement and a specific example of his work. It accurately captures the key information from the notes and directly addresses the student's goal.

11. B: In the passage, the sentence describes what soldiers, sailors, airmen, and marines learn to do during their rigorous training. The word *while* is sufficient to convey the intended meaning that these personnel learn to operate machinery, execute maneuvers, and adapt to challenging environments while upholding core values. The other choices introduce unnecessary phrasing and do not add clarity or improve the sentence's structure.

12. D: The word *reside* is the most logical and precise choice. It accurately conveys that episodic memories are located in the prefrontal cortex. It aligns with the description of memory storage occurring in different brain regions based on their type. The other choices do not accurately represent the process of memory storage. These words suggest processes of destruction, creation, or elimination, which are not in line with the description of memory storage in the passage.

13. A: The sentence is describing the park, which is a singular entity, so the appropriate word to use is *It*. The park is a place where various activities occur, but it is treated as a single location.

14. A: Choice A is correct because it directly correlates the low luminosity and low temperature of stars (e.g., Star B and Star E) with their smaller sizes, aligning with the researchers' claim that luminosity and temperature affect a star's size. This choice effectively references the data in the table and maintains logical consistency.

15. A: The passage describes a series of events that occurred in the past, including the causes of the Great Depression. To maintain proper tense and sentence structure, the completion should use the past tense to indicate the sequence of events. *Leading* in choice A is the past participle form of the verb *lead*, and it effectively communicates the idea that these causes initiated a chain of events that resulted in a massive economic downturn.

16. C. The passage describes Wendy's mother as a "lovely lady" with a "romantic mind" and a "sweet mocking mouth." Her "romantic mind" is likened to nested boxes from the East, suggesting complexity and depth. Additionally, it mentions a kiss on her mouth that Wendy could never get, implying a playful or teasing aspect to her personality.

17. D: The transition "On the other hand" is appropriate because it clearly signals a contrast between the famous authors and the lesser-recognized ones, highlighting a shift in perspective. It effectively conveys the intended message that there are two different sides to the literary world in terms of recognition.

18. C: This is the most effective choice, as it provides both an explanation and an example of oceanomics. It defines oceanomics as a term coined by Dr. Lisa Patel for her research that blends oceanography and genomics and presents "Coral Genomes" as a specific and notable instance of her work in this field, aligning with the student's goal.

19. C: "As a result of" is the most appropriate choice here because it indicates a cause-and-effect relationship. The discovery of the double helix structure of DNA is presented as a cause of the significant advancement in genetics research. This transition logically connects the two sentences by explaining that the groundbreaking discovery led to the subsequent advancement of genetics research.

20. B: The study's findings suggest that daily meditation has a positive impact on reducing stress and anxiety levels. The passage mentions significant reductions in stress and anxiety levels among participants who meditated for at least 20 minutes a day, and it highlights a strong correlation between meditation frequency and improved mental well-being.

21. B: The speaker in the text expresses strong emotions of love and devotion, stating that he would do anything for Miss Manette and her loved ones, even to the extent of sacrificing his life to keep a life she loves beside her. This deep emotional connection and willingness to make sacrifices are the central themes of the text, making choice B correct.

22. C: In the passage, the author discusses how empires and dynasties have left lasting legacies that persist for centuries and have shaped societies, cultures, and economies significantly. The passage suggests that these historical examples provide insights into the development of human civilization. Therefore, Choice C is the most logical choice, as it directly aligns with the passage's content. Choice D, while partially correct, does not encompass the full meaning conveyed in the passage, as it focuses more on the enduring effects rather than the insights and lessons.

23. A: The comma in "practical, as" is the correct punctuation to indicate that the clause "as it is helping us understand and care for our planet's most mysterious realms" is providing an explanation or clarification for the preceding clause. Here, the word *as* is used to mean *because*. It effectively conveys the idea that the research is both academic and practical, and the comma helps maintain the sentence's flow and readability.

24. A: The passage states that in 1900, *Starry Night* found a new home at the Galerie Bernheim-Jeune in Paris. It then goes on to state that the painting was placed at the Museum of Modern Art in New York City in 1941, so it must have been in the Galerie Bernheim-Jeune from 1900 to 1941, which includes the year 1926.

25. D: The phrase *a somber* effectively conveys the mood and atmosphere of Puritan society in *The Scarlet Letter*. It accurately describes the solemn, grave, and serious nature of the setting and society where Hester Prynne's story unfolds.

Mathematics—Module 1

1. $179,625: The ratio of new car sales to used car sales is $3 : 5$. This means that the total number of cars sold (both new and used) is $3 + 5 = 8$. The used car sales are $\frac{5}{8}$ of the total sales:

$$\frac{5}{8} \times \$287,400 = \$179,625$$

2. C: The formula for the volume of a pyramid is $V = \frac{1}{3}Bh$, where B is the area of the base and h is the height of the pyramid. The base is a square with a length of 756 feet on each side. So, the area of the base is $A = s^2 = (756 \text{ ft})^2 = 571,536 \text{ ft}^2$. With a base of $571,536 \text{ ft}^2$ and a height of 481 ft, the volume of the pyramid is $V = \frac{1}{3}(571,536 \text{ ft}^2)(481 \text{ ft}) \approx 9.16 \times 10^7 \text{ ft}^3$.

3. A: $(2x^2 + 3x + 2) - (x^2 + 2x - 3) = (2x^2 + 3x + 2) + (-1)(x^2 + 2x - 3)$. First, distribute the -1 to remove the parentheses: $2x^2 + 3x + 2 - x^2 - 2x + 3$. Next, combine like terms: $(2x^2 - x^2) + (3x - 2x) + (2 + 3) = x^2 + x + 5$.

4. D: To add the two fractions, first rewrite them with the least common denominator, which is in this case y^3. This is already the denominator in $\frac{x}{y^3}$, and we can rewrite $\frac{x^2}{y^2}$ as $\frac{x^2 \times y}{y^2 \times y} = \frac{x^2 y}{y^3}$. Thus, $\frac{x^2}{y^2} + \frac{x}{y^3} = \frac{x^2 y}{y^3} + \frac{x}{y^3} = \frac{x^2 y + x}{y^3}$.

5. 6: We can find the points of intersection by setting the two equations equal to each other.

$$-x^2 + 5x = 2x$$

We combine like terms by subtracting $2x$ from each side.

$$-x^2 + 3x = 0$$

We can factor the left side of the equation.

$$(-x)(x - 3) = 0$$

Setting the first term equal to 0 yields $-x = 0$. Thus, $x = 0$. This corresponds with the point we were given, (0,0). Now we set the second term equal to 0: $x - 3 = 0$. We add 3 to each side to yield $x = 3$. This is a. To find b, we plug in 3 for x to either of the two equations and solve for y. Using the second equation: $y = 2(3)$, or $y = 6$. So, our point is (3,6) and $b = 6$.

6. C: To find the average, we need to add up each part and divide by the number of parts. If Max reads 3 books and Lucy reads 5 books, there are 8 books in total. We can find the total number of pages by multiplying 360 by 3 and 200 by 5, and then dividing the sum by 8.

$$\frac{360 \times 3 + 200 \times 5}{8} = \frac{1,080 + 1,000}{8} = \frac{2,080}{8} = 260$$

Therefore, the average length of all the books that Max and Lucy read is 260 pages.

7. D: There are many ways to solve quadratic equations in the form $ax^2 + bx + c = 0$. However, some methods, such as graphing and factoring, are not useful for equations with irrational or complex roots. Solve this equation by using the quadratic formula, $x = \frac{-b \pm \sqrt{b^2 - 4ac}}{2a}$. Set the given equation equal to zero, so $7x^2 + 6x + 2 = 0$. Substitute the values $a = 7$, $b = 6$, and $c = 2$ into the quadratic formula.

$$x = \frac{-b \pm \sqrt{b^2 - 4ac}}{2a}$$

$$x = \frac{-6 \pm \sqrt{6^2 - 4(7)(2)}}{2(7)}$$

$$x = \frac{-6 \pm \sqrt{36 - 56}}{14}$$

$$x = \frac{-6 \pm \sqrt{-20}}{14}$$

$$x = \frac{-6 \pm 2i\sqrt{5}}{14}$$

$$x = \frac{-3 \pm i\sqrt{5}}{7}$$

8. C: The expression representing the charge for Ride Service A is $\$10 + \$0.25(m - 10)$, where m is the number of miles. Set this expression equal to the charge for Ride Service B, which is $\$0.40m$. Solve for m to find the number of miles the two companies charge the same amount.

$$\$10 + \$0.25(m - 10) = \$0.40m$$

$$\$10 + \$0.25m - \$2.50 = \$0.40m$$

$$\$7.50 = \$0.15m$$

$$m = 50$$

So, the cost of the two services would be the same for a 50-mile ride.

9. C: In a 45-45-90 triangle, the legs can be found by dividing the hypotenuse by $\sqrt{2}$, so one leg is $\frac{4}{\sqrt{2}}$. We simplify $\frac{4}{\sqrt{2}}$ by multiplying by $\frac{\sqrt{2}}{\sqrt{2}}$.

$$\frac{4\sqrt{2}}{\sqrt{2}\sqrt{2}} = \frac{4\sqrt{2}}{2} = 2\sqrt{2}$$

Therefore, the three sides of the triangle are $2\sqrt{2}$, $2\sqrt{2}$, and 4. We add these sides together to obtain the perimeter: $4 + 4\sqrt{2}$.

Answer choice A is incorrect because it is the area rather than the perimeter. Answer choice B is incorrect because it is the area without the last step of dividing by 2. Answer choice D is incorrect because it is only two of the three sides.

10. B: To simplify the given inequality, first move all the terms to one side.

$$x^2 + 3 > 2x + 2$$

$$x^2 + 3 - 2x - 2 > 0$$

$$x^2 - 2x + 1 > 0$$

Mometrix

Now, factor the left-hand side.

$$x^2 - 2x + 1 = (x-1)(x-1) = (x-1)^2$$

The original inequality is equivalent to $(x-1)^2 > 0$. Since the square of a negative number is positive, $(x-1)^2 > 0$ everywhere except where $x - 1 = 0$, i.e. at $x = 1$. Therefore, $x \neq 1$ is equivalent to $x^2 + 3 > 2x + 2$.

11. D: The solution(s) to a system of equations is the point or points at which the graphs of the two equations cross. If a system has no solution, this means that the graphs never cross. In other words, the two graphs are parallel. In the system here, we know the lines will be parallel if the slopes are identical. We can look at the first equation to find the slope by moving the x-value to the right and solving for y.

$$y = 3x - 2$$

Thus, the slope of the second equation needs to also be 3. We again move the x-value to the right and solve for y.

$$y = \frac{-n}{3}x - \frac{5}{3}$$

Therefore, the slope here is $-\frac{n}{3}$. We can set the slopes equal to each other to solve for n.

$$-\frac{n}{3} = \frac{3}{1}$$

Then we cross-multiply.

$$-n(1) = 3(3)$$

Finally, we divide both sides by –1 to find that $n = -9$. Answer choice B is incorrect because it is the value of the slope. Answer choice A is the negative reciprocal of the slope, which would be used if we were looking for a perpendicular line, not a parallel one. Answer choice C is the y-intercept of the second line.

12. D: The expression representing the monthly charge for Plan A is $\$20 + \$15(d - 2.5)$, where d is the data used. This can be found by adding the flat rate to the price of any data used over the provided amount. Set this expression equal to the monthly charge for Plan B, which is $50. Solve for d to find the number of GB for which the two plans charge the same amount.

$$\$20 + \$15(d - 2.5) = \$50$$
$$\$15(d - 2.5) = \$30$$
$$d - 2.5 = 2$$
$$d = 4.5$$

So, the plans have the same cost when Gillian uses 4.5 GB of data.

13. B: Call the number of people present at the meeting x. If each person hands out a card to every other person (that is, every person besides himself), then each person hands out $x - 1$ cards. The total number of cards handed out is therefore $x(x - 1)$. Since we are told there are a total of 30 cards handed out, we have the equation $x(x - 1) = 30$, which we can rewrite as the quadratic equation $x^2 - x - 30 = 0$. We can solve this equation by factoring the quadratic expression. One

282

way to do this is to find two numbers that add up to the coefficient of x (in this case, –1) and that multiply to the constant term (in this case, –30). Those two numbers are 5 and –6. Our factored equation is therefore $(x + 5)(x - 6) = 0$. To make the equation true, one or both of the factors must be zero: either $x + 5 = 0$, in which case $x = -5$, or $x - 6 = 0$, in which case $x = 6$. Obviously, the number of people at the meeting cannot be negative, so the second solution, $x = 6$, must be correct. There are 6 people at the meeting.

14. D: Manipulate the inequality to isolate the variable. Start by adding 12 to each side.

$$4x - 12 < 4$$
$$4x - 12 + 12 < 4 + 12$$
$$4x < 16$$

Then divide both sides by 4.

$$\frac{4x}{4} < \frac{16}{4}$$
$$x < 4$$

Since x must be less than and not equal to 4, only choice D works.

15. D: We can see from the table that 8 people ordered a cup of veggie soup and that a total of 42 orders were placed. So, the probability is 8 out of 42, or $\frac{8}{42}$. We can divide both numerator and denominator by 2 to reduce the fraction to $\frac{4}{21}$. Choice A is the probability of choosing veggie soup given that a cup was selected (not the overall probability). Choice B is the probability of choosing a cup of chicken soup ($\frac{7}{42}$ reduces to $\frac{1}{6}$). Choice C is the probability of choosing a cup, given that veggie soup was selected ($\frac{8}{20}$ reduces to $\frac{2}{5}$).

16. C: If there is one white petunia for every three red petunias, we can write that red petunias = 3(white petunias). We can then substitute 8 for the white petunias and r for the red petunias: $r = 3(8)$. We look through the answer choices to see which matches this. Answer choice A can be rewritten as $r = \frac{8}{3}$. Answer choice B can be rewritten as $r = \frac{3}{8}$. Answer choice C can be rewritten as $r = 3(8)$. Answer choice D can be rewritten as $r = 8 - 3$. So only answer choice C matches.

17. C: When solving radical equations, check for extraneous solutions.

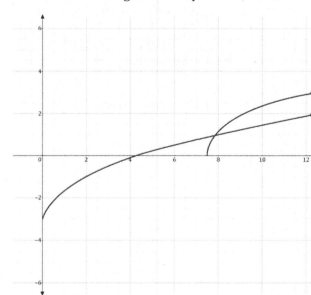

$$\sqrt{2x} - 3 = \sqrt{2x - 15}$$
$$\left(\sqrt{2x} - 3\right)^2 = \left(\sqrt{2x - 15}\right)^2$$
$$2x - 6\sqrt{2x} + 9 = 2x - 15$$
$$-6\sqrt{2x} + 9 = -15$$
$$-6\sqrt{2x} = -24$$
$$\sqrt{2x} = 4$$
$$2x = 16$$
$$x = 8$$

Check:
$$\sqrt{2(8)} - 3 = \sqrt{2(8) - 15}$$
$$\sqrt{16} - 3 = \sqrt{16 - 15}$$
$$4 - 3 = \sqrt{1}$$
$$1 = 1$$

Since the solution checks, it is a valid solution. Notice that the graphs $y = \sqrt{2x} - 3$ and $y = \sqrt{2x - 15}$ intersect, which confirms there is a solution.

18. D: The radical equation may be solved by first subtracting 8 from both sides of the equation.

$$4\sqrt{x} + 8 = 24$$

$$4\sqrt{x} = 16$$

Then, divide both sides of the equation by 4.

$$\sqrt{x} = 4$$

Finally, square both sides.

$$x = 16$$

19. C: We need to simplify the equation so we can factor it. First, we subtract 2 from each side.

$$3x^2 - 3x - 36 = 0$$

Then we can divide each term by 3.

$$x^2 - x - 12 = 0$$

Finally, we can factor.

$$(x + 3)(x - 4) = 0$$

Setting each factored term equal to 0 yields $x + 3 = 0$ and $x - 4 = 0$, or $x = -3$ and $x = 4$. The sum of –3 and 4 is 1.

20. C: A rectangle's area is found by multiplying length by width. Here, length is $5x$ and width is x.

$$245 \text{ in}^2 = x \cdot 5x$$
$$245 \text{ in}^2 = 5x^2$$
$$49 \text{ in}^2 = x^2$$
$$7 \text{ in} = x$$

Therefore, the longest side is $5 \times 7 \text{ in} = 35 \text{ in}$.

21. D: We can use the table to find the linear equation in slope-intercept form, $y = mx + b$, where m is the slope and b is the y-intercept. The table shows the y-intercept (the y value at $x = 0$) to be -5. The slope is the ratio of the change in y-values to the corresponding change in x-values. As the x-value increases by 1, the y-value increases by 3. Thus, the slope is $\frac{3}{1}$, or 3. So the equation is $y = 3x - 5$.

Only the graphs in choices B and D have a y-intercept at -5. Of these two graphs, only choice D has a y-value increase of 3 for each x-value increase of 1, indicating a slope of 3.

22. 140: If the distance between the two houses is 10 cm on the map, then the actual distance between the houses is 100 m. To find x, use the Pythagorean theorem:

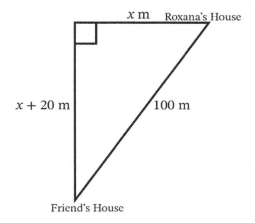

$$x^2 + (x + 20)^2 = (100)^2$$
$$x^2 + x^2 + 40x + 400 = 10{,}000$$
$$2x^2 + 40x - 9{,}600 = 0$$
$$2(x^2 + 20x - 4{,}800) = 0$$
$$2(x - 60)(x + 80) = 0$$
$$x = 60 \quad x = -80$$

Since x represents a distance, it cannot equal -80. Since $x = 60$, $x + 20 = 80$. Roxana walks a total of 140 m to get to her friend's house.

Mathematics—Module 2

1. D: To solve, we first rewrite the equation. We can write $\sqrt[3]{x}$ as $x^{\frac{1}{3}}$ and rewrite the fraction by making the exponent negative: $\frac{1}{x^{\frac{1}{3}}} = x^{-\frac{1}{3}}$. Then we can raise each side to the -3 power. This yields

$\left(x^{-\frac{1}{3}}\right)^{-3} = a^{-3}$. We can simplify to $x = \frac{1}{a^3}$. Answer choice A is incorrect because it raises a to the power of 3, not –3. Answer choice B is incorrect because it adds in a constant (1) and does not raise a to the power of –3. Answer choice C is incorrect because it raises a to the power of –2, not –3.

2. A: We can graph the two lines on a coordinate plane by plotting the y-intercept and then finding another point based on the slope. For the first equation, the y-intercept is –2, so we plot the point $(0, -2)$. Then we use the slope $\left(\frac{1}{4}\right)$ to plot another point by moving up 1 and 4 to the right, to $(4, -1)$. Now we can draw a line passing through the two points. It is a solid line because the solution is less than or equal to the equation. Next, we graph the second line. The y-intercept is $-\frac{7}{5}$, so we plot the point $\left(0, -\frac{7}{5}\right)$. Then we use the slope (3) to plot another point by moving up 3 and over 1, to $\left(1, \frac{8}{5}\right)$. Now we can draw a line passing through the two points. It is a dotted line because the solution is greater than the equation. We shade the area that is both below the graph of the first line and above the graph of the second line. When we do this, we can see that the overlap of the shaded area is only in quadrant III.

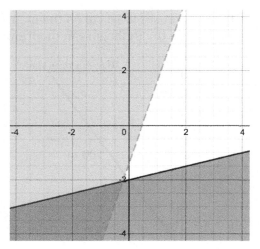

3. C: To make $820 in profit, Nursery B needs to earn $5,500 + $820 = $6,320 to compensate for overhead costs. We can calculate the amount earned by selling plants: $100(30) + 100(20) = $5,000. We subtract this from $6,320 to find that they need to earn an additional $1,320 from landscaping charges. Letting the number of hours be x, we can write out our equation: $55x = 1,320$. We divide each side by 55 to find that $x = 24$. So, Nursery B needs at least 24 hours of work.

4. D: We can calculate the cost of each nursery's trees and bushes. Nursery A's cost is:

$$25(10) + 15(8) = 250 + 120 = \$370$$

Nursery C's cost is:

$$20(10) + 15(8) = 200 + 120 = \$320$$

So, we can set up an inequality, letting x be the number of hours to plant the bushes and trees. For Nursery A's services to be a better deal, they must cost less than Nursery C's.

$$370 + 45x < 320 + 50x$$

We solve for x by subtracting $45x$ and 320 from each side.

$$50 < 5x$$

We rewrite this as $5x > 50$ and divide each side by 5 to obtain $x > 10$. It is important to remember to reverse the inequality sign when we move the x to the left so we don't end up with $x < 10$ (answer choice B).

5. C: The side of the square is equal to the diameter of the circle, or twice the radius, $2r$. The area of the square is this quantity squared, or $4r^2$. The area of the circle is πr^2. Subtracting the area of the circle from the area of the square gives the difference between the two areas.

$$4r^2 - \pi r^2$$

A common r^2 can be factored out of each term to get the expression $r^2(4 - \pi)$.

6. A: The equation can be translated:

$$\text{investment} = (\text{initial lump sum}) + 4{,}500(\text{number of months since beginning})$$

In other words, it grows 4,500 cents every month. The answer choices are in dollars, so we divide by 100 to obtain $45 per month.

7. D: To solve, isolate n by putting all the other terms on the other side of the equal sign.

$$4n - p = 3r$$

$$4n = 3r + p$$

$$n = \frac{3r}{4} + \frac{p}{4}$$

8. D: We solve for x and y by using elimination. We can multiply the first equation by 2 to eliminate the y-terms.

$$6x - 4y = 0$$

$$-2x + 4y = -8$$

Adding these two equations together yields $4x = -8$, or $x = -2$. We can solve for y by plugging the x-value back into one of the equations. Using the first equation, this yields:

$$3(-2) - 2y = 0$$

We add 6 to each side.

$$-2y = 6$$

Divide each side by –2.

$$y = -3$$

So, the solution is $(-2, -3)$. Now we can use these values to find $2x^2 - y$.

$$2(-2)^2 - (-3) = 8 + 3 = 11$$

Choices A and B are incorrect because they are the values of y and x, respectively. Choice C is incorrect because it involves adding the negative term instead of subtracting it.

9. $\frac{1}{2}$: We need to rewrite the equation to be in standard form of a circle.

$$(x - h)^2 + (y - k)^2 = r^2$$

First, we isolate the x- and y-terms.

$$(x^2 - 6x) + (y^2 - y) = -\frac{21}{4}$$

Next, we can complete the square to simplify the equation.

$$(x^2 - 6x + 9) - 9 + \left(y^2 - y + \frac{1}{4}\right) - \frac{1}{4} = -\frac{21}{4}$$
$$(x - 3)^2 + \left(y - \frac{1}{2}\right)^2 - \frac{37}{4} = -\frac{21}{4}$$
$$(x - 3)^2 + \left(y - \frac{1}{2}\right)^2 = \frac{16}{4}$$
$$(x - 3)^2 + \left(y - \frac{1}{2}\right)^2 = 4$$

Now we can solve for the center point of the circle by setting the parts of the equations in parentheses equal to 0.

$$x - 3 = 0 \text{ becomes } x = 3$$

$$y - \frac{1}{2} = 0 \text{ becomes } y = \frac{1}{2}$$

So, the coordinates of the center are $\left(3, \frac{1}{2}\right)$, meaning that the y-coordinate is $\frac{1}{2}$.

10. 6: Since the total is a multiple of ten and the $5 bill is the only one that is not already a multiple of $10, we can conclude that Riley must have an even number of $5 bills. Since we are looking for the greatest number, we should begin at the top and check each number to see if it is possible.

If there are eight $5 bills, this leaves only one other bill to make up the difference.

$$\$80 - 8(\$5) = \$80 - \$40 = \$40$$

Since there is no such thing as a $40 bill, there cannot be eight $5 bills.

If there are six $5 bills, this leaves three other bills to make up the difference.

$$\$80 - 6(\$5) = \$80 - \$30 = \$50$$

This $50, made up of three bills, could be formed by a combination of two $20 bills and one $10 bill. Since this satisfies the parameters, Riley has a maximum of six $5 bills.

11. A: The expression may be factored as $(x - 8)(x + 5)$. The factorization may be checked by distributing each term in the first factor to each term in the second factor by using the FOIL method. Doing so gives $x^2 + 5x - 8x - 40$, which can be rewritten as $x^2 - 3x - 40$.

12. D: We need to find the point at which d is equal to p, so set the two equations equal to each other.

$$4a = 9,660 + 1.2a$$

Subtract $1.2a$ from each side.

$$2.8a = 9,660$$

Divide each side by 2.8.

$$a = 3,450$$

We then plug a into the first equation to find that $d = 9,660 + 1.2(3,450) = 13,800$. Therefore, $13,800$ of investment is required.

13. C: Write the first part of the sentence as an equation.

$$3x^2 = 48$$

Then, divide each side by 3.

$$x^2 = 16$$

Take the square root of each side.

$$x = \pm 4$$

Since we are told that it is a positive number, we know the answer is 4. Finally, we multiply the number by 2 and subtract from 15.

$$15 - 2(4) = 7$$

Choice A is incorrect because it is obtained by subtracting 15 from 8 rather than vice versa. Choice B is incorrect because it is the value of x, not the final answer. Choice D is incorrect because it is obtained by subtracting x from 15 without first doubling x.

14. B: The point marked on the scatterplot for Day 8 shows that Zac worked for 3 hours, while the line of best fit crosses the 2-hour mark on the same day. The difference between 3 and 2 is 1 hour.

15. 4: Solve for x in the equation by first adding 7 to each side.

$$x^2 = 16$$

Then, solve by taking the square root of each side to yield $x = \pm 4$. Since $x > 0$, this means that $x = 4$.

16. A: We solve for q by dividing each side by $\frac{3}{7}$. We do this by multiplying each side by the reciprocal, $\frac{7}{3}$.

$$q = -\frac{6}{1} \times \frac{7}{3} = -\frac{42}{3} = -14$$

Choice B is incorrect because it involves multiplying $\frac{3}{7}$ instead of dividing. Choice C is incorrect because it involves subtracting $\frac{3}{7}$ from each side instead of dividing. Choice D is incorrect because it is only the numerator of the multiplied fraction.

17. D: Use the difference of squares rule that states that $(a+b)(a-b)=a^2-b^2$, or multiply the binomials using the FOIL method: multiply together the *first* term of each factor, then the *outer* terms, then the *inner* terms, and finally the *last* terms. Then add the products together.

$$(x+6)(x-6) = x \times x + x \times (-6) + 6 \times x + 6 \times (-6)$$
$$= x^2 - 6x + 6x - 36$$
$$= x^2 - 36$$

18. A: The graph shows that Miguel had 6 quarters in the jar at the end of the day on Sunday, and there were still 6 at the end of Monday. So, he did not add any quarters that day.

19. C: The line climbs the most sharply between Wednesday and Thursday, growing by 3 (from 9 to 12). Since the measurement is taken at the end of each day, we know there were 9 quarters in the jar at the end of Wednesday and 12 at the end of Thursday, so 3 quarters were added on Thursday.

20. 38: We start with the formula $y(t) = ae^{kt}$ where a is the starting amount and t is the time in hours. Since the half-life is 5, we can write $0.5 = 1e^{k(5)}$. We then solve by taking the natural logarithm of each side.

$$\ln(0.5) = \ln\left(e^{5k}\right)$$
$$\ln(0.5) = 5k$$
$$-0.693 \approx 5k$$
$$-0.139 \approx k$$

At 2:00 p.m., it has been 7 hours since Rafe drank the cup of coffee, so we can put that into the equation.

$$y(7) = 1e^{(-0.139)(7)} \approx 0.378$$

This translates to 37.8%, or approximately 38%.

21. 0.8: The sine of an angle can be calculated as the opposite side (4) divided by the hypotenuse (5). If angle Z measures $z°$, then angle X measures $(90-z)°$, so we are looking for the cosine of angle X. We can find the cosine of angle X by taking the adjacent side (4) and dividing by the hypotenuse (5). So, the answer is $\frac{4}{5}$, or 0.8.

22. 15: If $WX = XZ$, we can write $WX = XY + YZ$. We then substitute the expressions into this equation.

$$a + 9 = 4a - 9 + 2a + 3$$

Moving a-values to the left and numerical values to the right yields $-5a = -15$, or $a = 3$. Now we can solve for WX and XY.

$$WX = a + 9 = 3 + 9 = 12$$

$$XY = 4a - 9 = 4(3) - 9 = 3$$

290

So $WY = WX + XY = 12 + 3 = 15$.

SAT Practice Test #3

To take this additional SAT practice tests, visit our bonus page:
mometrix.com/bonus948/sat

How to Overcome Test Anxiety

Just the thought of taking a test is enough to make most people a little nervous. A test is an important event that can have a long-term impact on your future, so it's important to take it seriously and it's natural to feel anxious about performing well. But just because anxiety is normal, that doesn't mean that it's helpful in test taking, or that you should simply accept it as part of your life. Anxiety can have a variety of effects. These effects can be mild, like making you feel slightly nervous, or severe, like blocking your ability to focus or remember even a simple detail.

If you experience test anxiety—whether severe or mild—it's important to know how to beat it. To discover this, first you need to understand what causes test anxiety.

Causes of Test Anxiety

While we often think of anxiety as an uncontrollable emotional state, it can actually be caused by simple, practical things. One of the most common causes of test anxiety is that a person does not feel adequately prepared for their test. This feeling can be the result of many different issues such as poor study habits or lack of organization, but the most common culprit is time management. Starting to study too late, failing to organize your study time to cover all of the material, or being distracted while you study will mean that you're not well prepared for the test. This may lead to cramming the night before, which will cause you to be physically and mentally exhausted for the test. Poor time management also contributes to feelings of stress, fear, and hopelessness as you realize you are not well prepared but don't know what to do about it.

Other times, test anxiety is not related to your preparation for the test but comes from unresolved fear. This may be a past failure on a test, or poor performance on tests in general. It may come from comparing yourself to others who seem to be performing better or from the stress of living up to expectations. Anxiety may be driven by fears of the future—how failure on this test would affect your educational and career goals. These fears are often completely irrational, but they can still negatively impact your test performance.

Elements of Test Anxiety

As mentioned earlier, test anxiety is considered to be an emotional state, but it has physical and mental components as well. Sometimes you may not even realize that you are suffering from test anxiety until you notice the physical symptoms. These can include trembling hands, rapid heartbeat, sweating, nausea, and tense muscles. Extreme anxiety may lead to fainting or vomiting. Obviously, any of these symptoms can have a negative impact on testing. It is important to recognize them as soon as they begin to occur so that you can address the problem before it damages your performance.

The mental components of test anxiety include trouble focusing and inability to remember learned information. During a test, your mind is on high alert, which can help you recall information and stay focused for an extended period of time. However, anxiety interferes with your mind's natural processes, causing you to blank out, even on the questions you know well. The strain of testing during anxiety makes it difficult to stay focused, especially on a test that may take several hours. Extreme anxiety can take a huge mental toll, making it difficult not only to recall test information but even to understand the test questions or pull your thoughts together.

293

Effects of Test Anxiety

Test anxiety is like a disease—if left untreated, it will get progressively worse. Anxiety leads to poor performance, and this reinforces the feelings of fear and failure, which in turn lead to poor performances on subsequent tests. It can grow from a mild nervousness to a crippling condition. If allowed to progress, test anxiety can have a big impact on your schooling, and consequently on your future.

Test anxiety can spread to other parts of your life. Anxiety on tests can become anxiety in any stressful situation, and blanking on a test can turn into panicking in a job situation. But fortunately, you don't have to let anxiety rule your testing and determine your grades. There are a number of relatively simple steps you can take to move past anxiety and function normally on a test and in the rest of life.

Physical Steps for Beating Test Anxiety

While test anxiety is a serious problem, the good news is that it can be overcome. It doesn't have to control your ability to think and remember information. While it may take time, you can begin taking steps today to beat anxiety.

Just as your first hint that you may be struggling with anxiety comes from the physical symptoms, the first step to treating it is also physical. Rest is crucial for having a clear, strong mind. If you are tired, it is much easier to give in to anxiety. But if you establish good sleep habits, your body and mind will be ready to perform optimally, without the strain of exhaustion. Additionally, sleeping well helps you to retain information better, so you're more likely to recall the answers when you see the test questions.

Getting good sleep means more than going to bed on time. It's important to allow your brain time to relax. Take study breaks from time to time so it doesn't get overworked, and don't study right before bed. Take time to rest your mind before trying to rest your body, or you may find it difficult to fall asleep.

Along with sleep, other aspects of physical health are important in preparing for a test. Good nutrition is vital for good brain function. Sugary foods and drinks may give a burst of energy but this burst is followed by a crash, both physically and emotionally. Instead, fuel your body with protein and vitamin-rich foods.

Also, drink plenty of water. Dehydration can lead to headaches and exhaustion, especially if your brain is already under stress from the rigors of the test. Particularly if your test is a long one, drink water during the breaks. And if possible, take an energy-boosting snack to eat between sections.

Along with sleep and diet, a third important part of physical health is exercise. Maintaining a steady workout schedule is helpful, but even taking 5-minute study breaks to walk can help get your blood pumping faster and clear your head. Exercise also releases endorphins, which contribute to a positive feeling and can help combat test anxiety.

When you nurture your physical health, you are also contributing to your mental health. If your body is healthy, your mind is much more likely to be healthy as well. So take time to rest, nourish your body with healthy food and water, and get moving as much as possible. Taking these physical steps will make you stronger and more able to take the mental steps necessary to overcome test anxiety.

Mental Steps for Beating Test Anxiety

Working on the mental side of test anxiety can be more challenging, but as with the physical side, there are clear steps you can take to overcome it. As mentioned earlier, test anxiety often stems from lack of preparation, so the obvious solution is to prepare for the test. Effective studying may be the most important weapon you have for beating test anxiety, but you can and should employ several other mental tools to combat fear.

First, boost your confidence by reminding yourself of past success—tests or projects that you aced. If you're putting as much effort into preparing for this test as you did for those, there's no reason you should expect to fail here. Work hard to prepare; then trust your preparation.

Second, surround yourself with encouraging people. It can be helpful to find a study group, but be sure that the people you're around will encourage a positive attitude. If you spend time with others who are anxious or cynical, this will only contribute to your own anxiety. Look for others who are motivated to study hard from a desire to succeed, not from a fear of failure.

Third, reward yourself. A test is physically and mentally tiring, even without anxiety, and it can be helpful to have something to look forward to. Plan an activity following the test, regardless of the outcome, such as going to a movie or getting ice cream.

When you are taking the test, if you find yourself beginning to feel anxious, remind yourself that you know the material. Visualize successfully completing the test. Then take a few deep, relaxing breaths and return to it. Work through the questions carefully but with confidence, knowing that you are capable of succeeding.

Developing a healthy mental approach to test taking will also aid in other areas of life. Test anxiety affects more than just the actual test—it can be damaging to your mental health and even contribute to depression. It's important to beat test anxiety before it becomes a problem for more than testing.

Study Strategy

Being prepared for the test is necessary to combat anxiety, but what does being prepared look like? You may study for hours on end and still not feel prepared. What you need is a strategy for test prep. The next few pages outline our recommended steps to help you plan out and conquer the challenge of preparation.

STEP 1: SCOPE OUT THE TEST

Learn everything you can about the format (multiple choice, essay, etc.) and what will be on the test. Gather any study materials, course outlines, or sample exams that may be available. Not only will this help you to prepare, but knowing what to expect can help to alleviate test anxiety.

STEP 2: MAP OUT THE MATERIAL

Look through the textbook or study guide and make note of how many chapters or sections it has. Then divide these over the time you have. For example, if a book has 15 chapters and you have five days to study, you need to cover three chapters each day. Even better, if you have the time, leave an extra day at the end for overall review after you have gone through the material in depth.

If time is limited, you may need to prioritize the material. Look through it and make note of which sections you think you already have a good grasp on, and which need review. While you are studying, skim quickly through the familiar sections and take more time on the challenging parts.

Write out your plan so you don't get lost as you go. Having a written plan also helps you feel more in control of the study, so anxiety is less likely to arise from feeling overwhelmed at the amount to cover.

STEP 3: GATHER YOUR TOOLS

Decide what study method works best for you. Do you prefer to highlight in the book as you study and then go back over the highlighted portions? Or do you type out notes of the important information? Or is it helpful to make flashcards that you can carry with you? Assemble the pens, index cards, highlighters, post-it notes, and any other materials you may need so you won't be distracted by getting up to find things while you study.

If you're having a hard time retaining the information or organizing your notes, experiment with different methods. For example, try color-coding by subject with colored pens, highlighters, or post-it notes. If you learn better by hearing, try recording yourself reading your notes so you can listen while in the car, working out, or simply sitting at your desk. Ask a friend to quiz you from your flashcards, or try teaching someone the material to solidify it in your mind.

STEP 4: CREATE YOUR ENVIRONMENT

It's important to avoid distractions while you study. This includes both the obvious distractions like visitors and the subtle distractions like an uncomfortable chair (or a too-comfortable couch that makes you want to fall asleep). Set up the best study environment possible: good lighting and a comfortable work area. If background music helps you focus, you may want to turn it on, but otherwise keep the room quiet. If you are using a computer to take notes, be sure you don't have any other windows open, especially applications like social media, games, or anything else that could distract you. Silence your phone and turn off notifications. Be sure to keep water close by so you stay hydrated while you study (but avoid unhealthy drinks and snacks).

Also, take into account the best time of day to study. Are you freshest first thing in the morning? Try to set aside some time then to work through the material. Is your mind clearer in the afternoon or evening? Schedule your study session then. Another method is to study at the same time of day that you will take the test, so that your brain gets used to working on the material at that time and will be ready to focus at test time.

STEP 5: STUDY!

Once you have done all the study preparation, it's time to settle into the actual studying. Sit down, take a few moments to settle your mind so you can focus, and begin to follow your study plan. Don't give in to distractions or let yourself procrastinate. This is your time to prepare so you'll be ready to fearlessly approach the test. Make the most of the time and stay focused.

Of course, you don't want to burn out. If you study too long you may find that you're not retaining the information very well. Take regular study breaks. For example, taking five minutes out of every hour to walk briskly, breathing deeply and swinging your arms, can help your mind stay fresh.

As you get to the end of each chapter or section, it's a good idea to do a quick review. Remind yourself of what you learned and work on any difficult parts. When you feel that you've mastered the material, move on to the next part. At the end of your study session, briefly skim through your notes again.

But while review is helpful, cramming last minute is NOT. If at all possible, work ahead so that you won't need to fit all your study into the last day. Cramming overloads your brain with more information than it can process and retain, and your tired mind may struggle to recall even

Copyright © Mometrix Media. You have been licensed one copy of this document for personal use only. Any other reproduction or redistribution is strictly prohibited. All rights reserved. This content is provided for test preparation purposes only and does not imply an endorsement by Mometrix of any particular political, scientific, or religious point of view.

previously learned information when it is overwhelmed with last-minute study. Also, the urgent nature of cramming and the stress placed on your brain contribute to anxiety. You'll be more likely to go to the test feeling unprepared and having trouble thinking clearly.

So don't cram, and don't stay up late before the test, even just to review your notes at a leisurely pace. Your brain needs rest more than it needs to go over the information again. In fact, plan to finish your studies by noon or early afternoon the day before the test. Give your brain the rest of the day to relax or focus on other things, and get a good night's sleep. Then you will be fresh for the test and better able to recall what you've studied.

STEP 6: TAKE A PRACTICE TEST

Many courses offer sample tests, either online or in the study materials. This is an excellent resource to check whether you have mastered the material, as well as to prepare for the test format and environment.

Check the test format ahead of time: the number of questions, the type (multiple choice, free response, etc.), and the time limit. Then create a plan for working through them. For example, if you have 30 minutes to take a 60-question test, your limit is 30 seconds per question. Spend less time on the questions you know well so that you can take more time on the difficult ones.

If you have time to take several practice tests, take the first one open book, with no time limit. Work through the questions at your own pace and make sure you fully understand them. Gradually work up to taking a test under test conditions: sit at a desk with all study materials put away and set a timer. Pace yourself to make sure you finish the test with time to spare and go back to check your answers if you have time.

After each test, check your answers. On the questions you missed, be sure you understand why you missed them. Did you misread the question (tests can use tricky wording)? Did you forget the information? Or was it something you hadn't learned? Go back and study any shaky areas that the practice tests reveal.

Taking these tests not only helps with your grade, but also aids in combating test anxiety. If you're already used to the test conditions, you're less likely to worry about it, and working through tests until you're scoring well gives you a confidence boost. Go through the practice tests until you feel comfortable, and then you can go into the test knowing that you're ready for it.

Test Tips

On test day, you should be confident, knowing that you've prepared well and are ready to answer the questions. But aside from preparation, there are several test day strategies you can employ to maximize your performance.

First, as stated before, get a good night's sleep the night before the test (and for several nights before that, if possible). Go into the test with a fresh, alert mind rather than staying up late to study.

Try not to change too much about your normal routine on the day of the test. It's important to eat a nutritious breakfast, but if you normally don't eat breakfast at all, consider eating just a protein bar. If you're a coffee drinker, go ahead and have your normal coffee. Just make sure you time it so that the caffeine doesn't wear off right in the middle of your test. Avoid sugary beverages, and drink enough water to stay hydrated but not so much that you need a restroom break 10 minutes into the test. If your test isn't first thing in the morning, consider going for a walk or doing a light workout before the test to get your blood flowing.

Allow yourself enough time to get ready, and leave for the test with plenty of time to spare so you won't have the anxiety of scrambling to arrive in time. Another reason to be early is to select a good seat. It's helpful to sit away from doors and windows, which can be distracting. Find a good seat, get out your supplies, and settle your mind before the test begins.

When the test begins, start by going over the instructions carefully, even if you already know what to expect. Make sure you avoid any careless mistakes by following the directions.

Then begin working through the questions, pacing yourself as you've practiced. If you're not sure on an answer, don't spend too much time on it, and don't let it shake your confidence. Either skip it and come back later, or eliminate as many wrong answers as possible and guess among the remaining ones. Don't dwell on these questions as you continue—put them out of your mind and focus on what lies ahead.

Be sure to read all of the answer choices, even if you're sure the first one is the right answer. Sometimes you'll find a better one if you keep reading. But don't second-guess yourself if you do immediately know the answer. Your gut instinct is usually right. Don't let test anxiety rob you of the information you know.

If you have time at the end of the test (and if the test format allows), go back and review your answers. Be cautious about changing any, since your first instinct tends to be correct, but make sure you didn't misread any of the questions or accidentally mark the wrong answer choice. Look over any you skipped and make an educated guess.

At the end, leave the test feeling confident. You've done your best, so don't waste time worrying about your performance or wishing you could change anything. Instead, celebrate the successful completion of this test. And finally, use this test to learn how to deal with anxiety even better next time.

> **Review Video: Test Anxiety**
> Visit mometrix.com/academy and enter code: 100340

Important Qualification

Not all anxiety is created equal. If your test anxiety is causing major issues in your life beyond the classroom or testing center, or if you are experiencing troubling physical symptoms related to your anxiety, it may be a sign of a serious physiological or psychological condition. If this sounds like your situation, we strongly encourage you to seek professional help.

Additional Bonus Material

Due to our efforts to try to keep this book to a manageable length, we've created a link that will give you access to all of your additional bonus material:

mometrix.com/bonus948/sat

Made in United States
North Haven, CT
24 May 2024

52911700R00170